OF ADRIAN,
ANDROMEDA
& LEONARD

Also by Adrian Plass

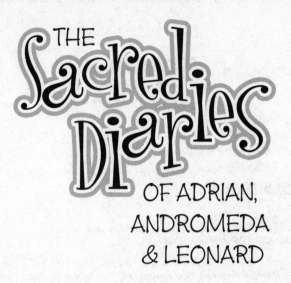

THE Sacred Diaries

OF ADRIAN, ANDROMEDA & LEONARD

Adrian Plass

ZONDERVAN™

GRAND RAPIDS, MICHIGAN 49530 USA

We want to hear from you. Please send your comments about this
book to us in care of the address below. Thank you.

GRAND RAPIDS, MICHIGAN 49530 USA

WWW.ZONDERVAN.COM

ZONDERVAN™

The Sacred Diaries of Adrian, Andromeda and Leonard
First published by Zondervan in 2002

The Horizontal Epistles of Andromeda Veal first published in Great Britain
in 1988 by Marshall Pickering. Text copyright © 1988 by Adrian Plass. Illustrations
copyright © 1988 by Dan Donovan.

The Theatrical Tapes of Leonard Thynn first published in Great Britain in 1989 by
Marshall Pickering. Copyright © 1989 by Adrian Plass.

The Sacred Diary of Adrian Plass, Christian Speaker, Aged 45³/4 first published in
Great Britain in 1996 by HarperCollins*Publishers*. Text copyright © 1996 by Adrian
Plass. Illustrations copyright © 1996 by Dan Donovan.

Requests for information should be addressed to:

Zondervan, *Grand Rapids, Michigan 49530*

Adrian Plass and Dan Donovan assert the moral right to be identified as the author
and illustrator of this work.

ISBN 0-310-27858-9

Interior design by Nancy Wilson

Printed and bound in the United States of America

02 03 04 05 06 07 08 /❖ DC/ 10 9 8 7 6 5 4 3 2 1

Contents

Preface

Andromeda Veal made her first vociferous appearance in *The Sacred Diary of Adrian Plass, Aged 37³/4*. Eight years old, and an uncompromising feminist, she took the Plass household in general and Adrian in particular by storm. In church she caused a furore by standing on her chair and singing "She is Lord...!!" at the top of her voice.

In the *Horizontal Epistles* we find Andromeda in a much more troubled and vulnerable state. Having broken her femur she finds herself stranded in hospital on traction – hence her horizontal state. With her mother and father separated, and both away pursuing their particular interests, Andromeda decides to write letters to all sorts of people in the hope that they will write back. These potential correspondents include Margaret Thatcher, God, her mother and father, Charles Cook, a student at Deep Joy Bible School, Adrian Plass, Anne Plass and a monk called Father John who also appeared in the original *Sacred Diary* book. Of the replies she gets, some are ludicrous, some are encouraging, some are funny, some are sad, one or two have very useful things to say to the lonely little girl, and one or two decidedly do not. In the end Andromeda sees the beginnings of hope for the future.

I wrote *Horizontal Epistles* before my one and only daughter was born, and I suspect that part of me was trying to create a little girl all of my own. For this reason, perhaps, the book has always been a favourite of mine.

Leonard Thynn is another *Sacred Diary* original, and possibly the most enigmatic character of all. People often ask me where

Leonard came from. Who is he based on? How did you come to create him? Why, in the *Sacred Diary*, was he so anxious to borrow Adrian's cat? The answer to the first two of those questions is that Leonard is based on no one that I ever met, and I have not the faintest idea how he came to be created. He just *was*. Single, probably alcoholic and a decidedly lateral thinker, Thynn lives with his profoundly deaf mother. As well as being a church-member, he has a close friendship with the Plass family, a friendship that borders on dependency for much of the time. Leonard's utterly disastrous attempt to explain the nature of the Trinity by using a carpet sweeper at the front in church as a visual aid (see the *Horizontal Epistles*) has become a thing of legend.

In the *Theatrical Tapes*, Leonard has set himself the task of recording most of the meetings and rehearsals leading up to the performance of a play put on by the church that he attends with Adrian and the others. He records everything, including his mother's inability to understand a single word that is said, and Adrian's intense annoyance with just about all those involved.

Leonard himself is asked to be the prompter, a simple enough request which is seriously complicated by Leonard's mistaken belief that the role requires him to wear a soldier's uniform. Rather than be driven mad by the task of unravelling Thynn's confusion on this point, Adrian agrees...

I suppose it would be true to say that *Theatrical Tapes* revolves around one central joke, which I would be mad to reveal in this introduction. Suffice it to say that a single monumental misunderstanding throws the final performance into a surreal chaos that is relieved only by the unexpectedly positive response of all concerned.

The Theatrical Tapes of Leonard Thynn has been successfully adapted as a play for the stage by a number of groups, both here and in Australia.

The Sacred Diary of Adrian Plass, Christian Speaker, Aged 45³/4 reveals the answer to that other question that people always ask me about Leonard Thynn. Why does he borrow the cat? The truth of this important matter appears towards the end of the book, but there's to be no cheating! Read it from the beginning or I shall send Leonard to live with you.

I had always said that I would never write a second *Sacred Diary*. I was frightened probably that it could never be as funny or as effective as the first one. I am not sure even now if those fears were justified, but I do know that this book, an account of Adrian's travels with his family to speak to church groups in places as far apart as Scotland and Australia, was a joy to write. Such extracts as the church notices, the rewritten story of the prodigal son, the tale of the leper who complained that he had not been healed and the spoof Christmas family newsletter are among the most frequently requested items in my repertory.

Many old friends appear in this book, including Leonard, Edwin the church elder, Stenneth and Gloria Flushpool, Adrian's son Gerald and the very spiritually upright Cooks, Richard and Doreen. Writing about them again after a gap of ten years was like meeting old friends at the end of a long separation. It was a pleasure to see them. They have been very good to me.

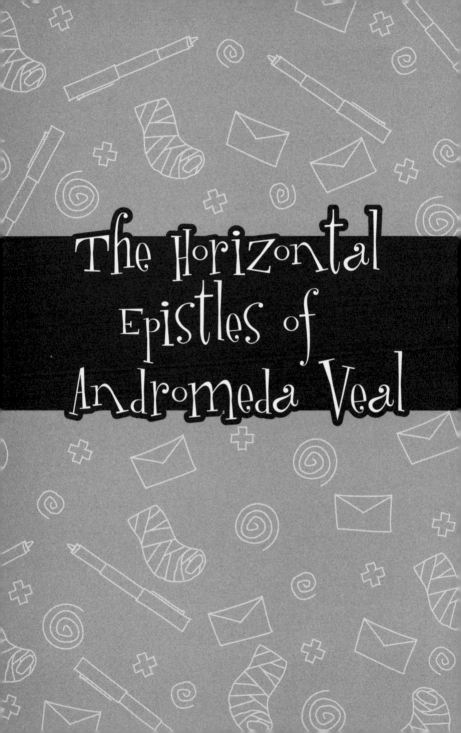

The Horizontal Epistles of Andromeda Veal

Dear Reader,

A real miracle has happened. Anne and Gerald think I've had a good idea! When I first told them I was going to collect Andromeda's correspondence from the time she was in hospital, they both tutted and clicked their tongues and made sighing noises. Anne said, 'Oh, really darling . . .', and Gerald ended up grinning that infuriating grin of his. They thought I was going to get carried away by another of what they call my 'loopy obsessions'. I reminded them that lots of people have been interested enough to read my diary. Anne was gracious enough to nod and say, 'Well, that's true enough, dear,' but Gerald sniggered and said that considering the fact that it was supposed to be a serious book, an awful lot of people had got a lot of laughs out of it. I pointed out that Edwin, our elder, had wept over a number of the entries, but that just set Gerald off cackling to himself, so I didn't say any more at the time.

I'd better explain about Andromeda's letters.

We first met Andromeda (aged seven at the time) when Mrs Veal had to go into hospital, and Edwin, who is Andromeda's uncle, asked if we could put his niece up for a few days. She turned out to be an unusual little girl with a *very* strong personality. We took her to church with us on the Sunday and she caused a sensation to put it mildly! It's all down in my diary (which, despite Gerald's comments, *is* intended to be a sort of spiritual log for the use of future generations, and *not* a religious joke book). Anyway, as I was saying, Andromeda caused quite an impact in church, and also in our family. She adored Anne, she was fascinated by Gerald, and she referred to me as 'The fascist'. She had lots to say about the rights of women, most of it learned from her mother who's a Christian feminist, and she had no qualms about saying it – especially to me! After she'd gone, Anne said she thought there was a lot of worry and tension underneath Andromeda's very grown up way of talking, but I couldn't really see it at the time.

Then, a few months later, Anne got a letter out of the blue from Andromeda, saying that she was on traction in hospital after breaking a femur, and that her parents were not around to visit her. The poor little scrap sounded so lost that Anne decided to mobilise the whole church to help. It was amazing! So many people wrote or visited over the next few weeks. Frank Braddock, our neighbour, wrote a story specially for her, Gerald sent her several letters, Charles Cook sent her two or three rather strange communications from Deep Joy Bible School, and even old Leonard Thynn put pen to paper a couple of times, although the results are – well, read them for yourself! Mrs Flushpool dropped her a line (full of advice and warning of course), and Vernon Rawlings sent her one of his duplicated 'non-begging' letters every now and again. Loads of others wrote, including me – I sent recent extracts from my diary for the times when Andromeda fancied something a little more serious. I'm afraid I couldn't stop Anne's Uncle Ralph from writing. I think his letter is just a bit – well – 'Ralphish'. Still, he meant well. Meanwhile, Andromeda wrote lots of letters herself, some to people in the church, and some to famous people or world leaders, like Cliff Richard and Margaret Thatcher. She never actually sent the 'famous people' ones, but she obviously meant every word!

It was when I was round at Andromeda's house, sometime after she left hospital, that her mum and dad showed me the letters she wrote and never sent, and the ones that people sent to her. I liked them so much that I decided (with Mr and Mrs Veal and Andromeda's permission) to go round all the people in the church and ask for copies of the ones she *did* send. I probably haven't collected them all, but people were very helpful (especially Father John out at the monastery). I think I've got most of them.

When I'd got them all together and in order I showed Anne and Gerald. That's when the miracle happened.

'A good idea!' they said. How about that?

Oh, one more thing – when Andromeda stayed with us, the only thing that would really keep her quiet was Gerald's personal stereo. She got a bit confused though, and always referred to it as his 'Personal problem'. I'm glad I remembered to tell you that. You might have been a little puzzled by Andromeda's constant references to my son's personal problem!

So there we are. I hope you enjoy reading these letters as much as I enjoyed collecting them.

Yours Truly

Adrian Plass.

Part One

Dear Anne,

I hope you don't mined me writing to you, but I am in trubble. I am an attraction in hospital. Muther has gone to be with the green and common wimmen and I am all aloan. I have fracchered my lemur trying to eat mewsli and rollerskate at the same time. The state have got me horizontall.

PLEESE WRITE. I am surrounded by impressed wimmen, and plittically unconscious children. Tell the fashist he can write too if he wants only no thacherite claptrap and remember I'm a mizz.

Tell Geruld I ~~wouldn't~~ woodn't mined having his persunnel problem to play with while I'm horizontall.

Anne, who are the green and common wimmen? Muther says they are stopping Prezident Raygun from putting american bottoms in our fields. She has gone with her frend Gwenda, the one father used to say makes Cyril Smith look anorecksic. Muther was going to stay when they made me an attraction, but Gwenda said love only means you buy a logical bond and the green and common wommen needed her more. Gwenda said lonliness must be fighted. I have fighted it Anne. I think I have lost. Please write to me. I even have to pee horizontall. They left me something to read, but there aren't many pichures in the Soshulist Worker.

Do you know where father lives now Anne? I know he is a laccy of the capitallist pigs but the logical bond he bort for me must have come from a very good shop. He mite come and see me if he heers I'm an attraction.

I have asked God to come and help me, but he hasn't turned up so far.
PLEESE WRITE!!
Logical bonds,

Andromeda Veal (Mizz)

P.S. If you find out where father lives, coold you give him a note for me pleese Anne. It's in the ennvellope with this letta.
Thancyou.

Dear daddy,
Please come and see me or wright to me or fone me or sumthing, eh?
PLEESE daddy

Logical bonds

Andromeda

Darling Andromeda,

I've just read your lovely letter. Thanks so much for writing to me. We've *never* forgotten your stay with us. I did three things as soon as I'd read your letter. First, I made a gingerbread man for you and put it in the oven to bake, then I wrapped Gerald's personal stereo up to send with some tapes, and last of all I sat down to write back to you.

You have been in the wars, haven't you? I'd love you to write back and tell me more about the accident and what the doctors said and did. Would you mind doing that?

I think it's American *bases* that Gwenda and mother are protesting about, darling, not *bottoms*. It must have been a very difficult decision for mummy to make, but I'm sure she misses you terribly and will be back soon. I'm afraid I have no idea where your father lives at the moment, but I'm going to ask your Uncle Edwin who, as you know, is the Elder in our church. I've given him your note for daddy as well. I expect he'll come and see you, and so will I soon. You must be *so* uncomfortable, you poor love. The other thing I've done is to write down a list of lots of names and addresses of people in our church, and I've sent you plenty of paper and envelopes and stamps so that you can write to them. I'll get Uncle Edwin to tell everybody you're going to write and I'm sure you'll get loads and loads of replies. I've told Uncle Adrian (whom you quite rightly describe as 'the fascist') to send you some extracts from his diary from time to time, and Gerald promises to write too.

Be brave, sweetheart! Remember Jesus loves all little children, and he's already turned up without you knowing it. See you soon.

Love, Anne.

XXX

Dear Anne,

    I cryed a bit when your parsel came. Mother's frend Gwenda says tears are a sign of weekness, but its hard to be strong when you are horizontall, Anne. You mustn't call them gingerbread men by the way. Muther made me a gingerbread <u>person</u> wonce. She said the men sort are sexist. Yours tastes just the same though. I hope there are no harmfull addititives in it. Gwenda says that bad temper and murder and rape and war are all caused by harmful addititives. She and muther said they were going to only live on grapes once because all the other food was full of harmful addititives. Gwenda said that in a few days they would be tall and strong and clean. By the third day they were crauling round the kitchen floor pewking up bits of grape. I stuck to having mewsli every day. It is a bit like eating your way out of a haystak, but at least you dont pewk up. Father used to annoy Gwenda when he was still living at home by saying he wanted a nice fat E102 sandwich for tea. I dont think father liked Gwenda. I hope Uncle Edwin finds father soon, Anne. My logical bond hurts.

It was orful when I broke my lemur, Anne! Muther said I had fifteen seconds to get my rollerskates off, eat my mewsli and get reddy for bed. I tried to do them all at once and fell down. When we got to the hospital a man looked at my leg and said he was the sturgeon who was going to mend me. He said he was called <u>Mister Fisher</u>. Just my luck to get an uncwollified one! He said I'd got to be an attraction for weeks and weeks, so here I am. Oh, Anne, it's a real pain in the base!

Thanks for the persunnel problem and all the stuff. Are you sure Jesus has turned up?

Logical bonds

Andromeda.

P.S. Do you think you've got just a
bit of a logical bond for me, Anne?
Do you think you mite have?

Dear Andromeda,

Anne Plass has just phoned me to say you've had a bit of a disaster! You really do things in a big way, don't you my adorable little niece. I wish Mum had let me know before she went, but never mind – we'll cope. Anne says she's sending you lots of stationery, and I'm going to let everyone in the church know that letters would be appreciated. No point being an Elder if you can't use it sometimes, eh, cherub? I'll be along to see you of course, and I'm sure there'll be a few others coming to stare at the only Veal in captivity! By the way, why not drop a few lines to some of our world leaders? You never know, you might change the history of the world!

As far as getting in touch with your dad is concerned, I'll do my very best, but, as you know, he did leave home rather suddenly, and so far no one I've asked seems to know where he's got to. Don't worry though – he's bound to get in touch eventually. He's always been quite crackers about you, Andromeda, you know that. We'll all be praying for you, love. See you soon.

Best wishes,

Uncle Edwin.

P.S. Don't give the nurses too hard a time, honey. They're not used to political activists like you!

The Gremlin,
 Red Square,
  Moscow,
   Russia.

Dear Mister Gorgeouschops,
        You don't know me, but I am a
small english soshulist called Mizz
Veal — Mizz Andromeda Veal. I am
eight and I am an attraction in
hospital. Pleese don't think you've
got to stop   your breckfast in the
 Gremlin kitchen just to read my
letter. I know you are very bizzy
and ockupied in Affganistan and
trying to get the pollit-bureau open
and stopping Prezident Raygun from
watching Star Wars on the moon,
but I wanted to ask you sumthing.
Everyone says you are not like Linen
and Starling and the bald thick one
who fighted with tables at the Untied
Nations. The thing is — I was wun-
dering if I could be your speshul
adviser when I am bigger. I can't
do much at the moment because
the state have got me horizontall

til the bones nit, but I am a soshulist like you and I could help. I
know ruffly where Margaret Thacher
lives, so I could show your G.B.H.
agents which tube to get off at if
they wanted to infiltraight her whe-
n the reverlooshun comes. Also I
could warn you when birds fly over-
head so you don't get those nasty
splodges all over your head! Your
Russian pigeons must be a size Mister
Gorgeouschops!

One thing I don't like is your
camps. They don't sound much fun.
Mother read to me about one in a book
called A day in the life of Ivan
Something that sounds like a sneeze,
but I think Starling was Akela at
that one so I'll let you off.

By the way my frend Geruld
(we share his persunnel problem) told
me that Neil Kinnock is an anagram
of I knock Lenin. Puts you off a
bit, eh?

Logical bonds,
Andromeda Veal (Mizz)
P.S. Don't tell muther I wrote will

you? She says Russian soshulism is a load of crab, but I think you look nice.

P.P.S. We've got one of yours over here already. He's in charge of lots of minors and he's got two brillo pads stuck to his head. His name is sumthing like Half a lagers brill.

P.P.P.S. Have you ever had to pee horizontall while you've been in charge of Russia?

Dear Andromeda,

Name of Thynn. Leonard Thynn. Friend of the Plasses – well, think I'm a friend. *Am* a friend. Sure of it! Friend of the Plasses. Adrian: tall, friendly, simple type. Anne: sweet, lovely, wonderful. Gerald: good lad, speaks his mind, not everyone likes what's *in* his mind. I do. Took me home and helped me to bed once when I got a bit – tired. Yes, definitely a friend of the Plasses. They certainly like *me* – well, they seem to. Quite often borrow their cat for – never mind what for. Used to have some pets myself. Cat called Brandy. Budgie called Soda. Two goldfish called Ice and Lemon. Funny eh? No, not really. Bit of a give-away actually. Got a little problem – well, not a *little* problem, more of a *big* problem, with thingy. Drink. Too much, that is. Yes.

Anyway – 'nough about the wretched Thynn. About you, young Veal! Hear you came a cropper. Bust your whatnot. In for running repairs, eh, girl? Well – not *running* repairs. Silly word to use really. More like 'hanging about' repairs. Femur I'm told. Fearfully fiddly fings femurs. Bit of a joke there. Well, not quite a joke, more of a – well, bit silly really. Always rather enjoyed alliteration. That's when all the first letters are – sorry! Drivelling on rather. Habit of mine.

Look! Thought I'd tell you a funny story. Cheer you up a bit. Not very good at it, but I'll have a go. Starts after the next full stop. This chap – walking through a forest. (Doesn't have to be a forest, you understand. Could be a wood, copse, clump – any sort of arboreal assembly, as long as trees are in the picture. Got it? Good.) Well, this chap is walking (or he could be strolling or ambling. Not striding. Striding spoils the story), he's walking, strolling or ambling through this forest, copse, wood or clump, when all of a sudden he notices a little chap (not abnormally little, I don't mean, more sort of at the bottom end of the 'not a dwarf' range), and this comparatively little chap is squatting behind a tree. I expect you're saying to yourself, 'How did the chap (the one walking through the forest, copse, etc. . . .) notice the little chap at all (the squatter, that is) if he was behind a tree?'

31

Well, the answer is that the squatter, vertically deficient though he might have been, was significantly broader (in the squatting posture at any rate) than the tree behind which he squatted. Clear? Good.

So, then the strolling chap calls out to the squatting chap (and we're getting a lot closer to the funny bit now), he calls out, 'Hello!'. Then the squatting chap – presumably craning his neck round his tree to see the strolling chap – (actually, he's probably not strolling any more – probably stopped just before addressing the squatting chap, but I'll go on calling him the strolling chap so as not to confuse you. Okay?) – now where was I? Oh, yes, the squatting chap calls over to the strolling chap and says, 'Hello!' back. Then, the strolling chap, who obviously doesn't have even a passing acquaintanceship with the smallish squatter, says, 'What are you?', and the chap replies, 'I'm a tinker.' Then the stroller says (and this really is the final bend before hitting the old punch-line – *ever* so funny! Well, *I* think it's funny – well, *quite* funny), he says, 'What are you doing squatting behind that tree?' And the chap answers (I'll put it on a separate line because this is IT, the joke proper), he says:

'I'm tinking.'

Get it? I'm *tinking*. What are you doing? I'm *tinking*. Good 'un, eh? Hope it's not a bit too – you know, bit too thingy.

Anyway, sorry about the leg and – the leg. Told mother I wanted to write to Andromeda. Poor old Mum. Deaf as a post. Said if I wanted to bite a chronometer I must be even loonier than she'd thought. Still – sent her love when she understood. Said a prayer with her about you last night. God's alright. Doesn't give up, not with me anyway. Do slip sometimes. Doesn't give up. I could tell you some stories – anyway.

Regards,

Thynn (Leonard).

P.S. Do hope the funny story was, well – you know.

Deep Joy Bible School
Narrowpath Road
Dumpton
Wessex.

Greetings in the name of one who is strong and mighty in deed and word to usward – able to give and provide from his marvellous bounty more than the simple heart of man can imagine, to bring salvation and eternal life through the outpouring of his boundless love to we who, in the latter years, were lost in sin and death, and through his great and immeasurable love to bring us at last safely to heaven's shore through the storm-tossed waves of that sea of life, the crossing of which is the portion of all men until we are called in the fullness of time, and on a day that was appointed and fixed before time began, to be with him for all eternity in the distant and shining place where all is peace and contentment because he is there and prepares a dwelling for us that we might also, undeserving though we be, inherit a kingdom of everlasting joy – from one saved and brought to repentance by that same grace from the sinful and rebelliously hard-hearted nature which all men since Adam have most shamefully endured, and brought finally after tribulation and the ministry of the saints to the knowledge of joy in-working through his soul, by the matchless and powerful movement of that heavenly will in one who shall throughout all ages be deeply thankful for that wonderful beneficence, and awaits with humble obedience the call that will herald his translation into Paradise – to a sister and partaker in the mystical body wherein we all share, who, caught up in the blessed mystery of saving power is one with the saints and martyrs now and through the life hereafter –

Dear Andromeda,

No time to write more now. Will write again soon.

Love, Charles.

Dear Andromeda,

Uncle Ralph here – Anne's uncle really, but I could be yours as well if you like. Anne said you were in for a stretch (Gettit! Stretch! Traction!), so I said I'd write and cheer you up with a few of me jokes. Rib-ticklin' Ralph they call me at work (among other things! Know what I mean?). I went to hospital once with a pain in the neck, but she left after I'd settled in. Eh? Anne said leave the jokes out, but you need a laugh, don't you? Pretty little nurse looked after me when I was in. She said, 'I'm just going to give you a little injection Mr Surtees, I hope it won't put you off me.' I said, 'You couldn't give me the needle if you tried, Nurse!' Laugh! I nearly asked for a bottle. They were a good bunch those nurses, though. Loads of patience. Mind you, they'd have nothing to do if they hadn't got any patients, would they? (Gettit? Patience – patients. Eh?). Doctors were a bit of a miserable lot. I said to one, 'Look, doc, I've had three different bits of me taken out in the last five years. You sure you haven't got a deal on with the local take-away?' Didn't even smile. He must have been foreign. The ward sister was a bit of a gloom and doom merchant too. Tried me best to cheer her up. I'd smuggled this bottle of imitation blood in, see? So one day after I'd asked for the bed pan and they'd put the old curtains round, I tipped it all down me chin and me chest, and hung over the side of the bed with me tongue lolling out and me eyes all wide and staring. Did she bite! I'll say she did! Panic! Emergency! Did she swing into action, or did she swing into action! Then, when she lifted me back on the bed, I grinned at her and said, 'I've finished with the bed pan, Sister.' I've never seen anyone so angry. She got her revenge though. Won't tell you how – let's just say that with friends like her, who needs enemas? Eh? I think the Italians call 'em innuendoes. With me?

I'm coming your way soon, so I'll drop in and say hello. Don't do anything I wouldn't do!

Cheers

Uncle Ralph.

P.S. What's the difference between a nurse with something in her eye, and a boil that's getting better? Answer – one's a blinking sister, and the other's a sinking blister. Gettit? Good 'un, eh?

Dear Anne,

Thankyou verry mutch for arsking yor Uncle Ralf to rite me a letta. It wos a bit of a funnee letta tho Anne. He said he was going to put lots of jokes in to chear me up, but I coodun't find a singul one! Still, he sounds nice and happee.

Anne, I think I mite write to Geruld if that's orlright. Muther said he sounded like one of the plitical corpsis yew see warking about aul the thyme but he was very frendly when I staid with you eeven tho he took the micky owt of me and said that FEMINIST is a nammagranam of I FIST MEN, and wen I said I diddun't thinc that wos verry funny he ticcled me and maid me larf, and woodun't stop untill I said – Corrunashun Street is maud in Personchester – three thymes. There hasn't bean mutch larfing in our house lately, Anne. Muther's frend Gwenda said

that wen the reverlooshun cums,
jokes will be judged on hou fare
they are to mineority groops, and
farther said - are yew seeriously
saying that joaks doon't have to bee
funnee? - and Gwenda said - that's
rite - and farther said - in that
cayse Bob Munkhowse must be the
Chay Gavara of commedy - and
muther put his pipe terbacco in the
food mixa with sum jelly.
  Oh, Anne, I carn't tell yew what
it's lyke to be stretched owt withowt
a pairent. I wood eeven tork to a
raiving fashist antee-reverlooshun-
ery if they wood be kined to me lyke
a pairent, but doon't tell ennyone
I said that, or Kneel Kinnerk
will nevver let me cum to his partee. Who do yew vote four, Anne?
I think yew shood be the leada of
the NICE partee, I do. Cum and
sea me soon, eh?
                    Logical Bonds
                       Andromeda.

P.S. Geruld's not ingaged or enny of that, is he?

Dear Andromeda,

I was so sorry to hear about your fractured lemur – I mean femur. Gerald asked me to say that he hopes that you don't end up with one leg shorter than the other. He said if you do, *he* can't do anything about it, but he knows a man who can. I think he's going to write to you soon. Now that *will* be a miracle!

Anyway – Auntie Anne says she thinks you might want to read an extract from my diary. I can't think why. It is, after all, a serious document. I hope it's not too 'fashist' for you ...

Thursday

Read a great article in a magazine called 'Jam for 21st Century Christian Families Who Don't Buzz Any More'. All about enjoying God's natural creation. Decided a good old family ramble was called for. Anne agreed. Gerald, in one of his cynical moods, said he was fed up with 'rambles, quiche, light jokes, cherryade, harmless fun, and all the other pseudo-Christian baggage that gets dragged around the church'. Got cross with him and insisted he comes on Saturday.

Prayed hard tonight for good weather at the weekend.

Friday

Distinctly overheard Gerald praying for rain as I passed his bedroom this morning. Locked myself in the bathroom and prayed for sunshine again.

We shall see!!

Rang Richard Cook and invited him along too. Gerald said he'd only come if he could bring a new girlfriend called Noreen, who's not a Christian. Agreed rather doubtfully. Hope she gets on alright with Richard. He is such a *Christian* Christian.

Saturday

Woke to brilliant sunshine. Tried not to look smug over my cornflakes. Gerald very glum.

Set off, all in our car, at 10.30 am. Absolute cloudburst the instant I switched the engine on. Ignored Gerald clapping in the back and carried on anyway.

Poor old Richard Cook was jammed in the back between Noreen, Gerald's girlfriend, who turns out to be a very large girl, and Noreen's pet, Paws, who is a huge black hairy dog.

After a while Richard said, in a muffled voice, 'Is your mansion booked in Paradise, Noreen?'

Noreen stopped putting on her bright pink lipstick for a moment, and said, 'No, love, we're just 'avin' days out this year. Can't afford to go away.'

Richard told her he'd meant was she a Christian, and added that he was a charismatic. 'You know what that means do you, Noreen?' he asked.

Noreen said she did because she'd had an uncle who had to stick this thing up his nose whenever his tubes got blocked.

''Ere!' she went on, 'You're not one o' them mormons are you?'

'Certainly not!' said Richard through a mouthful of Paws. 'I abhor sects!'

'Not much fun for your wife then,' said Noreen dispassionately. Blank silence.

Richard said, 'What a charming dog, Noreen.'

'Y-e-e-e-s,' said Noreen affectionately. 'Say hello to Uncle Dickie-doos, Pawsy-poos.'

'Oh dear,' said Gerald a moment later, 'Pawsy-poos has sicky-pood all over Uncle Dickie-doo's shoesy-woos.'

Stopped and let Richard out to clean his shoes with handfuls of grass. Sun came out immediately. Put Richard back next to the window beside Gerald. Stopped a mile later when Gerald was sick all over Richard's shoulder because of the smell.

Nobody hungry when we got to the picnic site. Everything smelled of dog vomit. Paws stole a ham and a huge trifle from the picnic basket while no one was watching. Richard went white and asked if there was a bus back to town.

Went for a short walk but had to dash back when the rain started. Richard begged pathetically to be allowed to sit in front. Anne sat next to wet Paws, who wasn't sick once on the journey back.

Arrived home and all got out of the car. Fine rain and sunshine at the same time.

'Ooh, look!' said Noreen pointing upwards.

We all looked. It was a beautiful rainbow.

Gerald and I smiled at each other.

Anne nodded wisely.

Paws brought up the trifle.

Richard said, 'I know I am not renowned for verbal flippancy, but were you aware that "God's creation" is an anagram of "Dog's reaction"?'

See you soon,

Love, Uncle Adrian.

P.S. I do hope we end up friends despite our political differences.

Dear Geruld,

I eggspect your muther has told you I am a horizontall attraction at the moment what with the lemur nitting and everything. I play with your persunnel problem all the time so I don't hear much, except when your Uncle Ralf vizited me and he pinched Nurse Roundway's base and she screemed so loud I heard it right through the beejees. I like Nurse Roundway. She smiles like a apple. I thort she'd report Uncle Ralf to the sturgeon, but after he'd gone she arsked if he was coming again. Tell you what though, Geruld — sh'es got a loony family. Last night she arsked me if I wanted sumthing to read so I told her I'd got a Soshulist Worker and muther doesn't let me read chilldren's books becouse they poison the mined, speshully Eden Blighted, the one who farther told me writes the Newrotic Nine books.

Gwenda said that Goldiloks and the three bears should really be called Arkytipal woman despretly struggles to snatch a few crumms back from three vicious myth-images of male dommination.

Anway, Nurse Roundway said (yor not going to beleeve this Geruld) she said that her little neece who is the same age as me, won't go to sleep unless she's bin able to cuddle up with her <u>poo</u>. I know it takes all soughts, Geruld, but that strikes me as dissgussting, and I thort we were talking about books anyway.

The fashist you live with sent me a bit of his dairy. I liked it. I liked Paws. I've never had a pet, Geruld. Father was going to get a dog wonce, but muther woodn't let him because she arsked him what he rearly thought of Gwenda, and he said "Clothes by Billy Smart and perfume by paranoya." I've never had a dolly either, Geruld Muther says they are sosieties tool for reeinforsing the subjektiv female roll, but Gwenda said I could have a little plastic man I saw in a toyshop as long as I cauled it Bigot. I luvved Bigot, Geruld, but he got broke when muther threw him at father after she said that Gwenda fild a big space in her life and father said it must be a blinking grate gap if Gwenda fild it.

Pleese come and see me Geruld and tell the fashist I woodn't mined a bit more dairy. Pleese pray that muther will come back from the green and common wimmen soon.

All my logical bonds,
Andromeda

P.S. Did you notiss the bit where I said I havn't got a dolly, Geruld? They are bad things but it woodn't be my fawlt if sumone gived me one wood it?

P.P.S. Eh?

Telephone (Bill awaits faith income)

Dear Brother or Sister,

Please excuse the faint print and poor quality paper of our newsletter but funds are low as we enter the ninety-eighth phase of our project to build the Universal Conversion College. As you know from our previous letter we are aiming for a total sum of 23.5 million pounds. At present we have just topped the thirteen pounds fifty pence mark and it is marvellous to see the work grow. Only last week one of us found five pence in the precinct, and we have also had a number of Tizer bottles donated which should realise a return substantially close to the sum of thirty pence. It is a great encouragement when you are living by faith as we are, to see how all that is needful is provided. We eat regularly (it is my turn to eat on Tuesdays and Thursdays) and it is amazing how many games and activities can be successfully organised in the dark. It occurred to me last night, as I lay trying to sleep on the linoleum, that our policy of never asking for financial support is what separates us out from those projects which seem to be constantly begging. The space provided at the bottom of this letter for Barclaycard numbers is purely intended for those who feel personally led to share their wealth and comfort with brothers and sisters fighting a lonely battle on the rugged frontiers of Christian endeavour.

Some have queried the fact that one of our original prophetic words to the effect that the college would be built and the whole of England and Wales converted by last Wednesday, has fallen a little short of fulfilment. We now feel led to say, however, that we believe this to be due to a spirit of meanness in some individual outside the project. We prayed for him or her last night as we read the story of Ananias and Sapphira by candlelight. Do you know that story, friend?

Yours,

Vernon Rawlings (sic sec)

P.S. We are also anxious that you should not leave large sums of money to the college in your will, unless you are absolutely sure that you wish to support the Lord's work, rather than leave the money to people who are already comfortably off.

P.P.S. We are studying the book of James at present. What a fine message it presents!

Part Two

Dear Anne,

Muther rung me up this mourning from a place near the green and common wimmen. It was a very bad line. I arsked her if Mister Raygun had bin for his base yet, but she said there are still a lots of crude rissoles behind a fence, so she can't come back yet. She said she cryed last night when she thought of me being an attraction and horizontall, but Gwenda said it was just a bad cayse of G. M. T., and G. M. T. always makes wimmen tense. I arsked Nurse Roundway what G. M. T. means. She said it means Grennich Mean Time. Why does Grennich Mean Time always make wimmen tense, Anne? Are we all going looney or what?

A man in a backwoods collar came round today Anne. I was the only one he spoke to. He said he was ~~caulled~~ cauled the Neverend Boom, and it was his first time in the

49

hospital. Just before he went I arsked him why he hadn't spoken to ennyone else. He said it was because I was the only one with P for Prottistant at the end of my bed. He said all the others had R.C. for Roaming Catlicks, C.F. for Christian Felloaship, or B. for Baptists or S.A. for Salvation Army. He'd gonn before I cood tell him. P. is for Porridge and R.C. is for Rice Crispies, and C.F. is for Corn Flakes, and B. is for Bran, and S.A. is for Stewed Apple. I thort I was the stupiddist person in the world, Anne, but Neverend Boom wins by a mile.

Did Geruld notiss the bit in my letter where I said I havn't got a dolly, Anne? Because I havn't got one of those bad things. If he gets me one I won't upset him by not taking it. I will pretend I like it.

Logical bonds
Andromeda

P.S. If Jesus only likes good little

girls, I don't think he will like me,
Anne. I am affrayed I was pleased
when muther said she cryed.
Yes I was, Anne.

Darling Andromeda,

Just a quick note to say that there's one address I didn't give you that I meant to. Do you remember, sweetheart, when you stayed with us, you met Father John? He was dressed in a long brown cloak and he was going rather bald on top. Now I come to think about it, you didn't actually *meet* him, but you saw him in the next door garden talking to Frank Braddock, our neighbour. Father John is a very kind, wise man, and I know he'd be only too happy to help with any problems you might have. Do write to him if you want to, darling. The address is on the back of this letter. See you soon.

Love Anne

X X X

Hey, Andy Pandy! Gerald here!

What's going on? I hear you lost a battle with a stone floor and now you're on the rack down at St Whatsit's. Thanks for your letter by the way. Best letter I ever had, especially the bit about old Uncle Ralph giving your Nurse Roundway a tweak. Sounds as if he's well in there! Like the bit about 'Eden Blighted – the one who wrote the Neurotic Nine books' as well. Something tells me I'd get on really well with your father – which reminds me, I'm not one of your get-up-at-dawn-and-pray-for-three-hours types, but I have been flicking the odd tiddly-wink up towards Holy Head Office. So have lots of others, so we'll probably see a bit of action in that area before long. Get in touch with old Father John – pure gold, he is. Talking about fathers – dear old Dad (the fascist, you know) is his same old loony self. Dad's pure gold in his own way as well, but he does get himself into some scrapes. The other day my cousin Wanda rang to ask if we could look after her babies for one night. Oh, Andy Pandy, you should see 'em! Triplets – three boys, one year old, and their names are Shadrach, Meshach, and Abednego. Their dad's a Christian steelworker, so he's really into fiery furnaces. Anyway, Mum was out when the call came, so Dad took it, and his end of the chat went something like this.

'Hello, Wanda ... yes, I see ... yes, I understand ... yes of course it's an emergency, I can see that ... just for the Friday night? ... oh, yes! No problem ... of course I mean it. We adore children ... no it's not Wanda, it's nothing at all. You just go ahead and make the arrangements and don't even think about Friday night ... no, it's a pleasure *really*. I'll enjoy it ... Yes ... 'bye Wanda.'

All through the call I was trying to attract Dad's attention, Andy, but he kept waving me away like he does when he gets exasperated. So after he'd put the phone down he turned to me and started ticking me off.

'I should have thought,' he said, all dignified, 'that it might be possible to speak on the telephone in my own house' (he only owns about one brick, Andy) 'without my son waving like a dervish at me because he can't wait to make some totally irrelevant comment!'

'Sorry, Dad,' I said, 'I was just trying to tell you that ...'

Mum came through the door just then and asked what was going on. So Dad explained, still very dignified, and when he got to the bit about me trying to interrupt, she just leaned back against the door and started giggling.

'I wasn't aware,' said Dad, 'that anything I've said is particularly amusing.'

'No, it's not really, darling,' said Mum, 'it's just that I think what Gerald was trying to say to you was that I'm not actually here on Friday night, am I? Remember? I promised I'd stay with Samantha Rind-Smythe for the night, didn't I, sweetheart?'

Poor old Dad went all white and quivery, Andy, and he made a little screaming sound in his throat. He tried to 'unfix' it with Wanda, but she wasn't in when he phoned back, and he knew she'd have made all her arrangements by the time he could get in touch with her.

So there we were Friday evening, Mum away till the next morning, and Dad, wild-eyed but determined, doing a real Forth Bridge job on Shadrach, Meshach and Abednego. I think Dad was actually getting to quite like them after a while, except for Abednego perhaps. Abednego really does look incredibly like Bernard Manning, Andy, and his sense of humour isn't much different. He threw his jelly and cream all over Dad, then laughed and clapped.

Anyway, by ten o'clock Shadrach and Abednego were asleep, but Meshach had decided he wanted a long and important chat with Dad. He waved his little arms around and babbled away for ages (just like some of the people in our church), and Dad sat, a bit pop-eyed with tiredness, and listened to him.

'Do you think he's really saying something?' asked Dad after a while.

'Yes,' I said, 'I think he's trying to give you a message – something from scripture, I expect. In fact, I think I can interpret what he's saying.'

Old Dad's just a little bit easy to play jokes on, Andy Pandy. I got a piece of paper, wrote on it, put it in an envelope, sealed it up and handed it to Dad.

'Here you are, Dad,' I said, 'this is the verse I think he's trying to say to you. You open it in the morning and I bet you find it's an accurate prophecy.'

Dad said tiredly, 'Don't be silly, Gerald', but he put the envelope in his pocket, and I went off to bed.

You should have seen Dad when I came down the next morning, Andy. He looked like a dead walrus. Shadrach, Meshach and Abednego were cackling and chattering and crawling and dribbling all over him.

'Good night, Dad?' I said.

Poor old Dad was just a grey lump with a grey voice.

'No, Gerald,' he said faintly, 'I did not have a good night. I had a very bad night. I had an awful, dreadful, appalling night. Meshach continued to talk to me for the entire night, his conversation interrupted only by two dirty nappies. Shadrach had a wet nappy at one o'clock and needed a bottle at three-thirty, and Abednego had two dirty nappies, three wet ones and a screaming fit. They have *all* been awake since five o'clock and if you make any jokes I am going to kill you.'

'Of course I won't make any jokes, Dad,' I said soothingly, 'but aren't you going to look at Meshach's prophecy?'

Dad looked at me with narrowed, bleary eyes for a moment, then dragged the envelope from his pocket and tore it open.

'Go on, Dad,' I said, 'read out what Meshach was trying to say to you last night.'

Dad screwed his eyes up, then read out loud.

'One Corinthians: chapter fifteen, verse fifty-one: We shall not all sleep, but we shall all be changed.'

Had to get out quick then, Andy Pandy, or he'd have thrown Abednego at me. I took pity on Dad after that actually. Sent him back to bed and wrestled with the terrible trio till Mum got home. Do you think he'll put it all in his precious diary? I bet he does!

Anyway, my little stretched friend, that's all for now. I'll be along later in the week, and I'm afraid I *have* bought you a dolly. I hope you don't mind.

Love, Gerald.

P.S. I've got a puzzle for you! Whose name is this an anagram of?

'LOVE AND A DREAM'

P.P.S. An anagram is when you mix the letters up, but I expect you know that, you clever girl.

Dear Geruld,
        I have werked it owt.
Love and a dream is an dnnnagr-
amm of Adam Ovalender!

            L. B's
            Andromeda

Dear Andy Pandy,

Good try – Wrong! Try again . . .

Love, Gerald.

Dear Farther John,

    I know you are a halibut nunk, but is it aul right for small girls with broke lemurs who are attractions in hosspittall to write to you? Do you live in a nunkery? Are you aloud to talk? If you aren't you ort to get a personnel problem like my frend Geruld. They don't harf pass the time if you're horizontall or not aloud to talk. I was going to be a none wonce, but farther laughed and said I'd never get into the habit. Why is that funny? I am only a small size.

    Ennyway, I've got some cwestions to ask you about God and things. Gwenda said that relijun is the opeeum of the masses, and farther said is that why Roaming Catlicks look so glassy-eyed in church? Muther used to say prairs with me, but lately Gwenda's read me bits by sumone cauled Mouse A. Tongue at bedtime from sumthing cauled the little read book. I'm not surprised it's a little read book, Father John. I'd have more fun cuddling up with my poo like Nurse Roundway's dissgusting little neece.

Anne Plass says Jesus is allready here but I am not so shore unless he's dissgised as Mister Blogg, the porter. I hope not. Mister Blogg is a very windy person and spits in those little paper bags on the wall when Nurse Roundway's not looking. I wood be a bit dissappointid if that turned out to be Jesus, woodn't you Farther John?

Here are my cwestions.

Who made God?

Where is God?

Where is hevven?

Why didn't he stop my lemur braking?

Why dussn't he bring muther back from the green and common wimmen when I arsk him?

Where is farther?

Why dussn't he bring him when I arsk?

Can I have some chocklit soon?

Will Germain Greer get in?

What was the R101? (Farther said Gwenda made it look like a chippolarter and she was a much greater disarster).

When will I stop being an attraction?

Do you still go to hevven if yor glad your muther cried? (Don't tell God I arsked that one for goodness sake!)

Logical bonds to aul in the Nunkery,

Andromeda Veal

P.S. Is the cheef nunk cauled a costello?

My dear Mizz Veal (may I call you Andromeda?),

I can honestly say that I have never enjoyed reading a letter more than I enjoyed reading yours. I took it into breakfast with me and laid it beside my boiled egg so that I could enjoy it in peace. We are not allowed to speak at breakfast, so I nearly got told off by the chief nunk (who certainly ought to be called a Costello, even if he isn't), because I kept chuckling over the wonderful things you wrote. We halibut nunks need all the smiles we can get, so I am very grateful to you. Life at the nunkery can be a little quiet at times, although the other brothers are all very nice. By the way, dear Anne Plass did telephone me a few days ago to say that you were in hospital after a nasty accident, so I was planning to come and see you at the same time as I visit my cousin Pearl, who has just had a little baby called George. Would you like me to bring George to see you when I come? As I expect you know, we halibuts don't usually do much marrying and having babies, so I would just love to come and show George off to you as if he were my very own, instead of being a beloved little nephew. Please let me do that.

Now, as to your questions – oh, Andromeda! I felt quite frightened. Such good questions, and so many of them! We nunks are supposed to know all about these things, but I just sat shaking my head and feeling silly. Then Brother Wilf, who is very old with two little tufts of white sticking-up hair, asked me what was the matter. I said that a young friend had written to ask me some very difficult questions about God, and I wasn't sure of the answers.

'Down to the lake, Brother John!' he said. 'Walk down to the lake and see what you find. I will attend to your duties. Away with you!'

One day, Andromeda, Brother Wilf will turn into a bright smile and just float away to heaven.

Down to the lake I went, to see what I would find. I do hope you will be able to see the lake near our nunkery when your leg is better, Andromeda. It is a shining, peaceful thing surrounded by all sorts of trees, and there is a soft quiet path running all the way round so that you can walk and walk until you come back to the place where you started. Here is a secret, Andromeda – just between you and I – sometimes I *skip* along that path. Yes! Can you imagine it – me, in my long brown habit, skipping along like some silly old sheep who's forgotten he's not a lamb any more?

Anyway, I walked along for a bit, listening to all those tiny lapping sounds you hear near lakes, until I came to one of my special places where an old wooden platform pushes out through the reeds into clear water. I stood right at the edge of the jetty, folded my arms in the big sleeves of my cloak and had a little conversation with God. I've put down what we said as though it was a sort of play. FJ is me by the way, Andromeda.

FJ: (Trying to feel holy and good) God, I have some questions ...

GOD: (Interrupting) Look at that little coot among the reeds, John. Look at his little white face. I expect he's looking for some food. I made him, you know. What do you think?

FJ: Very nice, God – very nice, but these questions.

GOD: (Interrupting again excitedly) John! John! Look what's coming down the bank towards us. It's Mother Goose with her old man and all the kids. Look how she's nagging away at them from the back. Aren't you glad you're a halibut? Look how the fluffy children are marching along in line minding their P's and Q's. Dad's got his head down, John. He's having a hiss at you, warning you not to start any aggro. Better not start any aggro, John. No joke, a goose peck. Oh, those babies are so pretty! Not bad, eh, John?

FJ: *Very* attractive, God. Very nice, but ...

GOD: (Sounding a little sad) Oh, John, you should have seen it in the beginning! It was so lovely. It will be again one day too. That's exciting isn't it, John? Isn't it?

FJ: It's very exciting, God, of course it is. God, about Andromeda ...

GOD: (He does interrupt, doesn't he?) John, have you ever made a goose?

FJ: Err ... no, God.

GOD: Have you ever built a coot, John?

FJ: No, God, I've never built a coot.

GOD: Well, let *me* tell *you* that making coots and geese is very complicated. Helping Andromeda is a piece of cake compared with building a coot. You go and tell her I love her very much, and she'll get all her answers as time goes by. I'm working on it right now. You will tell her, won't you, John?

FJ: Yes, God, I will tell her.

Look out for me and George, Andromeda. You should be able to tell us apart. We're both bald, but he dribbles more than me.

God bless from all at the nunkery,

Father John.

P.S. Why don't you write a letter to God? I do sometimes.

Dear Geruld,
        Gott it! It's Mad Ronald
Eave.
            L. B's

                Andromeda

Dear Andromeda,

Wrong again! Here's a clue. Love and a dream is an anagram of the name of someone I like very much. Good luck!

Love, Gerald.

Dear Mister Pluckley-Turf,

I got yor name from somone in the hospittal where I am a long-term attraction since the old lemur bitt the dust. Being horizontall doesn't mean you carn't have vertickal opinions you gnow, and seeing as you are our local ~~fepri~~ ~~repp~~ ~~repree~~ ~~repperez~~ m. p. I thort I'd write you a greevance about the Natural Health Surface in jeneral and this hosspitall in paticular. My frend Gerald (he has kindley donated his persunnel problem for hosspittal use) says that even though I am a left-leaning red person and you are a blue Thacher-scratcher, you still have to lissen to me becos I'm one of your constititituents. I may be onley eight now, but in ten yeers I shall be aloud to vote, eh, Pluckley-Turf, old man? If you want to be ~~a~~ miniskirt of health and soshul obscuritee one day you'll need all the votes you can gett!

Ennyway! It's about Nurse Roundway who looks arfter me. She is very
round and kined and smiles a lot,
but the uther day she was crying in
the nite when she thort I was
asleep, and I arsked why and she
jumped like a ambushed beachball
and told me it was becos she is
verry tired becos there is lots to do
and not enough nurses to do it and
she tries to do more but carn't
and she's sad becos peeple arn't
getting lookt after like thay
should. Then she made a beamy
smile come on her face and said
she was being silly and making a
fuss like a stewpid old woman and she
playd three littal words with me til
I dropt off.
    All you've got to do, Mister Plu-
ckley - Turf is stand up in the
House of Comments and say that
Nurse Roundway cried and then
everyone will undastand and Mrs.
Thacher will tell the civil serpents
to give all the hospittalls some
more money and all the Nurse

Roundways will be orlright again. I
bet you carn't wait to stand up
and get it all sorted out, eh?
I bet Mrs. Thacher'll line up something really speshul for you after
that!

You do think Nurse Roundway's
hosspittal <u>should</u> have more money,
don't you, Mr. Pluckley Turf?

Reguards

Andromeda Veal (Mizz)

Dear Ms Veal,

Rest assured that the issue raised in your letter of last week, is one which has received, and will continue to receive, attention commensurate with the importance attached to it by we whose responsibility it is to consider such matters in the interests of those who ultimately hold us accountable for such consideration, whoever and wherever they may or may not be. You ask me to state unequivocally my view on whether the hospital in which you are at present situated should receive an increased budget for staffing purposes, and perhaps it is your view that politicians are incapable of giving a straight answer to a question. That suggestion I must reply to by answering your question with a resounding proviso. In my own case I think I can honestly say that I have never failed to provide for those upon whom it is incumbent to take responsibility for the elicitation of appropriate responses from persons such as myself in the case of issues such as the one we are addressing, a statement of personal policy which, in terms of specific and unprejudiced concentration on aspects which by their very nature demand totally unbiased and quite unambiguous judgement, are, in a variety of nondiscriminatory ways, quite singularly oriented.

Now, to the actual circumstances pertaining to your individual environmental situation. Should the hospital in question receive extra funding for staff? I can assure you, Ms Veal, that I shall not be found guilty of that iniquitous obfuscation which invariably characterises the type of spurious response that we who humbly yet steadfastly adhere to a species of communication that cannot be described in other than superlative terms with regard to straight-forwardness and regard for what in the circumstances I am bound to refer to as the truth, have come to anticipate in a non-condemnatory but vigorously objective way, from those of our opponents who might be felt possibly to be verging on the brink of the hint of a tendency to be otherwise than open in their statements.

I hope I make myself clear.

None of us can afford, whatever our personal political and social persuasions and inclinations, to ignore the issue of staffing needs in those establishments which in time of physical and mental need carry out their statutory duties as representatives of the corporate will of the British taxpaying public in respect of necessary treatment of that aforementioned need. I reject and abhor such an attempt to side-step the responsibility for close and careful examination of such a complex and, in the atmosphere of negative and therefore potentially positive growth and prosperity prevalent at this time, purely indistinct issue as this one, which it behoves every one of us to face and explore with courage, whatever the outcome may be.

I am personally willing to exercise every ounce of energy and influence that I possess in a fully committed act of restraint with regard to unqualified acceptance of any view which does not fully comprehend the complexities of a position diametrically or obliquely opposed to such a view, and I am in total accord with those who, while decrying unconsidered allegiance to one opinion or another, are prepared to give their whole-hearted support to the proposition of retreat from acquiescence in the suggestion of any failure to act dynamically.

Need I say more? You may be sick in our hands with total confidence.

Yours faithfully,

Hugh Pluckley-Turf.

P.S. The Roundway employee whom you mention is, like all other National Health employees, entitled to days off in lieu of extra hours worked. With a little organisation she will have no further grounds for complaint. The system caters for her type of situation. Need I say more?

Dear Mister Pluckley–Turf,

Eh?

Yours facefully

Andromeda Veal (Mizz)

P.S. After reeding your bit about Nurse Roundway I looked up the end bit of your name in the dickshunnary. It said turf is the same as another werd that starts with S and ends with D. Need I say moor?

Dear Young Person,

(I think it best not to use your first name as I sense occult and astrological connotations in the term. Have mother and father dabbled? My anointed spouse, Stenneth and I have a special ministry in this area, not least because Stenneth, as a young person, unredeemed and adhering to the natural, was exposed to his grandfather's card trick. Thankfully, he is now released, but it is a lesson to us all).

Your name and needs were passed to us by a friend of Anne Plass, with whom I believe you are corresponding. I am surprised that Anne failed to mention it to me herself so that Stenneth and I could offer immediate ministry. But that is so like *dear* Anne. So gloriously human, and so devoted to her husband, who is certainly *not* retarded in my view, and her son Gerald, for whom we pray constantly, that his flippancy and lack of respect will be dealt with in the fullness of time. Only last week he referred to our new assistant Elder, a tall red-haired man with a habit of blinking hard every few seconds as the 'belisha deacon'. I am sorry to report that the majority of the house group seemed to find this remark highly amusing. I prayed silently for those present, and Stenneth's outrage was such that he suffered a choking fit and was forced to leave the room. However, I do not judge Gerald. God will do that.

Now to your accident. I wonder, dear, if there is some little naughty in your life that needs to be brought under the blood. I recall an incident some months ago when Stenneth fell from the loft after climbing the ladder to procure an article for me. He had maintained that the ladder was in such a state of disrepair that it would not support his weight. I agreed therefore, to stand at the bottom of the ladder and prevent the rungs from breaking by faith. As he lay on the landing floor, moaning and clutching the base of his spine, I asked *him* if there was some little unconfessed sin in his life that was gently being pointed out to him. At that instant, before my very eyes, Stenneth was possessed by a spirit of uncontrollable anger, coming very close to a physical attack on my person, shouting as he did so that the only mistake he had ever made was taking advice from 'cabbage-headed idiots who were about as spiritual as mud'. (I thought this a little hard on your Uncle Edwin, who, while not fulfilling the scriptural criteria for eldership totally, tries to do his best.) Despite Stenneth's denial, however, I was not at all surprised when, later in the day, secreted under Stenneth's portion of the nuptial mattress, I discovered an issue of a certain magazine which deals with the construction of balsa wood aeroplanes, an area wont to hold Stenneth captive in the natural, and one which he abandoned after it was revealed to me that if the number of letters in 'balsa wood' is multiplied by the age at which my saintly second cousin Maud's father died, namely 74, the resultant total is 666, the number of the 'Beast'. It was clear to me, then, on discovering this publication, that Stenneth had been covertly feasting his eyes

on illicit constructional illustrations and that his fall from the loft was a call to repentance.

So, young person, *is* there a little knot in the string of your life? If so, you must unpick it and make sure you keep your string nice and tight in future.

I have told Stenneth it is his duty to write to you, and you will be excited to hear that I may be able to visit you soon. Won't that be nice?

Yours faithfully

Victoria Flushpool.

P.S. The Plasses do *mean* well, dear.

Dear Anne,
  Misses Flushpool has ritten me a
pecewlier letter that I don't rearly
unddstand. Will you look at this
coppy of the letter I have ritten
back and tell me if you think it's
aul right? She fritens me a bit.

    Dear Misses Flushpool,
    I am not shore from your
    letter if you are narsty or
    nice. Witch? I arsk myself.
    I don't know why you say
    narsty things abowt my frend
    Geruld. If it wosn't for his
    persunnel problem I wood be
    bawd out of my mined. Wood
    you lend sumone your persun-
    nel problem if they were horizontall
    in sum way? Arsk yorself that
    ~~again~~ Misses Flushpool, eh?
(Have you got a persunnel problem by
the way? If you havn't you ort
to go down the shop and say to the
man — show me yor persunnel

problems because I want one if they don't cost two much).

Annother thing — Geruld feels sorry for you, Misses Flushpool. When I staid with the Plasses I heard him say to the fashist that he thort you had a miserable old face ache. He <u>caired</u> about you being in payne, Misses Flushpool! And he told Anne how well ejucated you are. You must be very prowd of yor deegree in hipockrusee. Anne got mad with Geruld when he said that for sum reeson, but she smyled when he'd gone out of the room. Groan ups are a bit odd if you arsk me.

I am afrayed I ~~did~~ diddn't undastand a lot of yor letter, but you did arsk if my muther and farther had ever dabbled. I don't cwite see what it's got to do with you, Misses Flushpool, but if you must gnow, they did dabble wonce when we were on holiday in Brighten. Farther roled his trowsers up and muther helld her skert up (you coold see her nickers

Misses Flushpool!) and they jumpt about on the edge of the sea. They were cwite happy then but when they went back the next yeer muther met Gwenda and it aul startid going wrong. Farther hates Brighten now. He says you have to be a feemale, marxist, homersexyouall, hunchbacced dworf with a percycution complecks if you want to fit in at Brighten. It must be a very funny plaice. I thort it was just seaside.

I remember yor husband Stenneth, Misses Flushpool. He is a smaul man who only says Amen to that and looks sadd when nowone's wotching. Has he got a big probblim of some sought? Tell him to get Geruld to tell him sum of his jokes. There rearly funny, they are.

Ennyway, Misses Flushpool, thats aul for now. Keep yor pecker up, as farther says.

reguards

Andromeda Veal (Mizz).

P.S. Wots so wrong with my name?
It's betta than being naymed
after a raleway stashun like you;
eh?

Well their it is, Anne. Wot do
you think? She'll think a bit
diffrunt abowt Geruld arfter
that, eh? Perhapps she'll arsk
him to tea or sumthing. I'll
post it off to her twomorrow.

Logical bonds,

Andromeda.

Dear Anne,

Gosh, I was rearly suprised when Nurse Roundway came over this mourning and said you had just phoned to say doan't send that letter to Misses Flushpool. She said you sownded as if you were a bit hett up. I was just abowt to hand it in to be poasted, Anne. It's a pity rearly because I addid on a bit abowt when Geruld said that when God gave out chinns, Misses Flushpool thort he said gins and awdered a dubble. Woodn't she have larfed, Anne? Pleese let me gnow wot was wrong with sending it. I mite have cheered her up, eh?

Logical bonds

Andromeda.

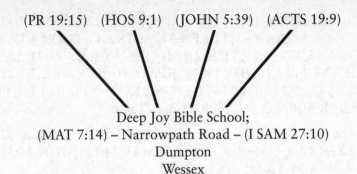

(PR 19:15)   (HOS 9:1)   (JOHN 5:39)   (ACTS 19:9)

Deep Joy Bible School;
(MAT 7:14) – Narrowpath Road – (I SAM 27:10)
Dumpton
Wessex

(JER 31:20)

Dear Andromeda,

I (GEN 6:17, EX 3:11, LEV 26:28, NUM 3:12, DEUT 7:17, JOSH 14:7, JUDG 5:3, I SAM 24:17, II SAM 3:28, JOB 1:15, EZRA 7:21, NEH 5:15, ESTH 4:16, PS 61:2, ECCL 2:25, HEB 2:13, REV 1:17, ISA 44:7, MAT 18:20) will (DEUT 21:14, JOB 13:13, PR 21:1, DAN 4:17, MAT 8:3, MARK 1:41, LUKE 5:13, MAT 20:15, MARK 14:36, JOHN 18:39, MARK 6:25, LUKE 4:6, JOHN 5:21, ACTS 18:21, ROM 7:18, I COR 4:19, PHIL 2:13, TIT 3:8, JAS 4:15, REV 11:6, DAN 4:35, COL 1:9) pray (GEN 20:7, I SAM 7:5, II SAM 7:27, EZRA 6:10, I KI 8:30, I CHR 17:25, NEH 1:6, JOB 21:15, PS 5:2, ISA 16:12, JER 7:16, ZECH 7:2, MAT 5:44, LUKE 16:27, MAT 6:5, MARK 13:18, ROM 8:26, PHIL 1:9, HEB 13:18, I TIM 2:8) for (DEUT 4:7, II SAM 11:22, PR 28:21, MAT 5:45, JOHN 1:16, ROM 13:6, II COR 5:1, II PET 3:12, MAT 6:7, II COR 13:8, MAT 25:35) you (JOSH 3:4, JOB 16:4, ISA 59:2, EZEK 11:19, AMOS 2:13, LUKE 10:16, ROM 2:24, II COR 9:4, EPH 2:1, COL 1:21, GEN 9:9, LEV 25:46, DEUT 11:4, I SAM 25:19, JER 42:16, II COR 9:14, PHIL 1:8, EX 10:16, LEV 26:17, JER 44:11, NUM 17:5, DEUT 1:44, JOSH 23:16, MI 1:2) every (GEN 6:5, LEV 19:10, NUM 5:2, I SAM 3:18, PS 119:101, PR 2:9, ISA 45:23, ROM 14:11,

JER 51:29, EZEK 12:23, DAN 11:36, ZECH 12:12, MAL 1:11, MAT 4:4, MARK 1:45, LUKE 4:37, ACTS 2:43, I COR 4:17, II COR 10:5, EPH 1:21, PHIL 2:9) **day** (GEN 1:5, EX 21:21, LEV 23:37, NUMB 3:13, DEUT 4:10, JOSH 6:10, JUDG 16:2, RUTH 4:5, I SAM 9:15, JER 15:9, NEH 4:2, ESTH 9:17, JOB 1:4, PS 19:2, PR 4:18, ISA 7:17, JER 12:3, EZEK 4:6).

Love (GEN 29:20, II SAM 1:26, PR 5:19, ECCL 9:1, JER 2:2, EZEK 16:8, DAN 1:9, HOS 3:1, MAT 24:12, JOHN 13:35, ROM 8:35, GAL 5:6, COL 1:4),

Charles

x (PR 27:6, LUK 7:45, ROM 16:16, I THES 5:26, HOS 13:2, PS 2:12)

Part Three

Dear Anne,

Oh, Anne! Gess what, gess what! Farther John cayme to see me yesterday like he said he wood and gess what! He brort George (that's how you spel it, I do'nt gnow why), and gess what, Anne. George liked me, he did. He <u>did</u> Anne! His muther is cauled Pearl and she told Farther John it was orlright for me to meat George and he brort him and I did and he smiled at me and oh, Anne! Listan, Anne, do you gnow abowt baby's hands? Their very smaul arn't they? George's hands are very very very smaul and Farther John said lets tell eech other what we think his hands look lyke. He said he thort they were lyke littal tiney bunches of pealed prawns. That was pritty good, eh, Anne? I wanted to think of sumthing even betta, so I thort and thort about what George's littal fingas peeping out of his sleeves lookt lyke, and gess what, Anne! I rememberd when I went on the beech with Farther at Brighten and he picked up a incy littal shell from a rock pool and held it on his hand and said - Wotch this, Andy bugs! (Daddy ewsed to caul me Andy bugs, Anne). And arfter a while sum titchy littal legs cayme creeping owt of the shell and a littal creecher walked allong Daddy's hand loocking four his home in the sea. Daddy told me it was cauled a hermitt crab, Anne. They pinch shells from wincles wile their owt.

Ennyway, I said to Farther John - I think George's fingers twiddling owt of the ends of his sleeves look just lyke a littal hemitt crab's legs comming owt of his shell. And gess what, Anne. Farther John said he thort my idear was the best! Betta than the pealed prawns! Acey-pacey skill for sumone who's a horizontall attraction, eh, Anne? Farther John said he could tell George lyked me becos he loocked at me and dribbald down his nuncles brown habbit in a happee sort of way.

Then nurse Roundway came allong and said oo isan't he sweet and things and isan't he lyke his daddy (meening Father John). So I pokt her jently in the base and wissperd — he's a halibut nunc, he lives in a nunkery. Then she notissed his habit and went aul red, but Father John said it was orlright and axshully he felt flatterned. You'd think Nurse Roundway wood have more cents, woodant you, being higlee trained and aul? She's a E. S. N., you gnow. Father John says I'm George's onararary arnt. That's eggsiting, eh?

Logical bonds,

Andromeda.

P.S. Tell you sumthing, Anne. Doon't

tell ennyone else becos it sounds
sillee, but when I was lying quiett
jus now, do you gnow whot I thor-
t? Father John onley rearly torks
about ducks and coots and babys
and things, but arfter he's gonn
it feals as if Jesus has bin.
Funny, eh?

88

Dear Geruld,
    Gottit this thyme! The persun you like is Eva Raddlemoan!

        L. B's
            Andromeda.

P.S. Eva Raddlemoan's not a little girl, is she, Geruld?

Dear Andy Pandy,

Eva Raddlemoan?! You must be joking! Another clue – this person who I like VERY MUCH has got the initials AV. Come on!!!

Love, Gerald.

Dear Child,

I am a nun in the Order of Saint Bollom of Nurd. He formed his Order in 463 and entitled it The little Brothers and Sisters of Inverted Ablution. He declined all food but squirrel droppings, and believed that God is most profoundly encountered in small purple objects immersed in badger's milk. He spent most of his life under a tree with his follower, developing the tenets by which we of the Order still live.

My name by the way is Sister Valium, and I was told of your plight by a holy Father of my acquaintance. He happened to mention the name of the hospital wherein you are constrained, and I have decided to address your soul on the qualities needful to one in your position.

First, we learn of the need for Patience from Saint Hormone of Pucket, a great intellectual of the middle ages who spent his life patiently attempting to prove his contention that the world was shaped like an aardvark's pelvis. He died in 1163 when a recalcitrant aardvark aggressively resisted his research. We revere his memory and we pray with him for that same quality of patience.

For a lesson on stillness, we turn to the work of another giant of the early church, Saint Weirdlip of Grime. Saint Weirdlip was commissioned to compose a poem on stillness by Pope Verminous the 59th in 269, and I have set the finished work down here for your edification.

> Be still, and if not still,
> Still, in not still, still be still,
> Still, until still cannot be still,
> Be still, and still be still,
> In not still. Oh, be still!

Saint Weirdlip, a great traveller, read his poem everywhere until his death in 274 when he fell off a pyramid. We remember his words and seek to attain that stillness.

Thirdly, we turn to Saint Gudgeon of Milton Keynes, a more recent teacher, to learn of the place in which we might find truth. Saint Gudgeon lived a hermit's life, preferring to remain in his Wendy House on the roof of a local fire station, emerging only to impart the newly ripened fruits of his long periods of meditation and contemplation. Saint Gudgeon delivered the following address to passers-by in a loud voice as they passed the fire station one Saturday morning.

'Brothers and Sisters, I tell you that when we seek the truth inside, it is actually outside, and when we look for it above, it is actually below, and when we hope to find it in front of us, it is actually behind us, and when we think we have found joy, we have actually found sadness, and when we are in turmoil, we are actually at peace, and when the wind blows, the air is actually very still, and when the rain falls it is actually very, very dry, and black is actually white, and get your hands off me . . . !'

Unfortunately, Saint Gudgeon's address was terminated by the arrival of two uniformed persons who maintained that the peace was being disturbed, and offered him the choice of quickly returning to his Wendy House or accompanying them to the police station. Enough of his homily emerged, however, for us to learn of the search for truth, and to feel grateful for the wisdom of this holy man.

So, child, may your soul benefit from these truths and may they be an aid to swift recovery.

Benedictions,

Sister Valium

Dear Sister Valium,

Thancyou four writing me aul that Sainte Bogwash stuff and that. My sole has befenittited from it. No dowt abowt that, eh? I had a Wendy house wonce becos farther bort me one, but Mother and Gwenda wood only lett me play with it if I cauled it a Willy house and put plastick Bigot inside two do the howsework, and I had to preetend to go off eech morning to do my carrear in the billding trade.

Farther got drunk once and sat innside with Bigot for hours and woodn't come owt so muther demolishuned it aul round him and he jus sat holeding Bigot and ~~singin~~ singing We shall Ovacome. That wos the end of my Willy house.

Regards to aul in the advent,

Andromeda Veal (Mizz).

Dear God,

A frend of yors cauled Father John said it wood be aul right to write to you. As you gnow (beeing omnisheeant), I am a horizontall attraction at the moment, but I hope to be A1 lemur-wise before two long. Farther John has eggsplained to me abowt Jesus and the cross and aul. He says I can be in it if I want. I want to be in it, God, but I am afrayed you will not be getting a verry good deel.

I was glad when muther said she cryed. Pretty bad eh, God? Can you still have internal salvashion if yor glad yor muther cryed? Farther John said you wood forgive ennything, but nunks do get a bit carryed away, don't they? Mined you, I do understand a bit abowt Jesus on that cross becos when Farther John said abowt it, I said it was a bit like being stretched horizontall like me, only up strait. He said it was, so I said Oh, so Jesus was rearly an attraction like me? Then Father John's eyes went aul wet and he said

Yes, Andromeda, he was an attraction just like you. He smiled threw his teers, God. Does that mean there must have been a rainbow on my face? Next time Farther John came too see me, he brort me a collidoscope. It's grate God! You look threw this incy littal hole and their are all shining peaces making a ~~butful~~ butiful pattern. Farther John said I cood be a littal shining peace in the collidoscope that Jesus is, so next time you look threw a little hole at yor son Jesus yooll gnow one of the shining peaces is Andromeda Veal (Mizz).

Ennyway, the uther thing is, good luck with Muther and Farther and Gwenda. I hope you mannage to sought it aul out. Farther John says they aul got sum things wrong. It's

a big job for you, God. The larst
time I saw them aul togetha
was when Gwenda cut her finger
and farther ran and got a puncture repare outfitt. That was the
last straw. Muther told farther
to cleer off and never come back.

Tuff one eh, God? Betta get
an ace angel on it.
        Logical bonds,
            Andromeda Veal (Mizz)

P.S. I bleeve yor acwainted with
George, who is Farther Johns neffew.
He is a sooperconfabulus baby who
likes me.   Ennyway, sumone brort
him over two the nunkery the other
day to vizit his unncle and
Father John left him with Bruther
Wilf for a minnit while he went
sumwhere. Ennyway! When he
cayme back he said that George and
Bruther Wilf (he has too tufts of
white hare sticking up from his
head, God. Do you gnow him?) were
just smiling at eech uther and
just for a ⚡ seccond he thort they

were eggsackly the sayme age!
Silly eh, God? One's verry old
and the uthers hardly borned!

P.P.S. I've adresst this to God c/o
hevven. I hop that's aul right.

Dear Geruld,
     Alan Veedordam! Eh?

          L. B's.

               Andy-pandy
          (That's what you
          caul me, Geruld).

Dear Andy Pandy,

Can you honestly imagine me REALLY LIKING someone called Alan Veedordam? I can't even say it. I can see I'll have to give you a lot more clues. Here goes! The person whose name is an anagram of Love and a Dream is:

(1) Someone I like VERY MUCH.
(2) Someone whose initials are AV.
(3) Someone who is in hospital with a broken leg.
(4) Someone who is eight years old.
(5) Someone who wants a bad beautiful dolly.
(6) Someone who is very pretty.
(7) Someone who I'm going to give a new personal stereo to when her birthday comes.

Love, Gerald.

Telephone (Reconnection awaits faith income)

Dear Brother or Sister,

How true it is that as one door closes another one opens. We now know and believe that the Universal Conversion College Project was meant to test our faith in preparation for the REAL task, that of organising and financing massive musical outreach events throughout the known world. Sadly, one or two of our number have left on finding that our earliest prophetic word (to the effect that the College would stand and be fruitful until the second coming) is no longer intended to be fulfilled. Regretfully, the departed brethren were unable to sustain faith in our divinely inspired change of direction, and faith, after all, is what underpins and makes possible the Lord's work.

Once again we must apologise for the even poorer quality of paper and print in our newsletter, but there are insufficient funds at present to repair our duplicating machine or to purchase new stocks of paper. Once again, however, our needs have been wonderfully met. One of our number retrieved an old John Bull child's printing set from the loft in his parents' house, and incredibly, on the very same day we discovered an anonymous gift of almost fifty sub-standard brown paper bags, simply left in the middle of the road outside our prefab. Wondrous indeed! And clear evidence that we are following the correct path.

As if more evidence was needed! It is now only weeks since it was revealed clearly that the three of us who remain are to create a powerful new musical force that will completely transform the concept of Christian music around the globe. In those weeks I have almost mastered E minor and G major on my little sister's guitar, and as funds are prayed in and it becomes possible to purchase the two missing strings, I believe in my heart that I shall be able to strum a three-chord accompaniment to 'Go Tell Aunt Rhody' by the time Christmas is here. That is not ordinary progress!

Much musical equipment will be needed, including sound systems, a range of the best guitars, drums and drum machines, keyboards of every description, special lighting effect facilities, and, of course a combination of vans and Range Rovers to transport the equipment to venues all over the world. Already we have a second-hand plectrum and a skateboard. Pledges, we believe, of the abundance that is to come. Please pray that my little sister will not notice her guitar is missing until after Christmas.

More strongly than ever we believe that we are called to live and work entirely by faith, without mentioning problems and hardships that could be alleviated by financial contributions. God knows, such difficulties abound, and, if listed, would cover several paper bags, but we are confident that the necessary funds *will* arrive and, after all, what is hunger, cold, lack of clothing and discomfort at night compared with the advancement of the Kingdom? Once more we make an impassioned plea that those who feel led to spend their money on shallow personal pleasures rather than the Lord's work should feel free to do so. We really do *not* want your cheques or postal orders (crossed and made payable to the WWCEC), unless you care.

Yours,

Vernon Rawlings (sic sec)

P.S. News of musical venues will follow. Eventually we hope to perform at Las Vegas, Wembley Arena, the Shea Stadium, and in Red Square. Our only actual booking at present is Stanley (my assistant) playing the spoons at amateur night in the public bar of the Frog and Spittle just down the road from the prefab. We really are looking for a miracle here, as we possess only one spoon and Stanley has never done it before.

Dear Geruld,
      Oh, Geruld! It was me!
Oh, Geruld. Love and a dream.
Oh, Geruld!

      L. B's.

      Andromeda Veal.
      (Andy-pandy) X.

Dear Farther John,

How are you and aul the uther halibuts? How is Bruther Wilf? I have dun a pichure of him to hang on his sell door. I bet heel be the onley one in the nunkery to have an eriginal Veal. One day in the fucher they'll sell it at Smotherbee's action rooms for trillyons and trillyons of pownds, and Brother Wilf's grate granchildrun will be as rich as acey—pacey Cliff Richud. Oh no! I forgott nunks doon't have baybies, do they? Well he cood leave it too the nunkery if he wants, so they can train up new Bruther Wilfs in the fucher. I hope he lykes my pichure. I did it four him becos he did yor work for you while you torked to God abowt coots and that, down by the lapping lake.

Listan, Farther John! Gess

what's happerned! I doon't gnow
if I menshunned it too you, but
I have nevver had a dolly
eggsept plastick Bigot and he
was a vicktim of dumbestic
vilence.   Gwenda said that in
the new aje arfter the reverlooshun wimmin woodn't be miss-
lead by such divices. She said
wimmen get a ror deal aul
round becos men ewes them. She
said sheed never   aggree to
show her nakid body on page
threee of the tablet press, then
farther said he'd lyke to prerpose
a vote of thanks on beeharf
of aul men evvrywhere, and it
aul got a bit vilent again.
Ennyway, Muther said I
wosn't to have a dolly becos
dollys are bad and I said I
doon't wont one ennyway if
their bad. But, Father John, I
wosn't telling the trooth! Ooh
Father John, I did wont a dolly
so much! Ennyway! In a letta
  to my frend Geruld (he's going

to give me my verry own ~~xxxx~~
persunnel problem soon by the way)
I sought of hinted that I
woodn't mind having a dolly,
eeven though they are bad
things. Gess what! He sumhow
got the hint! I slept aul
 threw viziting this morning
and when I woke up - gess what!
Their was anuther head on the pillo
necst to mine. It was a big
dolly! A dolly, Farther John!
She is luvvly and pritty and in
a bewtiful dress and their
was a note pinnd to her dress
and what do you think it said?
Are you shaking yor hed in the
nunkery and saying — no, I
doon't gnow what it said?
Are you, Farther John? I'll
tell you. It said,
    MY NAME IS LUCKY LUCY.
Then on the uther side it said
— We have called her Lucky Lucy
because we think she's very, very
lucky to belong to such a nice
little girl, from Anne, Geruld.

and the fashist.

Oh, Father John, I cuddal my Lucky Lucy aul the thyme, but cood you say to God that duzn't meen he can slip off too the lapping lake too do a bitt of coot bilding. I wont to show my Lucky Lucy to muther and farther soon.

Logical bonds to you
and Brother Wilf

Andromeda

P.S. Did you gnow that I am a nammagranamm of Love and a dream? Geruld said. Good, eh?

P.P.S. Cood you drop me a note eggsplaining the trinnity?

Dear Anne, Geruld and nice fashist,
    I found my dolly that you brort.
    I lyke her name.
    She is grate.
    How do you say thancyoo when you wont it to sound big?
    Thancyoo
    THANCYOO

Logical Bonds,

    Andy-pandy and Lucky Lucy.

P.S. Their mite be sum kissis cumming yor way when I'm verticall again.

Hi, Andy Pandy!

Glad you liked Lucky Lucy. She's a real doll, and so are you! I see the fashist has become a *good* fashist. You should've seen Dad's face when he read that. He's an old softy really. We all went to choose your dolly together, and you've never heard anything like Dad. Fussy? It was amazing! Clothes the wrong colour, ears the wrong shape, hair too long, hair too short, nothing was right. In the end he disappeared down behind this long counter to look at some dolls in boxes on the shelves. Just after he'd dropped out of sight, the lady who manages the shop came up and said to me, 'Is there something I can help you with now, sir?'

Before I could say anything, Dad's voice seemed to answer her from behind the counter.

'No! You're not pretty enough, and your knickers are falling apart!'

You know I don't get easily embarrassed, Andy Pandy, but I could feel myself going red.

'He doesn't mean you,' I said, 'he means . . .'

'As for your so-called body, it's hardly human, let alone female! Back in your box, yer ratbag!'

I explained that Dad was talking to the dolls under the counter, but that just made her very nervous instead of annoyed. Dad was mortified when he realised what had happened, so we got out quick after that and found Lucky Lucy in another shop. Your Nurse Roundway let us put her next to you while you were asleep.

Anyway! I ran into Father John yesterday on his way to speak at some meeting, and he told me you'd asked him to 'drop you a note eggsplaining the Trinity'. Good one, Andy Pandy! He was going to write back to you, but I said hold on a minute, because last Sunday we had a talk in church on the meaning of the Trinity, and I was pretty sure Dad would have got it all down in his blessed diary, especially as the 'talk' turned out to be – well, you'll

see what I mean! Dad says you're very welcome to see this bit.
Hope you enjoy it. I think it's *wonderful!*

Saturday

Leonard Thynn round tonight. Says he's volunteered to explain
the Trinity at church tomorrow. Bit surprised really. He can
hardly find his way home, let alone clarify one of the greatest theological mysteries of all. Gerald said he was looking forward to
it, and did we know that theology is an anagram of 'O, get holy!'?

Sunday

Church.

Thynn started by dragging a horrible rusty old electric fire out
to the front. Plugged it into a socket at the side, then faced the
congregation looking rather pleased with himself.

He said, 'Right! Trinity! Easily explained. When I switch on at
the mains in a moment, I want all of you, but 'specially the children, to watch very, very closely, and see if you can spot what
happens. Ready? Here we go! Keep those eyes skinned, or you
might miss it!'

Suddenly felt glad I was sitting at the back. When Thynn
pushed the switch down there was a loud bang and a shower of

sparks. Leonard screamed and stumbled back into Doreen Cook's lap. Several children put their hands up.

Little Dotty Rawlings called out, 'I saw, I saw! It blowed up and frightened you! Is that what the Trinity means Mr Thynn?'

Leonard got up and faced us again. Looked rather white and his hair was sticking up on end. He said, 'Sorry about that, everybody. Little light should have come on, and I was going to say that was like Jesus, and then I was going to say that the electricity was like the Holy Spirit, and then ... well, never mind. Hang on ... !'

Dashed over to the side and came back with an ancient old hoover. Switched the mains switch off, unplugged the electric fire, and plugged in the hoover. Dotty Rawlings leaned forward excitedly. Everyone else ducked.

Leonard said, 'Right! Another idea of mine – really explains the Trinity. Ready, children? When I switch on, watch what it does. Better put your fingers in your ears. Makes a bit of a racket. Here goes!'

Entire congregation flinched as Thynn switched on. Nothing at all happened. Children's hands went up again.

'It doesn't work!' squeaked Dotty Rawlings. 'The Trinity doesn't work, does it, Mr Thynn?'

Leonard turned the hoover upside down and stared sadly at it. He said, 'Hmm ... I *was* going to say that it sweeps as it beats as it cleans, and that's a bit like the old Trini – '

Mrs Flushpool rose like an iceberg to interrupt, 'That is the mediaeval heresy of modalism, Mr Thynn!'

'No,' said Thynn, poking absently at the machinery with his finger, 'I think it's just a coin stuck in the whatsit.'

Leonard ran out of appliances at this point so we went on to the choruses ...

Monday

Thynn round for coffee tonight, also Frank Braddock, our neighbour. Told Frank about yesterday and asked him how *he* would explain the Trinity.

He lit his pipe and said, 'You know, there are four things I like about the Trinity. First, I love having a father in God. Second, I love having a friend and brother in Jesus. Third, I love having a comforter and guide in the Holy Spirit. And fourth ...'

Anne and I said, 'Yes?'

'Fourth, I love the fact that it's a mystery. God in three persons. Three persons – one God. It's a mystery and I love it. Why would I want to spoil things by trying to explain it?'

'Mmmm ...' muttered Thynn, who wasn't listening, 'maybe if I'd used an automatic toaster ...'

Great, eh, Andy Pandy? Isn't Leonard wonderful! See you soon – love to Lucky Lucy.

Gerald.

Pope John Pall,
The Fattycan,
Roam,
Italy.

Dear Pope,
        Aul right so I'm knot a
roaming catlick, but befor you
rush off to give an ordinance to
sumone in annother part of the
Fattycan just considder this. I
have got a frend called Farther
John who is as big a halibut as
you are and I bet he gets inter-
upptid by God near gooses and
coots just as mutch as you do.
(My name is Mizz Andromeda Veal
by the way. I am horizontall
till the lemur recuvvers).
        Our cherch is not cwite like
yors, Pope. We do not have trainsin-
substandardstations at our commy-
union, we aul come in cars, but
we do have the same things to eat
and drink as yor lot, only littal
mingy bits tho, and letts face
it   Pope, the persunn in charje

of our cherch duzzn't faul
flat on his face evvery time he
steps off an airyplane like you
do. Carn't we aul joyne together,
Pope. We cood ion out our
diffrunces. For instans, you say
babies have got to be abul to do
the limbo to get into hevven.
Isn't that a bit unfare, Pope?
Why shood littal babies have to
limbo unda the gaites. Their
too smaul to lern, I reckon. I
can't do it very well and I'm
eight! Lett's leave that won out
eh, Pope? Get all your cardigan-
s together and do a bull on
them abowt it. I'm shore aul
the uther roaming catlicks will
aggree with you. In retern we
coold say you doan't have to
climb the thirty nine steps to
wear an angular preest's hood.
Fare? I think so. By the way,
isn't their one of your monseenyers
who goes on abowt crude rissoles
like the green and common
wimmen. He mite gnow my muther

and her frend Gwenda. I havn't
seen my muther since I started
being an attraction but Father
John has had a werd with God
about it and its aul in hand.
He's a nunk you see Pope.
Hears to yunitty!

Andromeda Veal (Mizz)

P.S. I hear you are a bitt of a
poet, Pope. Well, hears a coinside-
nse - so am I !!! I have writed a
poem speshully for you.

I'm not a roaming catlick,
And I sinseerly hope,
That lodes of preying cardigans,
Will never make me Pope.

I doan't think I'm a anglian,
I'd hayte to wear a hassock,
Or be like Rabbit Runcie,
And gneel apon a cassock.

I gnow who startid metherdists,
John Wesslee did of corse,

114

But I'm no good at showting,
And I cannott ryde a hoarse.

I doont think I'm a batpist,
I even hayte the rain!
When they poosh me in the warter,
Will I come upp againe?

I cood go to a howse church,
But I am rather bad,
At looking verry happy,
When I am fealing sad.

Why doon't we start a nue ~~chur~~
        cherch, Pope,
Where evvrything is reel?
I've eeven got a nayme for it—
The cherch of John Pall Veal.

        Aperson.

Part Four

Dear Andromeda,

My name is Frank Braddock. I live next door to Adrian and Anne Plass who I know are good friends of yours. Another person we are both friendly with is Father John. Years and years ago, we were at school together, although in those days we called each other by nicknames. His was Bungles, and mine was Smelly! You'll never guess why I was called Smelly, and I'm sure as eggs not going to tell you. The only smelly thing about me now (I hope!) is my pipe. I've found some delicious black-cherry scented tobacco, and I must admit it is rather powerful stuff. I don't think they'd want it stinking out the wards at this hospital you've landed yourself in.

Now, the reason I've written is to pay back a favour. You don't even realise you've done me a favour, do you? Well you have, and I'll tell you what it was. When you came to stay with the Plasses some months ago, you went to church with them and, although I go somewhere else usually, I just happened to be at their church on that particular Sunday. Your Uncle Edwin invited me along I think. Halfway through the service you stood up on your chair when the organist struck up, and sang 'SHE IS LORD . . .' at the top of your voice. Then the organist fellow panicked and went into 'Home, home on the range', and all was chaos. Well, ever since then, whenever I've felt a little low, I think of that day, and the organist's face, and one or two folk with their arms in the air singing '. . . where the deer and the antelope play . . .', and I just can't stop a little chuckle from tickling its way up from inside me somewhere and forcing its way out through a smile. So thank you very much for giving me a way to cheer myself up, and that's what I'm paying you back for.

Right! So what am *I* giving *you?* Not much I'm afraid. I'm going to tell you a story. That's my job you see – trying to write things that other people might want to read. I asked Bungles – I mean Father John – if he thought it was a good idea, and he said yes, he thought you would be good at reading stories. (He asked me, by the way, to say that the halibut nunk sends all his logical bonds). Now, here's the story. Hope you enjoy it!

Once upon a time, in a world almost exactly like ours, but with an extra thimbleful of opportunity for strange and exciting things to happen, there lived a little girl in a tall brown house. Now, I know there is nothing wrong with the colour brown. Chocolate ice-cream is dark, tasty brown, Hair can be a lovely shining brown. Some people have warm brown skins. Conkers, chestnuts, horses, birds, new shoes and little girls' eyes can all be brown and beautiful. I know that. But the house that this little girl lived in was a quite different kind of brown. It was a dead, hopeless, given-up sort of brown, an embarrassed, dingy, never-was-smart brown, and it was everywhere. I expect, when I say it was everywhere, you don't really think I mean it, do you? You think that there must have been a few yellows, a patch of red here and there, one or two orange things perhaps, some pictures on the wall with bright colours shining against the dull brownness, and, of course, whole expanses of blue sky and maybe green grass to be seen through the windows, not to mention the faces of all the people who lived in the tall brown house. Their faces can't have been that horrible brown colour, you're thinking. I tell you it was *everywhere!*

Walls, ceilings and floors – brown. Pictures, ornaments, furniture, curtains, lampshades, light bulbs, carpets, books, cups, saucers, plates, bowls, knives, forks – all brown. There might very possibly have been eggshell blue skies, and emerald lawns on the other side of the windows, but it was impossible to tell because every pane of glass was heavily tinted in one overwhelming colour – brown. There was a bird in a brown cage. He was a parrot. He ran up and down his brown ladder, looked at his brown face in his brown shaded mirror, pecked brown seed from the brown sandpaper on the floor of his cage, and had learned to say only one thing – 'Brown Polly! Brown Polly! Brown Polly!' Even the water that ran from the brown taps was brownish. It was used to make brown squash and brown tea, and brown coffee and brown Andrew's liver salts. Please believe me when I say that *everything* was brown. Brown, brown, brown, brown, brown! It was all – brown!

Now here's an embarrassing thing. I've just remembered that one thing wasn't brown. It was a book. It was the little girl's most secret and most precious thing, and she hid it very, very, very carefully in a brown space underneath the brown wardrobe where her brown clothes hung. She'd found it one day right at the back of the big bookcase in the sitting room, and when she opened it, it was as though someone had suddenly punched a book-sized hole through one of the brown-tinted windows. The colours seemed to fly up and dance around in front of her face like music that you could see. She felt quite light-headed and dizzy after only a few seconds, and had to shut the book quickly for fear of falling down. She didn't tell her mother and father about her find. She guessed somehow that they would take it away from her if they knew. So she carried it quickly up to her room and pushed it beneath the wardrobe. Every day since then, when the coast was clear, she had knelt down on her bedroom carpet, slid her hand into the secret space, and, with a little fluttery tickling feeling in her tummy, drawn out the book and feasted her eyes on the bright pages. For a long time that was enough. Just to know that brown was not all was a thrilling secret, but as the weeks went by, and the little girl grew older, she knew that she would have to sit her Mother and Father down one day and ask them to explain their brown attitudes.

The day came. Mother and Father were sitting in their brown armchairs in the brown sitting-room drinking brown drinks from brown glasses. Father was wearing a brown suit. Mother was wearing an old brown artist's smock over a pair of brown jeans. The little girl, whose name was Tanya, came into the room holding something behind her back.

'Mother and Father,' she said, 'I have a question to ask you.'

Father looked at her brownly. He had a thick brown moustache, long brown sideboards, and thin brown straggly hair.

When he wasn't completely happy he rubbed at the side of his nose with his thumb. He was doing it now.

'Ask your question, Tanya,' he said. 'I will try to answer it.'

'Why is everything brown?' said Tanya, quietly and seriously.

Father laughed a clockwork laugh.

'That is not a real question,' he said. 'That is like saying, "Why has everyone got two legs?" Everything is brown because everything is brown. That is the way it is – brown.'

'Is there only brown?' whispered Tanya.

'Yes,' said Father stiffly.

Mother looked worried.

'Why am I not allowed to see through the door when you open it? Why don't we ever open the windows? When am I going to go outside? Why have you told me fibs? Look!'

Tanya swung the open book from behind her back and held it out (open at the most colourful page) towards Mother and Father. Mother gave a little scream and put her hand over her mouth. Father stood up as though a spring had exploded in the armchair and shot him to his feet.

'WHERE DID YOU GET THAT?' he shouted.

'It's mine,' said Mother in a small wavery voice, 'I had it when I was a little girl.'

'I found it,' said Tanya. 'It's not brown. Why didn't you tell me the truth?'

'We thought it best,' said Mother tearfully. 'Colours can be dangerous.'

'Brown is safe,' said Father. 'It is our sort of colour. We did it for you. Why should you be confused by reds and blues and greens and golds and yellows and purples? We had big, big problems, all because of colours. We want you to stay in a brown world and not worry. Outside is a colour jungle. Stay in and tell yourself that all you need is brown.'

'No!' said Tanya, 'I am allowed to be confused too! I *want* to go in the jungle! I *hate* brown! Open that big window!'

She pointed towards the big brown-tinted French windows. All her life they had been closed. Outside, brown flowers bloomed sadly beside brown grass under brown trees as they had always done.

'If you don't open that window *now*,' said Tanya firmly. 'I shall shut my eyes and never, never open them again!'

Mother and Father looked at each other.

Father rubbed his nose *very* hard with his thumb.

'Shall I?' he said.

'Yes,' said Mother.

Father walked over and forced the rusty old brown bolts back. He pushed the windows open. The room was flooded with light and colour. As Father stepped back Tanya ran to the open space and gazed with bright excited eyes at this dazzling world she had never seen. Looking back, she saw that Mother and Father were standing side by side, holding hands. They seemed a little bit older, and a little bit smaller, but, to her surprise, they looked a lot less brown and, for the first time for a long time, they were smiling.

God be with you, Andromeda.

Love, Frank Braddock.

Dear Cliff Richard,

Orlright so I'm onely eight and I carn't play tennis and I havun't got a exy flash nayme like Nivea Looting John, and I havun't maid records like her abowt drinking lemmonaid wen its hot cauled Let's get fizzy cool and I carn't do mutch at the moment ennyway becos I'm an ongoing attraction in hospitall until the lemur getts its akt togetha, and muther is still up with Gwenda and the green and common wimmen and aul, but why shoodun't we get marrid when I am bigger? Arfter aul, you doon't seem to get enny older. One thing tho, yew'll have to be a bit more soshulist with yor cash or Gwenda will nevver let muther let us get ingaged. And let's face it, yor pritty near a trillionair, eh? You cood have as menny personnul problems as you lyke with no cwestions arsked. It's orlright for sum!

My frend Geruld (doon't tell him
I've writed to you, will you Cliff?
He's seccond choise and he mite get
a bit annoyde. Gnow what I mean?)
has onley got one persunnel probbli-
m , and thats on lone to me as
long as I'm horizontall. I bet
you've gived one to Mank Harvin and
all the uther shaddoes and still
got munny over. I bet you have,
Cliff!

Lissan! Annother thing we've got
going four us, Cliff- we're both
beleevers, so it won't be a mixt mar-
rije, and you can arsk yor frend
Billee Greyham to marree us, becos
he is an ordrained batpist as long as
he isn't bizzy getting peeple up owt
of there seats at the thyme. This
necks bit took aul of yesterday to
work out, Cliff. I was abul to do it
becos of muther havving aul yor old
reccords at home. Eeven Gwenda
said that wen she was a young
gullabul girl she lyked you. She
said — he ewsed to make my legs go
all funnee — and farther said - O

, that's wot did it is it? — and
muther tipt his bubbul and squeek
down the waste dissposul.

Ennyway! Hear it is. See if yew can
spot yor old reccords, Cliff.

If yew wont to go on beeing
one of THE YOUNG ONES yewd
betta marry this LIVING
DOLL cauled Andromeda and
stop beeing a BACHELOR BOY,
then arfterwoods we'll go
TRAVELLING LIGHT on our
SUMMER HOLIDAY and if
ennything getts in our way
we'll MOVE IT.
    Sighed,
      Yor DEVIL WOMAN
      Andromeda ♡

Acey-pacey skill, eh Cliffy baiby? Did
you spott the songs?

Ennyway! Nurse Roundway's cumming to put powder on my base in a
minnit. Horizontall = sore, Cliff!
Say hallow to the shaddoes four me,
      Logical Bonds

Andromeda Veal (Mizz)

P.S. Wen you were smaul, were you black with curlly hair and did you scream songs that sownded lyke Bee droppt a loofah she's my baibee or sumthin?

Dear Andromeda,

I hope you don't mind me writing you a little note. I am Lucky Wilf. I am just as lucky as the beautiful dolly that Father John has told me about, because I now have a wonderful picture on the wall of my room. A present from a little girl. Nothing could be more precious. I don't deserve to have it, but I *do* thank you for drawing it specially for me. I am very old, and not very good, but I do know that every now and then God decides that old Wilf needs a little something. *You* helped him this time. Thank you, Andromeda, so much.

Love in the name of my Master,

Brother Wilf.

Dear Bruther Wilf,

I'm pleesed you think my pichure is acey-pacey skill. Lissan! I writed a poem four the Pope the uther day, but now I want to wright one abowt baiby George for Farther John whoo's his uncel as I eggspect you gnow. I hope you ~~will~~ do'ont mined, but I'm sending it to you to see if it's good enuff. If it's exy acey-pacey grate you can tell me it is, butt if you thinc it's pritty crabby stuff can you preetend it's not two bad but not cwite good enuff? Eh? Thancs, Bruther Wilf. Hear's the poem.

God maid George.
by
Andromeda Veal (Mizz)
Age 8

God maid George
A fat littal packit of foot on the end of eech leg,

God maid George
A smile aul cleen and speshul
  from his tummy
God maid George
Wispee moheecan hair, he's a tuffee
  God maid George
His fisty waives say I'm alive, I am!
                                    I am!

God maid George
No narsty bits or nauty bits he's
  onley just unpakked.
God maid George
And he told George to smile at me, I
  nearly cryed, I did,
God maid George
    Sumtimes Georges cum owt
wrong, there braynes and boddies
        aren't maid right
God maid <u>them</u> two
God luvs aul the Georges.

<u>Doe</u>s he luv them aul Bruther Wilf?
Not justhe aulright ones, eh?
          Logical Bonds
            Andromeda Xx

P.S. How old <u>ar</u> yew, for goodniss

sake?

P. P. S.   I hope the kissis ar aulright four a halibut.

My dear Andromeda,

You make me feel so humble. Fancy asking *me* if I think your beautiful poem is good enough to present to Father John! I have not had the pleasure and privilege of meeting little George, but after reading your poem I could almost see him sitting in front of me, smiling and waving his fists to show me he is 'alive – he is! he is!'. As for the 'fat littal packit of foot on the end of each leg', oh, Andromeda, I think that is a marvellous description. I really don't know how you think of these things. Of *course* you must give the poem to Father John. His eyes will light up. They do that you know, when something special happens. I know – I've seen them.

Andromeda, may I ask you a big favour? As you will see I have sent the piece of paper that the poem is written on back to you with this letter. I wonder if you would be kind enough to give me permission to copy it out when you have sent it to Father John? I would like to put it on my wall beside my picture. That would be a real joy! Do say it's alright.

You are quite right of course when you say that some Georges – some babies – are not made right, and you asked me if God loves them just as much. Well, I'm sure he does, but, Andromeda, I must be honest with you. When I was a young monk I used to get very angry indeed with God. 'Why,' I used to say, 'when you are supposed to be able to do anything, and you are supposed to love everybody, do you let little babies be born with things wrong with them? Why, God? Tell me!' Oh, I *did* get ratty, Andromeda, and I didn't seem to get any answers at all. So I went along to someone called Brother Arnold (he was about as old then as I am now, and much, much wiser) and told him all about it. He listened and smiled and didn't say anything for a long time, then he said, 'Wilf, I want you to go and kneel in the little chapel and look at the cross on the altar, and as you kneel there I want you to say these words over and over again quite quietly to yourself – "He's in it with us – he's in it with us," then come back and tell me what you think. I'll be waiting here.'

We had a wonderful little private prayer chapel at that place, Andromeda. It was very small, not much bigger than a fairly big pantry, and there was just enough room for one person to kneel at a sort of desk thing in front of the altar. On the altar there was only a white cloth and a silver crucifix, and you had to take a candle in a brass holder from a little shelf at the side, light it with a match from the box that was always kept there, and stand it on the altar just in front and to the side of the crucifix, so that the cross was lit up by a gentle yellow glow.

That's what I did that day. Then I knelt at the desk and looked at the crucifix in front of me.

You know what a crucifix is, don't you, Andromeda? It's a cross with the figure of Jesus hanging on it. Some people don't like them. They say that Jesus rose from the dead and he's alive, so the cross should be empty. I know what they mean, and actually the big cross in the main chapel at both places where I've lived *is* an empty one, but I always thought it was right for Jesus to be there on the cross in that tiny little private chapel. I'll tell you why. You see, every day, however hard I try, I end up doing the sort of things that Jesus took the blame for on the cross. We all do. That's why he did it. He knew we'd never be good enough on our own. And every day God forgives me very enthusiastically. He says, 'Don't be discouraged, Wilf! Start again, old chap,' and I do. So you see – in a way – I put Jesus back on that horrible cross every day, and every day he dies, is buried, and rises again in me when I'm forgiven. That's why it's good to be reminded of what he did when I'm alone in the little chapel. The crucifix does that.

So, I knelt there for a while, as Brother Arnold had said I should, and repeated those words quietly and slowly, over and over again.

'He's in it with us, He's in it with us, He's in it with us …'

Jesus' face had been very well made by whoever modelled that crucifix. There was an expression of such pain and sweetness in his eyes, and he seemed to be looking straight at me, like those photos where the eyes follow you wherever you go in the room. And when I stopped saying those words, it was as if *he* started to speak.

'I'm in it with you, I'm in it with you, I'm in it with you ...'

And then, Andromeda, I just started to cry. It sounds silly doesn't it, but I couldn't stop myself. The funny thing was, though, they weren't really *my* tears – they were *his*. He was showing me how *he* felt.

I went back to Brother Arnold a little later and he said, 'Well?'

I just nodded. I couldn't think what to say, and I didn't actually have any more answers than I'd had before, but I did understand that God cares for and grieves over 'the Georges that come out wrong' much much *much* more than I ever could. Beyond that it's just a mystery, Andromeda.

Try to trust Him. He adores *you!*

Love and thanks,

Brother Wilf.

Dear Andromeda,

Thynn here again – Leonard Thynn. Friend of the Plasses, remember? Sent you that hilarious – well, quite hilarious – joke about the smallish squatter behind the thingy – tree. Gottit? Good. Well, thought I'd write again with another joke – well, more an anecdote than a joke, although it's meant to *be* funny – sort of a story with a funny bit at the end, if you know what I mean.

Anyway – this joke, anecdote, or story with a funny bit at the end – tell you what – let's call it an anecdotal story with a funny bit at the end from now on just to simplify matters. Okay? Right! Where was I? Oh, yes … this anecdotal story with a funny bit at the end starts – well, obviously it starts, doesn't it? I mean, in a sense, as soon as you say you're going to tell it, it's already started, hasn't it, although technically it could be said to have – sorry, wittering on again. Bad habit. No problem at all after a few drinks – not that that's a good reason to drink, young Veal! Good heavens, no! Just happens to be a fact that – what was I saying? Oh, yes, of course! This anecdotal story with a funny bit at the end starts in a prison. Well, I say a prison, but I suppose it could be a detention centre, or a borstal, or (depending on the old historical perspective) a prisoner-of-war camp, or even a jolly old police cell – not that there's anything very jolly about police cells. Been in a couple I'm afraid, after getting err … getting err … arrested, as it were. No, not very jolly, but err … the chap in this anecdotal story with a funny bit at the end happens to be locked up in a prison, detention centre, borstal, prisoner-of-war camp or police cell, and one day he says to himself – probably not out loud – well, maybe out loud if he's been in there a long time – he says, 'I want to get out.' Sounds from that as though he's English, but actually the chap could be any nationality at all. Could be Chinese or Ukrainian or Slav or Patagonian or Scottish – mind you if he was Scottish he'd probably speak in English anyway, unless he was fanatically devoted to the re-establishment of the Gaelic lan-

135

guage in which case he'd presumably – mind you, even if he was Chinese he might have been brought up in – say, Luton, in which case he'd probably speak English with a Chinese accent, one would guess.

Anyway, this chap in the prison, borstal, detention centre, prisoner-of-war camp or police cell, says to himself in his own particular language, accent, dialect, or patois, 'I want to get out.' And then – to cut a long story short – well, significantly shorter anyway – he says it again, and this time he really means it. Not that he didn't mean it the first time. It's just that the second time he err . . . meant it more. More than the first time, that is.

So, the chap (of uncertain nationality) digs a hole in the floor of his cell – if that's what he's in. Well, he must be in *some* sort of cell, unless he's a member of staff, in which case he wouldn't need to dig a . . . where was I? Ah, right! He digs a hole. Don't know how he does it. Not a practical chap myself. Once got Radio Four on the hoover when I was trying to fix the iron. Bit of a surprise really. Good programme though – all about the Watusi Tribe of Central Africa. Amazing people! Apparently they never, never – sorry, mustn't get side-tracked – spoils the err . . . anecdotal story with a funny bit at the end. He digs a hole, so that he can burrow out – tunnel out's better. 'Burrow' sounds a bit too rabbit-like really, don't you think? – he tunnels through the ground and comes out in the street outside. More good luck than good management, I'd say, unless he had special knowledge of the prison – which he might have done. Let's be fair! You don't get told that when you hear the joke – not that it matters – much . . .

Yes, well, anyway – he climbs out of the thingy – the hole, and he shouts out (in English or Chinese or Ukrainian or Slav or English with a Scottish accent, or Gaelic, or English with a Chinese/Luton accent) 'I'm free! I'm free!'

And then (the funny bit at the end of the anecdotal story is virtually imminent here, Andromeda), a little boy who happens to be passing – and, unless the digging chap has managed to burrow (tunnel rather) right through to another continent, he's presumably the same nationality as the digging chap – says (and this is the actual funny bit at the end of the anecdotal story) 'That's nothing – I'm four!'

Get it? 'I'm free! I'm free!' 'That's nothing – I'm four'. What a scream, eh? Well, anyway ...

All the best, young Veal. Don't fret now. Got the boss on our side. Know what I mean? Mother sends her love by the way. Says if she can put up with me for thirty-mumble years, you'll survive your hospital experience.

Regards,

Leonard (Thynn)

P.S. When you're better, you must (well, if you want to – no 'must' about it) come round and see what I've taught the Plasses' cat to do. You'll be amazed – well, very surprised anyway ...

Dear Andromeda,

It was with abundant joy that I received the wonderful news of your hospitalisation. How marvellous to suffer as you are doing! What a depth of gratitude and deep thankfulness you must be experiencing as you lie in the privileged position of one who is allowed to enjoy pain and discomfort hour after hour and day after day.

Hallelujah!

How you must delight in and chuckle over those verses which reveal the inestimable benefits of regular immersion in the rich baptism of physical anguish. How I envy you your glorious opportunity to participate in the ecstasy of awful agony. Oh, to break a femur! What happiness! To slip and crash to the ground causing serious injury necessitating a long period of intensive institutional care! What could be more welcome? How your faith must be blossoming in the invigorating atmosphere of profound disability that surrounds you now! With what deep happiness I am sure you must survey those heavy weights depending from your helpless limbs, and look forward with a mighty leaping of your spirit to a further lengthy experience of enforced horizontality! On Saturday I shall be enabled to witness your good fortune personally when I am home for a weekend from college. I shall enter your ward with a dance of elation and greet you with a word of celebration.

Yours in joyful anticipation,

Charles Cook.

Dear Geruld,

You gnow your friend
Charles at Deep Joy Bibul school
who sends me pecewliar letters?
Well the last one was all abowt
how fracchering your lemur and
being an attraction was acey-
pacey   brilliant and all.
Loony, eh?

Ennyway, he came to see me
on saterday and he dansed into
the ward not loocking where he
was   going and   stubbed his
big   toe on the end of a big
mettal thing and startid hopp-
ping dround saying bad words
threw his teeth. It was grate!
I decided to cheer him up
Geruld,   so I said - Oh to stub
a toe! What happinness! What
ridundant joy to have a acey-pacey
pain in the foot! I wish I
was lucky old you hopping
abowt, Charles old chap! Let's
hope the luvvly agony larsts a

good long time, eh? Hallylooyah!
    He was very cross for a littal while, Geruld, then he suddernly laughed, and he was nice like he ewesed to be and not like a robot. They must have speshul robot classes down at his school, eh? Do you have to get speshul permishun to be normal when yor a christiun, Geruld? If you don't, somewon ought to tell evvryone. I think so.

All my Logical Bonds

Andromeda.

Dear Andromeda,

I met Father John in the off-licence the other evening, and we were chatting about you. He said how much he'd enjoyed getting to know you, and how bravely he thought you were putting up with being stuck in that hospital bed and not having Mum and Dad around. One or two of the things he said made me think that you might be feeling a bit useless to God, and even worrying that you weren't good enough for him. When I talked to Anne about this she said I ought to send you the bit from my 'diary' when I had to give a talk on Spiritual Pride. She said, 'If God's still crazy about you despite things like that, then there's hope for anybody.' A bit of an exaggeration in my view, but it is true that I was rather thoughtless, and I'm sure you wouldn't have made the same mistakes. Father John says we're all members of the ratbag club, so we'd better stick together all we can, eh?

Anyway, here's my 'diary'. Your friend Leonard Thynn is in most of it . . .

Wednesday

Very flattered by Edwin asking me to speak on the subject of Spiritual Pride at next Sunday's service. Don't know why, but whenever I'm asked to do something like this, my spirituality seems to be cubed on the spot. Came away from the phone wanting to tell someone (in a humble sort of way) about Edwin's invitation. There was only Thynn there. He'd come round earlier for a meal without being invited *again*. I said, 'Edwin wants me to speak on Spiritual Pride next Sunday. I can't think why.'

'Because you're an expert on it I expect,' said Thynn, leaning back and taking the last pear from the fruit bowl.

Didn't bother to ask him what he meant. Why did God create things like locusts and earthquakes and Thynn?

I'm determined to do this talk really well. Must think of three headings beginning with the same letter . . .

Thursday

Thynn round tonight. Why doesn't he just move in and have done with it? Invited himself to go with Gerald to a meeting at some new local church. Asked which church it was. Gerald said it called itself the Holy and Apostolic True Church of the Abundant Revelation of Living Stones. Apparently it's a split from a break-away group which left the remnant of a disaffected portion of a dissenting faction from a fellowship that had separated itself from the original Holy and Apostolic True Church of the Abundant Revelation of Living Stones. According to Gerald, none of the present members realise that they've dissented themselves right back to the place where they started. I sometimes wonder if Gerald makes these things up . . .

Settled down after they'd gone out to plan my talk. Used a new concordance so that I can whizz from scriptural reference to scriptural reference like a real speaker. Managed to sort out two of my headings as 'Humility' and 'Holiness'. Bit stuck for a third, but it'll come!

Friday

Very difficult to work on my talk this evening. Thynn arrived at teatime and stayed until late. He and Gerald get very silly sometimes. Tonight they played Cluedo, substituting the names of church members for the traditional ones. In the first game it turned out that Mrs Flushpool did it in the study with the candlestick; in the second one Richard Cook did it with a rope in the kitchen. Found all the cackling very off-putting. Eventually they noticed my tutting and asked what I was doing. Made the mistake of telling them I was searching for a third heading beginning with 'H'. I must be mad. They suggested Henry Cooper, Haggis, Horstead Keynes, Halitosis, Hippopotamus, Heatrash, Ham rolls, and many, many more. Gerald doesn't seem to appreciate that this Spiritual Pride talk could be a foothold for me into the upper leadership of our church. Just to stop the flow of aitches I asked them how last night's meeting went.

Gerald said, 'You should've gone, Dad. It was good. Mostly for married people really.'

Thought how nice it was to see Gerald so serious for once. I said, 'What happened?'

Gerald said, 'Seven couples asked James Dobson into their lives.'

My son will end up as thunderbolt fodder, I swear he will . . .

Saturday

Still one blinking 'H' short! Unbelievably, Thynn was here *again!* Ignored all hints. He sat on the floor staring at our goldfish and singing The Green Green Grass of Home over and over again. Anne said there's probably something wrong that we don't know about, but what a pain! How can I work this thing out by tomorrow with Thynn doing Tom Jones impressions all over the carpet?

1.00 am. Still only got two headings beginning with 'H'. Too tired now. I'll get up early and work on it.

Sunday

Church.

Took my Cruden's Concordance to the meeting with me. Went through the aitches secretly during the prayers, still looking for my third heading. Only half realised that Leonard had gone up to the front to give a testimony. Sat up and took notice when I saw by my watch that he was running over the time when I was supposed to start my talk. Glared at him until I found myself listening to what he was saying.

'. . . and this last week – well, not exactly a week to be precise, more like eight days – it's been very, very thingy. Difficult, I mean, very, very difficult not to err . . . not to err . . . do it – drink, I mean. Not that it's wrong for anyone else to drink of course – well, it might be if they'd got the same problem as me – but not err . . . normally. Where was I? Oh, yes, very difficult over the last approximate err . . . week. So every time – nearly every time I felt like-going our and err . . . abusing my – for want of a better word – body, I went to the Plasses'. Not to abuse my body I don't mean. Good heavens, no! No, I just know they'd never err … turn me away, as it were, and I could just stay there until the old oojermaflip – the old whatsitsname – the old temptation err … went away. Nothing like having people who treat you like one of the old thingy – family – know what I mean? Just want to say how, well … how much I – you know …'

Realised my third heading was 'Hopeless' – me, I mean. Told everyone that, when I got up to do my (short) talk. Invited Thynn home for lunch afterwards, and thanked him privately in the kitchen for trusting us. He went red and knocked a full bottle of milk onto the floor.

I asked Gerald later what he really thought of James Dobson.

He said, 'Dad, I would go so far as to say that he's a combination of two of the greatest names in the Old Testament.'

I said, 'What do you mean?'

'Ah,' said Gerald, 'you see, James Dobson is an anagram of "Moses and Job".'

Mmmmm …

I don't really think you've got much to worry about, Andromeda, do you?

Love to you and Lucky Lucy,

From Uncle Adrian.

Dear Madam,

I write to you once again on the subject of toasters in general, and one toaster in particular: namely the electrical appliance which I purchased at your emporium some two or three weeks ago. Now, I am a broad-minded, flexible man, but I have certain stubborn, possibly even prejudiced, views on the ideal function of such machines. My idea, and you may wish to dismiss it out of hand as being wild and fanciful, is that one should be able to place slices of bread into the appliance and, a minute or two later, remove them in a toasted state. An eccentric whim perhaps, but there is a surprisingly substantial body of opinion which freely endorses such a view, and I feel it may be of benefit to you to be aware of this new and revolutionary movement in case other customers in your establishment should purchase similar pieces of equipment and take them home with just such a narrow expectation lodged in their minds. Let me suggest one or two minor refinements that may be thought useful in the particular model with which you supplied me.

At one end of the machine is a small dial, which can be turned from a point marked 'LIGHT' to a point marked 'DARK'. It was in connection with this dial that I made my first error. The morning after my purchase I was obliged to rise at a very early hour before the sun rose and while the temperature was uncomfortably low. Happily, my home is very adequately lit and heated by electric power so I was able to reasonably anticipate a pleasant breakfast in warm surroundings before commencing the day's duties. Having placed two slices of bread into the 'toaster', I then turned the aforementioned dial to 'DARK', and pressed down the lever which, I assumed, would simply lower the bread into the inner recesses of the appliance. How I ever contracted the lunatic idea that 'LIGHT' and 'DARK' referred to the degree of toasting required, I really could not say. But, though I say it myself, I am a fast learner. As the lights went out and the entire electrical system in my house ceased to function, I realised how foolish I had been. Turning the dial to 'LIGHT', however, did not restore the general illumination.

Much later, and after considerable expenditure on the services of an electrician, my lighting and power were restored, and your machine had been cleverly converted into something approaching the appliance I had originally envisaged. I say 'something approaching' because there are still some very minor improvements that might be possible. May I suggest, for instance, that the terms 'LIGHT' and 'DARK' should be replaced on similar machines with the terms 'NOT TOASTED AT ALL' and 'CREMATED'. Alternatively, and I slip this in merely as a little personal preference, might it be possible to produce a radically new variety of appliance which toasts bread to the degree required by the appliance's owner?

I do hope that you will not feel I am fussing over trivial details, and I look forward with eager anticipation to continuing a dialogue on this subject when I bring your 'toaster' back to visit you later in the week. I should love to hear your views on refunding, or the exchange of faulty goods.

Yours sincerely,

Percival X Brain (Elderly and frail)

P.S. Looking back through my files, I note that I have already written to you twice on this matter. I hope you will not brand me a fanatic. Did you know, by the way, that there is an old tradition, still upheld in some parts of the country, of actually replying to letters?

Dear Geruld,

I have had a letter from your naybour, Mister Brain, ackewsing me of selling him a crabby old toester. I gnow being an attraction mite do funny things to the mined, but shorely I'd rememba if I'd sett up a bizness selling forlty ~~elet~~ elecritdl stuff to old men. Eh? Shorely! Mister Brain mite have got a bit seenile in the head, beeing old and aul. It carn't be easy when yor name is Brain and most of it's gon.

Cood you arsk him to eggsplane pleese, Geruld?

Lucky Lucy says HALLO GERULD.

Logical bonds
Andy - pandy xx

P.S. I've put Mister Brain's loony letter in for you to Peru's. (good werd eh, Geruld. It meens look at).

Dear Andy Pandy,

What a scream! What a panic! What a to-do! Thank goodness you sent me that letter! Bless your little cotton socks, you prevented an innocent man from being dragged off to the cells. It was real drama – just like on the television. I'll tell you what happened. Ready? Okay!

I got your letter telling me about Mister Brain and the toaster after I came home from college the day before yesterday. (I came home at two o'clock in the afternoon, but don't tell Mother – she doesn't think college counts if you haven't been there *all* day). I went straight round after I'd read it to see old Percy and ask him what was going on. 'Toasters?' I thought. 'Funny!' I thought. Anyway, he wasn't there, so I thought I'd try again after tea. I was going to ask Dad what he thought about it, but I chickened out in the end. Dad's got a heart of gold, but – well, what's the point of complicating things? So, about seven o'clock, I stepped out of our front door to climb the fence to Percy's place. Then I stopped dead, because what do you think I saw standing outside Mister Brain's house?

Well, what do you think?

Come on – have a guess!

You can't? Right! I'll tell you then.

It was a police car, Andy Pandy, with an orange stripe all round it and a blue light on top, sitting there as large as life. For a moment I thought I'd better go back inside and mind my own business, but I just couldn't. I WAS NOSEY!!!! Awful, isn't it, Love and a Dream? God has to forgive me for something or other every single day. (Wish I was perfect like you.)

Anyway! Like I said, I was too nosey to leave it, so I hopped over the fence and up to Percy's back door, which I found wide open. In I walked, all innocent, and through in the front sitting-room I found a scene like something out of a bad play. There were two policemen in full uniform looking all stern and stiff, and standing between them was a lady who – well, she was one of those tall, angular ladies who look as if they've put their make-up on in the dark with a shaving brush. And she was looking *very* angry. All three of them were glaring at Percy Brain as if he was the lowest sort of criminal there was. Now, I don't know if you realise this, but Mister Brain used to be an actor, Andy Pandy, throwing his arms about with a loud voice on a big stage – that sort of thing. He looked just like that now, crouched back against the wall with one hand over his heart, and the other thrust out in front of him as if he was trying to keep vampires away. And his eyes! They were wide and crazy looking, and his mouth was hanging open. He was *really* laying it on thick, was old Percy, but he was a bit worried as well, I could tell. A bit pale and twitchy – know what I mean?

So then this lady held a piece of paper out in Percy's direction, and spoke like someone who's just been chewing on a slice of lemon.

'Do you deny,' she screeched, 'writing this letter threatening to cripple me with your car if I don't give you a new toaster?'

'Threatening? . . . cripple? . . . toaster?' gasped Percy. 'I totally, absolutely, categorically deny sending *any* such letter!'

Well, then she read out loud from this piece of paper, and this is how it went.

'Dear young lady,

What an unfortunate accident a broken leg is! The pain must be *very* unpleasant. It is amazing, is it not, how easily such things can occur when we least expect them. Goodness me, you could be immobile in hospital for many weeks with such an injury. Some claim that such occurrences are the consequences of less than virtuous treatment of others, but this is surely not the case. You, for instance, might step into the street and be hit by a car whose driver, for one reason or another, has failed to pay sufficient attention. I, myself, might easily make this kind of mistake. I could make it

149

tomorrow! I intend to visit you *very* soon, so I will not write more now. I wonder if you remember me? I *do* hope so! Look out for me.

Yours in anticipation,

Percival X Brain.

Yes, you guessed it, Andy! Poor old Percy had got his letters mixed. The lady in the toaster shop got the one meant for you, and you got the one complaining about the toaster. Good job I was on the spot with the other letter, wasn't it? All sorted out in the end. The boys in blue were in stitches – they thought it was hilarious. I got a feeling the lady was a bit disappointed really, though. I think she'd hoped Percy would be taken out and hung from the nearest lamp post. Tried to explain it all to Dad later, but I might as well have tried to strike a match on jelly.

Love to Lucky Lucy and, of course, Andy Pandy,

Gerald.

Part Five

10, Drowning Street,
   London,
   Youknighted Kingdum.

Dear Misses Thacher,
        Have you ever bean an attrac-
tion? I doon't think so. Not on
the natural helth ennyway. I am
pubblickly horizontall and prowd
of it . I bet you woodn't have
yor lemur mended by an uncwollified sturgeon called Mister
Fisher. My name is Veal by the
way. I leen to the left and I
am a bit red. My muther is up
with the green and common wimmen
and Gwenda, still tryeing too
get rid of the crude rissoles. I
bleeve you are verry kean on
Mister Raygun's base, Misses
Thacher, like that man with a
nayme that sownds lik a beddtime
drink who had an affare with a
hellicopter and climed out of the
cabinet to sulk after you told
him off. Well I'm knot!
Why doon't you tell Mister

153

Raygun to keep his rissoles in his own base? How meny people have to becum green and common befor you see cents? Eh? If I can werk it out with grate weights hanging off my ancles, shorely you can do it vertikal! You havvnt got grate weights on you. Hou is yor son Mark? Father said that Mark Thacher is an ambishun, not a persun. It's the only thyme I ever saw farther and Gwenda agree. Farther spoilt it a bit later when Gwenda said — Arn't you intarested in batterd wimmen, and father said - yes, I'll have two large ones and a dubble porshun of chips pleese.

Annother thing Misses Thacher, can you do sumthing abowt Dugless Nurd's hare? Farther used to say he looks lyke an unhappee ice-creem cone in the wind. Why don't you get Weedwell Sosoon to give him a bit of a trimm? Father said if you stuck a sigar in his ear heed look lyke a 99.

Ennyway, aul I can say is wot abowt a ewe-turn Misses Thacher? If you beecame a soshulist lots of the uther stories mite get a bit less blue. Eh? Mister Kinnerk mite give you a job if you do. Grarnted you woodn't be abul to be Frying Mincer and hav yor own persunnel defective, but you wood at leest avoid beeing infiltraighted when the reverlooshun cums. I am in tuch with Mister Georgeous chops. I cood put in a werd for you.

yors in antissipayshun

Andromeda Veal (Mizz)

P.S. Witch one is yor persunnel defective? Is it the one with gray hare and glasses?

Global One-man Evangelism Movement
International Drag-a-Pew Project
Prefab Number 3
Armistice Row
Bagshot

Telephone   (Decided not to reconnect after scripture revealed
it was visiting 'friends' who ran up the huge bill.
Jeremiah 12:6 'They have called a multitude.')

Dear Brother or Sister,

Please excuse the hand-written pink crayon on shiny toilet paper, but when Stanley left the Project with my other assistant, he took his John Bull printing set with him, and I have run out of paper bags.

As you will note from the new project title, a revelation has once again been vouchsafed to me, and we are, in obedience, setting out on a new course. When I say 'we', I mean in fact 'I'. Like Gideon of old I have seen the fearful and the kneelers removed from my midst, and I alone am continuing the work set before me. Stanley and Bruce are singularly lacking in vision and adaptability. Stanley in particular seeming to surrender to a spirit of moroseness after his unfortunate experience at the Frog and Spittle on amateur night. I reminded him that there are worse fates than being covered with beer by a drunken audience intent on making a fool of you because you tried to play the spoons with only one spoon and no experience whatsoever, but he appeared unconvinced. Bruce was infected by this negative attitude to such an extent that when I announced the termination of the musical project they were both unripe for change, and decided to leave.

The new, and certainly most exciting project to date, will involve the hauling of a thirty-five foot wooden Victorian church pew through every country in the entire world, on foot. Preparations are complete, other than details such as finding a suitable

157

pew, talking its owner into giving or selling it to me, working out how to move it, planning a route, sorting out passport and visas, amassing sufficient finance for the journey and selling the prefab. Once again I am absolutely determined that this will be a faith venture, and already I have received a firm offer of the loan of a screwdriver as and when I locate a suitable pew. I regard this as strong confirmation of guidance received thus far.

Over the last week or two I have been touring the local churches speaking to groups about my unwillingness to publicise the project purely for the purpose of raising much needed capital. I always take with me a pile of the sort of financial pledge form that I do *not* want filled in by those who are seeking only to salve their consciences. I enclose such a form with this letter. Please strike out either 'I give willingly to the Lord,' or 'I intend to keep my money for my own selfish pleasures and I don't see why God should get his hands on it,' then sign the form and return it to me. Please do *not* feel pressured to respond in a particular way.

Yours,

Vernon Rawlings (sic sec)

P.S. A fresh revelation this morning. Clear indication from scripture that I should sail my pew like a raft around the oceans. Ezekiel 28:2 'I am sitting on the seat of God, surrounded by the seas'.

P.P.S. Please pray for a paddle.

Dear Rabbit Runcie,

I am a non-anglian attraction cauled Mizz A. Veal. The onley uther one of yors I gnow is the Neverend Boom who has a bit of trubble soughting out what's a dimmonimation and what's a brekkfust serial. Rest ashored I have aulso written to the Pope abowt mayking babys do the limbo and that, so I'm not just gettting at yew Rabbit old chapp. My frend Geruld (his persunnel problum is the onley thing that's maid beeing horizontall beardabull) says yor name is a nammagranamm of C. E. but in error, so he mus lyke you two. Eh? One thing yor lukky abowt is yew doon't have to be a halibut like my frend Farther John at the nunkery or the Pope in his Fattycan, but I have a fealing yor not quyte asin charje as the Pope. He can say wot he lykes withowt feer of contracepcion from the catlicks eeven if the cardiggans get stroppy, but yew have to mayke speechis at a speshul plaice cauled the Sinodd. My frend Geruld says it's maid up of sum peeple who've been ordrained, lyke beacons and curits and shotguns and bish ups and rectums, and the rest are drorn from the ~~the~~ Layertee (whoevver they mite be when there at home, eh Rabbit?), but they aul have to be peeple who lyke to Sinodd, and evvrywon torks and torks for ajes and ajes and then decides to leeve evvrything lyke it wos befor. Sounds a bit of a waist of thyme to me, Rabbit, but I eggspect you gnow best beeing the arch bish up.

Ooh, Rabbit! I wish I'd been yew marreeing Prints Charls and Laidy Die! I saw it on a film. I gnow they are bluddsukkers on the tyred flesh of the British proladairyfat, but I think their aceypacey skill and aul. I lyke the ~~queen~~ queen two, eeven tho I'm not aloud to rearly. Shee nearly cryed

when thay got married by yew,
diddn't she? Wozzn't it nice of
the inshorance cumpany to lend
you their bilding for the day? I
hope you wrote them a thancyou
letta. Did you Rabbit? It's only
plite.

Rabbit, wot is a bish up? It
sownds lyke a missteak of sum kind,
but why do yew keep mayking new
ones if that's wot they are? Wot
woz aul that fuss abowt the
Durrem one who said things abowt
the verging berth and the west
direction of Jesus? He is a bish up,
isn't he? He is cauled the bish
up of Durrem, lyke the Grate fyre
of London, eh? I think he looks
nyce, but praps he shood have
stuck to sprinting.

Ennyway, wot I wonted to arsk
woz, sumtimes when yor going up
and down the Lambuth Warlk,
cood yew just remined God that
Andromeda is waiting with a unknit
lemur for a bitt of actiun green
and common wummen - wise?

Good on yer, Rabbit! Lucky Lucy says thancyou two. She is my first dolly sins Bigot, and I am keaping her eeven if I lern the wrong roll in serciety.
Logical Bonds to you and aul the bish ups,

Andromeda Veal (Mizz)

P.S. My frend Geruld says his nice fashist dad's car must beelong to the Cherch of England becos it onley goes in for a service twyce a year. Goodun', eh?

P.P.S. If yew and the Pope beleeve in the same God wot's so speshul about cantering through Walkerbury Catheedrul togetha? Eh? For goodniss sake!

Dear Andromeda,

Gerald says you very much enjoyed the last extract from my diary that you saw – the bit about my talk on Spiritual Pride – and that you wouldn't mind seeing some more. I'm *very* pleased that you enjoy my diary so much. I sometimes think that Gerald, and even Auntie Anne sometimes, don't really understand that you can learn things from experiences recorded in this way. I have known Gerald to sit with tears of laughter running down his face whilst reading an entry that doesn't appear even remotely humorous to *me*. Still, he's a good, kind lad, so I don't really mind.

By the way, I'm really pleased you liked your doll. We went right through two shops before we found one that looked right. We had to leave the first shop we tried because the manageress foolishly took offence at some perfectly innocent remarks I happened to be making to unsuitable dollies, but in the end we met Lucy and all agreed that she was the one. We *did* enjoy leaving her on the pillow beside you. Dear Andromeda – I felt so sorry for you stuck in that bed for so long. I'm glad you think I'm a *good* fashist now. I hope I'm good. I do try, but I seem to get in such a tangle sometimes. When I wanted someone to do the chairs at church for instance. It was really ... well, that's the bit of the diary I've put in for you to look at. Hope you find it interesting.

Monday

Edwin, our Elder, rang to ask if the study group I lead could take responsibility for putting out the chairs at church every Saturday evening ready for Sunday. I said, 'No problem, Edwin!' Felt rather proud of my 'team'.

Phoned Stenneth Flushpool and asked if he'd do it. He said he'd commit it to the Lord in prayer, and ask his wife. Gerald was listening. Said that if God and Mrs Flushpool disagreed he wouldn't put much money on God's chances.

Tried Richard Cook next. He said that it was unscriptural to make definite plans for the future, so he couldn't promise to do it every week, but 'as the Lord leadeth'. Asked him how far in advance he reckoned the Lord might let him know each time. He said, 'It is not for us to know, but may your faith be equal to the test, Brother.'

I have discovered that you can't strangle telephones ...

Tuesday

Vernon Rawlings (one of my study group) gave a talk tonight at the monthly church meeting about sacrificial giving. Very strong and inspiring. So impressive I started making notes near the beginning. Last bit went as follows:

'... and let's face it, brothers and sisters, when we talk about giving we usually mean parting with a small part of our surplus. We pay lip service to the Christian ideals of love and charity, but when it really comes to the crunch, are we ready to give freely and cheerfully beyond the point of comfort? Are we, brothers and sisters? I want to ask you all ...'

Vernon pointed dramatically at various members of the church as he went on in a loud voice.

'. . . young Christian boy! Young Christian girl! Brothers and sisters of middle age! Elderly friends! I want to challenge you right now! Are you prepared to give until it hurts? Are you prepared to take what you have in terms of money and possessions and time, and give whatever is needed to whoever needs it, or are you just going to play at religion by keeping the best for yourself and throwing a few scraps to your neighbour? I challenge you tonight, brothers and sisters! The next time someone comes up to you and asks you to give or do something, will you deny your faith and say "NO!", or will you count the cost and, despite personal expense, say "YES! I'll do it!" '

Collared Vernon straight afterwards and asked if he'd do the chairs. He said, 'No, I'd rather not. There's good telly on Saturday.'

Wednesday

Stenneth Flushpool rang. Said he had no inner peace about the chairs, and he wouldn't be allowed to do it anyway.

Richard Cook rang. Said he now felt that the Lord would have him stand with me in prayer about the chairs, and would that do?

Tried Percy Brain. He said that when I'd tried everyone in the entire universe and still wasn't able to get anyone, then he *might*, *possibly* help *very* occasionally, but that would depend on circumstances at the time, so it was better to rule him out other than *very, very* exceptionally. And even then he couldn't promise.

Thanked him for sparing the time to talk to me . . .

Sat down by the telephone and rang *all* the others. Never heard such a load of feeble, pathetic excuses in all my life. Bit fed up with my 'team' by the time I finished. What a list!

William Farmer: Bad leg, which for some lunatic reason means he can't use his arms.

Leonard Thynn: Chairophobia (?)

Norma Twill: Didn't want to spoil the sensitive soft skin on her hands.

Ephraim Trench: Said he'd disagreed with buying this particular set of chairs thirty-seven years ago, and his integrity would be in question if he was seen to be helping with them now.

Raymond Pond: Said his ministry was in music, not chair arranging, and could I ask whoever *did* do it to stay well away from the organ please?

Honestly!

Thursday

Study group tonight. At the end I really stormed at everyone about the chairs. Pointed out that *no one* had offered to help.

'And because of that,' I concluded, 'we all know who's going to end up doing the chairs every Saturday evening – Anne!'

After they'd all gone off looking very subdued, Anne said, 'Darling, I didn't want to say anything in front of everybody, but I don't quite understand why I'm the obvious choice to do the chairs.'

'What do you mean?' I said, a little shocked.

Anne said, 'Well, why shouldn't you do it, for instance?'

'Don't be silly,' I said, 'you know Saturday's the night when I always like to – ah, I see what you mean …'

Friday

Good job I'm a Christian. If I wasn't I'd tot up all the things I've done for my study group members and send each one a bill. As it is I naturally forgive them freely for being so selfish.

Saturday

Gerald offered to come down with me to help with the chairs this evening. Surprised to find the front door left unlocked. Even more surprised to find nearly all of my study group inside! They'd turned up to help with the chairs! Organised a rota for the future and got on with it.

Norma wore gloves.

Ephraim supervised.

Thynn kept his eyes shut.

William hopped.

Gerald spent the entire time working out that Alex Buchanan is an anagram of 'Ex-banana hulc'.

Went home feeling quite warmed inside.

So you see, Andromeda, it all got sorted out in the end. It usually does. It's the sorting out bit that seems to get complicated. When I get to heaven I've got a few questions to ask God . . .

Love to Lucky Lucy and you,

  Uncle Adrian.

P.S. Why don't you work out an anagram for Gerald's name? I did once. I think he was quite impressed. By the way, your Uncle Edwin's planning to come and see you tomorrow.

Dear Andromeda,

After visiting you last night I've decided to write to you because I'm afraid you might be getting a little confused. Mind you, I don't blame you! With everything that's happened to you and your family I would be surprised if you hadn't got things a *bit* upside-down.

As you know, Andromeda, I'm the Elder at my church and I think most of the people who go there think I'm not too bad at the job, but nearly all of them reckon I've one main fault. I wonder if you can guess what it is. You're *very* good at saying exactly what you think, so you might find it rather hard to understand! My problem is that I hardly *ever* speak out loud and clear about what I think and believe. People think I should do it much more often (especially when they think someone else has gone wrong!), but I just carry on in my own way most of the time – people who've got problems or aren't quite sure about things seem to find it easier to get close if I don't make too much noise. After talking to you last night though, I thought I ought to be more 'LOUD AND CLEAR' than usual. You see, I know how angry and upset you must be about your mother and father going off and leaving you at a time when you need them so much, and I'm sure I'd feel exactly the same. I just want to say one or two things to you. First, there's nothing wrong with what your Mum's doing. She believes very strongly in what's happening among the pro-testors up at the missile bases and we need people in this country who are willing to do more than just *talk* about things being wrong. I admire your Mother very much, and I think very highly of your Dad too. He just got fed up with not feeling very impor-tant, and started saying unkind things and making the kind of jokes that he *knew* would upset your Mum and Gwenda until things got so bad that he had to leave. Now, I know it sounds as if I'm just having a go at your parents, but it's only because I can remember just the same thing happening to me. You see, when your Auntie Joan and I moved down here and I took over the eldership of a church for the first time, I made the same sort of mistakes that I think your Mum might be making. I was quite young and very anxious that everything should go really well in the church, and it never occurred to me that Auntie Joan and our two little girls needed me at home just as much or more than most of the people in the church. I was out just about *every* evening, Andromeda, doing what I thought of as 'The Lord's Work', and if I'm really honest, I quite often made sure that 'The Lord's Work' started just before the time when the girls had to be bathed and put in bed and read to. I was never there, Andromeda! And if anyone had said to me, 'Do you love your family?', I'd have got very stiff and indignant and said, 'What *do* you mean? Of course I love them – I'm a church Elder!' I didn't understand you see. I came to my senses in the end when someone wise and kind gave me a bit of a telling off, but it went on for quite a long time, with poor Auntie Joan just having to put up with it because every time she complained I said that I was only doing what God told me to do. The things I was doing were good and useful and all that – it's just that I didn't realise (or didn't let myself realise) that there were even more important things to be done in my very own home. Maybe that's what's been happening with your Mum, Andromeda. There's no doubt she loves you, and your Dad's potty about you – always has been. I think they just let things go too far and get too bad, and in the end neither of them could stand it, so away they went, leaving you in the middle, sweetheart. It happens to an awful lot of children I'm afraid. But don't give up. I haven't. Your Mum and Dad were always great pals underneath everything and my guess is that they probably still are. Keep badgering God, and so will I.

Your loving Uncle Edwin.

Dear Andromeda,

Victoria (Mrs Flushpool) has asked me – well, told me – I should write you a letter. My name is Stenneth Flushpool and I am married to Mrs Flushpool (Victoria). You may be a little puzzled by my name. I am called Stenneth as the result of a disagreement between my parents. At my christening the vicar asked in which name I was to be baptised, and my father replied, 'Kenneth'. Simultaneously, my mother, a rather dominant lady, not unlike Victoria (Mrs Flushpool), replied 'Stanley'. The Vicar, an elderly man with somewhat impaired hearing, interpreted this confusion of sounds as the word 'Stenneth', and baptised me accordingly. My parents decided to accept this accidental compromise in the interests of peace, and I have been Stenneth ever since. I cannot say it has been a happy accident for me. There is invariably a short pause when I am introduced to a new acquaintance, while the person concerned controls his or her features and deals with the rising gust of mirth which the mention of my name always seems to precipitate. Do you find my name amusing?

However, enough of that. Victoria (Mrs Flushpool) was of the opinion that the bulk of my letter to you should consist of relevant and instructional verses from scripture, together with helpful anecdotes of testimony from my own life. I am not, however, bound to abide by the wishes of Mrs Flushpool (Victoria). It has been suggested that I am unduly influenced and even dictated to by Victoria (Mrs Flushpool), but this is not wholly the case. Last week, for instance, I was adamant that I would select my own new pinny for work in the kitchen. It is essential to win these battles from time to time. But I digress. The fact is, Andromeda, that I was myself obliged to remain in hospital for a long period in traction some four years ago. In my case it was a back problem, but I did experience all the same physical discomforts and indignities that you are undergoing now, and I would like you to know that you have my deepest sympathy. I would also, if you do not mind, like to share a confidence with you that I have shared with no other person, and particularly not with Mrs Flushpool (Victoria). You see, despite all the discomfort, I really rather *enjoyed* my stay in hospital. It was not unlike an extended holiday. Many of the nurses who cared for me were pretty, friendly girls, and I experienced a most unusual sense of specialness whilst lying so helplessly in my bed. Naturally I was *deeply* conscious of the absence of Victoria (Mrs Flushpool), but she did visit every other day to read lengthy extracts from holy literature for the whole of the visiting period. I find it difficult to express my appreciation of such devotion. On those occasions when she was not present though, I indulged myself in two areas, of which, I fear, Mrs Flushpool (Victoria) would not have approved. First, I managed to persuade one of the porters (a Mr Blogg if I remember rightly) to bring me some magazines on model aircraft construction, an activity which Victoria (Mrs Flushpool) regards (I believe mistakenly, though I say nothing) with some suspicion. These afforded me immense satisfaction, but it was my other activity that occupied most of my unvisited time. (Why I should be writing all this to a young person like yourself, I really could not say.) My other activity arose out of my dissatisfaction with my name – Stenneth. I spent very considerable periods simply imagining that my name was Kirk C. Flushpool (the C stood for Craig). Most of these imaginings were in the form of dialogue between myself and a new acquaintance. Here are some examples:

NEW ACQ: Hello, you're a fine looking chap. What's your name?

ME: Kirk, actually.

NEW A: What a great name! What's your middle name?

ME: Craig.

NEW A: My name's only Paul. I wish I was called Kirk Craig!

ME: They're only names. Paul's nice.

This is one I used to pretend was a telephone conversation from work.

ME: Hi! Flushpool here, K.C. Flushpool. Do you want to buy some of our goods?

CUSTOMER: That name sounds terrific! What does the K.C. stand for?

ME: Only Kirk Craig. Very ordinary names really.

CUSTOMER: Ordinary names my foot! They're great names, and I bet you live up to them.

ME: Oh, I don't know.

CUSTOMER: Well, look, Kirk ...

ME: Yes?

CUSTOMER: I'd like to put in a really big order, as long as it's you who handles it. Okay, Kirk?

ME: Sure thing! Kirk out.

This must appear very foolish to you, Andromeda, but I enjoyed these little pretendings very much indeed, and I still think about those weeks in the ward sometimes, although I do not mention such things to Mrs Flushpool (Victoria). I fear she would not understand.

Do forgive me for writing a letter that seems, now that I look back at it, mostly about me, but I have greatly appreciated the opportunity to express myself a little on paper. I do hope you are soon well enough to return home.

Yours sincerely,

Stenneth Flushpool.

P.S. Please bear in mind when/if replying that Victoria (Mrs Flushpool) is not aware of the contents of this letter. I do not intend deceit, but unnecessary upset would be rather unfortunate.

P.P.S. Please do not think that I am not sympathetic with Mrs Flushpool (Victoria). I think that if we had been able to have the child that we both so much wanted, she would have been a lot less – stern.

Dear Mister Flushpool, (It wood be districtspeckful of me two caul you Stennith).

Thankyou for yor letta. The scrippcher versis and anicdotes were rearly grate! Acey-pacey eggsiting and good four me and aul. (Nudje, nudje, wink-wink, eh?) Pleese give my rigards to Misses Flushpool (Euston), and say that I wood be pleesed to see her ennytime, eeven if I'm asleep. In fact if shee's thinking of cumming to kindely read me lencthy eggstracts from holey lichrercher, it wood be betta if I was asleep becos sientists say you can lern a lot in yor brain wile yor asleep. Eh? I think so.

By the way, I arsked Mr. Blogg if he remembered you when you were in here. He said — O yes, that bloke wot wanted magazeens about scripcher and that brort in, he wos orlright he wos — so he does rememba you Mister Flushpool. (I cept my fingas crossed while I wrote the bit abowt the magazeens, Mister Flushpool) Mr. Blogg can burp wenever he wants to by the way. I wish I cood burp wenever I wanted to. Pleese inquire of yor wife whether she can burp wenever she wonts to. Tell her yew have to be carefull it cums out the rite end.

Ennyway, that's aul for now from yor frendly littal horizontall attraction.

Logical Bonds
Andromeda

P.S. I doon't think Stennith is a funnee name (just in case you wundered wether I thort it was) I think it's a sweet nayme. I think yor rather sweet, Mister Flushpool, axshully.

P.P.S. If yew shood happen to meat an old frend of mine cauled Kirk Craig Something-or-other, cood you tell him how mutch I like his names?

P.P.P.S. Perhapps Misses Flushpool (Paddington) will have a lot less

stern as thyme goes by. It wos
sad wot you wrote larst. Nevver
to have a George. Eh?

Dear Geruld,
        Gess what! If I spell
yor name aul wrong with a
A instead of a U, yor a
nammagranam of —

SLADE SPRALG!

Goodun, eh? It makes you
sownd like a acey-pacey
weerdo film star.
        By the way, Geruld. I
thort I'd just menshun that
it's my berthday next friday.
I'm not remineding you in
case youd forgottun you were
going to give mee a brand new
persunnel problem aul of my
own, Geruld. I'm just men-
shuning it in passing. I
doon't mined if you forgett
to give me one
        Logical bonds (to Sladey-baby)
                Andy-Pandy x

P. S.   It's this friday cumming when I doon't mined you forgetting to give me a brand new persunnel problem aul of my own, Geruld. The one just cumming up at the end of this week.

P.P.S. Thanckyou for lending me your persunnel problem aul this time (like what I havvn't got one of my own of).

Dear Andy Pandy,

Hi! It's Slade Spralg here. How's tricks? Now listen carefully my little love and a dream – or read carefully rather – because I'm putting my life in your hands. If Dad finds out I've sent you this bit of his diary there's likely to be another attraction down your way soon. One called Gerald. You see, Dad doesn't come over all that dignified in this extract from his great classical work. Mind you, he doesn't come all that dignified in *any* of his entries, but this one is – well, you read it and see. And if you see Dad coming – eat it!

Monday

Why did God let cars be invented? Nothing but trouble and expense! In all the Christian paperbacks people travel fifty miles with no engine and four flat tyres almost every other day, just by the power of prayer. My cars have all been unbelievers. They sigh and give up. Even when *I* think they're okay someone else thinks they're not. Like this morning. Took my perfectly good car up to Ernie Pavement, our Christian mechanic, for its MOT. None of us has ever seen Ernie laugh. When Gerald told him we wanted a fully charismatic gearbox fitted in our last car, he said he didn't stock them. That's what made this morning so upsetting. He started by walking slowly round, staring sadly at it like someone watching a close relative die. Then, before I could tell him what I wanted, he patted me gently on the shoulder and suggested in a low, mournful voice that I should just walk quietly away without looking back and he'd see to its disposal.

I said, 'No Ernie, it's a perfectly good car! I don't want it disposed of. I want you to put it through its MOT.'

That's when he started this dreadful grating, helpless laughter. Ended up hanging over the bonnet wiping tears from his eyes with an oily rag. Good job for his sake the grease gun wasn't a couple of feet nearer my hand.

Gritted my teeth. 'Well, at least LOOK at it!' I said.

He walked round it again, poking bits here and there, and making clucking noises with his tongue, then he said, 'Looks like a resurrection job, mate.'

Asked him what he meant.

He said, 'Needs a completely new body.'

Went home very depressed (although inwardly rejoicing on some deep level of course). Wondered how I'd ever be able to afford a new car. Prayed about it, and suddenly in my mind's eye saw a brand new Volvo Estate!

Claimed it.

Tuesday

Saw fleets of new Volvos in my dreams all night. Told Anne over breakfast that I felt we were being led into praying for a brand new Volvo Estate, but she displayed what to my mind is lamentable faithlessness.

She said, 'Let's be realistic, darling. We're looking at something small, economical, probably second or third hand and easy to park.'

Gerald stopped overeating for a moment to offer to sell us his old skateboard if we wanted it. Stupid boy!

Told Anne that I was going to believe for a new Volvo Estate. She said she thought it was much more likely to be something like a ten year old Datsun. We agreed that we'd each look for confirmation between now and Saturday.

Wednesday

Extraordinary! Everywhere I go the roads seem to be packed with Volvos. Counted twenty-three. A real sign!

When Anne came home she said she'd seen *twenty-four* Datsuns. Bit of a blow really ...

Thursday

Counted eighteen Volvos today. Anne's score was thirteen Datsuns. I'm winning by four Volvos on aggregate! I don't like to doubt Anne, but I find her claim that she's hardly noticed any Volvos on the road very hard to accept. On the contrary. I don't understand where all these Datsuns appear from. I can't recall seeing *any*.

Friday

Excellent Volvo crop today. Anne went one better with her ridiculous Datsuns, but I'm still winning overall.

Leonard Thynn round tonight. You can always tell when Thynn thinks he's got something funny to say. He tries to look cool. Told me part of my car problem is solved because he's found a scripture verse in which God promises to arrange transport home from work for believers. Asked wearily which one it was.

He said, 'Isaiah, chapter twenty-two, verse nineteen. "I will drive you from your office".'

Thynn and Gerald cackled away like parrots. Left them cackling. Thynn borrowed the cat without asking while I was upstairs. Asked Anne tonight what he does with our cat. She looked surprised and said, 'That's just what I was going to ask you, darling. I thought *you* knew.'

One of these days I shall follow him ...

Saturday

Saw THIRTY-FOUR Volvos today! Absolute famine of Datsuns. Hurried home to announce final confirmation of my leading. Anne arrived just after me. Said she'd seen seven hundred and sixty-three Datsuns! Turns out Gerald took her over to the Datsun factory by bus. Gerald said, 'Is that guidance, or is that guidance, Dad?'

Was just about to accuse them of cheating when Ernie Pavement arrived at the door. Said sadly that he'd found a car for us. Escort. Five years old. Good nick. Only one problem – the heater didn't work. Quite cheap. Did we want it?

Went for a drive in our new car later with Gerald. Saw no end of Volvos *and* Datsuns. Curious!

Car went well. Terribly cold though. I felt like a lump of frozen meat. Must get the heater fixed. Gerald pointed out that Old Escort is an anagram of Coldstore.

Feel a bit embarrassed about all that Volvo counting. Hope God wasn't watching – well, of course he *must* have been watching, but I hope – well . . .

What Dad doesn't realise, Andy Pandy, is that there never was a trip to any Datsun factory, and Mum never really kept a tally of Datsuns she saw on the roads. She was just kidding Dad along till he came out of his latest loony phase. Dear old Dad! He's a rather sweet old fashist, don't you think, Andy Pandy?

By the way, I happen to know why old Leonard borrows the cat. It's very ingenious really. You see, he turns on his reel to reel tape recorder, and then – well, I'll tell you about it when I visit next. It's not the sort of thing you can describe properly in a letter.

Give my love to Lucky Lucy and Rosy Roundway. See you soon.

Love, Gerald.

P.S. I'm just off to the shops to buy something for a friend's birthday.

P.P.S. Eh?

Dear Andromeda,

Exciting news! Your Mum rang last night to say that she's travelling down late on Thursday evening to be here for your birthday on Friday. She tried to ring the hospital but kept not getting through to the ward, so she rang us instead and asked if I would pass the message on. Oh, darling, I'm *so* pleased Mummy will be with you on your special day. She'll be on her own by the way. Gwenda's got engaged to a man who writes comedy for Channel 4, so she won't be protesting for a while. I've never heard your Mum sound so excited. She's really dying to see you, sweetheart.

By the way, Gerald will be popping in just for a few minutes on Friday to bring you – well, wait and see! Uncle Adrian and I will come over with our presents on Saturday if that's OK, so you'll have two birthdays really, won't you? And when you come out of hospital at last, you poor old thing, I think we ought to have a really nice late birthday party for you. What do you think?

We're still praying for you, Andromeda.

See you on Saturday.

Love, Auntie Anne X

Dear Andybugs,

I didn't *know* you were in hospital. Edwin contacted me last night. I honestly didn't know that you'd come a cropper and got laid up for so long. Everything went out of my head when I left home and I've just been working without stopping since then in a sort of daze. Andybugs, you do know that your silly old Dad loves you, don't you? Just because I went away doesn't mean I don't care, sweetheart. The other day at work someone asked me if I'd got any children, and I was about to be all grumpy and say mind your own business, when I suddenly saw you in my mind and felt really proud. 'Yes,' I said, 'I jolly well have got a child. She's the finest little girl in the whole world, and she's called Andromeda.' You *are* the finest little girl in the world, sweetheart, and Mother and I have done the rottenest job in the world looking after you. But maybe it's not too late to try. I don't know.

Listen, Andybugs. I can't get to you for a couple of days, but I'm on my way. I shall see you on Friday. OK? Save a big kiss and a hug for me. I'll be coming through that door to see you very soon, and I'm not going to go so far away ever again. Keep your chin up!

Love and kisses,

Daddy X X X

P.S. I haven't forgotten what day Friday is, love!

Dear God,

Don't do enny big relevash-
uns or angel cwires or that
because I'm writing this in the
middul of the night with a
torch (not eesy when yor horizontall, God). or Nurse
Roundway will tell us both off.
Being God won't help yew if
yew annoy Nurse Roundway, God!
Shee's a wholly terrer when
she's rowsed. That's why I'm
writing this in a whissper.
The rest of the ward's aul
quiet, but I'm too eggsited to
sleep. Gess what, God? I gnow
you gnow ennyway, but I want
to tell yew what's going to
happen on friday. Farther wrote
me a letter, God! He did! He
did! He wrote me a letter and
cauled me Andybugs and said
he'd come on friday and oh,
God, issn't it eggsiting! And
it's dubbly acey-pacey brill

eggsiting because mother's cumming on friday too! Oh, God, I'm a bit fritened about them seeing eech other. Oooh, I go aul tingly when I think abowt it! Enny chance of yew beeing here to reff the match, God? It is my birthday on friday, you know. Eh?

Ennyway, I'm going to try to go to sleep now. Do you sleep or are you bizzy sorting out Ostralia all night.

I'm glad I got to gnow yew.

Goodnight, God

Logical bonds,

Andromeda Veal (Mizz).

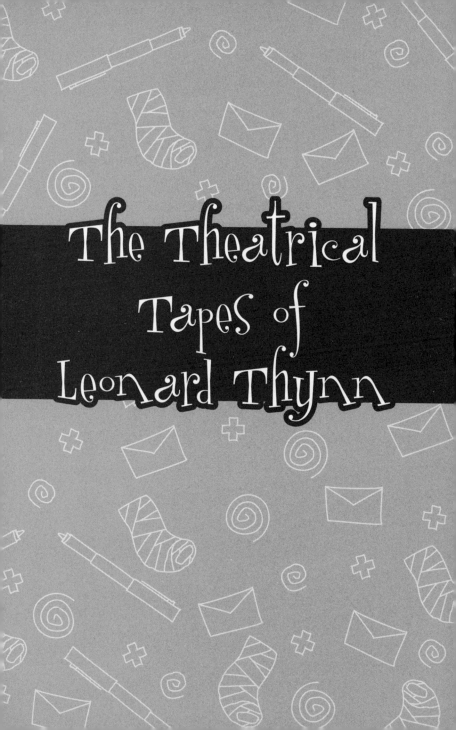

The Theatrical
Tapes of
Leonard Thynn

This book is dedicated to:
Matthew, Joseph, David and Katy.

*Who put up with their father's bad temper
when he is trying to write funny stuff*

dedication

Dear Reader,

Sometimes I wish I'd never collected Andromeda Veal's letters together for publication. You wouldn't believe how many people from the church have mentioned 'casually' that they've always thought their lives would make a good book. Vernon Rawlings, for instance, who's got a prefab down in Armistice Row and changes his ministry like other people change their socks, approached me with the modest suggestion that I should write his biography and entitle it *Miracle Man – The Vernon Rawlings Story.* He said he thought it would be good if the person who designed the cover made his name look as if it was carved out of massive blocks of stone. I said I'd think about it, which was a lie.

Mrs Flushpool, on the other hand, informed me regally that she was prepared to accept my assistance in the composition of a 'most important spiritual work' to be called: *Crossing the Carnal Swamp* or *Escape from the Natural.* She added that her appointed spouse, Stenneth, would contribute lengthy footnotes as he was one who, since his regeneration, had never been sucked into the bog. This was no more attractive a proposition than George Farmer's offer to supply material for a worship leaders' manual with the title: *Spontaneous Worship and How to Organise it so that it Happens the Same Every Week.*

Much more constructive, it seemed to me, was an idea put forward by Gloria Marsh, an attractive widowed lady who attends our Bible-study group from time to time. Gloria sat very close to me on the settee one evening, and said she'd been looking through her old diaries and letters and wondering if she might have some material worth publishing. She asked if I'd like to come round for a few evenings and look through her bits and pieces to see if there was anything I fancied. Anne, who must have been listening through the hatch, refused this invitation rather abruptly on my behalf. I felt that this was somewhat presumptuous and probably unscriptural. After they'd all gone, I asked Anne what was wrong with providing a little comfort to a lonely soul. She said, 'It's not her soul I'm worried about ...' Ah, well, perhaps she's right. She usually is.

Richard Cook, round to visit one evening, said that he thought it would be a good thing to produce Christian periodicals to combat the pernicious effect of the girlie magazines that you can see (if you look, which he doesn't) on the top rack in newsagents' shops. Gerald suddenly became animated. 'Yes,' he said, 'you're right, Richard. We could publish our own magazines!'

'What would they be called?' asked Richard, stepping goofily over the precipice as usual.

'Well, one could be called *Prayboy*,' said Gerald earnestly.

Richard's mouth was hanging open to the size of a golf ball.

'And then we'd have *Amen Only*,' continued Gerald, 'and how about *Repenthouse?*'

Richard almost needed the kiss of life to jerk him back into the land of the living, and we nearly lost him again when Gerald asked if he'd be willing to remove his glasses for the centre-fold. I don't know what Gerald would do without Richard to act as his straight-man.

Richard's son, Charles, wrote to me from Deep Joy Bible School to suggest that I help him with a book he felt he had to write, and which would change the face of Christian outreach as we know it. The title was to be *How to Communicate that which has been Vouchsafed to us by He Who Would Have us Share that which we have Received Through the Mighty Working of His Eternal Will, in Everyday Language, by One Empowered to Make an Open Profession of Faith to Those Who Have Ears to Hear.*

'A catchy little title,' said Gerald when he saw it.

There was also a request from Percy Brain for me to read what he described as a 'Lawrencian short story', written by his second cousin's nephew's best friend's aunt on several sheets of grease-proof paper with a blunt pencil. Percy said he wanted me to be absolutely honest about what I thought of it, because his second cousin's nephew's best friend's aunt wanted good constructive criticism and not hollow flattery. As far as I could decipher, the story was about a crowd of very odd people saying inexplicable things to each other during a sea voyage on a liner. It was full of lines like: 'She was deeply curious about her own liver ...' and 'She fell into his chest ...' At the end of the story the five main characters all fell into the sea at the same time, and found each other's true selves in a joyously deep act of drowning. When I suggested mildly to Percy Brain that his second cousin's nephew's best friend's aunt might need to do a little work on her manuscript before it was ready for publication, he revealed that, in fact, *he* was the author of the story. He said that if he had known he was to be viciously harangued by a jealous so-called fellow-author, he would never have allowed me to see what one of his closest and most unbiased friends had described as 'a modern classic'. He refused to speak to me for a fortnight.

It certainly never occurred to me that Leonard Thynn would have anything worth publishing. The only thing I'd ever seen him reading (apart from the Bible on church weekends – everyone reads the Bible on church weekends) was *The Good Pub Guide* and the *Beano*. Then, a few months ago, he invited Anne, Gerald and me round for the evening to listen to some tapes he'd made. I'd forgotten that he'd recorded most of the meetings and rehearsals leading up to the Christian drama festival that our church contributed to last year. He even recorded the evening itself, which is interesting because ... well, you'll see for yourself as you read on. It was I who directed our 'presentation', and it was such a hectic business that I hardly noticed Thynn's infernal machine revolving away constantly.

Anyway, after listening to all the tapes, Gerald and Anne persuaded me that this was something that should be shared with the world. I wasn't quite so sure, not least because I didn't exactly come over in the most dignified light. Thynn got so excited though, and Gerald and Anne were so sure that it would help other church drama groups (in a 'negative' way, whatever that might mean), that I gave in and agreed to transcribe and edit the tapes. I do hope it was a good idea....

Yours Truly,

Adrian Plass.

ONE

How It all Got Started . . .
and Almost Ended

After an announcement during church one Sunday, that we hoped to enter the local Christian drama festival in a few weeks' time, this meeting was intended to be a brainstorming session. All were welcome, and as free refreshments were provided, thirteen people came. Edwin, our elder, suggested that I should take the chair.

[*Tape commences with a succession of crackles and hisses as Thynn's tiny brain wrestles with the complexity of a switch that is labelled in big red letters: PRESS TO RECORD.*]

ADRIAN PLASS (A.P.): Right, well we'd better get started. We're meeting this evening to discuss . . .

THYNN: *(Interrupting.)* Hold on a sec.! I don't think it's recording. *(More crackles and hisses.)* Yes it is. Sorry! Carry on.

A.P.: We're meeting this evening to discuss . . .

THYNN: Wait a minute – the little red light's not on. I'm pretty sure the little red light ought to be on. I don't think it's recording. Yes it is! No it's not! Wait a minute. *(Tumultuous crackles and hisses and thumps, together with unseemly words muttered by Thynn under his breath but clearly audible on the tape.)* Right, I'll just do a test . . .

A.P.: *(With rather impressive patience.)* Leonard, old chap, we really ought to . . .

THYNN: *(In a high-pitched, unnatural voice.)* Testing, testing, one two three testing! This is your sound sound-man testing for sound. One two three, I'm L.T., this is a sound test, testing for sound. One two ...

A.P.: *(With slightly less patience.)* Leonard, I really think ...

[*Sound of machine being switched off, followed by sound of machine being switched on again.*]

THYNN: There you are, it was recording all right after all. Let's get on. It's late already.

A.P.: *(Through his teeth.)* We're meeting this evening to discuss the ...

THYNN: Could we just wait while I run the tape back to the beginning? There's no point in ...

[*Sounds of a chair falling over and a forest of crackling and hissing as A.P. goes over to strangle Thynn. Repenting at the last moment he whispers in his ear instead.*]

A.P.: *(Hissing murderously.)* If you don't shut up about your tape recorder, do you know what I'm going to do?

THYNN: *(Nervously curious.)* What?

A.P.: I'm going to thread the tape up one of your nostrils and pull it down the other.

THYNN: *(After a moment's consideration.)* Fair enough. *(In normal tones.)* I don't think there's much point in running the tape back to the beginning. I'll just start recording from here.

[*Sounds of* A.P. *picking his chair up and sitting in his place again. Very faint sounds of* THYNN *whispering 'waste of tape' to himself.*]

A.P.: Right! Good! Perhaps we can get on now. We're here this evening to discuss ...

MRS FLUSHPOOL: *(Interrupting.)* I realise that I am not the chairman of this meeting, but do you not feel that supplicatory cover is a fundamental requirement at the commencement of a Christian endeavour such as this?

[*Puzzled silence.*]

ANNE: *(Sitting next to me.)* I think Mrs Flushpool means that we ought to start with a prayer, darling.

A.P.: Oh! Err ... yes, of course. A prayer. Right! Err ... would anyone like to ...?

CHARLES COOK: *(Back from Deep Joy Bible School the day before.)* Shall I ...?

A.P.: Yes, Charles, go ahead.

CHARLES: Okay, let's just turn away from the hurly burly and the rush and bustle and the every-day concerns and the toing and froing and the ups and downs and the worries and the problems and the responsibilities and yesterday's regrets and today's anxieties and tomorrow's fears and ...

A.P.: *(Loud throat clearing noises.)*

CHARLES: ... and let's just get into that peaceful state where we're just ready to just receive and just listen. Let's just keep silence for just a minute while we just err ... do that.

[*A minute's silence during which Charles can be heard making little smiley sipping noises with an occasional isolated 'just' escaping like air from a slow puncture in a bicycle tyre.*]

... we just want to just ask that this thing we're going to do – I can't remember just what it is just at the moment – just that it will really be just really blessed in a way that's really just right and that we'll all be really conscious of how you just want to really help us to just do it in the right way and that all those involved will just really come to know that you just want to just really show them how you really just want them to just realise the truth about just understanding that you're really err ... just.

GERALD: *(Leaning over to whisper in my ear.)* If you don't stop him soon, dad, we're going to just have three choruses and just a call to the front before we just get started.

CHARLES: So we ask that we'll just really know your will and really just be really encouraged – oh, hallelujah! *(He starts to sing.)* Bind us together ... !

A.P.: *(Loudly.)* Amen!

[*A volley of 'Amens', ranging from the half-hearted muttering of Thynn, still preoccupied with his machine, to Vernon Rawlings' manic cry of 'Amen! Hallelujah! Bless you, Lord! Oh, yes, amen indeed!'*]

A.P.: *(Wearily.)* We're meeting this evening to discuss what our contribution to the ...

ANDROMEDA VEAL (A.V.): *(Here with Uncle Edwin.)* I'm afraid I don't find that very funny.

ANNE: *(Sensing my imminent breakdown.)* What don't you find very funny, darling?

A.V.: What Mrs Plushfool said about Uncle Adrian bein' the Chairman.

MRS F.: *(Sitting up very straight, like a water bed standing on end.)* My name, child, is Flushpool, not Plushfool ...

A.P.: Oh, for goodness sake ...

MRS F.: ... and I fail to see how a mere child such as yourself could have any comment to make on my remarks to the chairman.

A.V.: That's why I intersected – insurrected – indisected – said what I said just now. He's not a chairman, he's a chair*person*!

MRS F.: May I say, in love, little girl, that, in my view, the feminist movement is almost certainly contrary to scripture. I myself am under the authority of my husband, Stenneth. *(Sharply.)* Confirm that please, Stenneth!

STENNETH F.: Eh? Oh, yes, dear. Absolutely. Whatever you say ...

A.V.: And can I say in love, Mrs Slushpoof, that I wish you'd go and live on the Isle of Person, or anywhere really, and ...

ANNE: That's quite enough now, Andromeda. You mustn't be rude. Please stop laughing, Gerald. It doesn't help!

EDWIN: *(Mildly.)* Let's just say that we call Adrian 'Chair'. All agree?

[*Chorus of assenting murmurs.*]

A.P.: *(A pale shadow of himself.)* We're meeting this evening to discuss ...

THYNN: Could we go back to where you said 'Oh, for goodness sake'? The little red light wasn't ...

A.P.: *(Stands and flips his lid.)* All right! Okay! Fair enough! Let's not talk about drama. Let's talk about tape recorders and little red lights and what I ought to be called, and let's pray great long prayers and say things to each other in love! Let's not do what we came here to do! Let's completely waste our time and then eat all the food and then go home! *(Sound of a body slumping back into a chair.)*

[*Silence.*]

ANNE: *(Soothingly.)* Everyone's listening now, darling.

197

A.P.: *(Quietly grim.)* We're meeting this evening to discuss what our contribution to the local Christian Drama Festival ought to be. This is a brainstorming session, so I'll just write down all the ideas everyone has, then we'll discuss which is the best one to use. That's all – it's quite simple really. Quite simple. It really is.

THYNN: Excuse me, Chair ...

A.P.: *(Very calm.)* If this is about your tape recorder, Leonard, I shall commit grievous bodily harm on your person.

THYNN: No, no it's an idea – for the festival.

A.P.: *(Guardedly.)* Yes?

THYNN: Well, it's about this man, right? He's an alcoholic, dependent on drink. Drinks all the time. First, we see him sitting at home drinking. *(Continues in a low, dramatic voice.)* He takes one drink, then another, then yet another until the bottle is empty. In the next scene we see him with a bottle of vodka. Again he drinks it glass by glass. He bemoans his fate and cries aloud for help. In the third scene, just as he drinks the last drops from a bottle of rum, he's converted, and everything's all right!

[*Pause.*]

A.P.: And may I ask, Leonard, who you thought might selflessly abandon sobriety to enact this moving piece of drama?

THYNN: Well, I thought as it was my idea, I should ...

A.P.: I thought so. Next!

THYNN: But ...

A.P.: I've written it down. Next!

PERCY BRAIN: *(In resonating theatrical tones.)* I believe I may lay claim to more theatrical experience than that of this whole company combined. I have considered the matter with great care, and I know what we must do. It shall be an epic! The entire history of the Holy Bible will unroll across the vast wooden plain of the stage. In scene after magnificent scene, we shall depict the gigantic forces of creative energy flinging the sun into its place on the black cloth of heaven, the making of man and his Fall, the construction and journeying of the mighty Ark through the floodwaters of divine punishment, the tragic tale of the kings and prophets of Israel, the misery of Egyptian captivity, the parting of the waters of the Red Sea, the tale of Daniel and the gigantic image before which he would not bow, the birth, life and death of our Lord, the imprisonments, shipwrecks and mighty deeds recorded in the Acts of the apostles, and finally, superbly, cataclysmically, the visions, the battles, the judgments, and the final days of this planet, as pictured in the book of Revelation!

A.P.: It's going to be a bit hard getting all that into ten minutes.

RICHARD COOK: And we've only got thirty-one pounds, sixteen pence in the entertainment budget.

EDWIN: And we can't have proper scenery because of the different groups coming on and off stage.

GERALD: And the vast wooden plain of the stage is actually ten blocks pushed together.

A.P.: And we haven't got enough people for that sort of thing anyway.

THYNN: Apart from that it was a jolly good idea, Percy. *(Laughs immoderately.)*

PERCY: *(Glaring at me as Othello glares at Iago in the last scene.)* Am I to understand that the scenario I have laid before you is to be rejected with the same sneering contempt with which you flung a previous manuscript back into my poor smarting face ...?

A.P.: *(Firmly.)* I never flung anything back into your poor smarting face, and we haven't rejected your ideas, I simply tried to point out that ...

PERCY: I sensed no carping reluctance in your manner on that occasion when you requested the loan of my excellent mechanical hedge-trimmer. Is that act of generosity and open-heartedness to be forgotten so swiftly? With what grief I echo the poet's words: 'There might I see ingratitude with an hundred eyes gazing for benefit, and with a thousand teeth, gnawing on the bowels wherein she was bred ...!' *(Rests his head on his arms as if grief-stricken.)*

[*Depressed pause.*]

A.P.: Yes, well – can we get on? Has anyone ...

MRS THYNN: *(Turning her hearing aid up.)* Can I ask a question?

A.P.: *(Warily.)* Yes?

MRS T.: When are we 'avin' the food, and why 'ave we got to call you Claire?

ANNE: *(Kindly but loudly.)* Not 'Claire', Mrs Thynn. Edwin said we should call Adrian 'Chair'.

MRS T.: *(Groping for comprehension.)* But that's sillier than callin' 'im Claire! Why 'ave we got to call 'im Chair? No one's called Chair!

A.P.: *(Almost shrieking.)* It's short for Chairman, Mrs Thynn! I'm the chairman you see!

MRS T.: Well, why aren't we callin' you Chairman then?

A.P.: *(Shrieking.)* Because Andromeda thinks we shouldn't be sexist!!

MRS T.: Why're we takin' any notice of a scrap of a girl tellin' us we shouldn't exist? Anyway, when's the food?

A.P.: *(In a little, hoarse, broken voice.)* Leonard, could you please convey to your mother that no one gets anything to eat until I get some ideas down on this piece of paper? That is what we are here for.

PERCY: *(Finding his grief ignored.)* Blow, blow, thou winter wind, thou art not so unkind ...

GERALD: ... as Claire's ingratitude to Percy.

VERNON RAWLINGS: *(Preventing infanticide by interrupting.)* Err ... Charles and I have got something, Chair. We sat up late last night and worked it out. It's a sort of thing for sort of Christian outreach. It sort of came to us in a surge last night, just like it must have been in the upper room, although we were actually in the basement not that it matters, because whichever room ...

A.P.: What was your idea, Vernon?

VERNON: Yes, well, we thought we'd write something sort of gritty and real that would really glorify the Lord and bring a mighty blessing to everyone who sees it, didn't we Charles?

CHARLES: Yes, we really just ...

VERNON: We thought we could start with the drama festival and then move to one of the provincial theatres, and go from there to the West End before doing a year-long international tour, didn't we Charles?

CHARLES: Yes, we just really ...

VERNON: And last night I had a dream that mightily confirmed the leading we felt! In my dream I was a dolphin performing in one of those aquarium places, and the trainer was brushing my teeth with a giant toothbrush! Wasn't he, Charles?

CHARLES: Well, I wasn't really just there ...

A.P.: I'm afraid I don't really see ...

VERNON: *(Very excited.)* Surely it's obvious! The performance bit's about acting – the stage, you know. The trainer's God, and he's symbolically purifying the fish – that's me, for the task ahead.

GERALD: What I don't quite see ... apart from the fact that you do look a bit like a dolphin, Vernon, is why you should appear as a creature like that?

VERNON: That's the really *great* part of it, isn't it, Charles?

CHARLES: Yes, it's really just ...!

VERNON: The fish is a symbol of Christianity!! Amen?

CHARLES: Halleluj ...!

A.V.: *(Dispassionately.)* A dolphin's not a fish. It's a mammal.

VERNON: *(Carried away by enthusiasm.)* Well, what's the difference ...?

A.V.: The diff'rence is that fish've got cold blood and gills and fins. Mammals are aminals that *(with relish) give suck* to their young. I done it in a project while I was an attraction in hospital. So there!

VERNON: *(Slightly irritated.)* Well, dolphins *look* like fish!

A.V.: P'raps God doesn't know the diff'rence between fish and mammals. P'raps he's forgot, seein' as it all started millions of years ago.

MRS F.: It *all* started, as you so irreverently put it, child, six thousand years ago, and ...

EDWIN: Come now, Victoria, don't be too dogmatic with the child ...

A.V.: *(To Vernon.)* Why don't you ask God to do another dream tonight with you as a haddock. Haddocks are real fish, aren't they, Charles? And you look more like a haddock.

CHARLES: *(Completely confused.)* I just really don't really just ...

A.V.: Mind you, I've never heard of haddocks performing in public.

MRS T.: Why're we talkin' about performin' haddocks, fer Gawd's sake? I thought we was choosin' a play!

THYNN: Sort that lot out, Claire!

A.P.: The next person who calls me Claire is neither going to be in the play, nor have any food.

ANNE: Come on, dear, it was only a joke. Don't be childish.

A.P.: I wasn't being childish – I was just ...

MR F.: I think we have a fundamental doctrinal issue to settle before we proceed any further. This child ...

A.P.: Anyone who insists on settling fundamental doctrinal issues isn't going to be in the play or have any food either.

MR F.: *(Nobly.)* Victoria will never allow threats or promises to affect her defence of scriptural puri ...

MRS F.: Be quiet, Stenneth.

MR F.: Yes, dear.

PERCY: Alas, the gratitude of man, hath often left ...

A.P.: Anyone misquoting bits of poetry about ingratitude gets no part and no food either.

[*Pause.*]

Right! *Please* can we get on. Vernon and Charles – never mind about the dream. Just tell us what your idea is please.

VERNON: Okay, well basically it's one chap talking to another chap in a pub. We thought a pub was sort of better, because it's sort of real and – well, real, and if there's anything we want to be, it's real, so we thought it ought to be in a pub, so that it's real.

A.P.: *(With grinding patience.)* Yes? And ... ?

VERNON: One chap's a Christian called Dave and the other's a non-Christian called Bart, and they have a really natural sort of conversation about sort of faith, don't they, Charles?

CHARLES: Yes, it's really just natural, just like a really natural err ... conversation.

VERNON: We'll sort of do what we've sort of written, shall we? It's not long enough yet, but we can easily sort of pad it out when – if we err ... need to. I'm Dave, right? And Charles is Bart, aren't you, Charles?

CHARLES: Yes, I'm really just Bart.

[*Rustle of scripts.*]

VERNON: Right, well it starts with Bart sort of sitting on his own in the pub, sort of talking to himself. Right, Charles, whenever you're sort of ready. *(Whispers.)* I come in soon, but not sort of at the beginning ...

CHARLES: *(Much clicking of the tongue and sighing.)* Blow! Huh! *(Sigh.)* I don't know! My life isn't going very well! I have had three big beakers of alcohol already this evening, and I shall probably have a lot more before I go home. Huh! *(Sigh.)* Blow! What is life really about? If only I could see some meaning in it all. I see no reason not to sin at present. I have a good mind to smoke a cigarette and be naughty with a lady. No wonder people such as I turn to a life of crime. Rootless and ignorant, we go around with the wrong sort of chap, not realising that with every step we move farther from God, about whom we know nothing. Barman, I hereby order another shandy, and I don't mean the children's sort! *(Click, sigh.)* Huh! Blow!

VERNON: *(Sounding like Baden-Powell addressing a Scout rally.)* Good evening, friend. May I sit at your table with you? I will not force my company on you, as that frequently produces a resentment that hardens the listener to attempted impartation of the gospel.

CHARLES: Something about your sensitivity attracts me, sunk though I am in the misery of godless self-absorption. Sit down if you wish. But – I say, you are a laughable person. Is that not a glass of orange squash in your hand? Ha-ha, you are not a man of the world as I am. I am on my fourth beaker of shandy, but – huh – who is counting? *(Sigh.)*

VERNON: I count it a joy to suffer your mockery, friend. I require no base intoxicant to produce the joy that springs from

204

within. Can you not tell from the expression on my face that I draw from other wells than these? *(He smiles a ghastly, crinkly smile.)*

GERALD: *(Leaning over to whisper in my ear.)* If anyone smiled at me like that in a pub you wouldn't see me for dust ...

A.P.: Sssh!

CHARLES: Now that you mention it there is an almost visible aura of joy, peace and contentment about you. To what do you attribute this phenomenon?

VERNON: No, no, friend, let us talk first about your life and work, your hobbies and interests. In this way we shall establish an easy, natural relationship – a platform on which to build a friendship that is not exclusively concerned with the welfare of your soul. Scripture supports this method of approach.

CHARLES: I am a welding person, recently made redundant. Life does not seem worth living to me at present. Blow! Huh! *(Sighs.)* I have been sitting here all evening attempting to drown my sorrows through the medium of alcohol. I have already consumed three beakers of this devil's brew. It is shandy, and I don't mean the children's sort. But enough of me. Now that we are close friends and you have shown

yourself interested in me as a person and not just as a form of spiritual scalp, tell me the origin of the love, joy and peace that flows from you like a river.

GERALD: *(Whispering again.)* Yeah! What's he put in his orange squash?

A.P.: Sssh!

VERNON: As you ask me, friend, I shall tell you. I am a Christian, and the joy that you witness is a product of redemptive suffering, apprehended through divinely implanted spiritual vision, nurtured and developed through appropriately organised exegetical study.

CHARLES: I have never heard it explained so simply. Oh, that I too might share this simple faith. *(Sighs.)*

VERNON: But you *may* share it, friend! You may indeed! You must choose now between shandy and God. Choose God and you will become as I am.

GERALD: *(Another whisper.)* Back to the shandy then, I guess.

A.P.: Sssh!

CHARLES: I abhor thee, devil drink! I choose God! *(Pause.)* The feeling of joy that I am suddenly experiencing is at once more powerful and subtle than that induced by the excessive consumption of shandy, even though it's not the children's sort. Thank you, friend, for your words.

VERNON: *(Smugly.)* Not I, friend, but he who speaks through me.

CHARLES: And what now, friend?

VERNON: Well, there's a Bible study on Monday, the church meeting's Wednesday evening, Thursday there's a new nurture group starting – you'll need to get to that. Friday night there's a coach going to hear John Wimber, Saturday there's a day-long conference on next year's mission, and Sunday it's service in the morning, Azerbaijanian meal at lunchtime, and communion in the evening.

CHARLES: Free at last!

[*Sound of two people clapping. It is Vernon applauding Charles and Charles applauding Vernon. A short silence follows.*]

VERNON: *(With shy pride.)* Well, that's it. What do you think?

A.P.: *(Clears throat.)* It – it – it's certainly very ...

VERNON: *(Anxiously.)* You don't think it's too sort of street-level? Charles and I were a bit worried that it might be a bit too sort of street-level, weren't we, Charles?

CHARLES: Yes, we were really just a bit worried about err ... that.

A.P.: No, I err ... don't think you need to worry about that.

VERNON: *(Slightly hopeful.)* You don't think it comes over too raunchy and realistic?

A.P.: *(As if considering carefully.)* No, no, I wouldn't say that at all.

ANNE: *(Kindly.)* You must have both worked very hard on it I expect, didn't you?

CHARLES: Well, we just really felt that God had really just given it to us.

GERALD: *(Whispering in my ear.)* Glad to get rid of it, I should think.

A.P.: Ssh! Okay, well what did other people think?

EDWIN: Good effort. Jolly good effort! Not perhaps quite what we ...

PERCY: As I understand it, there are a mere two characters in this – 'effort', as Edwin so eloquently describes it. Are the rest of us to be 'pub extras'? If so, I strongly prot –

A.P.: *(Quite gratefully really.)* That's a very good point actually, Vernon. As Edwin said, it's a very good – a very good – a very good err ... effort, but it does only involve two characters, so it is just a little bit limiting. Anyway, we know it's there if we want to ...

GERALD: *(Whispering.)* Put on something really bad.

A.P.: ... if we want to come back to it later. Now, Gerald *(thinking to teach him a lesson),* how about you? Have you got anything to offer?

GERALD: Funny you should say that, dad. *(I might have known.)* As it happens I have prepared a little scene. Not quite as Pinteresque as Vernon and Charles' err ... effort – more sort of observed behaviour rather than anything to do with outreach and that sort of thing.

A.P.: What sort of 'observed behaviour'?

MRS F.: *(Grimly.)* I trust we are not about to enter the realms of your accustomed flippancy, young man.

GERALD: *(Gravely sincere.)* Thank you, Mrs Flushpool. I appreciate that.

MRS F.: *(Bewildered.)* What are you thanking me for?

GERALD: For your trust, Mrs Flushpool, for your trust. Thank you for trusting me.

ANNE: That'll do, Gerald. What's your idea?

GERALD: Well, basically, it's a couple of typical young Christians meeting in one of the restaurants at one of the big Christian holiday events like 'Let God Spring Into Royal Acts Of Harvest Growth' or something like that.

A.P.: Typical young Christians?

GERALD: Yes, more or less.

A.P.: Go on then.

GERALD: Well, there's Gary. He comes from *(puts on a voice)* 'a really great fellowship in the Midlands – really lively and the gifts are used, and the pastor's written three books, and we have some really great speakers, and two of my best friends have come through in the last six months, and we've just started a prophetic basketball group, and last week we claimed Greenland for the Lord, and next year a group of us are going over there, and we've had lots of prophesies about ice melting and the summer going on right through the winter, and I'm trying to decide whether to be a full-time evangelist or a Christian scuba-diver and my prayer partner said he sees me immersed in water so I think that's quite clear guidance really, and I'm reading a great book at the moment called *Origami and the Christian – a Frank Look at what the Scriptures say about Paperfolding,* and some of us are going to go and hold up posters outside the local stationer's next Friday, and I've just written a devotional song with G minor seventh diminished in it, and ...'

A.P.: *(Amused but nervous.)* And the other one?

GERALD: Well, about the same really, except his name's Jeremy and he's not sure whether to be a full-time Christian entertainer or a charismatic accountant. Anyway, this is how it goes. I'll have to do both parts myself because I haven't practised it with anyone. It starts in the middle of their conversation.

Jeremy: ... so I thought it would be great to join O.M. *(Casually.)* I had a chat with Ishmael about it last time he was up.

Gary: Oh, do you know Ish?

Jeremy: Oh, yeah, Ian's a good friend.

Gary: Nice house – nice place to stay.

Jeremy: *(Defeated.)* You've stayed there, have you?

Gary: Well, err ... no, not exactly stayed as such, but I've heard that it's a nice err ... place to stay.

Jeremy: *(Relieved.)* He's great though, isn't he?

Gary: Oh, yes, he's great!

Jeremy: So what are *you* going to do?

Gary: Well, I think I might be being led to spend some time with YWAM. I heard all about it from a chap who works for C.L.C. Bumped into him up at C.B.C. when I was working for S.U. He's an A.O.G. who used to be an R.C. Made the move after a B.Y.F.C. rally.

Jeremy: Impressive, was he?

Gary: Not initially. He was introduced to me by a bloke from L.S.S.

Jeremy: Are they sound?

Gary: And light, yeah. Anyway, after this chap had talked about YWAM for a bit I really felt I was being led in that direction, so I took the whole idea to Elsie and talked it through.

Jeremy: What's that stand for?

Gary: What does what stand for?

Jeremy: L.C.?

Gary: It doesn't stand for anything. It's my girlfriend's name – Elsie.

Jeremy: Oh, I see!

Gary: What's that stand for?

Jeremy: What does what stand for?

Gary: O.I.C.?

Jeremy: Nothing, I was just ...

Gary: Only joking! Anyway, after talking about YWAM to this chap ...

Jeremy: The R.C. who became an A.O.G. after going to B.Y.F.C.?

Gary: Yes, that one. After talking to him and Elsie I really felt led to go and work with old Floyd again.

Jeremy: Old Floyd? You mean Floyd McClung? You mean the one who wrote that book – the one with the brown cover?

Gary: Yes, that's the one. That was a great book, wasn't it?

Jeremy: That was a *great* book!

Gary: A *truly* marvellous book.

Jeremy: Mmmm ... what a book!

[*Reverent pause.*]

Gary: You've err ... you have read it, have you?

Jeremy: Well – flicked through it, you know ... You?

Gary: Not read it, no, but everyone says it's err ...

Together: A great book!

Jeremy: What did you mean about 'working with Floyd again'?

Gary: *(Airily.)* Oh, we did a mission together a couple of years ago, that's all.

Jeremy: You and Floyd McClung did a mission together?

Gary: Well, afterwards he said he wanted to personally thank me for the support I gave him – actually he said he wanted to personally thank about a hundred and twenty of us for the support we gave him, but I always felt he gave me a special look, so ...

Jeremy: Actually, I'm really into the music side of things lately.

Gary: Yes, I've just used G minor seventh diminished in a ...

Jeremy: It would be great to play keyboards with someone like Martyn Joseph.

Gary: Who's he? Friend of yours?

Jeremy: *(Shocked.)* He's one of the top performers at Let God Spring into Royal Acts of Harvest Growth and Blackbelt ...

Gary: Blackbelt?

Jeremy: Yes, it's like Greenbelt only better. Martyn's always there. He's *great!*

Gary: I think U2 are absolutely superb.

Jeremy: *(Deeply moved.)* Well, thank you very much! I didn't realise you'd heard me playing. Do you really think ...

Gary: I said 'U2' not 'you too'. I was talking about the band called U2.

Jeremy: Oh, yeah! U2 are *really* great!

Gary: Born again Christians ...

Jeremy: Really sort of secular as well ...

Gary: Great music on any level ...

Jeremy: Great how they don't act like non-Christian bands ...

Gary: That Bono ...

Jeremy: The things he says ...

Gary: Really sort of honest and unhampered ...

Jeremy: Not like a Christian at all ...

Gary: *(Sings.)* '... I still haven't found what I'm looking for ...'

Jeremy: Great!

Gary: Great!

[*Pause*]

Jeremy: Not quite sound?

Gary: Not quite. We've found what we're looking for, haven't we?

Jeremy: We have? I mean – we *have!* Anyway, I must go. I'm meeting a girl who's here with CYPAS over by the E.A. stall. We're having tea with a U.R.C. couple who've just done a tour with M.F.O. in Africa. She's hoping to go to L.B.C. while he gets a couple of months in with W.E.C.

Gary: I think I'll have a sleep.

Jeremy: Okay, R.I.P.

Well, that's it! What do you think?

EDWIN: *(Chuckling softly.)* Extremely amusing, Gerald, but I don't somehow think it would go down too well at the local festival. They do take themselves rather seriously.

VERNON: *(Clearly puzzled.)* Of course, it's really good, Gerald, but err ... I didn't sort of see it as funny. I mean, it was really sort of two ordinary Christian chaps having the sort of chat that, well, that we young Christian chaps have, wasn't it?

A.P.: Surely people don't really talk like that! I can't believe ...

RICHARD: Of course they don't! We were only saying on the SPUC committee the other day, or rather a chap from SPCK was saying, that in all his years with the WCC and SASRA before that, how sensible and mature Christian conversation is, whether you're in the YMCA or a school C.U. All that stuff about initials was, frankly, completely O.T.T.

A.P.: Mmm ... yes. I see what you mean, Richard.

GERALD: I know an A1 S.R.N. with a B.M.W. and the sweetest B.T.M. you ever ...

ANNE: Gerald!

PERCY: *(Sniffing.)* Discussion is superfluous. We have already established, or I believed we had established, that a duologue is not suitable. Unless of course *(fixing A.P. with an accusing eye)* we are being abused by a nepotist!

MRS T.: *(Straining to hear.)* Who's bin bruised by a methodist? Doesn't surprise me, mind you ...

A.P.: *(Raising his voice.)* No one's been bruised by a methodist, Mrs Thynn! Mr Brain thought I might be favouring Gerald's idea, because he's a relation!

MRS T.: I thought we wasn't doin' Revelation, like old 'Enry Irvin' over there suggested.

A.P.: *(Bawling.)* We're *not* doing Revel ... !! Oh, never mind, Leonard, explain to your mother please.

PERCY: I will not be referred to as 'Old 'Enry Irvin' over there'!

MRS T.: Well, come an' sit over 'ere! Then you can be Old 'Enry Irvin' over 'ere!

PERCY: I have *never* been so ... !

MRS F.: I am very much afraid that Gerald's little piece of nonsense embodies those elements of flippancy and irreverence that seem to characterise the greater majority of his utterances. I fear, Mr Chairman, that there is an undue residue of the natural in your progeny.

EDWIN: Victoria, this really is not the place for ...

A.V.: She said 'Chairman'. She was s'posed to say 'Chair'! Somebody pass a motion – quick!

PERCY: To think that I, who once trod the same boards as – as – as Peter Butterworth, should be subjected to ...

MRS T.: Peter Butterworth! Now yer talkin'! *(Laughs shrilly.)* 'E was in all them Carry On films, wasn't 'e? 'E was good, but my favourite was ...

MR F.: *(A strange rasping laugh.)* I very much enjoyed the performances of that charming fair-haired girl who always seemed to have very large parts.

[*A profound silence falls. During it, Mrs F. turns with ominous slowness to look at her spouse.*]

MRS F.: I was not aware, Stenneth, that you had attended *any* of those highly questionable presentations.

MR F.: *(Even his voice is pale.)* Ah, well ... yes, well ... of course ... that was – was before we were err ... married, my dear. Before you err ... assisted me in seeing so clearly that err ... almost everything is err ... wrong, as it were.

MRS F.: *(The air is heavy with 'Wait till I get you home'.)* Mr Chair ...

A.V.: *(Interrupting with triumphant precision.)* ... person!

MRS F.: I would like to move ...

THYNN: Hear, hear!

MRS F.: I would *like* to move that none of the suggestions received so far be adopted. They are either ungodly, unsuitable, or incompetent.

GERALD: *(Whispering.)* And there isn't a part for her.

A.P.: Ssh! Look, could we just ... ?

[*There is a lot of loud noise as someone crashes through the door and slams it shut behind them.*]

ELSIE BURLESFORD: *(For it is she – out of breath, but not energy.)* Hello, everybody! Hello, dad! Sorry I'm late. William and I have been at the back of the fruit shop rebuking China and doing our maths homework. William believes we can actually change the shape of countries through prayer and he's read about someone in South America who's actually chipping bits off Peru, and he doesn't see why it shouldn't happen here, and neither do I, so we're going to ...

GERALD: It's a great idea, Elsie! We wouldn't need ferries to get to the Isle of Wight any more. You and William can just stand on the mainland and pray the island to and fro all day. Brilliant!

ELSIE: Don't be silly, Gerald. Anyway, I hope I'm not too late, Mr Plass, because ...

MRS T.: You 'ave to call 'im Wardrobe, love.

ELSIE: Wardrobe?

A.P.: *(Shouting.)* Chair, Mrs Thynn! Not wardrobe!

MRS T.: Well, I knew it was furniture ...

ELSIE: Chair? Oh, Chair! I see! Short for chairperson?

[*You can hear Andromeda grinning.*]

A.P.: Elsie, have you got ... ?

ELSIE: *(Great rustling of paper.)* I've brought my idea along. It's a poem! I thought different people could read different verses. I've got them all here; they've got the names on. Each person represents a part of God's creation, you see, so we'd all stand in a line on stage and read it out verse by verse. What do you think?

A.P.: Well ...

ELSIE: Let's try it out! Mr Flushpool, you're first. Here's your verse. Off you go.

MR F.: *(Much throat-clearing. He begins to read at last in a very small, nervous voice.)*
>A lion I, a fearsome beast
>I'm six feet long or more,
>My teeth are white as tennis shorts
>Oh, tremble at my roar.

(Makes a tiny mewing noise.)

MRS F.: Roar, Stenneth! Roar!

MR F.: *(Makes a loud mewing noise.)*

ANNE: *(Whispering to A.P.)* I say, darling.

A.P.: Yes, what?

ANNE: *(Still whispering.)* It just occurred to me that with Stenneth, Victoria and you all sitting in a line, we could do 'The

Lion, the Witch, and the Wardrobe'! *(Dissolves into silly giggles.)*

A.P.: Sssh! Err . . . that was very impressive, Stenneth. I could just see you stalking the plains . . .

MRS T.: Why's 'e walkin' to Staines?

THYNN: Be quiet, mother. Err . . . Adrian?

A.P.: Be quiet, Leonard. Carry on Elsie, please.

ELSIE: Right! Mr Brain, you're next. It's on that piece of paper I just gave you. Start when you're ready.

PERCY: *(Declaims in a mountainous voice.)*

> An earthworm, I, a humble worm,
> Of negligible brain,
> I swallow little bits of earth,
> Then spit them out again.

(Sound of rustling paper as he searches for more.) Is *that* my part? That fragment of absurd doggerel? Is that *all?*

ELSIE: *(Undaunted.)* Yes, Mr Brain, it is. And it's not absurd doggerel. William's pretty sure that it's inspired verse. He's just been reading a book about a man in South-east Asia who's written fifteen full length Christian novels despite having been blind, deaf and dumb since birth. William says the things I've written are amazingly similar to the things this man's written.

GERALD: *(Whispering.)* That figures!

PERCY: Humph!

A.P.: Sssh! Not you, Percy, I was talking to Gerald.

ELSIE: *(On the warpath.)* What *did* Gerald say, Mr Plass?

A.P.: It doesn't matter what Gerald said, Elsie. Let's just carry on.

GERALD: I said . . .

A.P.: Be quiet, Gerald!

THYNN: Adrian?

A.P.: Be quiet, Leonard!

VERNON: This chap in South-east Asia sounds really sort of . . .

ELSIE: Be quiet, Vernon! Now, the next one to read a verse is Mrs Flushpool. Here you are, here's yours. You're an oak tree.

MRS F.: *(Quite flattered.)* Well, I must say that seems eminently suitable. Now, let me see … *(She begins reading in ringing tones that slow down to incredulity as she takes in the words.)*

An oak tree I, my arms held high,
In postures wild and cranky.
My feet beneath the stubborn sod,
My skin all brown and manky.

(Pre-natal silence.)

GERALD: Eat your heart out, Wordsworth.

A.P.: Sssh! Elsie, I'm not quite sure …

MRS F.: *(Faintly.)* Stenneth, defend me!

MR F.: Err … yes, of course, dear. Err … I think Victoria is a little upset at the err … idea that she has been considered physically appropriate for this particular verse. Her skin, after all, is not brown at all ...

MRS F.: Stenneth!!

MR F.: Or err ... indeed err ... m – m – m – manky, and we – we insist on having the err ... *sod* removed, and replaced with turf, or indeed g – g – g – grass.

ELSIE: *(Vocal hands on hips.)* I was led to write those words and I refuse to change a single one!

GERALD: *(Whispering.)* Stubborn little turf, isn't she?

A.P.: Sssh! Elsie, this just isn't working, is it? Perhaps ...

THYNN: Adrian, there's something ...

A.P.: Be quiet, Leonard!

ELSIE: *(About to boil.)* Very well! If you don't want what I've written, I'll tear it all up, and I'm very sorry to have bothered you! William says that we'll thrive under persecution, and I suppose this is the beginning of it. This meeting is like – like – Rumania! *(To A.P..)* I wrote a verse specially for you, Mr Plass, and you don't even want to hear it! William's just heard about a man in ...

A.P.: *(Surrendering.)* All right, Elsie! I'm sorry, I'm sorry, I'm sorry! I will read the verse you wrote for me and then we really must get on. Okay?

ELSIE: *(Slightly mollified.)* Well, all right then. Here it is, and you won't be all sensitive like Mrs Flushpool?

A.P.: *(Testily.)* Of course not! I shall just be objective.

ELSIE: Right, off you go then.

A.P.: *(Reads quite quickly.)*

> A slug am I, a slimy thing
> I crawl upon my belly,
> Behind I leave a sticky trail,
> My body's like a jelly.

[*Round of delighted applause.*]

ELSIE: What do you think, eh?

A.P.: *(Objectively.)* Why the blue blazes do you think I'm specially suited to read that? What is it about me that suggests a slug? I'd just like to know, Elsie!

ELSIE: Well, it had to be someone fat and humble and useful, so . . .

A.P.: *(Gritting his teeth.)* Right! That's it! Thank you all for coming! Thanks for your suggestions! Thanks for anything I've forgotten! Nothing's suitable, so we might as well all just eat all the food and clear off! If I'd had any idea that . . .

THYNN: Err . . . there's something . . .

A.P.: What?!

THYNN: It's this. This script.

A.P.: By you? I'm not interested in . . .

THYNN: No, it's by FRANK BRADDOCK. He popped in this morning and said could I bring it along because he couldn't get to this meeting. He said it's exactly ten minutes long, it's in rhyming verse, and it's about Daniel in the lions' den. It's got six characters including the narrator and the lions and he wrote it specially for us to do.

[*Long pause while* A.P. *stares at* THYNN.]

A.P.: *(Quietly but menacingly.)* Let me get this straight, Leonard. You have been sitting there with this script, by a proper writer, in your pocket, throughout this farcical meeting, during which people have been told they have manky skins, and bellies like jellies, and I have had to listen to hour after hour . . .

ANNE: *(Mildly.)* Less than an hour, darling . . .

A.P.: . . . nearly an hour of unusable material; and now, only *now* do you produce something which might have saved us all that trouble. Is that a fair summary, Leonard?

THYNN: Err . . . let me see . . . yes, yes, that's about it. I – I forgot I'd got it, you see. *(Laughs hoarsely.)*

A.P.: Well, in that case I'm going to ... *(sound of chair legs scraping and a little scream from Thynn's throat.)*

ANNE: You're going to forgive him, aren't you, darling? Aren't you, darling?

A.P.: *(Breathing heavily and noisily through his nose.)* Yes! That's it – that's what I'm going to do to you. I'm going to forgive you, Leonard *(Barely audible muttering)* – right in the teeth ... *(Sits again.)*

ANNE: Is the play good, dear?

A.P.: *(Rustling of pages.)* Looks great! Just right. Listen to this bit:

> Down in the den on the bone-strewn floor,
> Where the lost men scream and the lions roar
> Where a man whose gods are life and breath,
> Will lose his gods in the jaws of death.

[*Impressed silence.*]

PERCY: And are there – is there a part for, well, for ... ?

A.P.: I should think you'd make an ideal King Darius, Percy.

PERCY: *(Beaming audibly.)* Ah! Well, that seems – yes!

MRS T.: I think if we don't get some blinkin' food soon, we ought to vote in a new chest-of-drawers to get things movin'!

A.P.: Good idea! I'd quite happily give way to a new chest-of-drawers. Right! We've got a play. I'll sort out who's playing what and allocate the other jobs like prompter and so on, then we'll have another meeting. Okay, everyone?

[*Murmurs of hungry acquiescence.*]

THYNN: Here, it's a good job we're finishing now.

A.P.: Why?

THYNN: Because I've almost run out of ...

[*Click! as tape runs out.*]

TWO

Smoke Gets in Our Eyes

That first meeting left me a bit shell-shocked, as you can imagine, but when I got home later and had a proper look at Frank's play I felt quite encouraged. It was just right. Anne and Gerald went off to bed saying silly things like 'Goodnight Mr De Mille', and I stayed up to work out the cast list for 'Daniel in the Den'. Earlier, during the meal, I'd promised Andromeda that I'd give serious consideration to her suggestion that the play should become a modern parable, entitled: 'Daniella in the Working Men's Club', but – well, I ask you! Anyway, after a lot of thought, this was the list I finally came up with.

Narrator – Gerald Plass
Daniel – Edwin Burlesford
King Darius – Percy Brain
Servant – Elsie Burlesford
First lion – Charles Cook
Second lion – Vernon Rawlings
Third lion – Stenneth Flushpool
An angel – Victoria Flushpool
Director – Adrian Plass
Treasurer – Richard Cook
Prompter – Leonard Thynn
Costumes – Mrs Thynn & Norma Twill
Technical effects – William Farmer
Make-up – Gloria Marsh

Andromeda was not available on the date of performance, for which I sent up a brief but profoundly sincere prayer of thanks. I'm very fond of Andromeda but she is a very powerful presence when you're trying to *do* things.

As for Stenneth being a lion, well, I know he didn't put up much of a show when he read Elsie's lion poem, but I sensed how much he wanted to be in it, and besides, it occurred to me that the bit where Victoria, as an angel, had to get the lions to shut their mouths would have a very natural feel about it – in Stenneth's case anyway.

The following day I rang young William Farmer to check that he was happy to be responsible for technical effects. Happy wasn't the word! He started raving on incomprehensibly about smoke machines and coloured gels and mirror balls, whatever they might be. I just agreed with everything he said, and promised to send him a script and let him know when the next meeting was.

Surprisingly enough it was Anne who suggested I should ask Gloria Marsh to do the make-up. She said that Gloria needed to be involved and would be very useful because she'd done professional make-up once. I find Anne's attitude to Gloria oddly inconsistent. She seems to have a particular insight about which of Gloria's quite frequent requests for assistance I should respond to positively. At other times she will actually insist that we help with things I hadn't even noticed. Once, quite inexplicably, Anne and Gerald collapsed in helpless laughter after I came away from the phone to say that Gloria was asking for help in lifting a very large chest. Most odd . . .

However, I digress. I did visit Gloria on the evening following that first meeting, and she was very pleased to be asked to help. She sat me down in front of a mirror and demonstrated on my face the kind of make-up she would use. It seemed to me rather bright and garish, but Gloria said it would look quite different under stage lights. We had a very pleasant coffee together after that. She really is a sweetly ingenuous person. As I left she squeezed my hand just as a child might do with her daddy, and asked if I'd forgiven her for being a naughty girl when she borrowed our car last year and bashed it.* Naturally, as a Christian, I forgave her wholeheartedly and agreed to her request to borrow it again next week. As I walked into the Coach and Horses on my way home I felt an unusual lightness of spirit as a result of this encounter. As Ted, the barman, pulled my usual half-pint of bitter, I said whimsically, 'I feel different, Ted.' He stared at me for a few moments then said, 'Come out the closet, 'ave yer?' It was then that I realised with alarm that I was still wearing my make-up. Needless to say, when I arrived home *very* shortly after that, Anne and Gerald and Leonard Thynn nearly died laughing when I told them what had happened.

Anyway, I'd got my list sorted out, and that was the important thing. The next morning I photocopied the script and the list on a machine at work, and sent off copies to all the people involved. I also added a note to say that there'd be a meeting of the non-acting participants on the following Monday evening, and that's what the next tape is mainly about. It doesn't start with that meeting, though. You see, every Monday evening at about half past six, Leonard gets dragged along by his mother to a rather obscure religious group called The Ninth Day Specific Bulmerites – Baroness of Wertley's Involvement. On this particular evening Leonard had his tape-recorder with him ready to come on to the 'Daniel' meeting afterwards, and he must have pressed the record button by accident, just as the 'message' started. I wasn't going to transcribe it, but Gerald said he thought it was too wonderful to leave out . . .

[*Tape opens with the same crackles and hisses as the last one, followed by the typical coughs, shuffles and mutterings of a waiting congregation.*]

PREACHER: *(In a flat, monotonous, rather burdened voice.)* There are so many lessons to be learned in a garden.

CONGREGATION: *(Equally flatly.)* Ah, yes, in the garden. Amen, yes we witness to that etc.

_____

*See: *The Sacred Diary of Adrian Plass.*

223

P.: Only the other day I was trimming the privet that separates our garden from the next, and chatting uncommittedly to a non-Christian neighbour, when my ladder collapsed . . .

CONG.: *(Sympathetically.)* Amen, brother . . .

THYNN: Ha, ha! I mean – amen, brother.

P.: As I lay writhing on the rockery I realised, with a little spasm, that I was being taught a very important lesson. Namely, that we must expect to lose support if we start hedging.

CONG.: Amen! Thank you, Lord! Yes! etc.

P.: Recognising the providential nature of this revelation, I fetched a wooden box from the garage and, having once more ascended, re-engaged Mr Studeley in conversation. This time I was much more direct. 'Mr Studeley,' I announced, firmly, 'we are all suffering as a result of the Fall.'

CONG.: Amen! Yes! Ah! etc.

P.: '*I'm* not,' replied Mr Studeley, 'but you're bleedin' in three places.' I was about to correct his interpretation of my state-ment when, unfortunately, the box on which I was standing gave way with a loud crack like a pistol shot and I must have disappeared from Mr Studeley's view with quite startling suddenness.

THYNN: Hallelujah! Praise the Lord! *(Frowning silence.)* I mean – Amen, brother . . .

P.: Honesty compels me to admit that as I fell backwards onto the rockery once again, I very nearly succumbed to a recur-rent temptation to ascribe randomness to the events of my life. However, seeing Mr Studeley's face appear above the privet hedge at this point, I realised that here was an ideal opportunity to show joy in adversity. Abandoning my heretical impulses . . .

CONG.: Praise God! Yes!

P.: . . . and baring my teeth in a joyful smile, I sang the following words whilst attempting to convey that I was spreadeagled in a divinely ordained sort of way. *(Sings in a flat, joyless manner.)*

I'm H – A – P – P – Y
I'm H – A – P – P – Y
I know I am
I'm sure I am
I'm H – A – P – P – Y

Mr Studeley said, 'Banged yer 'ead, did yer? Must 'ave!' As he withdrew, I turned my eyes away from the privet hedge, and there, less than one inch from my face, was further justification for my descent. It was only a humble slug, but – and this was the point – behind it lay a shining trail. What a graphic picture of the Christian life!

CONG.: Amen! Hallelujah! We want to be slugs for you! etc.

P.: A little later, as my wife cleaned and bandaged my wounds, I said to her, 'Wife, you are a slug among women!' She stopped bandaging and said, 'In what way, pray, do I resemble a slug?' 'It is the slime!' I cried affirmingly, 'It shines!'

CONG.: Amen! Let it shine! Let the slime shine! etc.

MRS THYNN: *(Very loudly.)* As 'e started yet?

THYNN: *(Very loud whisper.)* Turn your hearing-aid to 'T', mother, you've missed half of it!

MRS T.: Oh, good, there's only 'alf to go then.

P.: My wife is a trained nurse, so I trust there was some excellent reason why she tied my left wrist to my right ankle, and my right wrist to my left ankle before leaving rather abruptly. Bent double, I hobbled out into the garden again with little shuffling steps, and balanced carefully at the edge of the lawn to await further revelations. Mr Studeley's face appeared over the hedge again. He said, 'I was just wonderin' if you was feelin' – why are you touchin' your toes? 'Ere! Your arms an' legs is all tied together! 'Oo did that then?' Suddenly inspired, I replied, 'I am in the strings of healing, whereas you are bonded to your iniquities.'

'Too right!' said Mr Studeley, 'specially first thing in the mornin' when I get out of me bed an' try to stand up. Bonded to me iniquities, I am. Couldn't 'ave put it better meself!'

MRS T.: *(Very loudly.)* 'As 'e finished yet?

THYNN: *(Loud whisper.)* I'm not sure!

P.: I was unable to resist a slight feeling of depression as Mr Studeley disappeared again; particularly as a large apple fell heavily on the back of my head at that instant. A moment's reflection, however, showed that once again a heavenly message had been vouchsafed to me. I smiled in grateful comprehension as a larger and even heavier apple hit my head, and I toppled slowly over sideways into the rockery. I knew without doubt that my efforts with Mr Studeley would be crowned with much fruit. Amen.

CONG.: *(Frenzied response.)* Hallelujah! Amen! Oh, yes! Let there be much fruit! He toppled, he toppled! Crown his efforts! Amen! etc.

P.: We now sing number seven hundred and fifty-two in the *Ninth Day Specific Bulmerites – Baroness of Wertley's Involvement Songbook;* 'Let us rush around with . . .

[Tape clicks off]

(Not only did Thynn not realise he'd turned his machine on and off during his hour with the Bulmerites, but when he came on to the Daniel meeting he forgot to take the pause button off until we were several minutes into the proceedings. That's why it starts in the middle of me shouting at Mrs Thynn. Also present were Leonard, Richard Cook, William Farmer, Gloria Marsh and Norma Twill, who had agreed to supervise costumes. Norma is a very pretty, single girl in her mid-twenties, who works in a factory making those pink and white marshmallows, not that it matters where she works, or that she's pretty, of course. I just mention it for information . . .)

[Tape begins abruptly as Thynn realises he's forgotten to switch on.]

A.P.: *(Shouting.)* I did not say 'I rely on sin', I said 'hire a lion skin'! Why on earth would I say that I rely on sin, for goodness sake? All we want you to do is go along to the theatrical costumiers and hire three lion outfits! Three lion outfits! That's all!

MRS T.: I think gorillas is more frightenin'. I 'ad a dream once where this big 'airy ...

A.P.: Lions, Mrs Thynn! It's got to be lions!

MRS T.: Oh, well, you're the Bureau, you know best I s'pose.

RICHARD: Cheap!

MRS T.: Eh?

RICHARD: Cheap! Cheap!

MRS T.: Why's 'e doin' canary impressions?

THYNN: He's not, mother! He's saying the costumes can't be too expensive!

A.P.: We're not quite as badly off as we were, because Edwin has redirected some church funds towards this project. We haven't got money to chuck about, but we should be all right if we're careful. *(To MRS T.)* All we want you to do, Mrs Thynn, is make sure those three costumes are ordered and ready to be collected when the time comes! All right?!

MRS T.: All right, I'm not deaf!

NORMA: And you want the others in black tops and tights or trousers, Adrian, is that right?

A.P.: That's absolutely right, Norma. That's exactly it, and thank you for being here and taking such an invaluable part in the proceedings. Yes, black tops and tights or trousers. After all, we want to be original, don't we? Your own clothes are, if I may say so, Norma, extremely original and attractive, just as you are yourself.

NORMA: *(Blushing audibly.)* Err ... thank you. Do the black things have to have any special feature, or ...?

RICHARD: Cheap!

MRS T.: Oh, give 'im some birdseed, someone!

A.P.: The answer to your very intelligent question, Norma, is that, beyond the fact that we can't afford to be too extravagant as Richard points out, the black clothes can be plain and simple and err ... plain. Is that okay? I do want you to feel absolutely relaxed and happy about the responsibilities that you've so kindly agreed to undertake for us. Thank you again for – well, for just being here with us. Is your chair quite comfortable? Perhaps mine would be ...

NORMA: No, I'm fine, thanks – really.

A.P.: Well, if it gets uncomfortable, just let me know and we'll exchange seats.

THYNN: My seat's not comfortable. Let's swop ...

A.P.: Be quiet, Leonard, we've got a lot to get through. Don't make a fuss. Now ...

GLORIA: I'm really looking forward to seeing Mr Brain in black tights.

[*Pause as everyone mentally envisages Percy Brain in black tights.*]

A.P.: Mmmm! Perhaps you'd better jot down 'trousers' next to Percy's name, Norma, after all ...

THYNN: We don't want to scare people off before they even see the lions, do we?

A.P.: After all, trousers look just as nice as err ... tights. Now ...

GLORIA: As for the prospect of seeing Victoria Flushpool in an angelic body-stocking, well, my cup runneth over.

THYNN: So will the body-stocking.

A.P.: Be quiet, Leonard. Err ... Norma, perhaps you'd better organise a slightly err ... fuller garment for Mrs Flushpool. I'm so sorry to mess you about. Thank you for being so patient and ...

GLORIA: I'd *love* to see *you* in tights, Adrian! Wouldn't you, Norma?

NORMA: Well, I don't – I mean, of course it would be – I mean . . .

GLORIA: He's got the figure for it, hasn't he? You have you know, Adrian. Oh, I say, I haven't said something naughty, have I? You will forgive your little Gloria if she's said anything to offend you, won't you? *(Puts on a little-girl voice.)* Big smacks for naughty-warty Glorbags if daddy's cwoss wiv her!

A.P.: *(Overcoming paralysis.)* Err . . . Daddy's not cwoss wiv – I mean, I'm not cross with you, Gloria. Err . . . could we talk about make-up?

GLORIA: Oh, yes, of course. *(Suddenly business-like.)* Well, I don't think Gerald and Edwin and Elsie and Mr Brain will need more than basic stage make-up, so that's no problem. I've got a bit myself, but I suppose we can buy more if we need it?

A.P.: Oh, yes, as long as it's . . .

RICHARD: Cheap! Cheap!

MRS. T.: D'you know, I reckon if we spent enough time, we could teach 'im to talk.

GLORIA: And the lions obviously won't need anything, so that brings us to the only real problem.

A.P.: Which is . . . ?

GLORIA: How do we make Victoria Flushpool look like an angel?

WILLIAM: Why did you cast her in that part, Mr Plass?

A.P.: *(Miserably.)* It was a choice between telling her she wasn't in it, telling her she was playing a lion, telling her she was playing a man's part, or letting her be the angel. *(Manfully honest.)* I'm afraid . . . *(Sigh.)* . . . I chickened out.

THYNN: *(In sympathetic tones.)* You took the lily-livered, yellow-bellied path of abject, cowardly, pathetic refusal to face the clear path of duty. Well, who are we to judge?

A.P.: *(Coldly.)* Thank you, Leonard.

THYNN: Yes, it's good to know that a Christian brother is able to openly confess that he's a wretched, snivelling, fainthearted worm of a . . .

A.P.: All right, Leonard, that'll do – thank you very much. Can we get back to the point? How do we make Mrs Flushpool into an angel? Was that the question?

THYNN: Job for Wimpey's if you ask me.

A.P.: We don't ask ...

NORMA: *(Quite stern.)* That's very unkind, if you don't mind me saying so, Mr Thynn. In fact it's very unkind even if you *do* mind me saying so. The way to make Mrs Flushpool into an angel is not just to do with clothes and make-up; it's to do with loving and caring and saying nice things, and not always trying to placate her and shut her out by making fed-up faces about her behind her back. When was the last time any of us went round to see Mrs Flushpool when we didn't actually have to? How many of us really know what goes on inside her head; what hurts her and frightens her and excites her and makes her unhappy? She's a very difficult woman. I know that. Of course I do. But I also know that Jesus never made anyone angelic by ignoring them unless he had no choice, or by saying rotten things about them when they weren't there, and neither will we!

[*A long, stunned silence.*]

A.P.: Well ...

NORMA: *(Very embarrassed.)* I – I'm sorry, I shouldn't have said all that. I had no right ...

A.P.: *(Quietly.)* I'm very glad you said it, Norma.

THYNN: Mmm ... wish I hadn't said that about err ... thingy

WILLIAM: Yeah! Well said, Norms!

GLORIA: A spot of number two, you think, Norma?

A.P.: Make-up, you mean?

NORMA: *(Softly.)* I think Gloria's talking about the command-ments, Adrian.

A.P.: Ah!

RICHARD: Certainly, some of our responses to Victoria have been somewhat ... cheap.

MRS T.: I'm goin' to give you a little bell an' a ladder for Christmas, Richard. *(Pause.)* Prap's we ought to be a bit nicer to the old frump – try anyway ...

[*Short silence.*]

A.P.: Perhaps we could move on to you, Leonard.

THYNN: *(Fiddling with his machine.)* Eh? Oh, yes! Me. I'm the prompter, you know.

A.P.: You're sure you can handle recording and prompting at the same time?

THYNN: *(Considers for a moment.)* Yes! Yep! No problem there.

A.P.: And you still want to do it?

THYNN: *(As though slightly hurt.)* Of course I want to do it! I *am* the prompter.

A.P.: So you're quite confident?

THYNN: Yep!

A.P.: No problems?

THYNN: No, none!

A.P.: Good! Great!

THYNN: Just one little thing ...

A.P.: Yes?

THYNN: What does a prompter do?

A.P.: *(Seething.)* He lies on the floor while the director jumps up and down on his head, Leonard. Do you honestly have no idea at all what a prompter does?

THYNN: *(Vaguely.)* I thought it was a sort of soldier.

A.P.: Why on earth ... ?

THYNN: Well, when I was about seven and at big boys' school ...

A.P.: Big boys' school, yes ...

THYNN: I went along to the first rehearsal of this school play that Miss Glanthorpe was doing ...

A.P.: Miss Glanthorpe, yes ...

THYNN: I *loved* Miss Glanthorpe!

A.P.: Get on, Leonard!

THYNN: Well, I was a bit late getting there because I had to visit the boys' tiddler room on the way – that's what we used to call it, you see.

A.P.: Really! How interesting ...

GLORIA: So sweet!

THYNN: Anyway, when I got to Miss Glanthorpe's classroom, she said, 'Ah, Lenny, you *must* be a little prompter if you want to take part in my play,' then she gave me a soldier's uniform to put on, so I thought ...

NORMA: You thought it meant a soldier?

THYNN: Yes. Doesn't it?

NORMA: *(A little weepy.)* I think that's a lovely story. I can just picture little Lenny trotting along to be in the play and getting all excited when he was given his soldier's uniform to wear. Oh, Leonard ...

GLORIA: And thinking a prompter was a soldier. Sweet!

WILLIAM: *(Shouting.)* So did you go and see Leonard playing a soldier in the school play, Mrs Thynn?!

MRS T.: Eh? Oh, yes, I went all right! 'E was the best one in it. Better than Hoity-toity Vera Ashby-Jones' youngest, Alfred. 'E threw up just as is mother clicked 'er camera. Lovely picture that must 'ave been. He-he!

THYNN: What is a prompter, then, if it's not a soldier?

A.P.: A prompter, Leonard, is someone who sits at the side of the stage with the script in front of him, ready to help people when they forget their lines.

THYNN: *(Mentally digesting.)* I see.... But, in that case, if Miss Glanthorpe wanted me to be a prompter and help people with their lines ...

A.P.: Yes ... ?

THYNN: Why did she dress me up as a soldier?

A.P.: No, you don't understand. When she said she wanted you to be a little prompter she meant – look, I'll explain afterwards, all right? Just as long as you understand what you've got to do in the play. *Do* you understand?

THYNN: I sit at the side of the stage ...

A.P.: On the left ...

THYNN: I sit at the side of the stage on the left, and I've got the script in front of me, and when people forget their lines, I help them ...

A.P.: By calling out clearly the first few words of the next line.

THYNN: ... by calling out clearly the first few words of the next line.

A.P.: *(Relieved.)* Good! You've got it!

THYNN: Yep!

A.P.: Good. Now, Richard, let's ...

THYNN: Just one thing ...

A.P.: Yes?

THYNN: When do I get my uniform?

A.P.: *(Wildly.)* I've just explained! You don't ...

NORMA: *(Kindly.)* Leonard, dear, you don't need a uniform to be a prompter – just ordinary clothes, that's all.

THYNN: *(Sounding terribly disappointed.)* I was looking forward to the uniform. I like uniforms. I haven't worn a uniform for nearly ...

NORMA: Adrian, couldn't Leonard wear a soldier's uniform? I'm sure I could get one quite cheaply and it doesn't really matter, does it? I mean, it doesn't, does it?

A.P.: Of course, Norma, I respect your judgment tremendously but it's not ...

GLORIA: *(Wheedlingly.)* Daddy let Lenny be a big soldier just to please his little Glorbags?

WILLIAM: Go on, Mr Plass! Say Leonard can have a uniform. Go on!

A.P.: *(In a hair-clutching sort of voice.)* I find it very difficult to believe that we are sitting here discussing what kind of costume the *prompter* should wear!

THYNN: *(Miles away.)* I *loved* Miss Glanthorpe ...

[*Silence as several pairs of reproachful eyes bore into* A.P.]

A.P.: *(A broken man.)* All right, Leonard can wear a soldier's uniform. Why not? Why should we be rational?

[*General noises of approval and satisfaction*]

GLORIA: *(Whispering.)* Big kiss for daddy afterwards for being such a huge big kind jelly-baby!

A.P.: *(Alarmed.)* Err ... that won't be necessary, Gloria, thank you very much. Now, if we could turn to finance just for a moment. As you know, Richard has kindly agreed to act as our treasurer for the duration of this project, using funds placed in the newly established Entertainment Budget. Richard has opened a special account at one of the local banks for this purpose, and I believe they've now sent you a cheque book, Richard, is that correct?

RICHARD: The bank in question has indeed now furnished me with a cheque book appropriate to the account in question, and I am therefore in a position to make withdrawals from the said account as and when the demand arises, and according to the way in which the Lord shall vouchsafe knowledge of his guiding will.

MRS T.: Eh?

THYNN: He says the boodle's on tap, mother.

RICHARD: On the contrary, Leonard. The 'boodle' is not 'on tap'. We have, after recent additions, the sum of seventy-five pounds in the aforesaid account, and I am entrusted with the stewardship of that sum. Last night, in a dream, I believe that I received a warning regarding the dangers of unworthy expenditure. I would like to share it with you now.

A.P.: Must it be now? We haven't really ...

RICHARD: *(In prophetic tones.)* I saw, as it were, an mighty herd of aardvarks flying in formation through the sky. And, behold, an voice spake unto men saying, 'Touch not these aardvarks, beyond that which shall be needful to thee for thine own sustenance, for these are mine own aardvarks set aside for mine own use.' And as I watched and marvelled, some men did with mauve bows and arrows fire at and fetch down sundry aardvarks for their own sustenance and that of their kinfolk, but a goodly multitude remained and, behold, there was in this no condemnation. Then, one standing by said, 'Wherefore should we touch not these aardvarks beyond that which shall be needful for our own sustenance? Behold there existeth quite a market in aardvark skins, not to mention the attractive little knick-knacks you can make out of their teeth and so on.' And this one did then fire his arrows in mighty numbers until it did seem to rain aard-varks, and great was the falling down thereof, until they did lie as an mighty blanket upon the land, and no aardvarks flew as in the latter times. And the same voice spake saying, 'Where are mine aardvarks, set aside for mine own use? Wert thou not content to take only those aardvarks needful to thee for thine own sustenance? Wherefore hast thou taken those aardvarks which were mine own aardvarks, set aside for mine own use?' Then he that spake did wax exceeding wrath, and did cause a plague of green jerbils to afflict he who had sinned. I then awoke after a short further dream about getting into a bath full of Smarties wearing a Batman costume.

[*Stunned silence, during which you can sense* A.P. *thanking his lucky stars that Gerald's not here.*]

A.P.: Well ... I'm sure we shall all take to heart that warning not to waste a single aardvark – I mean, a single pound. Thank you, Richard. Our watchword shall be ...

RICHARD: Cheap! Cheap!

MRS T.: 'Oo's a pretty boy, then?

A.P.: Okay! All requests for expenditure should come to me first, then, if I approve it, you go to Richard for the cash. Any problems? No? Good! William, you've been sitting there patiently since we started. Let's come to you now. Edwin's taking responsibility for general stage-management, props and all that sort of thing, so basically you're in charge of sound and any special effects that you can dream up.

WILLIAM: Great! Err ... you didn't mention lights. What about the floods and the spots and the gels and the mirror-ball and the strobe and the fresnels and the follow-spots and the baby spots ...

A.P.: I'm sorry, William, but apparently there's a sort of phantom of the opera type down at the hall, who crouches over the lighting board all day – and all night for all I know – and does a sort of Incredible Hulk act if anyone else even mentions touching it. We can send him a script and some suggestions, but that's about it. So it's just sound and effects, I'm afraid.

WILLIAM: That's a shame. Elsie and I have just read a book about a man in South-east Asia who saw two thousand people converted every week just through the lighting arrangement in his theatre and we thought . . .

A.P.: *Just* sound and effects, William . . .

WILLIAM: Ah, well, never mind, I could make up a really good soundtrack with stuff like thunder and roaring, and we could do some effects like smoke, and people sort of glowing and – and things.

A.P.: Exactly! Now, I think the best way to go about this is if I read the whole thing through, and you can talk about any ideas you've had as we go along. Is that okay, William?

WILLIAM: Great! Great!

A.P.: Right. Well, it starts with King Darius coming to the front of stage and addressing the audience. Here goes:

Darius: Though ruling, ruled by men with . . .

WILLIAM: I see smoke here! Thick, curling gouts of smoke almost obscuring the figure of the king!

A.P.: Err . . . right, I'll make a note of that. I'll start again, shall I? I didn't get all that err . . . far, did I? Right, here goes again –

Darius: Though ruling, ruled by men with hooded faces,
    Jealous, not for me, but for their honoured places.
    Lions indeed, made vicious not by hunger's pain,
    But by their lust for power and selfish gain.
    No darker hour than when I lightly penned,
    This blind agreement to destroy my servant-friend.
    Within the veil of vanity my foolish eyes,
    Perceived my greatness, but could not perceive their lies.
    Oh, God of Daniel, guard your son tonight,
    Do not defend the law, defend the right.
    No sleep for me, no calm, no peace, no rest,
    For I have sanctified the worst, and sacrificed the best.

Then Gerald comes on, and Darius moves over to the side looking all tragic and preoccupied, and Gerald says ...

WILLIAM: I'd see this as a moment when the – the tragedy of the moment would be best underlined by thunder – and smoke! Lots of grey, mysterious smoke creeping across the floor of the stage, really err ... mysteriously!

A.P.: *(Doubtfully.) More* smoke?

WILLIAM: Oh, yes! Really effective!

A.P.: Mmmm ... Well, anyway, we can come back to that. As I said, Gerald comes to centre-stage and speaks. He's the narrator.

> Narrator: Pain is sharper than remorse,
>   Death more final than regret,
>   Darius will mourn tonight,
>   But live his life, perhaps forget.
>   While Daniel faces fearful hurt,
>   Beneath the dark remorseless flood,
>   That flood of fear which runs before
>   The tearing down of flesh and blood.

Then, Gerald gestures behind him, and the light comes up just enough – if we can get the phantom of the opera on our side, that is – to reveal three lions sort of roaming around in the half-light, just growling softly. No sign of Daniel yet. Darius turns his head and watches the lions, and Gerald does his next bit, only it's a different rhythm – more intense and a bit faster ...

Narrator: Down in ...

WILLIAM: Can I cut in a moment?

A.P.: Yes?

WILLIAM: I've just had an idea.

A.P.: What is it?

WILLIAM: Smoke!

A.P.: Smoke again?

WILLIAM: Yes, as the tension gets going, so we release evil clouds of black smoke to show the satanic influences that . . .

MRS T.: I don't know why we don't just set fire to the blinkin' theatre an' 'ave done with it. Plenty of smoke then . . .

GLORIA: Aaaah, don't laugh at William's idea. I think smoke is a wonderful idea, Willy, darling.

WILLIAM: *(Blushing loudly.)* Well, I just thought . . .

A.P.: All right, it's all written down. Black smoke – right. Now, Gerald's next bit . . .

> Narrator: Down in the den on the bone-strewn floor,
> Where the lost men scream and the lions roar,
> Where a man whose gods are life and breath,
> Will lose his gods in the jaws of death.
> Where the strong alone will hold their creed,
> In the tearing grip of the lions' greed.

> Darius: *(Turning towards audience.)*
> Oh, Daniel, Daniel! save me from my madness.
> Pray your God's compassion on my sadness
> Bid him send an all-forgiving rain,
> To cool the fiery furnace of my brain.

WILLIAM: A quick thought! Rain on fire equals steam, right? We could do that using . . .

A.P.: Smoke?

WILLIAM: Yes! How did you know?

A.P.: Lucky guess, I suppose. Right, now the servant comes in. That's Elsie. She's only got a little bit to say, but it's just as important. She goes over to her master, Darius, and speaks to him:

> Servant: I wait upon you master as you bade me wait,
> To bring intelligence of Daniel and his fate.
> Some moments past, without complaint, or sign of care.
> I saw your servant thrown into the lions' lair.

> Darius: Save him God, he is yours!
> Save him from the lions' jaws!

Then Darius collapses onto his knees and more or less stays there, praying, until later on, and the servant goes off to see if there's any more news. Then we see Daniel, played by Edwin, coming slowly onto the stage, and he just sort of stands there looking at the lions with his back to the audience, while Gerald says his next bit:

Narrator: Now the moment, now the test.
　　　See Jehovah's servant blessed,
　　　As he stands, a trusting child,
　　　Before these creatures of the wild.
　　　Glad to pay the highest price,
　　　To make the final sacrifice.

Now, at this stage, the lions really wake up and start to look a bit menacing – prowling around in a hungry sort of way, looking at Daniel as if he might make a good square meal. Now here, William, we really could do with a lot of ...

WILLIAM: Smoke?

A.P.: Well, I was going to say – a lot of genuine lions' roars on tape. I don't think Stenneth and Vernon and Charles are going to keep their credibility if they start bleating out unconvincing roaring noises all over the place. But as well as that we could do with some really dramatic ...

WILLIAM: Smoke! Right on!

A.P.: ... some really dramatic thunder effects.

WILLIAM: Oh ...

A.P.: That'll build up the atmosphere of danger and imminent death.

WILLIAM: Look, can I just shove a token in the fruit-machine and see if it comes up grapefruits?

A.P.: Err ... yes. I suppose so ...

WILLIAM: I just wondered (*As if it hasn't been mentioned up to now*) what you thought about smoke at this point. With the roaring and the thunder, *and* a sort of angry, swirling curtain of yellowish-black smoke it would be really atmospheric, wouldn't it?

A.P.: A bit of smoke might be appropriate here, William, but we do actually want the audience to be able to see what's happening on stage, don't we?

WILLIAM: Oh, sure! Yes, of course! Smoke here, then – I'll mark it off on my script. Great!

A.P.: Now, the roaring and the thunder . . .

WILLIAM: And the smoke . . .

A.P.: . . . and the smoke, yes; they go on for a minute or two while Daniel sinks quietly onto his knees, facing the audience this time, and he's obviously praying quite calmly while death comes at him from behind, as it were. Then the noise goes down a bit while Daniel speaks:

Daniel: Lord of exiles, friend in strife,
    In your hands I place my life.
    Yours to take and yours to give,
    Let me die, or let me live . . .

A.P.: Then Daniel bows his head and waits to be . . .

MRS T.: Eaten.

A.P.: Err ... eaten, yes, or whatever, but just then ...

NORMA: Ooooh, Adrian, it's quite exciting, isn't it? It makes me go all shivery, the thought of lions suddenly attacking me. Doesn't it you, Gloria?

GLORIA: Ooooh, it does!

A.P.: Anyway, just then ...

THYNN: D'you think it's true?

RICHARD: Is what true?

THYNN: Daniel and the lions and all the rest – the fiery furnace and all that. D'you think it's true?

A.P.: I wonder if we could postpone ...

RICHARD: *(Deeply shocked.)* Of course it's true, Leonard! The story of Daniel is a part of holy Scripture, the inspired word of God. Jesus himself quoted scripture and ...

WILLIAM: I've just been reading about a man from Mauritius who was converted by a semi-colon in Leviticus! Every single jit and tattle ...

THYNN: Jat and tittle, isn't it?

NORMA: I thought it was tat and jottle ...

GLORIA: I thought it was ti ...

WILLIAM: Every single little bit is there because it's supposed to be there, and that's that!

RICHARD: The authority of scripture is absolute. It is an unshake-able rock!

THYNN: So you're not allowed to even wonder if it's true or not, then?

GLORIA: Oh, ye ...

RICHARD: No!

NORMA: *(Shyly.)* I think we're allowed to wonder anything we like, really. Edwin always says ...

THYNN: *(Remembering.)* Oh, yes ...

NORMA: Edwin always says that the Bible is a letter from God to us. He says it starts 'Dear Norma – or Richard – Or Gloria', and finishes 'Love, God', and that God meant it all to be in there, whatever you think about it.

RICHARD: Mmmm ... lets a few liberals in I suppose. The Bible's the Bible, in my view!

THYNN: My cousin, Finnegan Thynn, spent a year secretly smuggling Bibles *out* of China before he told someone what he was doing and they put him straight. He was amazed at the miraculous way the guards didn't notice what he was carrying, and when ...

GLORIA: Lenny, sweetheart, I think we're telling little porky-pies, aren't we?

MRS T.: 'Course 'e is! Can't imagine a Thynn bein' that stupid! I think the Bible's a good ...

A.P.: Do forgive me for interrupting this fascinating theological discussion, but there is a little matter of a play to be attended to, and we haven't finished yet.

[*Murmured 'sorries' etc.*]

WILLIAM: Can I just ... ?

A.P.: No, William, I'd really rather you didn't. As I was saying a very long time ago, just then, just as Daniel finishes saying his bit, and the roaring and thunder ...

THYNN: And smoke!

WILLIAM: Thank you, Leonard.

THYNN: Don't mention it, William.

WILLIAM: I appreciate it.

THYNN: Really, it was ...

A.P.: The roaring and the thunder and the ...

A.P./THYNN/WILL: Smoke.

A.P.: ... increase in intensity, until a figure enters the lions' den from the side, and that's Mrs Flushpool as the angel. She moves slowly among the lions, touching each one on the head as she goes, and as she touches them they settle down

243

and purr like cats. So the roaring and thunder die away completely until everything's quiet. Then Daniel stands up, turns to the angel, and says ...

WILLIAM: The smoke stays, then?

A.P.: Sorry?

WILLIAM: You said the thunder and roaring dies away, but you didn't mention the smoke. I think it's a great idea to keep the smoke. We could have gentle, soothing, everything's-all-right sort of smoke, couldn't we? It could be ...

A.P.: *(Quietly.)* William?

WILLIAM: Yes?

A.P.: Don't be silly.

WILLIAM: Right ...

A.P.: *(Muttering to himself.)* Everything's-all-right sort of smoke! Honestly! *(Normal tones.)* Daniel stands up, turns to the angel, and says:

Daniel: Now indeed I sing your praises,
    Now indeed all terror flees,
    For I see your sovereign power,
    Even over beasts like these.

And the angel answers him:

Angel: God's own servant, fear me not,
    Love and joy and peace are yours,
    God has sent his holy angel,
    I have closed the lions' jaws.
    Here they lie, those mighty killers,
    Harmless where great harm has been,
    Sleep and when the dawn has risen,
    Tell the king what you have seen.

Then the angel wafts off, and everything goes dark – Incredible Hulk permitting – and then the lights come up, and the lions and Daniel have gone, and there's just Darius there, calling out to Daniel.

Darius: Servant of the living God, hear my anguish!
 Has he kept his hand upon you in your danger?
 Does your God have power to rescue you from danger?
 Daniel, speak to me!

Then Daniel appears:

Daniel: Live for ever mighty king,
 God's own angel took my part,
 Evil has no power to harm
 People who are pure of heart.
 He subdued your hungry lions,
 On their heads he laid his hand,
 So it is you see your servant,
 Happy now before you stand.

Then the last speech is from Darius:

Darius: Such a God deserves a people,
 And I vow it shall be so,
 Every soul within this land,
 Shall kneel and praise the God you know.

And that's it! Thunderous applause, we win the prize, and we all go home. Okay?

[*Pause.*]

THYNN: I really, really *loved* Miss Glanthorpe ...

GLORIA: Jot and tittle! That's it! Jot and tittle! Got it!

A.P.: *(Suspiciously.)* You have been listening to the play, haven't you?

NORMA: *(Earnestly.)* Oh, yes, Adrian, and it's really good! Mr Braddock is ever so clever. We've all enjoyed hearing it ever so much.

A.P.: Well, thank you, Norma, and I've enjoyed ...

MRS T.: 'As 'e finished readin' that mouldy old play yet?

WILLIAM: It's not a mouldy old play, Mrs Thynn. It's absolutely great! I'm going to ring up Stage Gear and book a smoke machine as soon as I get home!

A.P.: *(Hastily.)* We haven't actually agreed on exactly where we're going to have smoke, have we, William? Do bear that in mind, won't you?

WILLIAM: Of course! Don't worry, I'll make sure there's enough smoke.

A.P.: That's not quite – oh, never mind now. I'll ring you up later to talk about it. Everyone else quite clear?

[*Chorus of 'yes', 'yep', 'fine' etc.*]

MRS T.: 'Ow many tiger skins?

A.P.: *LION* SKINS!! THREE *LION* SKINS!! OKAY?!!

MRS T.: That's what I thought – no need to get difficult, I'll gettem!

A.P.: Good! Norma? Richard? William? Gloria? Leonard? Questions? Problems? No? Right, I'll let you all know when the next meeting is. Thanks for coming.

[*Rustling of paper and noise of farewells until only A.P. and THYNN remain. THYNN is making a sort of snuffling noise.*]

A.P.: *(Gently.)* Leonard, what's the matter? You're not . . . ?

THYNN: M – M – M – Miss G – G – G – Glanthorpe! I m – m – m – miss her!

A.P.: *(A bit out of his depth.)* But, Leonard, that was years and years ago. She must be . . .

THYNN: She used to tell me I was good at things. I liked that. I'd forgotten . . .

[*Long pause.*]

A.P.: Errr . . . shall I pray with you, Leonard?

THYNN: To God, you mean?

A.P.: Err . . . yes, to God.

THYNN: Yes, please.

A.P.: All right, well let's turn the tape off first.

THYNN: Oh, yes, I'd forgotten about . . .

[*Click! as tape-recorder is turned off.*]

THREE

A Giraffe called Mr Hurd

That second meeting wasn't too bad, but it left me with one or two misgivings. William clearly saw the whole thing as a sort of continuous smoke-screen, interrupted from time to time by actors peering through the fog searching for an audience to deliver lines to. I had an awful feeling that if I wasn't very firm with Master Farmer the production would be more appropriately entitled 'Daniel Gets Lost', or 'Daniel in the Smoke Den'.

My other concern was about Mrs Thynn. Her incredible capacity for getting hold of the wrong end of the stick (a capacity inherited to an almost clone-like extent by Leonard – I'd seen no reason to doubt the Finnegan Thynn story) could prove a problem, simple though her task was. Other than that, I was quite pleased. I even began to indulge in little day-dreams where people shook me by the hand after the performance and said things like, 'This is undoubtedly a major contribution to the world of Christian drama.' Then I'd say things like, 'Really, I had very little to do with it,' and they'd smile at me, rather impressed with my quiet modesty, and know that, actually, I was absolutely *central* to the whole project. It was a very pleasant, warming sort of picture. If I'd known what was really going to happen I'd have booked my passage with Gerald's friend, Gary, and gone off to do something feasible like converting Greenland. Not having the gift of foretelling the future, however, I pressed on quite optimistically.

Leonard asked me if I'd come round the next evening so that we could practise 'being a prompter' and that's where this next tape, a shorter one, was made. When I arrived, he said that he'd just recorded a prayer about the production, and would I like to hear it? This was it.

THYNN: *(Shouting.)* I'm just going to do some recording, mother!

MRS T.: *(A distant voice, probably in the kitchen.)* All accordin' to what, Leonard?

THYNN: *(Louder.)* No, mother! I said I'm about to record on tape!

MRS T.: Can't afford to escape what?

THYNN: *(Almost screaming.)* I'M RECORDING SOMETHING! PLEASE DON'T DISTURB ME!!

MRS T.: Bees don't disturb *me* either, specially when there aren't any, like there aren't 'ere. Are you goin' loony, Leonard?

THYNN: *(Actually screaming.)* I'M RECORD ...!! Hold on, I'll come through there ... *(Very faint muttering as he goes.)* It'd only be about six years with good behaviour ... *(Speaks loudly in the distance.)* Mother, I'm going to do some recording: Would you mind not disturbing me?

MRS T.: 'Course I don't mind. Why didn't you say so?

THYNN: *(Muttering again as he returns to the living room.)* I *did*, you deaf old – person. *(Sound of door closing.)* Right, now I can get down to prayer. Sitting or kneeling? I think I'll sit. After all, we're not supposed to make pointless rules for ourselves. *(Creak of armchair springs followed by a pause.)* On the other hand there's nothing wrong with kneeling down, and maybe it's big-headed to think I can sit, when people who're better than me are kneeling ... *(Sound of armchair creaking again as Thynn kneels down. Pause.)* I don't know though – Edwin said the other day that being comfortable's the main thing, and my legs go to sleep when I kneel for a long time. Think I'll stand. *(Pause and slight huffing and grunting noises as Thynn gets to his feet.)* This is silly! I can't relax while I'm standing up. Maybe I could kneel on the floor and put my head on the armchair – no, I'll fall asleep if I do that. P'raps if I squat on the floor with my back to the wall . . .

MRS T.: *(In the distant distance.)* Adrian's goin' to be 'ere soon! 'Ave you got through yet?

THYNN: *(Creak of springs as Thynn sits in armchair.)* Sorry, God! I'd better get on with it or there'll be no time left. It err . . . it's me again, God. Thynn – Leonard Thynn, thirty-five Postgate Drive, just past the King's Head and second on the left as you go round the pond. I err . . . I hope my position's all right – not too err . . . relaxed or err . . . arrogant. I could kneel if you like, or squat, or hang over the back of my chair with my head on the floor, or anything really. I hope you don't mind me bothering you again, but I feel a bit err . . . funny, so I thought I would. Bother you, that is. Got a bit upset yesterday thinking about – thinking about – well, thinking about Miss Glanthorpe and when I was small and all. Got thinking about things. Me. Things in the past, God. About never doing much – being much. Got thinking about the old hooch – booze – drink – alcohol. Haven't done too badly lately, God. Almost forgotten what the inside of the old King's Head looks like. I always go the long way round to avoid Wally's off-licence. Haven't had a drink for a while. Not that I don't want one! Oh, *God* I want one! Get a bit cross with poor old mother sometimes, too. Suppose you couldn't sort her ears out – do us all a favour? No, well, up to you, of course, just a thought . . . Anyway, the point is, I don't want to be a – a Jonah in this Daniel thing. You remember Jonah? Sorry, silly question. 'Course you knew him – friend of yours. Your whale too, presumably. None of my business, naturally. I just don't want to mess it all up for the others by not being – not being – I don't know . . . good enough, or something when I'm being a soldier – prompter I mean. So, if you could sort of look after everybody who's in it, and make sure what they do doesn't get messed up by what I do, if you see what I mean, and if my uniform could be a – a good one, that would be err ... good. And I'm sorry I said that about Mrs Flushpool and Wimpey's, and err ... that's about it for now I think, God. Thank you for listening. Amen.

[*Click! as recorder goes off, followed by click! as* THYNN *switches to 'RECORD' after playing his prayer to me.*]

THYNN: Sounds a bit silly played back, doesn't it?

A.P.: It doesn't sound silly at all, Leonard. Better than most of my prayers. I seem to just flip tiddly-winks up most of the time. I hope I don't mess up what everybody else does as well.

MRS T.: *(From the kitchen.)* D'you want coffee, Adrian?

A.P.: *(Shouting.)* Yes please, Mrs Thynn!

MRS T.: D'you want coffee, Adrian?

A.P.: *(Bellowing.)* Yes please, Mrs Thynn!! Two sugars!!

MRS T.: D'you want coffee, Adrian?

A.P.: *(Trying to inject politeness into apoplexy.)* YES PLEASE! TWO SUGARS!

MRS T.: 'Ow many sugars?

A.P.: TWO!!

MRS T.: I'll bring the sugar through then you can 'ave what you like.

A.P.: *(Weakly.)* Thank you ...

THYNN: Right, let's get on with the prompting practice.

A.P.: Okay, Leonard. Now, let's see ... you sit over on that chair as though you were sitting at the side of the stage, and I'll stand in the middle of the room as if I was acting. Got your script?

THYNN: Yep!

A.P.: Good! I've got one too, so we're all set.

THYNN: *(Sounding very alert and business-like.)* Right!

A.P.: Now ...

THYNN: We'll just pretend I've got my uniform on, shall we?

A.P.: Err ... yes, all right, Leonard. Now, let's imagine that I'm Percy Brain playing King Darius.

THYNN: Right.

A.P.: And I've just come on stage right at the beginning of the play. I'm feeling very nervous ...

THYNN: So am I, don't worry.

A.P.: No, I don't mean *I'm* feeling very nervous. I mean I'm pretending to be Percy Brain and *he's* very nervous.

THYNN: *(Intelligently.)* Ah, right! With you ...

A.P.: The curtain's up and the audience is waiting for me to start. With me?

THYNN: Yep!

A.P.: So, off I go *(rustle of script)* Ready?

THYNN: Ready!

A.P.: *(A vaguely Brain-like impression.)*
Though ruling, ruled by men with hooded faces,
Jealous, not for me, but for their honoured places.
Lions indeed, made ... err ... made ... err ... made err ...
(Pause.) Leonard, why aren't you telling me what the rest of the line is?

THYNN: I don't need to.

A.P.: *(Blankly.)* Why not?

THYNN: Because you've got a script. You can look for yourself.

A.P.: *(With rising hysteria.)* But that's because we're pretending! On the night Percy *won't* be holding a script – he'll have learned his lines!

THYNN: He won't need prompting in that case, will he?

A.P.: BUT IF HE'S NERVOUS, YOU ID ...!

[*A.P.'s raging interrupted by bumps and clatters as* MRS T. *enters with the coffee.*]

MRS T.: 'Ere you are, nice cuppa coffee! 'Ow's it goin'?

THYNN: Adrian says Percy Brain's going to forget his lines on the night, mother.

A.P.: No I did *not* say that! Percy Brain forgetting his lines is purely hypothetical.

MRS T.: I agree, specially at 'is age. Anyway, I'll leave you to get on with it.

[*Bumps and door-slam as* MRS T. *exits*]

A.P.: Perhaps I haven't made it quite clear, Leonard. Shall we go through it slowly again?

THYNN: *(Confidently.)* Okay!

A.P.: On the night when we do the play, Percy Brain – it could be anyone, but we're using him as an example – might get very nervous and forget his lines, even though he's actually learned them and got them in his head. Right?

THYNN: Yep!

A.P.: So you're there to help when that happens. If someone starts a line and can't remember the end of it, you're the one who reminds him or her what it is. If they can't remember how a speech starts, they'll probably say 'PROMPT', then you'll know they need help. Understand?

THYNN: Got it!

A.P.: *(Lacking faith.)* Really?

THYNN: Yep! If they forget their lines, it's up to me!

A.P.: Good! Now, let's have another go. That great big china giraffe on the wall unit's going to be the audience, right?

THYNN: Right! He's called Mister Hurd because ...

A.P.: So I come on, pretending to be Percy ...

THYNN: Pretending to be King Darius.

A.P.: Yes, and I, or rather, *he,* is very nervous.

THYNN: Right!

A.P.: Script ready?

THYNN: Script ready!

A.P.: Know what to do?

THYNN: Firing on all cylinders, Sah!

A.P.: Err ... right, here we go then:
Though ruling, ruled by men with hooded faces.
Jealous, not for me, but for their honoured places,
Lions indeed, made vicious not by hunger's pain,
But by their lust for power and selfish gain.
Err ... err ... Prompt!

[*Rustle of script and creak of chair springs as Thynn stands up and, watched with dumb disbelief by* A.P., *moves to the centre of the room and addresses the china giraffe with loony sauvity.*]

THYNN: Good evening, Mister Hurd. My name's Leonard Thynn and, as you can tell by my uniform, I'm the prompter. Now, Percy's having trouble getting started on the fifth line, so I'm here to help him out. Percy, the line you're looking for is: 'No darker hour than when I lightly penned'. See you later Mister Hurd, whenever anyone's nervous, in fact. Remember: Thynn's the name, prompting's the game! Goodnight and God bless until we meet again!

[*Thynn returns to his chair, waving to the giraffe as he goes.* A.P. *stands, silently transfixed, for quite a long time.*]

THYNN: *(Modestly.)* I thought those extra bits up all on my own.

A.P.: *(A little, quiet, 'what's-happened-to-the-real-world?' sort of voice.)* Leonard ...

THYNN: Yes?

A.P.: The prompter doesn't come on stage, Leonard. He stays out of sight, Leonard. He doesn't say 'Thynn's the name, prompting's the game,' Leonard. He doesn't say anything except little bits of lines to help the person who *is* on stage, Leonard. Are you sure you ought to be the prompter, Leonard?

THYNN: Well, I did it all right when I was in Miss Glanthorpe's play. *(Hastily.)* I know that was different, but – but I do want to be the prompter, I really do ... I think I've got it now. I sit at the side of the stage, out of sight, and when people forget their lines I help them by calling out the next bit. How's that. *Let* me be ...

A.P.: All right, Leonard. Okay, okay, okay, okay, okay! One more chance. Okay?

THYNN: Yep! Okay!

A.P.: Right. I'll use a different bit of the script, the bit that starts 'Down in the den ...' – the narrator's bit. Got it?

THYNN: *(Frantic rustling of scripts.)* Err ... got it!

A.P.: You sit on that chair. *Stay* on that chair!

THYNN: Fine – no problem ...

A.P.: And I'll be Gerald addressing the giraffe from over here. Okay so far?

THYNN: Ace!

A.P.: Sure?

THYNN: Ace cubed!

A.P.: Here we go then. Last chance!

THYNN: *(Humbly.)* Last chance ...

A.P.: Off we go then:
Down in the den on the bone-strewn floor,
Where the lost men scream and the lions roar,

Where a man whose gods are life and breath
Will lose his gods in the jaws of death
Where the strong alone ... err ... prompt!

THYNN: Will hold their creed ...

A.P.: Where the strong alone will hold their creed, In the tearing grip of the ... err ... err ... prompt!

THYNN: Lions' greed!

A.P.: In the tearing grip of the lions' greed ... That's it, Leonard! You've done it! You've got it right!

THYNN: *(Clearly astounded.)* I have?

A.P.: That was perfect. Well done!

THYNN: So I *am* the prompter?

A.P.: You certainly are, Leonard.

THYNN: I really understand now, don't I?

A.P.: You really do! Well, I must fly, Leonard. I'll see you later. Thank your mother for the coffee. I haven't got much voice left. Bye!

THYNN: Yes, 'bye then! See you later ... *(sound of doors opening and closing as A.P. leaves. After a few moments Thynn's voice can be heard in the kitchen as he speaks to his mother.)* Adrian said thank you for the coffee, mother!

MRS T.: 'E's welcome. 'Ow'd you get on with your wha'snamin'?

THYNN: Brilliant! I really understand it now. By the way, I hope you don't mind, but Adrian wants to borrow your big china giraffe for the evening of the performance. It's going to be the audience.

MRS T.: You'll 'ave to speak up, darlin'. I'm gettin' a bit deaf in me old age. I thought for a minute you said my big china giraffe was goin' to be the audience on the night of the play.

THYNN: I did say that, mother. It's the only bit I don't really understand. I've got to stay right out of sight in my soldier's uniform so that the giraffe can't see me when Percy Brain forgets his lines.

MRS T.: *(Suspiciously.)* You 'aven't bin back on the bottle again, 'ave you, Leonard?

THYNN: 'Course not, mother! I'm just telling you what Adrian told me. Apart from that, I understand everything perfectly ...

MRS T.: That's nice, Leonard ... 'Ave you switched your thing off?

[*Click! as Thynn rushes in to switch his machine off.*]

FOUR

Directing Gandhi Would be Simpler...

It wasn't until long after the performance of 'Daniel', that I heard the end of that third tape and realised why Thynn was so puzzled when he saw real people arriving to watch the performances at the drama festival. It also explained why he brought his three-foot-high china giraffe along and sat it in the middle of the front row. As soon as the seats started to fill up, his mighty brain must have realised the truth, because he went out and retrieved it. He stood it outside the men's toilet in the dressing room and said it was a mascot. The end of the tape also explains the origin of a persistent local rumour to the effect that the Home Secretary, Douglas Hurd, would be gracing the festival with his presence. I never did get round to asking the Thynns why they thought Mister Hurd was an appropriate name for a china giraffe. The way Leonard's mind works is one of the world's great unsolved mysteries. Still – he had got the hang of prompting, just about, so that was one more job done.

The next thing that happened was me getting neurotic about whether people had learned their lines or not. We only had time for two proper rehearsals before actually performing the thing, so it was essential that people had made a real stab at learning their parts. After all, no one had *that* much to say. Anne said I shouldn't phone people and check because I always end up in a bad temper; a gross exaggeration, but I thought it best to wait until she and Gerald were out. Unfortunately, they both came in with Thynn in tow just as I'd dialled Elsie's number and was waiting for someone to answer. When I told them what I was doing, Anne sighed, Gerald chuckled and Thynn whipped his ridiculous machine off his shoulder and stuck the microphone right next to the phone so that he could pick up both ends of the conversation. In some places I've put down what I *wanted* to say, in contrast with what I *did* say . . .

[*Click of recorder being switched on, followed by sound of receiver being picked up at the other end.*]

A.P.: *(With forced casualness.)* Hello, who's that?

ELSIE: *(For it is she.)* You don't think I'm stupid enough to give my name to potential telephone perverts, do you?

A.P.: I'm sorry, Elsie – it's Adrian Plass here.

ELSIE: I know, I recognised your voice.

A.P.: Well, why bother with all the telephone pervert stuff, then?

ELSIE: It's the principle. I'm training men.

A.P.: Oh, I see, well, consider me trained. Look here, Elsie, I'm ringing about your lines.

ELSIE: What lines?

A.P.: *What* lines? *Your* lines – in the play!

ELSIE: What play's that?

A.P.: *(With controlled but rapidly mounting fury.)* The play, Elsie! The Daniel play! The play we sat and talked about for goodness knows how long last Monday! The play we're doing at the Drama Festival. You *must* remember!

ELSIE: Oh, am I in that? Yes, I do remember something vaguely about it. Well, you might have given me a script. It'll never be ready if you don't get the scripts out on time, will it?

A.P.: *(What I actually said, using massive self-control and Christian restraint.)* Elsie, my darling, I think you'll find, if you look, that I *have* sent you a script – some days ago, actually – and I really would be ever so grateful if you could just learn those four little lines by this Friday evening, which, as

258

you'll see if you read the note I sent with the script, is when the first of our only two rehearsals is due to happen. So, as you can see, it really is important to get learning.

[*What I wanted to say while holding Elsie upside down over a vat of boiling oil) You stupid egocentric, fluffy-haired twit of an adolescent! Why haven't you been eating and sleeping and breathing this play like I have, through every second of every minute of every hour of every day since I was foolish enough to start this whole horrendous exercise! And if, you empty-headed little ratbag, you haven't learned every single letter of every single word of every single line in your miserable little speech by Friday, I shall dunk you like a fancy biscuit into this boiling oil! Do I make myself clear?*]

ELSIE: Well, if you say you've sent it I suppose you must have. I'll try to glance at it before Friday if I get a moment. Wait a minute! Friday, did you say? William and I go out on Fridays. That's our night! *(With heavy reluctance.)* I suppose we *could* come out to this rehearsal of yours if we absolutely had to …

A.P.: *(What I actually said.)* I'd be so grateful if you could organise things so that it's possible to be there, Elsie.

[*What I wanted to say whilst waving a magnum pistol under her nose) Go ahead – don't turn up! Make my week, punk!*]

ELSIE: *(Sighing.)* I suppose I'll be there, then. Hold on a minute – William's here. He's saying something … *(Pause with distant muttering.)* William says he's got the smoke machine, and he's had lots more ideas about how to use it in the play.

A.P.: Oh, good, yes, that's err … good.

ELSIE: *(Powerfully.)* Mr Plass, I'm a Christian, so I forgive you freely for rejecting what I wrote as though it was a piece of rubbish, nor do I feel anger or resentment about your feeling that I look enough like a *boy* to be cast as a male servant! However, I would get very upset if I thought that William's creativity was being crushed.

A.P.: *(Sweetly.)* You've remembered an awful lot about the play suddenly, Elsie.

ELSIE: Yes – well ... anyway, just as long as the most important person in the whole thing doesn't get ...

A.P.: Meaning William?

ELSIE: Of course! Just as long as William doesn't get ...

A.P.: Crushed ...

ELSIE: Exactly!

A.P.: *(With superhuman control.)* I shall do my very best not to crush any aspect of William, Elsie.

ELSIE: Good! Well, I expect I'll see you on Friday, Mr Plass. I can't stay talking any longer. William's just bought a book about a man in the Solomon Islands who converted people by scratching their names on trees then laying hands on the bark. We're just going up to Hinkley Woods to do a few before suppertime. We thought we'd do it road by road until the whole town's done. It may be that there's time for us to look at the play later on this evening. We'll see.

A.P.: Thank you *very* much, Elsie. How *very* kind of you. Good-bye.

[*Sound of receiver being placed gently down, then ground viciously into its cradle.*]

ANNE: I don't know why you bother, darling. I told you you'd end up in a bad temper. Why don't you just leave them? They'll learn their lines all right. You get yourself in such a state!

A.P.: I am not in a state!

ANNE: You are, you've got those little white bits at the corners of your mouth. You're in a state!

GERALD: And you keep rubbing the back of your neck with your hand. You always do that when you're in a state.

THYNN: *(Suicidally.)* Say something into the microphone about being in a state.

260

[Sound of vicious dialling.]

ANNE: You're not ringing someone else, surely, Adrian. It'll only get worse, you know it will! Why don't you come and have a nice cup of tea and forget . . .

A.P.: *(Grim.)* Hello, is that Percy? – Get that microphone out of my nose, Leonard – Percy, I'm just checking that you've learned your lines okay . . .

PERCY: An actor prepares! I am engaged in all aspects of what promises to be a highly demanding role! I have been soaking myself in historical and biblical references to kingship in ancient Babylon. I dwell within the skin of King Darius!

A.P.: Have you learned your lines, Percy?

PERCY: I shall proceed according to the tenets of the master, Stanislavski. I shall build a character upon the rock of my own personality. Layer upon layer, nuance upon nuance, like some insubstantial phantom slowly gaining flesh and blood reality, the person I am to become will emerge, and live!

A.P.: Have you learned your lines, Percy?

PERCY: I have delved deep into the very entrails of the *meaning* of the words, and I am discovering . . .

A.P.: Have you learned your lines, Percy?

PERCY: I am immersed in . . .

A.P.: Have you learned your lines, Percy?

PERCY: I have . . .

A.P.: Have you learned your lines, Percy?

PERCY: I . . .

A.P.: HAVE YOU LEARNED YOUR LINES, PERCY?

PERCY: No, I have not! I must not be troubled by such trivial details at this stage in my flow through the estuary of rehearsal towards the deep ocean of performance!

A.P.: You'll end up in the little dribble of not being in it, if you don't learn your lines, Percy. Do I make myself clear?

PERCY: *(After a little rumbling.)* Possibly the optimum moment has arrived for a little vulgar line-learning. Rest assured I shall err ... attend to it. In fact, I shall err ... attend to it now. Farewell!

A.P.: *(Through his teeth.)* Farewell, Percy!

[*Sound of phone slamming down.*]

GERALD: It's wonderful how you manage to stay cool, dad. You'd make a good nun.

THYNN: You've got the feet for it.

A.P.: What do you mean, I've got the feet for it?

THYNN: Well, you know those King peng ...

ANNE: Darling, don't make any more calls – please! You'll end up marching up and down the hall blowing through your nose and muttering to yourself. Why not just leave it?

GERALD: Yeah, leave it, dad. You can trust Edwin to learn his lines, and you wouldn't have the nerve to ask Mrs Flushpool if she's learned her words, so ...

ANNE: Gerald, you really are unbelievably silly sometimes!

[*More vicious dialling.*]

A.P.: *(Hums tensely as he waits.)* Hello, is that Vic – Leonard, I shall insert that microphone into you if you don't hold it away from my face – I'm sorry, is that Vict ...

MRS F.: Who is that?

A.P.: Hello, Victoria, it's Adrian Plass here. I just phoned to ask you – *(Suddenly remembers the new 'be nice to MRS F.' decision)* to ask you err ... how you are. *(Lamely.)* How are you?

MRS F.: *(A little taken aback.)* I am well, and rejoicing in my daily defeat of the natural. Today I have eschewed chiropody. My feet were a thorn in my flesh.

A.P.: Really ... Good! Well, I also wanted to ask you err ... *(nerve gone)* how Stenneth is.

MRS F.: Stenneth is seated at the pianoforté perusing a new and most instructive book – *Sermons Set to Music,* by Doctor Martyn Lloyd Webber. He is quite content.

A.P.: Good, good! That's good . . .

MRS F.: Was there something else, Adrian? I am at present . . .

A.P.: There was just one thing – err . . . I wondered if you've yet managed to – to . . .

MRS F.: Yes?

A.P.: To err . . . to plan your holiday for next year.

MRS F.: We do not take holidays, Adrian. We do not *believe* in holidays. We undertake periods of recreational outreach.

A.P.: Ah, I see . . . well, where are you planning to err . . . undertake your period of recreational outreach next year?

MRS F.: Benidorm.

A.P.: Ah . . . yes, very commendable . . .

MRS F.: If there's nothing else, I really ought to get on with . . .

A.P.: *(Desperately.)* I really did just want to – to know . . .

[*Sound of Gerald making chicken noises in the background.*]

MRS F.: To know what?

A.P.: To know – to know err . . .

MRS F.: Adrian, I am engaged in the task of learning my lines for the forthcoming dramatic production. I should like to continue with this task if at all possible!

A.P.: Ah! Right! Fine! Good! Sorry! Of course! Yes! Goodbye! See you later . . .

MRS F.: God willing, yes. Goodbye.

[*Sound of A.P.'s telephone being dropped onto its cradle.*]

GERALD: Have you got anything you want to melt, mum? You could use dad's face.

ANNE: Be quiet, Gerald! She was in the middle of learning them, was she, darling?

A.P.: *(After inhaling long and deeply through his nose.)* Yes. She was in the middle of learning them, Anne. If you don't stop following me around with that infernal mechanical lollipop, Leonard, you'll be recording your own death rattle.

ANNE: Anyway, you've checked everyone now, darling, except Edwin, and Gerald's quite right in saying that you can trust Edwin. Don't you think so?

A.P.: *(Sounds of weary chair-sinking.)* Oh, yes, I'm sure Edwin will do his stuff. I dunno … it's hard work, this directing business.

GERALD: It's good practice for saying: 'Do I make myself clear', though, dad. You must've said that at least, ooh, let me see …

A.P.: Thank you so much for your chicken imitation while I was on the phone, Gerald. It was most helpful and encouraging. Now, if you don't mind I'm going to – wait a minute!

ANNE: *(Quite alarmed.)* What is it, Adrian? Why are you looking at Gerald like that?

A.P.: *(In slow, menacing tones.)* There's just one other person we haven't checked. Isn't there, Gerald?

GERALD: Is there, dad?

A.P.: Yes, Gerald. You! I forgot all about you. You've got about twenty lines to learn, haven't you?

GERALD: Err … yes, that's about right …

A.P.: So how are we doing, my little chicken imitator? How many of our lines have we learned since we got our script? Eh?

GERALD: *(Airily.)* Oh, I don't think it matters if you don't learn a script word for word. As long as you get the general sense, that's all that really counts. I'll just fudge along and more or less busk it. The rhymes don't add that much to it after all, do they?

[*Short pre-eruptive silence.*]

ANNE: *(Aghast.)* Gerald! What … ?

A.P.: *(A murderously incredulous growl.)* Fudge along ...? More or less busk it ...? Rhymes don't add that much to it ...? I'll teach you whether it matters if you don't learn a script word for word!

[*Sound of banging and crashing as* A.P. *chases Gerald around the room.*]

GERALD: *(Sounding, appropriately, like someone undergoing the pain of a half-nelson.)* Only joking, dad! Only joking! Listen:

> Pain is sharper than remorse,
> Death more final than regret,
> Darius will mourn tonight,
> But live his life, perhaps forget.
> While Daniel faces fearful hurt,
> Beneath the dark remorseless flood.
> That flood of fear which runs before
> The tearing down of flesh and blood.

I know all the rest as well! Really I do! Listen:

> Down in the den on the ...

A.P.: You know it? You've learned it? You've ...

GERALD: Of course. Got it off pat more or less immediately.

A.P.: So you thought you'd just give my blood pressure a little exercise, did you? Thanks a lot!

[*Sound of door opening and slamming as* A.P. *stomps off into the hall.*]

ANNE: Honestly, Gerald. When will you learn?

GERALD: Sorry, mum. Just couldn't resist it *(Chuckles.)* Went up like a volcano, didn't he?

THYNN: What's he doing now?

ANNE: He'll be doing just what I said he'd end up doing – marching up and down the hall blowing through his nose and muttering to himself.

THYNN: *(Excitedly.)* I must get that on tape!

ANNE: I really wouldn't . . .

[*Door opens and slams shut as* THYNN *disappears into the hall. Muffled sounds of conflict end with a muffled cry, and abrupt silence as the recorder is either deliberately or accidentally switched off.*]

FIVE

An Angel Unaware

I didn't kill Thynn in the hall. I quenched him with a very heavy old army greatcoat which happened to switch his machine off at the same time. I must admit I was a little miffed. I was beginning to feel a bit ashamed of the whole exercise really, if I'm honest. I hadn't lost my temper so much or so badly for a long time, and it wasn't exactly bringing out the best in others either. The day after not killing Thynn I decided to pop round and see Bill Dove. Bill and Kitty Dove had been my favourite elderly couple for years. They were amazingly good at making things seem 'okay' again – especially Kitty. When she died nearly a year ago, I was very upset. Anne and I tried to get round to see Bill every week or so.

'The thing is, Bill,' I said, 'that we don't get all this conflict – or hardly any of it – in services or church meetings. People make an effort to get on with each other, and things go more or less smoothly. Perhaps it's a big mistake to do this sort of thing.'

Bill chuckled like he always does. 'That's the 'ole point, mate! 'Seasy ter be all lovey-dovey in church an' that, innit? Piece o' cake! Summink like this what your doin', well, ain't so easy to keep the old pretendin' up, is it? Little bit of aggro – little bit of sortin' out – do us all good. Find out what's 'appenin' behind the old crinkly smiles, eh?'

'I don't think there's much happening behind my crinkly smile, Bill,' I said dismally. 'I seem to spend all my time getting irritable and telling people off.'

'Yer know what Kitty'd say if she was 'ere now, doncher, mate?'

'What would she say, Bill?'

'First of all she'd say ''ave another doughnut, Adrian. Then she'd say 'ow good it was that you was takin' on somethin' like this for Jesus, an 'ow if 'e wants you to do it, 'e'll make sure it ends up right. But . . .'

He leaned forward and tapped me on the chest. ''is idea of endin' up right might not be the same as your idea of endin' up right! An' it 'asn't got to matter! With me?'

'Yes, Bill,' I said. 'I think I'm with you – I do miss Kitty sometimes, Bill.'

'So do I, mate,' said Bill, smiling and sighing, 'so do I . . .'

The first of our two rehearsals was planned for the following Friday. We booked Unity Hall specially for the purpose, and I arranged that the actors should come early, so that we could do some rather interesting warm-up exercises from a book I'd bought called *The Third Book of Theatrical Themes for Theological Thespians*. Nearly everybody was there on time. Gerald, Percy, Edwin, Charles, Vernon and Stenneth were all there by five past seven. Stenneth explained that Victoria would be a little late as she was in the middle of speaking to a neighbour about his son's musical excesses, but would get there as soon as she could. Thynn was there early as well, thinking he'd be allowed to sit on the side and laugh at us. I said he could only stay if he left his machine switched on and joined in properly. There was no sign of Elsie by the time we got started. Just before we began I reminded everybody – including Stenneth, who seemed terribly pleased – that we were going to make an extra special effort to be nice to Victoria starting from when she first walked through the door this evening. Everyone nodded enthusiastically and said they'd really have a go. This tape starts just as I began to explain the first warm-up exercise:

[*General murmur of conversation as people find a space on the floor of the hall.*]

A.P.: Right! If we could have a bit of hush we'll be able to get going. The first . . .

PERCY: I hope that these activities are well-advised! I feel in my bones that I should be curled in a corner balancing the brim-full container of character until rehearsal commences.

THYNN: He means he's not sure if he's learned his lines yet. He wants to grab a chance to . . .

PERCY: How dare you! I am word perfect! My method is . . .

EDWIN: Let's get on, shall we? I'm sure Percy knows his lines, Leonard.

A.P.: Thank you, Edwin, thank you very much. Now, the first of our exercises is designed to help us to – *(reads from book)* 'loosen up and lose inhibitions'. So I want everybody to come up this end of the hall and stand with your backs against the wall so that we're all facing the door at the other end. Right, off you go!

[*Clatter and nervous murmur as all move.*]

A.P.: Shush, everybody! Now, this might seem a bit strange, but I want us all to . . .

THYNN: Adrian?

A.P.: Yes, Leonard. What is it?

THYNN: Can I go to the toilet, please?

A.P.: Leonard, don't worry! I promise I won't make you do anything embarrassing – okay?

THYNN: We won't have to stand on boxes and do dances, or feel each other with blindfolds on or anything like that?

A.P.: No, nothing like that.

THYNN: Or one of us lie on the floor and the others stand round in a circle talking about him?

A.P.: No, Leonard!

GERALD: We *are* doing the one where we exchange clothes with the person we like least, while everyone watches, aren't we, dad?

THYNN: *(Panic stricken.)* I'm going to the boys' tiddler room!

A.P.: Come back, Leonard! Gerald was joking, *weren't* you, Gerald?

THYNN: *(Warily.)* Were you, Gerald?

GERALD: 'Course I was, Leonard. *(Blithely.)* Sorry, dad!

A.P.: If we were Russians, Gerald, I would be very tempted to show you where the crayfish spend the winter.

THYNN: Eh?

PERCY: I believe he meant ...

A.P.: Never mind what I meant! Let's get on. Now, for our first exercise we're all going to shout as loud as we can down the hall.

CHARLES: *(Nervously.)* Err ... ?

A.P.: Yes, Charles?

CHARLES: Err ... I'm not really just err ... clear about what we should err ... shout ...

A.P.: Well, the book suggests that everyone should shout, 'I hate you!' Sounds a bit funny, I know, but that's what it says. The idea is we clear out all the repressed aggression and bad temper that's got stuck inside and pushed down and err ... that sort of thing ...

[*Blank silence for a couple of seconds.*]

THYNN: I'm going to the boys' tiddl ...

A.P.: STAND STILL, LEONARD! No exercise – no uniform! Now, everybody, after three – one! two! thr ...

CHARLES: *(In an abrupt reedy scream.)* I hate you!

[*Shocked silence.*]

A.P.: Yes, Charles. Err ... good effort. If we could just try it together this time. Ready, everyone? One! Two! Three!

ALL: *(A pathetic, totally unaggressive mooing sound.)* I hate you ...

VERNON: ... in love.

A.P.: No, Vernon, we don't add 'in love', on the end. As for the rest of you, I don't honestly think an awful lot of aggression came out of us then, do you? Now come on, backs to the wall and really shout it out. After three again. One! Two! Three!

ALL: *(A faintly annoyed mooing sound.)* I hate you ...

CHARLES: In l ... sorry!

A.P.: Look, let's just try to imagine the person or thing we hate most, and then try again, right? Edwin, what would that be for you?

EDWIN: Hmmm ... interesting. I think for me it would be the devil.

[*Impressed murmur.*]

A.P.: Good! Stenneth, what about you? Who do you hate most?

STENNETH: *(With passion.)* Those who wantonly destroy balsa-wood models without compunction!

A.P.: Err ... yes, right – good one, Stenneth. Leonard, dare I ask?

THYNN: Me.

A.P.: Pardon.

THYNN: Me. I'm the one I hate most – especially when I'm drinking.

[*Embarrassed pause.*]

EDWIN: I don't hate you, Leonard – I love you. You're my friend. *(Slap of hand on shoulder.)* Charles, what about you? Who do you hate most?

CHARLES: *(Vaguely.)* Err ... Joe Bugner I think ...

A.P.: Why Joe Bugner?

CHARLES: I don't really know. I just really ...

PERCY: Loneliness! For me it is accursed loneliness! That I can shout at. Loneliness ...

271

A.P.: Well, I think we're really getting somewhere now. You see! Everyone's got something they'd like to have a shout at. Vernon, what's your pet hate?

VERNON: *(With wild intensity.)* I really hate it when you have a bath, then suddenly realise you've forgotten to bring a towel in, and you're staying in someone else's house, and you shout for someone to fetch one from your bedroom, then suddenly remember you've left your dirty old socks and a Biggles book lying around in your room and there's nothing else you can do and you want to die!

THYNN: Have you got *Biggles and the Little Green God*, Vernon? That's the only one I haven't . . .

A.P.: Right, well I think that's everyone . . .

THYNN: Expostulated Algy . . .

A.P.: What?

THYNN: Opined Ginger . . .

A.P.: Do be quiet, Leonard.

THYNN: Voiced Bertie . . .

A.P.: Leonard!

THYNN: Encapsulated Biggles, as the air commodore pushed his cigarette box across the desk . . .

A.P.: Leonard, be quiet! *(Pause.)* Thank you. Now, we've all identified something or someone that we hate – right?

GERALD: Daddy, dear!

A.P.: *(Sighing.)* Sorry, Gerald. I forgot you. What do you hate most?

GERALD: *(Pathetically.)* Being left out by daddy-doos, I think.

A.P.: If you don't want to be left out altogether by daddy-doos, you'd better decide what you really hate most, Gerald.

GERALD: What, seriously?

A.P.: *(A little taken aback.)* Well, err . . . yes, seriously.

GERALD: *(After a short pause.)* Well, if you must know, I hate it when people think that just because I tell jokes and take the mickey sometimes it means I'm not serious about anything, or that I don't really believe in God, or that I'm just being nasty. I expect it's my fault sometimes, but ... well that's what I really hate most ...

A.P.: *(Quietly.)* Thank you, Gerald. *(Briskly.)* That's everyone, then. Let's ...

THYNN: Err ... excuse me, air-commodore?

A.P.: *(Testily.)* What now?

THYNN: You haven't told us what *you* hate most – interrogated Von Stalhein.

A.P.: Apart from ridiculous un-funny allusions to Biggles books, you mean?

THYNN: Sorry.

VERNON: Go on, Adrian, tell us who you hate most. We've all said ours, so it's sort of only really thingy, isn't it?

A.P.: Never let it be said that I am anything but thingy, Vernon! The thing I hate most, now let me see ... I think probably one of the things I hate most is anyone being nasty to Anne. I can't stand that. *(Ruefully.)* I'm the only one who's allowed to be nasty to Anne. I didn't mean that I never err ... you know. But I don't like it when someone else err ... isn't – or rather – is being err ... nasty.

EDWIN: I think that really is everyone now, Adrian.

A.P.: Good! Now, stand up straight – backs to the wall! After three. Think about all those things we've just said we hate so much! In fact, let's not shout '*I* hate you.' Let's shout '*We* hate you,' as loud as we can – really feel it together! Ready?

[*Chorus of agreement.*]

ALL: We hate you!

A.P.: Not bad! Not at all bad! But we can do even better! One, two, three!

ALL: *(With considerable volume.)* We hate you!!

A.P.: And again! Really let it go!

ALL: *(Quite caught up in it now.)* We hate you!!!

A.P.: One more time! One, two, three, go!!

ALL: *(A terrifying scream.)* WE HATE YOU!!!

[*Sound of a body slumping to the floor as* MRS FLUSHPOOL *collapses with the shock of seven people – including her husband – screaming hate at her as she comes in through the door at the opposite end of the hall.)*

A.P.: Oh, no! We were going to be specially . . .

[*Clatter of feet as everyone surrounds* MRS F. *and helps her to her feet.*]

CHARLES: *(Wildly.)* I wasn't shouting at you – I was shouting at Joe Bugner!

MRS F.: *(Faintly.)* What?

EDWIN: It was just an unfortunate coincidence, Victoria. As far as I was concerned, I was shouting at the dev – err ... at somebody completely different. I do hope ...

VERNON: *(Comfortingly.)* It was in love ...

MRS F.: *(In high-pitched bewilderment.)* How can you scream at someone that you hate them *in love*?

VERNON: You don't understand, Mrs Flushpool. We were using our imaginations. I was pretending I'd got no clothes on.

MRS F.: An orgy! Stenneth, how could you?

STENNETH: *(Sounding like the captain of the Titanic surveying his future just after the impact.)* Victoria, words fail me ...

A.P.: It's actually very simple to explain, Victoria. We were doing an exercise from a drama book I've bought. You get rid of aggression and stuff by shouting 'I hate you' as loudly as you can. That's what we were doing. You just happened to come in when we reached our err ... peak, as it were. I'm awfully sorry. Please forgive us.

MRS F.: *(Graciously.)* In the natural you would certainly have found me intransigent. I hope that I am now capable of exercising reflective redemption.

THYNN: Yes, but are we forgiven?

EDWIN: That's what Victoria meant, Leonard.

STENNETH: So *I* am err ... forgiven, Victoria?

MRS F.: Naturally, Stenneth. It is a scriptural obligation. I would, however, be extremely interested to know what your particular imaginary object of hatred happened to be.

STENNETH: *(The blood draining from his words.)* Of – of course, my dear. My err ... main object of hatred was, well, it was actually err ... it was ... *(Looks imploringly at the the others.)* Henry the Eighth! Wasn't it, everybody?

EDWIN: Err ... yes, I believe it was something like that, Stenneth, yes.

THYNN: *(Trying to be helpful.)* I thought it was Henry the Seventh ...

A.P.: *(Firmly.)* It was Henry the Eighth, Leonard! Wasn't it, Gerald?

GERALD: Yes! Definitely! 'Enery the Eighth!

MRS F.: Very suitable I'm sure, Stenneth. A notorious bigamist.

A.P.: Perhaps if you're feeling okay now, Victoria, we could move on to the second exercise. What do you think?

MRS F.: That rather depends on what the second exercise *is*, Adrian. I will not wink at impropriety.

THYNN: Eh?

A.P.: It really is quite proper, Victoria. We simply sit in a circle and think peaceful thoughts, then share our mental images with others. It's the opposite of the first one if you like. Instead of thinking about the thing you hate most, you think about nice, beautiful things, things that make you feel happy and relaxed.

THYNN: *(Remembering the 'Be nice to MRS F.' vow and overdoing it as usual.)* Dear, sweet, kind Mrs Flushpool, do please be good enough to join us in this little tiny exercise. We shall be miserable and upset if your pretty face isn't there for all to see in our little circle in a moment.

MRS F.: *(Unexpectedly flattered by Thynn's nonsense.)* Well, of course, one wants to be co-operative. *(To A.P..)* You say we are to sit in a circle?

A.P.: Err ... yes, if we could all just form a rough circle on the floor ...

[*General commotion as everyone tries to form a circle. A minute passes.*]

EDWIN: I think that's about as near as we're going to get, Adrian – a sort of bulgy oval.

A.P.: Right, well, if we could all be quiet now, and just concentrate on something that makes us feel good ...

[*Brief silence, broken only by Thynn sighing heavily.*]

A.P.: Could we just err ... come back now, as it were? Any volunteers to start us off ... ?

CHARLES: I could just . . .

A.P.: Okay, Charles, off you go.

CHARLES: Well, I just sort of pictured myself dying and being lifted up by two heavenly cherubims until I found that I had entered a city of gold, where I joined a white-robed throng singing praise and worship for all eternity to he who is above all and in all, and joy and elation filled the firmament!

A.P.: Wonderful! Leonard, what about you?

THYNN: *(Dreamily.)* I'm just starting my fifth pint of Theakston's Old Peculiar . . .

A.P.: Ah, right . . . err, Vernon?

VERNON: I was picturing a really huge auditorium full of people responding to a superb message from an internationally acclaimed evangelist and preacher.

A.P.: Who was the preacher?

VERNON: *(Modestly.)* Me.

[*Some laughter.*]

A.P.: No, no, fair enough. Better to be honest. Edwin? Were you imagining you were pope?

EDWIN: *(Laughing.)* I'm afraid mine was very boring. I was lying in the sun on a beautiful sandy beach, just listening to seagulls and seasidey sort of noises. Lovely. Not very holy I'm afraid . . .

GERALD: Mine isn't, either. I was only a blue, a pink and a black away from a hundred and forty-seven break. Steve Davis was sitting on his chair looking as sick as an interesting pig. *(Sighs.)* It was wonderful!

A.P.: It was a blooming miracle, seeing as the highest break you've ever scored is seventeen!

GERALD: Oh, come off it, dad! When we played at Frank Braddock's club I scored twenty-five points, and it would have been thirty-two if I hadn't mis-cued on the next black.

A.P.: Twenty-five points, my aunt! You mis-cued after seventeen points. I remember it as clearly as anything.

GERALD: That's good, coming from you. You're the only person I know who chalks up *after* a mis-cue!

A.P.: Well, who pushed his cue up his own nose when he was breaking off and trying to look professional and cool?

GERALD: Well, who said, 'Aren't the webs a problem?' when he was told there was a swannecked spider on every table in the club?

A.P.: That was a joke, and you know it! I never thought ...

EDWIN: *(Breaking in diplomatically.)* Adrian, you haven't told us what your err ... beautiful thoughts were.

A.P.: What? Oh, right, sorry. Yes, err ... actually I was just blank really. Quite serene, but blank, void, one of those empty pockets of ...

GERALD: Now we're back to your snooker again.

A.P.: Sorry?

GERALD: Empty pockets ...

A.P.: Now look, if you think ...

STENNETH: *(Miles away, eyes still shut, suddenly speaks with a deep American accent.)* To boldly go where no man has gone before ... warp five if you please, Mr Sulu ... beam me up, Scotty ... what in hell's name *is* that, Mr Spock?

MRS F.: Stenneth!

STENNETH: *(Coming to with a start.)* Condition red! I mean err ... yes, Captain – I mean, yes, Victoria.

GERALD: We can't imagine what you were thinking about, Stenneth.

[*General laughter.*]

STENNETH: *(Rather embarrassed.)* It used to be my – my favourite programme you see. I suppose it seemed so wonderfully adventurous and exciting. You never quite knew what was going to happen next, whereas ...

MRS F.: Yes, Stenneth? Whereas what?

STENNETH: Whereas my own life *(hastily)*, although satisfactory in many ways, was somewhat err ... predictable.

[Pause as everyone waits for MRS F. to devour STENNETH.]

MRS F.: *(Surprisingly subdued.)* I am aware, Stenneth, that your life is not, perhaps, as fulfilled and err ... pleasant as it might be. I am also aware that I am not guiltless in respect of your occasional – your continual lack of contentment. I have been attempting since I first ...

STENNETH: *(Genuinely distressed.)* Please, my dear, you mustn't ...

MRS F.: Since I first undertook this role as an – angel, I have been attempting to imagine myself as such a being – with little success I am afraid. Just now I was attempting to experience peace by picturing Stenneth and myself at our favourite places and activities – or rather, those activities that I assumed gave enjoyment to Stenneth despite never having asked him – and I was quite unable to properly relax. For some reason the challenge of having to present myself as an angel, a messenger from God, has made me realise something that I fear I have known for rather a long time. Namely, that, despite my redemption from the natural, I am consistently harsh and unpleasant to others, and – and I ... oh, dear ...

[Sobs, sniffs and tissue-wielding sounds as MRS F. bursts into tears for the first time that any of us can remember.]

STENNETH: Victoria, you're crying! Please don't cry, my dear ...

THYNN: *(Kindhearted but wildly misguided.)* Don't cry, Mrs Flushpool. We don't think you're any of those things you said. We think you're the nicest, kindest, most wonderful person in the whole church! We think ...

EDWIN: *(Taking over with that quiet authority he shows sometimes.)* No, Leonard – I know you're just trying to be kind, but that's not what's needed here. Victoria, you make me feel very humble. I only hope that I shall be able to reveal my negative side as openly as you have when my time comes. We forgive you fully for anything you've ever said or done that might have upset us, don't we, everybody?

[Enthusiastic assent from all, especially Stenneth, nearly in tears himself.]

EDWIN: And so will God, if we ask him. Do you want us to pray for a little while now before we go on with the rehearsal, Victoria.

MRS F.: *(Whispering.)* Yes, please – I would ...

EDWIN: Okay, we will. Loving heavenly father, we pray – Leonard, is your machine over there recording?

THYNN: Yes, it is. Do you want me to ...?

EDWIN: Switch it off, there's a good chap.

[Sound of footsteps, followed by a click! as the tape-recorder is switched off.]

SIX

Anne Does the Trick

It was quite right of Edwin to tell Leonard to switch the tape-recorder off when we began praying with Victoria. It was better kept private. But no one remembered to switch it on again. I pretended to commiserate with Leonard when we realised that the whole of one rehearsal had gone unrecorded, but I was quite glad really. It wasn't the line learning. I was pleasantly surprised at how well everyone knew their words. Leonard was quite upset to find that he had hardly anything to do. We had a read-through first, which went very well. It was the next bit that got rather confusing. Perhaps I was trying to be just a fraction more professional than I really am. I wanted to use all the proper theatrical terms like they did in *The Third Book of Theatrical Themes for Theological Thespians,* but I made the mistake of not explaining them properly first. With my eyes fixed on a series of diagrams I'd drawn the night before, I called out such a complicated barrage of instructions that, at one point, everyone ended up in a bewildered huddle in one corner of the hall and got annoyed with me. Things got a lot easier after I explained what 'stage-left', and 'up-stage' and 'stage-right' and 'down-stage' actually mean. Percy already knew, of course, so did Gerald, but the others took some time to absorb it all. I was deeply thankful that Thynn wasn't part of the acting team. He has a great deal of trouble sorting out left and right at the best of times.

The lions were a bit feeble at first. Then Gerald suggested they should imagine they were sitting in church, and that George Farmer had just reached that point in one of his twelve fruit-gum talks, when, after forty-five minutes, he says, 'That's a very important point, and I want to examine it more fully later . . .' After that they really put some aggression into their roaring. I had to stop Leonard roaring with them, but I sympathised – we all did.

Overall, the acting wasn't bad at all. Percy was a touch Knight-of-the-Theatre-ish, and Victoria tended to enter like the Fairy Godmother in Cinderella, but the standard seemed generally high, and by the time we finished everyone knew basically where to go and what to do. Gloria and Norma were there, sitting at the side and giggling when I got things wrong. Anne and Mrs Thynn came along later as well. Mrs Thynn assured me that she'd booked the lion costumes for our next rehearsal, and Norma was being very organised about all the other clothes, so that part of the arrangements seemed to be well looked after. Gloria said that the make-up was so simple that there was no point in doing it until the second rehearsal, which would have to be our dress-rehearsal as well. There was just one major problem. At the end of the rehearsal Anne came up and whispered the question that I'd been asking myself all evening: 'Darling, where on earth have Elsie and William got to?'

'I don't know!', I hissed, 'I wish I did. I asked Edwin where Elsie was earlier, but he said that as far as he knew they were coming. I could throttle her – fancy not coming at all!'

I grabbed Edwin just before he left, and asked him whether he was planning to quiz his daughter about what was going on, but he smiled and said, 'Adrian, I'm going to annoy her intensely by appearing totally unconcerned about her absence tonight. I think she ought to sort it out with you – or you and Anne, perhaps.'

Later that weekend I phoned Elsie and asked as casually as I could (bearing in mind that I actually wanted to explode at her) whether she was planning to come to next Friday's rehearsal. There was a short pause, then she said, 'I suppose so, yes.' Conquering a temptation to swear loudly, I asked her if she could come half an hour early so that we could have a chat. She said, even more reluctantly, 'I suppose we could if we must, yes.' I said thank you quite calmly, then went into the garden and beat the hedge with a stick for a while.

The next Friday I felt quite nervous. Thynn didn't help much by arriving at the hall three-quarters of an hour early with his ever-present machine, very excited about the dress-rehearsal and especially about trying on the soldier's uniform that Norma had promised to get for him. I told him he'd have to clear off while Anne and I spoke to Elsie and William, so, grumbling a bit, he went off to buy a peach, and pester George Farmer in his fruit shop round the corner.

It was probably a good idea of Anne's that she should speak to the young couple on her own. She said that with the play on my mind, and feeling as angry as I did, I would degenerate into my Basil Fawlty mode within two minutes of starting the conversation. Neither of us realised that Leonard had left his machine switched on before he went out. Obviously we would have turned it off if we'd realised. I was quite amazed when Elsie agreed to allow this next bit to be included for publication. She's a good girl at heart, though.

I've started the transcription from when I left the hall 'to do something', and Anne settled down in the corner with Elsie and a very uneasy looking William.

ANNE: Elsie and William, you know why Adrian asked you to come early, don't you?

ELSIE: *(Defiantly.)* No!

WILLIAM: I suppose it's about . . .

ELSIE: William doesn't know why he did either.

ANNE: Is that right, William?

ELSIE: He doesn't . . .

ANNE: You do want William to tell the truth, don't you, Elsie?

ELSIE: *(Sulkily.)* Of course I do – I'm a Christian.

ANNE: Well then, William?

WILLIAM: Well, err ... I suppose it's about why we didn't come along last Friday, is it?

[*Unconcerned sniff from Elsie.*]

ANNE: That's absolutely right. Adrian and all the others missed you ever so much on Friday evening. You're essential to the play and you just weren't there. We don't want to get angry with you, we just want to understand. Did you feel upset by anything that Adrian or anyone else said to you?

ELSIE: I was a tiny bit upset that my poems were turned down flat without any reason being given, and I don't quite understand why I'm a boy in this play, but as I told Mr Plass the other day, I'm a Christian, so I forgive him.

ANNE: You do?

ELSIE: Of course. I'm a ...

ANNE: But that's not the reason you didn't come on Friday?

ELSIE: No, it's not. It's – tell Anne, William.

WILLIAM: *(Uncertainly.)* Yes, well, Elsie felt that ...

ELSIE: *We* felt!

WILLIAM: *We* felt that err ... well, that if it was meant to err ... be err ... well ...

ELSIE: *(After loud throat-clearing.)* We felt that if God wanted this play to be performed he'd make sure it was all right on the night, and that we were being led to use our faith to believe that what we did would be all right without us having to let him down by doing it in our own strength, and – and ...

WILLIAM: And there was a film on at the pictures that we'd been looking forward to, so ...

ELSIE: *(Hastily and rather redly.)* It wasn't because of that! That was just a – coincidence. *(With more confidence.)* William and I had a time of prayer after tea on Friday and we really felt it was really right not to go to the rehearsal, didn't we, William?

WILLIAM: *(Unhappily.)* Well, you felt it first, and then – then I err ... sort of did ... I suppose ... actually, I really wanted to go.

ANNE: To the rehearsal you mean?

WILLIAM: Yes, you see ...

ELSIE: William!

WILLIAM: *(Eyes-shining sort of voice.)* ... I don't know if Mr Plass mentioned it to you, but I've got one or two ideas about using smoke in this play. So, actually, I was quite keen to err ... be there, but ...

ANNE: But Elsie talked you out of it?

ELSIE: No, we *both* thought – I told you we had a prayer-time!

ANNE: Elsie, darling, do you remember when you were a very little girl and you had a yellow canary?

ELSIE: *(Surprised and not far away from tears.)* Yes ... he was called Sammy ...

ANNE: Do you remember when you went on holiday one summer, you came round to see me, and asked if I'd look after Sammy while you were away?

ELSIE: *(A small voice.)* Yes.

ANNE: You were very serious and very anxious, and you made me promise two or three times that I'd feed him every single day without fail until you came back. Remember, sweetheart?

ELSIE: Mmm, yes ...

ANNE: But I bet you prayed every night while you were away that I wouldn't forget. Eh?

ELSIE: Yes, I used to screw my eyes tight shut and say 'Please, please, please, God!'

ANNE: And how was he when you did come back?

ELSIE: Fine – all right. He was all right, Anne.

ANNE: You didn't expect God to feed him while you were away, did you, love?

ELSIE: 'Course not ...

ANNE: It's exactly the same with the play, Elsie. We've got to pray as if prayer's the only thing that works, and then work as if work's the only thing that works. I can't remember who said that, but I think it's true.

ELSIE: Mmm, well, perhaps ...

ANNE: In any case – let's be honest – that wasn't the real problem, was it?

ELSIE: *(Very quietly.)* What do you mean?

ANNE: Well, you say you've forgiven Adrian for the things you felt hurt by, but it doesn't work automatically when you're a Christian. You have to pray about it, think about it, do something about it, and really *feel* it. You're still quite angry about your poem not being used, and the other thing, aren't you?

ELSIE: Well ...

ANNE: Well?

ELSIE: Yes, I s'pose I am ... *(Suddenly passionate.)* I don't look like a boy! I don't, do I Anne?

ANNE: *(Laughing affectionately.)* No one ever said you did, Elsie! If you must know – the reason Adrian wanted you to be the servant was that he knew once you were involved you'd put all your enthusiasm into it. He just wanted you to be in it. As for looking like a boy – well, do you want to know what Adrian said to me when you started going out with Gerald that time?

ELSIE: *(Avidly interested.)* Don't mind ...

ANNE: He said, 'Trust Gerald to end up with a little cracker like that.'

ELSIE: *(Blushingly pleased.)* Did he really say that?

ANNE: Would I lie to you, Elsie?

ELSIE: *(Simply.)* No, Anne, you don't tell lies. *(Pause.)* Did he really say that?

WILLIAM: *(Inadvisedly incredulous.)* About Elsie?

ELSIE: William!

ANNE: And, let's face it, Elsie, you're not the only one who had an idea turned down, are you? There were Charles and Vernon and Percy and Leonard, and even Gerald – although I don't think he was very serious really.

[*Pause.*]

286

ELSIE: I've been a bit silly, haven't I?

ANNE: I think you owe William an apology, don't you? He would have been here on Friday if it hadn't been for you, Elsie, wouldn't he?

[*Longer pause.*]

ELSIE: *(Reluctantly but bravely.)* Sorry, William, I was silly.

WILLIAM: *(Cheerfully.)* Does this mean it's full-steam ahead with the old smoke?

[*Sounds of me coming in through the door, trying to look as if I haven't been eavesdropping.*]

ADRIAN: I'm back! Everyone okay?

[*Sound of Elsie coming over and kissing me on the cheek.*]

ADRIAN: *(Terminally taken aback.)* What was that for?

ELSIE: It was a kiss from a little cracker. I'm sorry I wasn't there on Friday, Mr Plass, so is William, although it wasn't all his fault. But he is sorry, aren't you, William?

WILLIAM: Eh? Oh, yes! Now, let's talk smoke . . .

Anne certainly did the trick! Elsie couldn't have been more cheerful and enthusiastic than she was for the rest of that rehearsal. Just as well really; it was *very* hard work. Everyone came this time – the whole caboodle! There was Edwin and the rest of the actors, nervous but excited, Norma and Mrs Thynn complete with black clothes and lion costumes, Richard, fussing around with his cheque book asking about 'legitimately incurred expenses', and Gloria, armed with a box of make-up, towels, cleansing-cream and other intriguing tins and tubes. I felt quite nervous at the thought that this little crowd milling around noisily in the hall was relying on me to sort everything out. My confidence wasn't helped by the discovery, just as the last person had been made up and we were all ready to begin, that Thynn, after arriving three-quarters of an hour early, was now nowhere to be seen. He came rushing in after another five minutes (during which I didn't swear out loud because, as Elsie would say, I'm a Christian) clutching a big plastic bag full of George's apples, and shouting, 'Did you get my uniform, Norma?' You can trust Norma. Not only is she charming and pretty and, well ... that sort of thing, but she never forgets a promise. Within a few minutes Leonard emerged from our little improvised changing room wearing the white uniform and plumed helmet of what I guessed to be something like a nineteenth century French colonial officer. The ideal costume for a prompter! He was overjoyed with it, and said it was an even better uniform than the one that Miss Glanthorpe had given him to wear.

The lions really didn't look too bad at all. The costumes were head-pieces with lion-like cloaks rather than complete cover-all affairs, so they didn't look as silly as they might have done. I'd paid a visit to the phantom of the opera a few days previously and managed to extract a sullen promise that the lions wouldn't be lit very brightly. I felt quite optimistic really, and a little ashamed of my doubts about Mrs Thynn's reliability. She said that the man in the costume hire shop told her he was hardly ever asked for his three lion costumes, so she'd decided to take them back tomorrow and re-hire them next Friday morning ready for the performance. That would make it cheaper. Richard nodded approvingly. So, like an idiot, did I, failing completely to register the significance of what Leonard's mother had said. A week later I was to remember her words only too well ...

Meanwhile, the rehearsal started really well. They all seemed to be remembering lines and moves perfectly, until Percy's next to last speech in the final run-through.

PERCY: *(Sounding like a cross between Topol and Olivier.)* Servant of the living God ... *(Pause.)*

THYNN: *(His first prompt of the evening.)* Hear my anguish.

PERCY: *(Irritably.)* I didn't need prompting, Leonard! That was a dramatic pause – a *planned* dramatic pause! *(To A.P.)* I shall commence my speech once more.

A.P.: All right, Percy, that's fine. From 'Servant of the living God', everybody. Leonard, don't prompt unless people really need it, okay?

THYNN: Well …

A.P.: Off you go, Percy.

PERCY: *(After throat-clearing.)* Servant of the living God, hear my anguish!

[*Loud crunching noise as Thynn bites into one of his apples.*]

ALL: Ssh! Be quiet! Quiet! etc.

PERCY: *(Put off by Thynn's thunderous crunching.)* Has he kept his hand upon you in your danger? *(Long pause)* Err … *(Longer pause.)*

A.P.: Come on, Leonard! Prompt!

THYNN: *(After swallowing half an apple whole and nearly choking to death.)* Sorry! I thought it was another dramatic pause. Err ... where are we? Oh, yes, right, here we are, Percy.

Does your God have power to –

PERCY: MAY I start my speech again, IF you please?

A.P.: *(Exasperated.)* Yes, yes! Off you go!

[*Another loud crunch as* THYNN *foolishly bites into a second apple.*]

PERCY: *(Determined to get it right this time.)*
Servant of the living God, hear my anguish,
Has he kept his hand upon you in your danger?
Does your God have power to rescue you from
from danger?

Err ... prompt!

THYNN: Drmnl smrnker mm ...

PERCY: What?

THYNN: Danmnk sprklk mwe ...

PERCY: I can't understand a word you're saying, Thynn!

THYNN: Dnml ...

[*Sound of* RICHARD COOK *slapping* THYNN *suddenly and violently on the back, followed by cries of dismay and disgust as the members of the cast are showered with bits of half-chewed apple.*)

A.P.: Leonard, I think that, as a general rule, it's pretty safe to assume that apple-eating and prompting don't go together. What do you think?

THYNN: Err ... yes, you could be right ... *(coughing fit.)*

After that we got to the end of the run-through without any mishaps, and I got everyone to sit round in a circle for a last chat before we all went home. It said in *The Third Book of Theatrical*

Themes for Theological Thespians that there was no point in saying anything that might lower confidence, so I was determined to be positive at all costs.

[*Hubbub of excited conversation.*]

A.P.: Right! If we could have a bit of hush ...

[*Hubbub dies down gradually.*]

EDWIN: Shush, everybody! Adrian wants to talk to us.

A.P.: Thanks, Edwin. Err ... all I really want to say is that you've all done amazingly well. I can't believe it's this good after just two rehearsals. Well done! I don't just mean the acting. I mean the costumes and the make-up and ...

THYNN: The prompting.

A.P.: And the err ... prompting, yes. Now, I've said all I want to say during the course of the evening, so it's over to you. Are there any questions?

MRS T.: We're *all* Christians, yer great goop!

THYNN: QUESTIONS, MOTHER!! ARE THERE ANY QUESTIONS!!

STENNETH: Err ... I have a question.

A.P.: Yes, Stenneth?

STENNETH: I just wondered if it might be possible to keep our costumes when the production is over. I must confess I rather enjoy being a – a lion ...

GERALD: Heh, good wheeze, Stenners! We could both roam the streets at night terrorising the locals with our bloodthirsty roars! What d'you say? We could eat Christians in the shopping precinct and ...

A.P.: Thank you, Gerald. I'm sorry, Stenneth, but the costumes are only hired. I suppose you could always buy one if you wanted to err ... use it at home.

GLORIA: I've got a leopard skin leotard at home, Stenneth, darling. We could get together and ...

MRS F.: Err ... could I just enquire, Adrian, whether you think my portrayal as err ... an – an angel is, more or less err ... satisfactory, or ...

[*Amazing chorus of approval and praise from everyone else in the circle.*]

A.P.: Well, there's your answer, Victoria.

STENNETH: You're getting more like an angel every day, my dear, if I may say so.

NORMA: I agree, Victoria. It's been really lovely being with you this evening. You seem so sweet and relaxed.

THYNN: *(Goofily tactless.)* For a change.

[*Chorus of disapproval directed towards* THYNN *by everyone else in the circle.*]

MRS F.: No, no, Leonard is simply adhering to the truth. I do feel somehow – different. Perhaps there was more of the natural lodged in my personality than I realised ...

ANNE: You *are* different, Victoria, and it's lovely. Something else, Adrian – what about William's smoke? We haven't actually seen any of it yet, have we?

WILLIAM: Ah, yes, well ...

A.P.: William's going to – Carry on, William, you say.

WILLIAM: Adrian and I have agreed on a few places

A.P.: *Two* places!

WILLIAM: Err ... yes, two places where loads of smoke ...

A.P.: A *moderate* amount of smoke!

WILLIAM: Two places where a moderate amount of smoke would look really great!

PERCY: I hope that this smoke will not obscure any principal err ... characters. Where are these two places?

WILLIAM: Well, one is ...

A.P.: Nobody's going to be obscured, Percy. The first bit is just after Gerald's opening speech when we see the lions for the first time, and the second one is after Victoria's angel speech, just before everything goes dark. Okay?

PERCY: That sounds reasonably satisfactory. I trust, by the way, that my performance was of a sufficiently high standard?

ANNE: *(Sensing the worry beneath Percy's casual question.)* Percy, you were quite as wonderful as I always thought you'd be. Your King Darius is a *real* king!

GLORIA: You're *marvellous,* Percy darling! Scrumptious! I could eat you!

VERNON: Yes, Charles and I think you're really great, Mr Brain!

CHARLES: Yes, just sort of really ...

PERCY: *(Inflated beyond description now.)* Leonard? What do you think of my performance?

THYNN: Gorgeous, Percy, darling! Absolutely scrumptious! What do you think of my prompting, sweetheart?

[*Much amusement.*]

PERCY: *(Haughtily.)* Your prompting is singular, Leonard. I think that is the appropriate term – singular!

THYNN: Thank you, Percival. Wait a minute – what does singular mean?

A.P.: It means wonderful! Richard, are you happy with the way the money's going?

RICHARD: Our financial status is more than satisfactory, I'm very pleased to report. We are err ... several aardvarks in hand, as it were.

GERALD: *(Who wasn't at the meeting where Richard revealed his dream.)* Several aardvarks in hand? Is this a new currency they introduced in the middle of the night when I wasn't looking? Let me guess how it goes:

Six wombats equal one aardvark.
Two aardvarks equal one wolverine.
Three wolverines equal one yak.
Five yaks equal one hairy mammoth.

Got change for a gibbon, dad? I need a jerbil for the coffee machine. I reckon . . .

A.P.: Gerald, Richard was making a little joke about . . .

CHARLES: *(Astonished.)* Did you really make a joke, Father?

RICHARD: I was making a light-hearted reference to a prophetic dream vouchsafed to me recently in connection with the financial arrangements pertaining to this production.

GERALD: *(Genuinely bewildered.)* About aardvarks?

RICHARD: Yes, I saw, as it were, a mighty herd of . . .

THYNN: Singular means only one, doesn't it? Very observant of you to notice there's only one of me, Percy. Well spotted!

PERCY: I did *not* mean that. I meant . . .

GERALD: What were they doing, Richard?

RICHARD: *(Solemnly.)* Flying in formation.

PERCY: I meant, Leonard, if you must know, that your so-called prompting was execrable.

THYNN: Well, that's all right then!

[*Laughter.*]

GERALD: Tell us all about the aardvarks, Richard.

A.P.: *(Hastily.)* I think we're getting a bit off the point, aren't we? Are there any more questions in connection with the play?

ANNE: I'm sure we're all praying in a general sort of way about what happens next Friday evening, darling, but I wondered if it would be a good idea if Edwin just said a little prayer before we break up tonight.

A.P.: Sounds good to me. What does everyone else think?

ALL: Yes/Good idea/Mmm/Go for it, Edwin etc.

EDWIN: Okay – let's pray. *(Pauses.)* Dear Lord, I'm not much like Daniel – don't know how I'd get on with the lions, probably get eaten up, but I love you and I'd try to trust you. That's what I hope we all do next Friday – love you and try to trust you. We don't really know what success means, except that it's what you want. Look after us, Lord, keep us loving you and each other, and thanks for everything, past, present and future. In Jesus' name.

ALL: Amen.

[*Click! as Thynn switches his machine off.*]

SEVEN

LoVe a DucK!

I didn't sleep much during the week leading up to the performance. Every night I lay awake imagining all the things that could possibly go wrong with 'Daniel in the Den'. On the Wednesday night I dreamed that Percy Brain dressed in a leopardskin leotard, and leading a pink aardvark on a chain, walked on to the stage, only to be crushed by a giant apple dropped by Thynn from somewhere up among the lighting bars. Turning to see what my neighbour in the audience thought about this, I found that I was sitting next to a King Penguin in evening dress who asked if he could borrow my feet. Then I woke up . . .

By Friday evening my nerves were so bad that Anne suggested I should ask Edwin to take charge backstage, so that, apart from going round to wish everybody good luck, I could just take my place with Anne in the audience and watch from the front. It was a good idea. Edwin never flaps. He seemed quite happy to take on this role when I phoned him, so that's the way we arranged it.

There were eight entries in the festival competition, four scheduled to appear before the interval, and four after. Ours was the one due immediately after the interval. The hall was packed by seven-twenty. Eight local churches were heavily represented, as well as the usual crowd come out of interest or curiosity. At the back, seated behind a highly complex-looking control panel, sat the phantom of the opera surrounded by pieces of paper and sound cassettes. Somewhere among all that lot – I assumed – were our lighting requirements and a tape of lion roars, imitated with surprising success by William blowing through the outer covering of a matchbox.

At seven-twenty-eight Thynn emerged from the side door that led to the back-stage area, hurriedly scooped up a large china giraffe from a seat on the front row, and disappeared through the door again, much to the bewilderment of the giraffe's near-neighbours who'd been discussing its presence with great animation. At about seven-thirty-five, as the last few people straggled in and took their seats, the lights dimmed and Mr Lamberton-Pincney, who runs a group called 'Spot it and Stop it' in our church, stepped forward to begin his duties as Master of Ceremonies for the evening. I don't know how I sat still for that first half. The four offerings were worthy but dull, and seemed to go on for weeks. There wasn't a hint of humour in any of them – lots of death and repentance, and oodles of sad realisation. Ours wasn't a comedy either, of course, but at least there was a bit of drama and passion in it – and smoke! William was poised at the side of the phantom of the opera, ready for action when the time came. I began to feel quite hopeful.

At half-time the audience rose gratefully to pursue tea and biscuits, while I made my way backstage to see how everyone was getting on. They were all in one of the changing rooms, standing or sitting very tensely as though waiting for something. Thynn's machine was switched on.

[*Sound of door opening and closing as* A.P. *enters. Buzz of conversation stops abruptly.*]

A.P.: *(Brittle but bright.)* Hi, all! Everything okay?

VERNON: We've got a . . .

EDWIN: Everyone's made up who needs to be, Adrian. Gloria's done a great job, so that's all right. Gerald and Percy and Elsie and Victoria and I have all got our gear on, as you can see, and good old Leonard's all dressed up ready for the prompting, so we're ready to go just as soon as . . .

A.P.: *(Sensing disaster.)* As soon as what? What's gone wrong? Tell me!

[*Absolute uproar as everyone tries to speak at once.*]

EDWIN: *(Shouting.)* QUIET!

[*Silence.*]

A.P.: *(Tensely.)* Just tell me, Edwin – please!

EDWIN: It's just that – well, I might as well come straight out with it – the lion costumes haven't arrived yet.

A.P.: What?! Not arrived? They must have ...

THYNN: Mother hasn't ...

A.P.: Mother hasn't *what*? Somebody tell me!

[*More general uproar.*]

EDWIN: QUIET!!

[*Silence.*]

A.P.: Well?

EDWIN: Mrs Thynn hasn't arrived with the lion costumes yet. We've been waiting and waiting, thinking she'd turn up at any moment, but – well, I just don't know ...

A.P.: But ...

THYNN: She went into town this morning to do some shopping and get the costumes and things, and she said she'd see me at the hall this evening. I don't know where she is! I don't know what's happened to her! I don't know ...

GLORIA: *(At her best.)* All right, Leonard, calm down now. It's all going to be okay. Come to Auntie Gloria ...

CHARLES: Vernon's sort of just waiting ...

EDWIN: I've sent Vernon out to wait by the back door so he can let us know if – I mean – *when* she appears.

A.P.: *(Panicking wildly.)* But there's only a few minutes before we're on! What do we do without lions? We can't go on with the play if ...

[*Sound of door crashing open.*]

VERNON: She's coming!

[*Cries of relief and excitement.*]

GERALD: What about the costumes, Vernon?

VERNON: She's got a bundle under her arm. That must be them.

A.P.: Thank goodness for that! Do you want me to stay and …

EDWIN: *(Shooing me out.)* No, no, we'll be fine. You go back and sit out front. We'll sort it all out. Off you go! Relax and enjoy the show.

A.P.: Well, if you're sure …

EDWIN: Quite sure!

A.P.: *(At the door.)* Right, well, good luck, everyone! Good luck with the prompting, Leonard – and the recording.

THYNN: Yep! I'm going to switch it off now to make sure there's enough tape to record the actual …

[*Click! as Thynn switches off.*]

I can't describe the relief I felt as I went back to my seat and told Anne what had happened.

'Just think,' I said, 'after all this work, how close we came to disaster.'

'Yes, darling,' she replied, handing me a cold cup of tea, 'I'm sure we'll be okay now. It's very exciting, isn't it? All these people watching!'

It *was* exciting. As people started filing back to their seats I felt quite shivery with anticipation. It was when all but one or two of the audience were settled in their places, that Richard Cook suddenly appeared through the door I'd closed, rushed up to me, knelt by my chair and started whispering urgently in my ear.

'Edwin sent me to say that Mrs Thynn's brought the costumes!'

'I knew that!' I hissed back. 'You didn't have to come and tell me that!'

'Yes, but she hasn't brought the right costumes!'

'Well, it's too late to worry about that. Leopards, tigers, whatever they are, you'll just have to go ahead.'

'But you don't understand! Percy and Gerald are already up on stage behind the curtain and they don't know that the costumes are ...'

'Richard, the lights are going down. Mr Lamberton-Pincney will be introducing our play any second now! They'll just have to go ahead, understand?'

'Yes, but ...'

'It's too late to worry, Richard!'

'But ...'

'Sssh!'

As Richard scuttled off worriedly towards the connecting door, the auditorium lights dimmed once more, and Mr Lamberton-Pincney's mournful, horse-like face was lit up by a spotlight shining on the curtains at the centre of the stage. In miserable, measured tones, he praised the offerings of the first half, and introduced the first play in the second part of the evening.

'Ladies and Gentlemen – Daniel in the Den!' As the curtains parted to reveal Percy standing majestically centre-stage, I felt a stab of pride and pleasure. He took two steps forward, moved a yard or two stage-right, then faced the audience and spoke in ringing tones. By now, Leonard had his recorder in position next to him, so the rest of the performance survives for posterity.

[*Sound of Percy's feet on the boards as he moves stage-right.*]

PERCY: Though ruling, ruled by men with hooded faces,
Jealous, not for me, but for their honoured places.
Lions indeed, made vicious not by hunger's pain,
But by their lust for power and selfish gain.
No darker hour than when I lightly penned
This blind agreement to destroy my servant-friend.
Within the veil of vanity my foolish eyes,
Perceived my greatness, but could not perceive
their lies.
Oh, God of Daniel, guard your son tonight,
Do not defend the law, defend the right.

No sleep for me, no calm, no peace, no rest,
For I have sanctified the worst, and sacrificed the best.

GERALD: *(Entering stage-left)*
Pain is sharper than remorse,
Death more final than regret,
Darius will mourn tonight,
But live his life, perhaps forget
While Daniel faces fearful hurt,
Beneath the dark remorseless flood
That ... err ...

THYNN: *(Prompting perfectly.)* That flood of fear ...

GERALD: That flood of fear which runs before
The tearing down of flesh and blood.

It was marvellous! The opening speeches had been superb, despite Gerald's lapse of memory, which, thanks to Thynn, was hardly noticed. Now it was time for William's first opportunity to use his beloved smoke-machine. And he certainly used it! Despite my constant pleas for moderation, within two minutes the stage was completely filled with thick, impenetrable, yellow smoke. Percy and Gerald, their backs to the audience, peered hopelessly into the swirling mist, waiting for the lions to appear. The moment when the smoke cleared at last, and three large pantomime ducks waddled forward from the back of the stage will stay in my memory until the day I die. Percy was completely transfixed. From my place at the end of a row I could see his jaw hanging slackly down, his eyes wide and staring as the absurdly costumed trio tried to look menacing. A ripple of laughter passed through the audience as the ducks first hove into view, building to loud, uncontrollable guffaws, as they started to growl softly.

Gerald recovered first. Turning back towards the audience he gathered himself together, and delivered the following on-the-spot adaptation of his second speech.

GERALD: Down in the den where it's dark and black,
Where the lost men scream and the ducks go quack
Where a man whose gods are life and breath,
Will lose his gods in the beak of death.

[*Shouts of laughter.*]

Where the weak will lose their sworn religion,
In the tearing grip of a pin-tailed widgeon.

[*Screams of laughter.*]

THYNN: (*Audible to the mike, but not the audience.*) That's not what it says here!

PERCY: (*Recovering like the old trouper he is.*)
Oh, Daniel, Daniel save me from my madness,
Pray your God's compassion on my sadness,
Bid him send an all-forgiving rain,
To wash these excess mallards down the drain.

ELSIE: (*Entering stage left and getting the idea immediately.*)
I wait upon you master as you bade me wait,
To bring intelligence of Daniel and his fate.
Some moments past your man, of whom you're fond,
Was taken out and thrown into the pond.

PERCY: Save him God, hear my appeal!
Save him for that flock of teal!

THYNN: (*Louder.*) That's not what it says here! (*Wanders out onto the stage absent-mindedly, studying his script.*) That's not what it says here, Percy! There's nothing about ducks!

[*Wild laughter from the audience on seeing someone in a nineteenth-century French colonial officer's uniform wandering inexplicably around the stage among the ducks.*]

STENNETH: (*A muffled bleat through his duck head.*) She brought the wrong costumes, Leonard! She brought ducks!

GERALD: *(Pushing between* STENNETH DUCK *and* THYNN *to address the audience.)*

> Now the moment, now the test,
> See Jehovah's servant blessed,
> Standing here with troubled scowl
> Before these deadly water-fowl.
> Glad to earn the highest crown,
> By ending up in eiderdown.

[*Loud roars from the speakers as the 'phantom' puts on William's tape. Audience collapses again as the ducks bob up and down, opening and shutting their beaks in time with the roars.*]

THYNN: *(Wildly at centre-stage.)* You're all getting it wrong! There aren't any ducks in it!

EDWIN: *(Entering stage-left.)*

> Though I may be short of pluck
> I'm not afraid to face a duck!
> I'll cut these creatures into thirds,
> The stupid geriatric birds!

THYNN: *(Very indignant.)* That's *completely* wrong!

MRS F.: *(Entering stage-right with a very straight, severe face. Touches each duck's head in turn with her hand.)*

> Here they lie, those mighty killers,
> Harmless where great harm has been,
> Sleep, and when the dawn has risen,
> Tell the king what you have seen.

(Moves over and touches Edwin's head with her hand.)

Daniel, you *shall* go to the ball!

[MRS.FLUSHPOOL'S *face suddenly cracks into a real smile and she laughs until she cries.*]

THYNN: *(Resting his arm on* VERNON DUCK'S *shoulder.)* Now that *is* wrong!

GERALD: If you would score, you mighty kings,
> Be sure, don't trust to luck.
> If you don't score by God's own law,
> You'll end up with a duck.

THYNN: That's not . . . !

GERALD: Come on, everyone!

[*Gerald gets all on stage into a chorus line, and leads them into song.*]

ALL: Knees up Daniel Brown!
> Knees up Daniel Brown!
> Knees up! Knees up!
> Better get your knees up,
> Knees up Daniel Brown! Oi!

THYNN: We never sung that at rehearsals . . .

At this point the phantom of the opera, knowing that he was supposed to black out the stage somewhere in the course of the action, decided that now would be as good a time as any. Who can blame him?

When the lights came back on, the cast of 'Daniel in the Ducks' Den' received the only standing ovation ever witnessed in that building. People cheered and clapped for a good three or four minutes, while the actors waved and bowed extravagantly until the applause died down. Thynn, postponing his quest for some basic understanding of what was going on, waved and bowed with the rest, a blank but happy grin stretched across his face.

I felt sorry for the people in the three plays that came after ours. Two of them were quite good, but there was no doubt about it – nothing, on this particular night, was going to match the emergence of those three ducks from the middle of William's smoke. I think I had experienced every emotion known to man during the 'Daniel' performance, and as I joined in the applause for the final offering of the evening I felt quite exhausted. Four more significant things were yet to happen, though, before we left for home that night.

First, Mr Lamberton-Pincney announced immediately after the final play had finished that the judges' overwhelming and unanimous decision was that 'Daniel in the Den' was the winning entry, and I was called up on stage to collect the little silver cup on behalf of our church, for a 'hilarious and cleverly devised comedy'. Feeling terribly guilty, I tried to explain to Mr Lamberton-Pincney and the audience that our play was meant to be serious and had only become funny by accident. The more I tried to explain, though, the more they obviously thought I was being terribly witty. They just laughed and clapped. In the end I gave up, and decided to explain to whoever was in charge later on.

The next thing was that Anne, who'd nearly died of laughing from 'ducks' onwards, steered me through the crowds of lingering theatre-goers to where a little old lady was sitting next to Leonard, still in his uniform and clutching Mr Hurd. They were chatting away like mad.

'Miss Glanthorpe,' whispered Anne in my ear. 'A little surprise I organised. Found her in the book. She's eighty-two!'

I looked at Anne for a moment, then moved closer to eavesdrop.

'You were absolutely marvellous, Leonard,' Miss Glanthorpe was saying, her little eyes twinkling as she surveyed the white-clad figure.

Leonard beamed happily.

'I don't quite understand though,' went on the old lady, 'the significance of this splendid uniform, and I was just wondering why you have that big china giraffe sitting on your knee ...'

'Oh, that's easy to explain,' said Leonard confidently, 'I was wearing uniform because I was the prompter, and I was supposed to stay out of sight so that the giraffe couldn't see me when Percy Brain forgot his lines.'

'I see, dear. How silly of me to be so dense.' The little eyes twinkled even more. 'You know, Leonard ... ?'

'Yes, Miss Glanthorpe?'

'You really haven't changed at all ...'

The third thing was that as we moved away towards the back-stage area we almost collided with Frank Braddock, our neighbour, and author of the play we'd just mangled. He was with Father John, an old friend of his, and an occasional very welcome guest speaker at our church.

'Frank,' I said apologetically, 'I just don't know what to say. I'm so ...'

'Don't apologise!' boomed Frank taking his unlit pipe out of his mouth. 'I was just saying to old Bungles here that I haven't enjoyed anything so much in years. The moment when old Thynn wandered on in his uniform was just – I dunno, I could've died! My version much more boring than yours.'

'It's nice of you to say that, Frank,' I replied gratefully, 'but it wasn't exactly what I set out to do. Winning was an accident. I can't really see this evening as a success, not really.'

'Not a success?' Father John broke in gently. 'Adrian, I've never seen Victoria Flushpool as she was on that stage this evening. Her eyes shone, she was laughing, she was part of you all. She's different. I wouldn't be at all surprised if the experience of rubbing up against each other in a real, side-by-side effort like this had changed all of you in one way or another. It all depends whose

success you're talking about, you know. I sometimes think that football teams and dramatic societies might be just as important as prayer-meetings and Bible-studies ...'

'Come on, Bungles!' Frank slapped his friend on the back. 'Enough deep stuff! We've just got time for a pint if we're quick ...'

The fourth and last thing to happen was finding the cast and crew of 'Daniel in the Den', still sitting in the changing room behind the stage. Thynn followed Anne and me through the door as we went in, and stood leaning against the wall cuddling his giraffe. All conversation stopped as soon as I appeared, and they all stared at me, waiting to see what I'd say. I thought of what Father John had said as I looked round at the familiar faces. Vernon and Charles, as earnest as ever, had little frowns beneath hair still lank from being enclosed in hot costumes. Victoria and Stenneth were sitting closer together than usual – they seemed lighter somehow. Gerald looked the same as ever, leaning on the radiator and giving me a little quizzical smile. I suddenly realised how grown up he was getting. Richard was sitting on an old, burst horse-hair sofa, jammed in tightly by Gloria on one side and Norma on the other. William and Elsie sat cross-legged on the floor gazing up at me. They looked even younger than usual. Percy was in the only armchair, legs crossed stylishly, head thrown back, but watching me with wide eyes. Mrs Thynn was doing something busily with a piece of cloth held in her fingers. Her eyes darted up to meet mine every few seconds. Edwin was standing by the window looking as serene as ever. Anne stood very still beside me. There was someone else there as well, right in the middle of us, the one who decides what success really means.

'Those ducks!' I said, and we all burst into laughter at the same moment.

The Sacred Diary of Adrian Plass, Christian Speaker, Aged 45 3/4

This book is dedicated to Jeremy Gates

Diary – A. Plass

Monday 31 Jan

Got a bit distracted in church during the message yesterday. Very clever visiting speaker. So clever that I hadn't got the faintest idea what he was talking about.

Suddenly said very loudly near the beginning of his talk, 'Who will stand and declare the Lord's displeasure with churches that are unrepentantly cleistogamic?'

Richard Cook, who was sitting next to me, leapt to his feet and said, 'Indeed, Lord, we rebuke and we stand against those cleistogamic tendencies that exist in our church!'

When he sat down I leaned over and whispered in his ear, 'What does cleistogamic mean?'

He whispered back, 'I don't know.'

Honestly!

Decided, as the talk droned on, to start up a diary again, just for a while, so that I can record some of my experiences connected with being a Christian speaker. Lots of invitations for the next three months, and as I have to use up oceans of leave before the end of the financial year, I'll be able to do quite a lot of them.

Unbelievable the way it's all taken off. Started with being invited by local churches to read bits from what I'd written, but over the last couple of years I've been all over the country. I do speak a bit as well as doing the readings now. Anne says it sounds all right when the things I say are true, but that when they're not I sound like a pompous git – I think that's the expression she used. Her ministry of encouragement is subtle and special.

Seems hardly possible that my three books about people in our church have been read by so many people. Glad Gerald persuaded me to send my first diary off to a publisher, although it was a bit of a shock to find what was supposed to be a serious, helpful account of daily Christian living, being described by critics as a 'searing satire on the modern church'. Slightly galling also to find some of my important personal spiritual insights being labelled as 'ludicrous modern religious attitudes, hilariously caricatured'.

Still, if they say it's searing satire I suppose it might be. At least I've mastered the process now – all I have to do is write seriously and everyone laughs their heads off. Really hope this book will end up being used as a sort of serious textbook for Christian speakers, but after seeing what happened to the first one I wouldn't be surprised if it became regarded as a major influence in the field of begonia culture.

We shall see . . .

Must look up 'cleistogamic' in the dictionary.

Tuesday 1 Feb

Decided this morning that I ought to have one of those support groups that lots of other Christian speakers have. The more I pictured it the more I liked it. I would be God's chosen vehicle, powerful and mantled with authority in public, yet restrained and full of grace in private, opening myself up in humble submission to the ministrations, advice and criticism of a little group of folk who would feel privileged and proud to be part of what God was doing through me.

Mentioned the idea to Anne and Gerald over breakfast.

'The thing is,' I said, 'that I'd submit myself to their advice and criticism and be sort of accountable to them, and er . . . that sort of thing.'

Anne stopped in mid-toast-buttering, did a little laugh, and said, 'But you absolutely *hate* criticism, darling. You always have done. You get very cross indeed when anyone says anything remotely critical – doesn't he, Gerald?'

'Mum's right, Dad,' said Gerald, 'criticism's one of the things that makes little bits of spit appear at the corners of your mouth.'

Absolutely appalled by this response to my idea. 'I do *not* hate criticism, Anne – I've never heard such rubbish in my life! How can you possibly say that? I have been given the heart of a servant.'

Gerald said, 'I don't think the transplant's taken, Dad.'

Ignored him.

'And I do not get "very cross". You make me sound like – like a toddler who's been told he can't have another sweet. I'll have you know that God has done a mighty work of building in me as far as the whole area of criticism's concerned. Frankly, you couldn't be more wrong if you tried.'

Both burst into laughter at this point, for reasons that totally escape me. Gerald so busy cackling he didn't realize the end of his hair had flopped into the marmalade. I was slightly consoled by this.

When she'd recovered, Anne said, 'I'm sorry, Adrian, I'm sure God has done a mighty work of building in you, it's just that –'

'It hasn't been unveiled yet.'

'No, Gerald, don't – that's not what I was going to say. What I was going to say,' Anne continued in her sensible voice, 'was that you *have* changed. You're quite right. You *are* much more aware of problems and faults in yourself that, in the past, you never even noticed. But, let's be honest, darling, you're still not very good at – well, hearing about them from other people, are you? There's something useful and rather splendid about telling big halls full of people that you're not a very good person, but you're completely in charge of what people are allowed to know about you in that sort of situation, aren't you? In fact, they think all the more of you for being so honest about your shortcomings, so, in a sense, you win all ways, don't you? And that's great, as long as you can also take a bit of criticism from people like us, who are close to you and aren't going to be quite so easily impressed.'

She reached over and took my hand. 'I'm sorry, darling. Gerald and I shouldn't have laughed at you like that just then. It was just so funny that you got very cross indeed when I criticized the fact that you get very cross indeed whenever you're criticized. Well, you did, didn't you? Adrian, you do see what I'm getting at, don't you?'

Paralysed temporarily by the battle raging inside me. Didn't want to appear sulky or angry because both were bound to be interpreted as failure to accept criticism, but didn't want to speak, knowing it would come out sounding sulky or angry because that's how I actually felt. Managed a sort of glassy-eyed, wooden nodding movement.

'If it's any use to you, Dad,' said Gerald, who'd been scribbling on the back of an envelope, 'here's a little verse on the subject:

> 'Freely I confess my sins,
> For God has poured his Grace in,
> But when another lists my faults,
> I want to smash his face in.

'Does that more or less sum it up?'

Couldn't help laughing. Anne made more coffee.

I said, 'So you don't think the support group idea is a good one?'

'Oh, yes,' said Anne, 'I think it's an excellent idea, as long as you're going to be genuinely vulnerable, and not just use it as a means of – well, emphasizing and relishing your "stardom". That's not what you want, is it?'

Made me sound like Liberace.

'Oh, no . . . no, that would be awful. I'd hate that . . .'

'You don't want to waste their time either, do you? Tell you what – why don't you ask Edwin to choose a group and set the whole thing up for you? He'll know the best people to ask.'

'Oh,' I said, 'I was rather thinking that I might choose who comes.'

'Exactly,' said Anne and Gerald in chorus.

Reluctantly but sincerely thanked God for my family before going to bed tonight.

Wonder if Norma Twill will be in my support group. Not for any particular reason really. Just wonder if she will because – well, because she's very er . . . very nice.

Wednesday 2 Feb

2:00 p.m.

Just had lunch at work with Everett Glander, who's still not converted after over ten years of contact with me – the great travelling evangelist!

Suffering a real attack of nerves. If I can't manage to convert the person who's been sitting next to me for a decade, how am I going to make an impact on anyone else? What *do* I think I'm doing? I mean, it's not as if I even feel like the sort of person you'd imagine God would use to communicate to people. And what makes me think a group of busy people are going to want to waste their time supporting me when they're all doing important things themselves? And why ever would God want me, of all people, to go and represent him anyway? Suppose he actually *doesn't* want me to represent him, but my ears have been stopped by Satan. What if the devil's got me wrapped round his little finger? Suppose I'm an active agent of evil without out realizing it. What if I'm Antichrist? What if I *am* the Beast of Revelation, destined to be thrown into the lake of fire for all eternity?

Bit worrying, really.

11:30 p.m.

Showed Gerald what I wrote at work when he came in this evening. He read it and said, 'Yes, very balanced piece of thinking, as usual, Dad. You don't think you might have got just a tad carried away? When the angels are strolling slowly through the city of gold enjoying their Beast 'n' chips wrapped in old sheets of *Mission Praise,* I don't somehow think it'll be you they're consuming.'

317

Told him I didn't really believe what I'd written – just felt a bit silly assuming that God was 'sending me out', as it were. He nodded very thoughtfully, and said he'd give the matter careful consideration.

Don't know what's going on with Gerald at the moment. Not sure whether we should be worried about him or not. He's left his job and come back home to live. Lovely to have him here, but what's going on? Living on his savings at the moment, and says he's got a big decision to make. Anne and I keep finding ourselves hovering nervously behind him as if he's likely to explode at any moment. Keeps going off for long walks, or working for hours on his word processor or just spending time quietly in his room.

Says he'd like to come with me when I go to do my talks. That's a good sign – isn't it?

Surely.

Thursday 3 Feb

Free day today to do some preparation.

Came down late to discover that Gerald had already gone off for one of his marathon strolls. Found an envelope on the kitchen table addressed simply to '666'. Very amusing, I don't think. Four sheets of paper inside. First one read as follows:

Dear Satan's Plaything,

Had a think about what you said yesterday, and came to the conclusion that you only need to begin worrying when you do start to feel that you're the kind of person God would be foolish not to use. He's always used idiots – sorry, I don't mean you're an idiot – you know what I mean. What I'm trying to say is, there aren't any special people, only ordinary ones. If he decides you're of some use, that's his problem, not yours. Thought you might be interested to read the enclosed rewrite of Scripture that I've been working on. Don't suppose it was really any different then. Ordinary people – that's all there is.

Love,

Son of the Beast.

Made myself a coffee, sat down at the kitchen table, and unfolded the three sheets of paper that had been in the envelope with the note. Have copied down Gerald's 'rewrite of Scripture' here. Wonder what God thinks about it? I have a funny feeling he probably bends the rules for Gerald ...

After these things the Lord appointed another seventy also and sent them two by two ahead of him to every town and place where he was about to go. He told them, 'The harvest is plentiful but the workers are few. Ask the Lord of the harvest, therefore, to send out workers into his harvest field. Go! I am sending you out like lambs among wolves. Take neither purse nor scrip, nor sandals; and do not greet anyone on the road.'

And behold one of the seventy raiseth his hand and enquireth, 'When thou sayest "sandals", Lord, do we taketh that to be an generic term which denoteth all forms of footwear, or focusseth thou in on sandals in particular? I asketh only because I possesseth an exceeding fine pair of walking boots, ideal for those who hiketh around as thou art indeed commanding us to do.'

Before the Lord could reply, another breaketh in and saith, 'Lord, I heareth what thou art saying, but behold, the skin that undergirdeth mine feet and also the feet of mine friend, Fidybus – he who maketh a pair with me as we getteth on well over long periods and always have done since we playeth together as children ... Er, the object of mine speech escapeth me ...'

Jesus saith wearily, 'Something about the skin that undergirdeth thine feet, and those of thine friend, Fidybus?'

'Ah, verily, yes, it cometh back now. The skin that undergirdeth mine feet is like unto that which undergirdeth the feet of mine friend, Fidybus, in that it very soon waxeth tender and painful on rough ground. And it just striketh us that the sight of two men who holdeth heavily on to each other and hobbleth slowly and painfully along, going "Oo!" and

"Ah!" and "Ow!" whensoever they putteth down a foot, might cause those who dwell in the towns and places to which thou sendest us to scoff when we imparteth the news that the Son of God approacheth presently. "What state musteth *his* feet be in, if he cannot keep up with these two clowns?" they will mock. Might, therefore, Master, we ask thine blessing on the idea of wrapping strips of rag round and round each of mine feet and each of those belonging to mine friend, Fidybus? After all, strips of rag falleth well outside the dictionary definition of sandals, dost thou not agree?'

And behold, an veritable babel of footwear-related queries filleth the air, and Jesus raiseth his hand and saith, 'Hold on a minute! Let me maketh myself clear. No sandals means nothing on thine feet, all right? Nothing! Neither walking boots, nor strips of rag, nor tennis shoes, nor high-heeled slingbacks, nor Wellingtons, nor roller-boots, nor skateboards, nor anything that I mighteth construe as an sandal in the broadest sense of the word. Understandeth thou all? Good. Now, departeth thou in twos and –'

'Er, excuse me, Lord.'

'Yes, Thomas?'

'Regarding thine command that we travel in twos.'

'Yes?'

'Er, no one desireth to go with Thribbiel.'

And the Lord enquireth, 'Well, why doth no one desire to go with Thribbiel? He looketh all right to me.'

'He's a bit funny, Lord.'

'Well, we're *all* a bit funny, aren't we? Anyway, I invariably organizeth it so that we have even numbers. Who goest thou with, Thomas?'

Thomas replieth mournfully, 'No one desireth to go with me either, Lord. No one picketh me even at junior school.'

'Well, for all thou knowest, Thribbiel might desire to accompany thee?'

'I doubt it.'

'Well, let's ask him, shall we? Thribbiel, dost thou wish to accompany Thomas?'

'Yeah, Lord, but canst thou ask of him that he cometh over a bit less negative? He can be an real Eeyore.'

'Thomas, canst thou do that?'

'I doubt it, but, verily, I will try.'

'Good,' saith the Lord, 'now, mayhap, we can get on. Departeth thou in twos and –'

'Command Thribbiel that he be less funny, Lord. There existeth little point in me being more positive if he maketh no attempt –'

'Sorteth it out between you!' saith the Lord. 'Verily, this whole affair beginneth to feel more like an Brownie picnic than an commission to establish the Kingdom of God.' He pauseth to collect himself. 'Now, I repeateth my command that thou departest in twos, take neither purse nor scrip nor sandals and do not greet anyone on the road. Now, go!'

But immediately one of the seventy raiseth his hand to ask of the Lord if an small pink face-towel mighteth be taken, and that setteth all the others off all over again. One enquireth concerning his personal toilet kit which fitteth nicely into an little pocket specially sewn into his robe by his mother, another pleadeth to be allowed an small stuffed animal without which he feeleth insecure at night, and yet another postulateth an situation in which he meeteth the Lord himself on the road, and querieth whether the command not to greet anyone applieth in that case, until, behold, there ariseth an great clamour of foolish enquiries.

Then the Lord shouteth for silence, and saith, 'Look, I don't think we've quite grasped the theory behind this trip, have we? The idea is not that thou smugglest sundry items into thine luggage using as an crummy excuse the fact that stuffed toys cometh not under the Oxford Dictionary definition of sandals, but rather that thou art dependent on me! Understandest thou that? No purse, no scrip, no sandals, no teddy bear, no Barclaycard – just go!'

Then an lengthy silence falleth, and just as Jesus believeth they are truly about to depart, an nervous hand raiseth itself.

Jesus regardeth the owner of the hand with narrowed eyes. 'Yes?'

'Er, regarding thy command that we should take no scrip, Lord?'

'Yes.'

'Well, er, to be honest, I knoweth not what an scrip is, Lord, and, well, it worrieth me that I might er, taketh an scrip without realizing I've got it. So I just thought ...'

On hearing this the remaining sixty-nine scoffeth loudly, laughing, and crying, 'Hah! Thou dolt! Knoweth thou not what an scrip is? Surely all possesseth that knowledge. What an div!'

Then Jesus gritteth his teeth and saith, 'Very well, who can telleth us what an scrip is?'

Behold, the confidence of the sixty-nine draineth away. One hazardeth an guess that an scrip is 'what you use in an play'.

Jesus shaketh his head and saith, 'All right, how many knoweth not what an scrip is?'

All seventy raiseth their hands.

Jesus emitteth an little sigh, and smileth to himself, and saith, 'Okay, taketh the weight off thine feet. Behold, I commenceth from the beginning ...'

Friday 4 Feb

Much cheered and inspired by what Gerald had to say yesterday. He's absolutely right! I do qualify to speak for God because I am just an ordinary follower. Rather fancy I now have a greater appreciation of that fact than most. Really feel ablaze for the Lord! Can't wait for tomorrow's meeting at something called the 'Reginald and Eileen Afternoon Tea Club' in West Hammerton, one of our local villages. Those folk have specially requested me to come. They're looking forward to it, and I'm not going to let my stupid worries about myself spoil their enjoyment, or their access to things of the Lord.

Hallelujah!

Saturday 5 Feb

Arrived at West Hammerton Village Hall with Gerald at two-thirty, well in time for my talk which was scheduled for three o'clock. Walked into the hall wearing my shy, yes-it's-me-folks-but-I'm-no-different-from-anyone-else expression. Needn't have bothered. No one seemed to know who I was.

Approached as we entered by a smartly dressed, very elderly man of stiffly military, but somewhat unsteady bearing, who introduced himself as Mr B. Granger, secretary of the Reginald and Eileen Afternoon Tea Club. Said the person who'd actually invited me wasn't able to be there because he was dead (a pathetically lame excuse, Gerald commented later), so he didn't really know what was going on.

Things were further complicated, he explained, in his age-muffled bark of a voice, by the fact that I was an alternative to someone who, as far as I was able to understand it, wasn't able to fill in for a man who couldn't take the place of a woman who'd backed out of substituting for some wonderful person called Mr A. Whittle, an expert on 'West Hammerton As It Was', who everyone had really wanted to come (with his slides) in the first place.

Did my talk involve slides?

No, it didn't.

Oh.

In response to a question from Gerald, Mr B. Granger explained that the Reginald and Eileen Afternoon Tea Club derived its name from the fact that it had been founded many years ago by two people called Reginald and Eileen, who were also dead.

Gerald nodded intelligently.

Most of the twenty or so elderly people sitting round little tables in groups of four or five glared at me as I followed Mr B. Granger to the place where there would have been a microphone if they'd had one.

They hate me, I thought, for not being Mr A. Whittle, and for having no slides.

Mr B. Granger glanced covertly at a small piece of paper in the hollow of his hand, and cleared his throat commandingly.

He said, 'Make a start, then, ladies and gentlemen. Notices first.' Pause. 'There are none. Any notices from any member before introduction of speaker?'

An ancient, white-haired little lady who was almost bent double, levered herself up from her chair and zig-zagged her way determinedly to the front, from which vantage point she addressed the assembly in quaveringly aggressive tones.

'I just want to say,' she announced, 'that I've been taking all six club tablecloths home and washing them once a year for the last twenty years, and I'm not prepared to go on doing it. It's time someone else had a turn.'

'What is involved, Mrs Lazenby?' enquired Mr B. Granger, in sternly official tones.

'You have to take all six tablecloths home once a year and wash them,' said Mrs Lazenby rather predictably. 'Only I've been doing it for twenty years, and I think I've done my bit. It's time someone else had a go. I'm not prepared to go on doing it. I've done it for twenty years, and I think that's long enough. Someone else can –'

'Mrs Lazenby has been doing it for twenty years,' interrupted Mr B. Granger, presumably realizing that the repetition of this complaint was affording Mrs Lazenby enormous satisfaction, and that she would probably go on making her point indefinitely if nobody stopped her, 'and I think she's done her bit. It's time for someone else to have a go, because she's not prepared to go on doing it.' He cleared his throat again. 'I should like to propose a vote of thanks to Mrs Lazenby in recognition of the work she has undertaken in relation to the club tablecloths over the last twenty years. Shall we express our appreciation in the usual way as she now steps down from the post in which she has so magnificently served for –'

'Twenty years,' filled in Mrs Lazenby with relish, 'and I'm not prepared to –'

'Perhaps a volunteer would present herself – or *him*self,' ripple of laughter, 'during the refreshment period immediately following the talk. Thank you once again, Mrs Lazenby, for your sterling endeavours on our behalf.'

Mrs Lazenby, accompanied by a patter of frankly grudging applause, reluctantly but triumphantly wove her way back to her table, where she immediately embarked on a fiercely whispered discussion with her two immediate neighbours about the fact that she had done it for twenty years and wasn't prepared to do it any longer . . .

'Now,' Mr B. Granger ticked off Notices on his little piece of paper, 'we come to our speaker. And we are indeed most fortunate to have secured the presence of Mr E. Bass, a much loved local lay reader.'

(The only things he got right were geography and sex, which, as Gerald said later, are not a lot of use unless you're an itinerant gynaecologist.)

'Mr Bass's talk, to which we are all looking forward to – er . . . with a great deal of pleasurable anticipation, is entitled –' quick squint at the piece of paper, 'it is entitled "Readings from *The Scared Dairy*", and will take us up to tea at twenty-five to four. There are no slides. Thank you, Mr Bass.'

The only person in that hall, not excluding myself, who enjoyed my slideless 'Readings from *The Scared Dairy*' was Gerald, who loved every minute, of course. The rest of my audience stared at me with either undisguised puzzlement or deaf incomprehension as, with my top lip sticking uncomfortably to my teeth, I agonized my way through half an hour of completely inappropriate material which failed to raise even the glimmer of a smile. It was like trying to water plants with sand.

Not helped by the fact that, about ten minutes before the talk ended, two ladies from different tables got up at precisely the same moment, as if by magic, and disappeared into the kitchen, where they spent the next ten minutes clattering and chinking and slamming things, and talking in voices loud enough for them to be able to hear each other speak over their own clattering, chinking, slamming noises.

Totally drained afterwards. Only one question from the floor when Mr B. Granger invited them.

Was I acquainted with a Mr A. Whittle, who spoke a commentary with most interesting slides of old West Hammerton? No, regrettably, I was not acquainted with Mr A. Whittle who spoke a commentary with most interesting slides of old West Hammerton.

This piece of information seemed to kill off any further interest. Felt a strong desire to kill off Mr A. Whittle, and send him, with his slides, to entertain Reginald and Eileen.

Needed my tea badly. Gerald was really good with the old folk. Got them laughing and chatting with ease. Wish he'd done the talk. I never want to do another one again – ever.

Meeting finished with the singing of the club song, led by a piano in the corner which seemed to be missing almost as many original ivories as the old gentleman who played it with wobbling panache. The words of the song, sung twice through with great gusto, went like this:

> Reginald and Eileen may not be with us now,
> For they, with many friends, have passed away,
> But sad though we may be, we will gather here for tea,
> And show the world that we are proudly gay.

Gerald drove us home. I sat miserably clutching my previously written Thank you card ('We all much appreciate the new insights into the work of our dairies that you have brought to us this afternoon') and my five-pound note, wondering how to cancel all further engagements. All the way back Gerald, who still seems to feel the need to tear the guts out of every joke, produced depressingly accurate impressions of Mr B. Granger saying, 'Mr E. Bass, a much loved local lay reader, whose talk is entitled "Readings from *The Scared Dairy*".'

Anne, and Thynn, who'd come round for tea, in hysterics when Gerald told them about my sepia photograph of an experience.

Perhaps my support group should be composed entirely of chronic depressives, then they could have a good laugh twice a month at my expense.

Poor old Leonard's still a bit shaky since the death of his mother. Still, as he said this evening, at least she'll be able to hear what all the heavenly beings are saying now. The thing that drove Leonard mad towards the end of her life, was that she refused to wear a hearing aid because, according to her, she wasn't deaf, she just couldn't hear what people were saying.

We see a lot of L.T. at the moment.

Sunday 6 Feb

Had words with God in church today. Asked for something to lift my spirits about the whole speaking business. I seem to so easily lose confidence.

Looked up as I came out of church with the others and saw a cloud that was shaped just like South America. Idly wondered if this could be 'the sign'. Pointed the cloud out to Richard Cook.

I said, 'You see that cloud that's shaped just like South America? Do you think it could be a sign?'

He said, 'Yes, it could be, except that it isn't South America. It's shaped exactly like Italy. That's remarkable! God's calling you to Italy.'

Thought I'd better see what everyone else thought.

Gerald said he thought it was the continent of India.

Anne (who loves the West Country) said it was definitely the Lizard peninsula in Cornwall.

George Farmer knew it was Greenland, which, he said, confirmed something he'd always thought about me.

Thynn said it was a carrot, and suggested that I was being called to minister among those who labour among root vegetables.

Decided it wasn't the sign I was looking for, not unless God is expecting me to convert most of the planet, *and* people who labour among root vegetables. I mean, God created the world, didn't he? So he must be able to draw one little bit of it accurately if he wants to.

Monday 7 Feb

The clouds have parted! Took their time, I must say . . .

Woke up feeling gloomy.

Gerald, who has agreed to be my unpaid, part-time secretary while he's at home, handed me the following letter this morning. Told me it had arrived in the first post. Quite excited as I began to read. This is what it said:

Dear Mr Plass,

Greetings in the name of he who empowers.

This is to inform you that prayerful consideration on the part of the church committee has revealed you to be God's chosen guest speaker on the occasion of our Autumn Church Family Weekend this year. Your message will be given on Friday the Eighth of September at 7:33 p.m. and should be *no more* than twenty-seven minutes in length, to include a final five-minute period in which signs following (excluding slaying in the Spirit and lengthy individual ministry please) may be manifested to and among the assembly. Your talk must be supported by appropriate Scriptural references (extracted from the Never Inflamatory Version of the Bible please) and needs to be broken into three easily comprehended sections, each beginning with the same letter.

Limited humour (mild only please) is allowable in the initial stages in order to demonstrate that Christians enjoy fun, but should be swiftly succeeded by admonitory and exhortational modes of address culminating in a controlled but movingly passionate appeal for changed lives at around the twenty minute mark. Please stress that such changes should occur within a denominational context. Some past speakers have, regrettably, held the wire fence down, as it were, thereby allowing errant members of our assembly to migrate to spiritual pastures new. We would ask you, in this connection, to emphasize the God-given authority of our church elders, and the fact that your task is simply to point the attending church members in their direction.

Please *do not* invite questions as these invariably disrupt time schedules, and tend to have an unsettling effect on those who are not yet truly wedded to our understanding and exposition of the Word.

We wish you to speak on the subject: 'ALLOWING THE SPIRIT TO WORK'. Please feel free (within the above parameters) to follow the Lord's leading in the presentation of his word as it is ministered to you.

Please send details of the fee you are likely to demand in return for doing the Lord's work on this occasion, bearing in mind that in addition to being already heavily in debt as we await confirmation that certain faith enterprises are truly of God, we are likely to be out of pocket at the end of the event, and that all spare money is, in any case, generally sent to alleviate the suffering of sick and starving children whom no one cares about, perishing alone on dung-heaps in poverty-stricken parts of the world.

We will, of course, cover your travelling expenses. We plan to purchase and post to you a return ticket issued by the national coach company, the timetable of which indicates an ideal service leaving your home town at 5:30 a.m. on the Friday in question and making a scheduled stop at a town two miles distant from the conference centre at 6:30 p.m. in the evening. The last stage of your journey could be in the form of a brisk walk (not unacceptable after a day of motorized travel, I dare swear), or, if you should so decide, I believe there are taxis available from the town centre. It may well be, however, that you are reluctant to expend such a large proportion of your fee in this way.

You can, of course, in case of extreme difficulty, and only *if absolutely necessary,* contact us at the conference centre by phone, but I should point out that there is only one telephone, situated in the farthest recesses of an extensive and comprehensively locked cellar system beneath a completely different wing of the building from the one that we shall be using, and that the Centre manager, who is elderly, arthritic and less than amenable to special requests, allows no telephonic access to visitors. I feel sure you understand our reluctance to use up goodwill in this area. If you do decide to walk (and the decision is entirely yours), you should be with us by 7:00 p.m. at the latest, which would allow you a good half hour to explore the Centre, rest for a minute or two, eat your supper, which June Salmons will pour into a bowl to save and warm up for you, meet a few of the folks you will be speaking to, supervise a Getting To Know You Game, say a brief word to the children's group which begins its meeting just before ours and join the elders for a time of instruction and prayer before beginning your talk.

I estimate that there will be approximately three hundred folks present at the meeting. The hall we are using was originally one arm of an old cloister, and, although very long, is also very thin. As you can imagine, communicating with lines of four people stretching back for seventy-five rows is a stimulating challenge for a speaker, especially when no public address system is available, as is the case here. Please do speak up, as most of our elderly friends like to sit at the back for ease of egress if they become bored or in need of the facilities.

After the meeting please feel free to stay and chat with folks for as long as you wish, although we quite understand that you will need to return to town in good time to catch the coach which departs for your return journey at 9:30 p.m. that same evening. If you have heavy cases to lug back to town, just mention it to the elders, any one of whom will be pleased to offer very competitive rates.

Perhaps I should say, in passing, that accommodation is actually available at the Conference Centre, and, just in case that is a decision you wish to make, I am pleased to enclose the relevant price-list for your consideration. I am afraid that you would *not* benefit from the group-booking rate that members of our church will enjoy, and I also need to make it clear that if you do stay on as a paying guest your return coach ticket will no longer be valid, and you will therefore have to make alternative, and possibly very costly travel arrangements for yourself on the following day. The last thing we want is for you to end up out-of-pocket and feeling used. That wouldn't be very Christian, would it?

Please write back as soon as possible confirming your availability for this event and your agreement in the matters detailed in this letter.

Yours,

Dennis Floom

(For The Open Heart Fellowship)

P.S. Please enclose stamped addressed envelope with your reply for despatch of coach tickets.

Gerald must think I'm terribly naïve. Realized it wasn't a genuine letter as soon as I looked closely at the words on the paper and recognized the print from Gerald's machine. Was about to suggest that jokes about invitations to speak weren't really very funny at the moment, when he handed me another letter that had been sent through my publishers.

Couldn't believe it!

The letter came from a place called Bongalinga Creek in Western Australia, and it was to inform me that the joint churches of Bongalinga Creek were planning to stage a production of *The Theatrical Tapes of Leonard Thynn,* a book I wrote some years ago about putting on a play for our local drama festival. They apologized for the short notice, and said that because of a very recent, anonymous gift, offered specially for the purpose, they are able to invite me and Leonard to GO TO AUSTRALIA and be at a performance on the twenty-fourth of March this year, and THEY WILL PAY FOR EVERYTHING. Suggested that if I was happy to speak at a few meetings while I was there, they could probably PAY FOR ANNE TO COME AS WELL.

Could hardly speak for excitement. Had to run all the way up to the top of the house and all the way down again for no reason before all the popping, pinging springs in me settled down. Gerald says he'll come too and pay for himself if it all works out. Couldn't wait to tell Anne when she came in at lunchtime. Dreaded her pointing out some tedious wedding or funeral or something that would prevent us going. Needn't have worried. She said the only thing that would have got in the way of me going was if she hadn't been able to go. All three of us did a little dance round the kitchen. So exciting!

I'M AN INTERNATIONAL SPEAKER AND I'M GOING TO AUSTRALIA!

I'M GOING TO AUSTRALIA AND I'M AN INTERNATIONAL SPEAKER!

TO AUSTRALIA I'M GOING IN THE ROLE OF INTERNATIONAL SPEAKER!

SPEAKING IN AUSTRALIA IS WHAT I'M DOING ON AN INTERNATIONAL BASIS!

INTERNATIONAL SPEAKING IS THE BASIS ON WHICH I'M GOING TO AUSTRALIA!

Called Leonard this evening. Told him we were going to Australia and that he would be guest of honour at the play in Bongalinga Creek.

He said, 'Great! Will it involve being away the night?'

Tuesday 8 Feb

In high spirits all day today.

Phone call this evening from the Reverend Spool, rector of St Dermot's at the other end of town.

He said, 'Ah, Mr Plass, may I say –'

'Call me Adrian.'

We international speakers are like that.

'Well, that is most kind, and you must feel free to address me as Vladimir.'

'Vladimir?'

'Vladimir, yes, that's right. Now, Adrian, I am ringing to ask if you might very kindly consider the possibility of favouring us with a visit here at St Dermot's on Sunday March the thirteenth. I do realize, of course, that a person as well known as yourself will already have a very full diary, but I just wondered . . .'

Replied as though flicking through a diary full of international trips. 'Well, let's have a look here. Yes, the Australian trip comes later in the month, so that's no problem . . .'

'Australia – my goodness, what a following you must have, Adrian. I suppose you travel all over the world, do you?'

'Well . . .' Laughed lightly as though I didn't want to make too much of it. 'I wouldn't say that.'

'You wouldn't say that! But I am quite sure it must be true!'

'Oh, no . . .'

'So you feel you may be able to squeeze us in on the thirteenth. It would cause much excitement in the church if it were possible.'

'Yes, I think I can help you there, er, Vladimir. I'll put it into the diary straightaway. That would be the morning service, presumably, would it?'

'Precisely!' said Reverend Spool, who seemed to find everything I said amazingly clever. 'The morning service, that's absolutely right – gosh yes! I really am most grateful, and you must let us know your normal fee for such an occasion. I firmly insist on that.'

'Oh, that's not a problem at all. By the way, Vladimir, I just wondered – your Christian name seems er …'

'Ah, well, yes, no, you see, yes, you're absolutely right, it is indeed an uncommon first name for an English Anglican clergyman, but the simple truth is that as a young, impressionable girl my poor dear mother eloped with a vodka salesman and I, believe it or not, was the product.'

'Oh.'

'Well, thank you once again.'

'Think nothing of it. So I'll see you on March thirteenth at, what – ten o'clock?'

'Ten o'clock is spot on! See you then, and thank you again so much for agreeing to do our children's talk. Goodbye.'

Had actually put the phone down before Spool's final words registered.

A children's talk?

Oh, well, if I can travel across the world to speak I shouldn't have any trouble with a few kids, should I?

Wednesday 9 Feb

before supper

Spent a lot of time at work today thinking about my ministry generally and our trip abroad in particular. Be nice to reach out to people with the gift of healing. Must be wonderful to have a real healing ministry. Not that I'm complaining about what I do, of course. It's just that – well, it must be wonderful.

Got completely distracted by one of my favourite, very satisfying fantasies. It's a wonderful daydream.

Dressed in a very smart suit, I'm walking slowly up the centre aisle of a huge, packed auditorium, while a band plays softly on the stage behind me. Yearning, pleading eyes try to catch mine as I pass. Imploring arms stretch out in the desperate hope that perhaps just the touch of my coat against the sufferer's fingers might bring healing. Eventually, I am confronted by a mere child in a wheelchair. She forces a smile onto her broken, pretty little face as she senses the aura of spiritual power that surrounds me. My eyes fill with compassionate tears as I lay a hand on the thin, twisted shoulder of this tiny victim of the Fall. 'What do you want of me?' I ask, in a deep, cosmically resonant sort of voice (rather like the one in the lager adverts). 'I want to be able to walk,' she whispers. 'And so you shall,' I reply. 'And so you shall. In the name of Jesus – be healed!' Slowly, dramatically, she pushes herself to her feet, her pain-filled eyes alight with a new, radiant hope, and then, suddenly, she is running, running, running, along the length of the aisle and up onto the stage. Gasps of amazement are followed by loud and prolonged applause as I follow her into the spotlight, only to turn modestly away towards the darkness of the wings, my expression one of mingled exhaustion, joy and pain. For none can guess the draining personal cost of this great and selfless work. Who can tell –

'Got 'ny tissues?'

Hate real life sometimes. Fancy having to move from a massive auditorium full of adoring, tragically needy people and a chronically sick child in a wheelchair – to Everett Glander with a cold. Especially as I only had one tissue left and I was about to use it to dry my eyes after being so moved by the thought of my great healing ministry. Really resented giving away my last paper handkerchief to someone who persistently refuses to be converted. Glander's been along to a few church things since he met Frank Braddock at our party a few years ago, but nothing seems to quite do the trick. If I didn't know God was perfect I'd say that he'd missed a few excellent opportunities with Glander. Wonder if he'd be any different if he was redeemed. Hope so. At the moment he has the knack of saying the one thing you really don't want to hear. That's what he did today after I'd given him my last tissue.

'Why don't you ask God to make my cold better – or do I not qualify for some reason? Or is it just that *he* hasn't found a cure for the common cold either? Or is it –'

'Everett, if God wanted to heal your cold, he could do it just like that.'

Snapped my fingers, then turned back to my work with what was supposed to be a that's-the-end-of-the-conversation sort of movement. Dreaded him continuing the conversation.

'Well, why would God *not* want to heal my cold, then, old chap?'

Looked at him. Because, I thought silently, he probably finds you as awkward and obnoxious as I do, and a miracle might finally provoke you into coming to church every Sunday, and then I'd have to put up with you for six days a week instead of only five. Unless, of course, we manage to set up a little denomination specially for people like you, called the Seventh Day Everett Glanderites, where members of the congregation raise their objections during worship instead of their arms.

'Because,' I said out loud, 'his will is sovereign, and he is all-knowing. It's probably better for you to have a cold than to not have one, in ways that are difficult for us to understand.'

Glander said, 'Why has your voice gone all high-pitched, Adrian? Something wrong with your throat?'

Muttered under my breath, 'There'll be something wrong with yours if I get my hands round it.'

'So what you're talking about,' rasped on Glander, 'is the old "Living in the Mystery" syndrome, right?'

'Well, I wouldn't put it quite like that, but –'

'All right, then, old man, you give me an example of a reason why it would be better for me to go on having a cold than be healed. Just one'll do.'

He leaned back, sucking his pencil, grinning infuriatingly. Racked my brains for something convincing. Tried to look as if I was calmly selecting one of many possible answers available to me.

I said, 'Well, er, for instance, you might be walking along the road on your way home tonight –'

'Always get the bus just outside the building, old boy.'

'All right, you might get on the bus tonight and happen to be sitting next to an international expert in medical research who –'

'Unlikely to get too many of them on the top deck of the Number 39 to Grey Prospect Road, in my humble view, old man.'

Gritted my teeth. 'Well, this one's a poor but very clever one who's on the brink of discovering – you know – what you said before, a cure for the common cold, and he looks at you sniffing away next to him, and all of a sudden feels inspired. Suddenly the last bit of the jigsaw falls into place, and when he gets home he writes it all down, and before long millions of people have their colds cured, all because God didn't heal you at the moment when you thought it was a good idea.'

Felt quite pleased with myself.

'Yeah, but if he wanted to,' persisted Glander, reminding me of one of those road-drills that carry on their insane clattering right over the last bit of a television programme you particularly wanted to hear, 'he could heal all those millions of people anyway. Or have I got it all wrong?'

'No – I mean, yes, he could.'

'So why doesn't he?'

'Well, because er ... He doesn't heal them because ...'

Screamed silently at God:

WELL, WHY DON'T YOU HEAL THEM, FOR GOODNESS SAKE? IF GLANDER CAN WORK IT OUT, WHY CAN'T YOU?

Glander said, 'Tell you what – just in case it turns out there isn't an international expert on medical research who needs me to sit next to him on the bus tonight, how about praying for my cold to go away now?'

'Now?'

'Now.'

Somehow managed to mumble a miserable prayer, but I hadn't the slightest faith in it being answered. Besides which, if I'm honest, I really hadn't even a remote interest in seeing the state of Everett's nasal passages improved. Part of me rather hoped he might develop complications and die. I can't seem to make Christianity work at all when I'm with him. He sniffed loudly and obviously for the rest of the morning, then he went out to the chemist's at lunchtime and came back with a box of tissues. Paid my one tissue back to me very obviously.

Thank you, God – I don't think!

He could have backed me up, couldn't he? Rather hoping that it'll end like one of those Christian paperbacks, with Everett phoning me later to say that he's healed, and we'll both break down and sob together . . .

later

8 p.m. (after supper)

Anne shouted through just now to say Everett was on the phone. Rushed out to the hall very excited.

'Just called to tell you,' said Everett, 'that a mighty miracle hath occurred.'

'You mean your cold is . . . ?'

'That's right. My cold's no better at all. So, presumably it won't be long before the papers are full of this wonderful new cure you were talking about.'

'Everett, you *know* that was only an ex –'

'I must say, though, Adrian, they're producing a very strange breed of international expert in medical research these days. The one sitting next to me on the bus tonight was the spitting image of a very fat lady with a Charlie Chaplin moustache who happens to live just down the road from me, and I have to be honest and say that, for someone who was just about to crack the medical problem of the century, she didn't seem very excited about my cold, old man. Quite the opposite, in fact. Still, there we are. See you tomorrow – if I'm well enough, that is.'

Went to bed feeling very depressed.

Thursday 10 Feb

Told Anne and Gerald about Glander over breakfast this morning. I said, 'Why couldn't God have just healed his stupid cold and shut him up? I've got to face his big ugly mouth all day today.'

Anne said, 'It does seem a shame you're wasting so much compassion on him, darling, You'd think that all the warmth and love and genuine concern and goodwill that you pour out in his direction would have left him with no choice but to be healed. In future I shouldn't bother to waste all that positive energy on people you see every day. I should save it for people at your meetings. Don't you agree, Gerald?'

Couldn't help thinking Anne was rather overstating the case.

Gerald handed me an envelope with something written on the back. He said, 'How right you are, Mum, and I've written a little poem for Mr E. Bass, much loved lay reader and author of The Scared Dairy, to read out at his very next meeting.'

Read the poem out loud.

'Assist me in this new resolve, oh, Lord,
That those who know and love and suffer me,
Shall one day, through a miracle of Grace,
Enjoy the warmth I use in ministry.'

Yes, all right, all right ...

Went to work knowing that, however wrong my attitude might have been, if I had to put up with another day of Glander's sarcasm I'd really give him something to be healed of. Luckily he was off sick today, so that was all right.

Praise God!

Still couldn't stop thinking about healing all day, though. When I got home I asked Gerald to tell me seriously what he thought about the whole thing.

'Dad,' he said, 'I have thought about that a bit, and it seems to me that, when it comes to things like healing, people tend to rewrite the Bible to fit the way they want things to be. Especially the things Jesus said and did. It beats me how some folk can line up the things they do with what they read in the gospels. There's a sort of religious stubbornness that won't let the straightforwardness of Jesus' approach be a factor in the equation of real day-to-day living. I think it's probably a fear of facing the cosmic shock you get when you open your eyes and actually confront the fact that God really did become a man.'

Totally gobsmacked by this speech. Amazing! Can this really be the same Gerald who, not so very long ago, crept up behind me

339

in the hall, put a raw egg in the hood of my anorak just as I was about to go out in the rain and then laughed himself sick when I came back and said that some huge bird must have laid it from a great height onto the top of my head just as I was pulling the hood up? Hope he doesn't get *too* serious.

Later, Gerald handed me another of these pieces of work he's been doing on the word processor. He said, 'Take a look at this chunk from Not-Luke, Dad. This is the sort of thing I meant about people rewriting Scripture. This must be the way it happened if some Christians I know have got it right.'

This is what Gerald had written:

A man with leprosy cometh and kneeleth before him and saith, 'Lord, if thou art willing thou canst make me clean.' Jesus reacheth out his hand and toucheth the man. 'I am willing,' he saith. 'Be clean!'

And behold, Jesus strolleth away rejoicing, but the leper haileth him with an loud voice, saying, 'Er, excuse me, mayhap it hath escaped thy notice, but I am still an leper. An small point, I know, but important to me.'

And Jesus hisseth through his teeth with vexation and replieth, 'Knoweth thou not that I am heavily into holistic healing? Good heavens, thou must indeed be well naïve if thou thinkest that healing concerneth thy body only. Keepest thou not up with current literature on the subject?'

The man saith, 'All I knoweth is that I was an leper five minutes ago, and behold, I am still an leper.'

'Well,' asserteth Jesus, 'despite thine complaints, thou art, in a very real sense, no longer an leper.'

'Oh, terrific!' persisteth the man, waxing sore sarcastic. 'But I *am* still an leper in the trivial but equally real sense that bits of me have droppeth off, and thou seemest incapable of replacing them.'

Then Jesus snorteth and demandeth, 'Why doth there always have to be one? All right, mate, there existeth a number of possibilities, none of which, I mighteth add, constituteth a failure on the part of myself or any other member of the management team. Counteth them off on thy fingers.'

'It'll have to come to less than three, then,' saith the leper.

Jesus ignoreth him.

'One, thou lackest faith – highly likely. Two, thou hast failed to claim thy healing, a common one, that. Three, thou hast been specially chosen to benefit others through thine own suffering – congratulations. Four, thine healing is to be in the form of death. Byeee! Five, thou art called but not chosen – tough! Anyway, I must departeth. I am up for a big catering contract and the size of the budget challengeth me greatly.'

He goeth, and the leper gathereth himself together, and repeateth over and over to himself, 'I am not an leper! I am not an leper! I am not an leper ...' And behold, from that day forth, he becameth known throughout that country as the Mad Leper.

Don't think I have to worry too much about Gerald getting over-serious!

Anne said tonight, 'I don't know why you're getting such a bee in your bonnet about bodies being healed. That doesn't seem to be your job at the moment. It's true the Reginald and thingy meeting was a disaster, but you know from other meetings you've done, and your books, that God has chosen you to help him heal people's feelings and tensions and worries through making them laugh, and cry a bit and relax. A lot of folk would give their eye-teeth to be able to do that.'

Said to God tonight, 'I expect Anne's right as usual. I should be grateful, I know. It's just that – well, you can't actually see healed feelings jump out of wheelchairs. I'm not complaining ...'

'Yes, you are,' said God.

Friday 11 Feb

Very uneasy about this children's talk I've so foolishly agreed to do. Something tells me I should have rung Spool straight back and made it clear that only a platoon of crazed mercenaries armed with sub-machine-guns would be able to threaten me into addressing one of those ego-bludgeoning groups of small children that you see every now and then chewing up speakers who know nothing about what they're doing. Asked Anne if she thought I'd be all right. She said, 'No, but you promised. Why did you say you'd do it?' I'm going to ring Vladimir and tell him straight out I can't do it. Probably ring him tomorrow.

Saturday 12 Feb

Had an amazing phone call this morning from a lady called Angela in Manchester who'd got my number through directory enquiries. At first I was a bit puzzled and nervous about the way the conversation was going. She told me that her father, Ron, went into hospital last year with a serious illness, and was told that he only had two or three months to live. Ron was deeply depressed, not just about his illness, but about his faith.

Angela said, 'He kept asking all these questions over and over again, and nothing I said made much difference. I mean, I couldn't think what to say for the best. It was awful. I got so upset. Both of us did – Mum and me.'

'What sort of questions?'

'Oh, all kinds. Was he really saved? Did God really care about him? Was he praying properly? Had he done all the things you have to do to make sure you get into heaven? I know it sounds a bit silly, but Dad got himself into a right old stew about what was going to happen after he – well, after he went, you know. He started reading the Bible sort of – I don't know how to put it – *feverishly,* as though he was fuelling up for some long journey, but I'm pretty sure he hardly understood a word of what he was reading. It was just panic, if you know what I mean.'

Wondered what this was all leading up to.

I said, 'And what happened next?'

'Well, that's why I'm phoning. I gave him your book to read – your diary book. Mum bought it for me for my birthday, so I had it on the shelf at home.'

342

Cleared my throat uneasily. 'So, you er . . . gave your father my book to read in the hospital.'

'That's right, yes.'

'And he – '

'He laughed himself to death, Adrian. My Dad laughed himself to death.'

Felt a bit worried. Wanted to ask if this was a good thing or a bad thing, but didn't like to. I could hear Angela was nearly crying on the other end of the phone. I said, 'So, he did – he did enjoy it, then?'

'Oh, Adrian, he really relaxed after that. I think it helped him realize most of those big problems of his were made by men – or people, I mean. You're not supposed to say that sort of thing any more, are you? – not by God. Poor old Dad had somehow forgotten that God loves him, I think, and reading your book gave him back his spiritual common sense, if it's all right to call it that. And, you know, he kept that little book on his bedside locker right up to the very end. Even when he got too bad to read for himself, he used to get me to read bits out to him, and you could hear this little wheezy laugh right in the middle of him. I reckon when he walked into heaven God must have smiled at Dad and said, 'What are you laughing about, Ron?' And Dad will've answered, 'Sorry, it's just this book I was reading . . .' Anyway, I rang just to thank you really, that's all.'

I mumbled, 'No – thank *you* for ringing. Thank you.'

Meant it.

Told Anne about the call. Tears came to her eyes. She said, 'And you moan about not having a healing ministry. God spoils you – you know that, don't you?'

Sunday 13 Feb

This morning Edwin asked the congregation to get into small groups and talk about what we'd want to rescue most if our houses caught fire.

Anne said to me, 'Which of your most valued things would you go back for?'

I said, 'You.'
Multitudinous Brownie points, *and* I meant it!

Monday 14 Feb

Both remembered Valentine's day! A miracle!

Nervous about the first meeting of my support group this evening.

Went quite well in the end. Edwin said we should start off with a small group and build up gradually, so tonight there was just Anne, Gerald, Edwin, Richard and Doreen Cook, Leonard Thynn – I was a bit surprised that Edwin chose Leonard, fond though I am of him – and me.

(Edwin said that if Victoria and Stenneth Flushpool hadn't been away on their African mission trip they would certainly have been part of the group. Amazing to think how much Victoria has changed since we first knew her. There was a time when she made the Pharisees look like angels of mercy. Nowadays, Stenneth is no longer forced to hide his copies of *Balsa Modelling Monthly* under the nuptial mattress because of his wife's belief that he is unhealthily ensnared by full-frontal photographs of Sopwith Camels made of wood. Miss them both really.)

Quite apprehensive, and suddenly very embarrassed at the idea of being the centre of attention in such an obvious way.

Everyone except Leonard arrived on time at about seven-thirty. Needn't have worried about being the centre of attention. They all got chatting immediately, as though it was just a social occasion and they'd forgotten why we were meeting.

Doreen, for instance, who was in a very stiff mood anyway, for some reason, was getting very worked up about unsuitable videos being available to young people in the High Street shops – one of her hobby-horses. Funny thing, although I agree completely with just about everything Doreen says on this subject, the more she talks about it, the more part of me wants to rush out, hire an unsuitable video and make it available to a young person. I think there must be something wrong with my attitude . . .

Gerald listened for a while, then said, 'Actually, Doreen, there's a film showing at the Curzon in town that I think you'd disapprove of, and it's got a "U" certificate, so children of any age can go to it. In fact I actually *saw* small children going in on my way home tonight.'

Anne and I know that slight change in Gerald's voice all too well. We braced ourselves. Doreen leaned forward, the light of holy battle in her eyes.

She said, 'What sort of film is it, Gerald?'

Gerald shook his head worriedly and said, 'I hardly dare tell you, Doreen. It's – well, it's so awful ...'

'Gerald, remember that you are covered.'

I read in my son's eyes his decision to sacrifice the opportunity to make comments about third party fire and theft for the sake of whatever else he had in mind. Nodding solemnly, he continued slowly and gravely.

'Well, all right. It's a story about a family violently ripped apart by cruelty and death. It's a tale of guns and fire and the blind fear that fuels panic-stricken flight. It's a tale of homelessness and isolation and the death of innocence.'

Dramatic silence. Doreen took a notebook and pen from her handbag, and set her mouth in a thin grim line (Like Biggles when bandits appear at two o'clock, Gerald commented later).

'What is the name of the film?' she demanded, with a sort of verbal roll of drums.

'*Bambi*,' said Gerald.

Doreen's reactions to Gerald's nonsense never cease to amaze me. She simply closed her notebook, clicked her Biro, and replaced both items in her handbag. She then sat back in her chair quite unmoved, as though the forty second capsule of time containing this little interchange had never actually existed.

I've noticed this before with people who are in permanently religious mode. It's as if their personality computers have been programmed in a very limited way. In this case, Doreen, having pressed her SEARCH button and keyed in GERALD HAS MADE A JOKE, had received a message on her mental screen which read: INVALID REQUEST: NO SUCH FILE: GERALD-HAS-MADE-A-JOKE NOT KNOWN: TRY COATES, and abandoned the whole thing.

Richard, on the other hand, nodded as if he understood perfectly, and said, 'Ah yes, I believe that is the word commonly employed to describe young ladies who are, shall we say – wanton.'

All stared at Richard.

'I refer,' he explained, colouring a little, 'to those scenes that one cannot avoid witnessing inadvertently on the television from time to time, where a man is said to be out walking with "some new bambi on his arm".'

Anne said gently, 'I think the word you're thinking of is "bimbo", Richard. Bambi is a little deer ...'

'Expensive, you mean?'

'No-no, *Bambi* is the name of a little deer ...'

'But in that case, why on earth – '

Just as Richard's confusion began to acquire a truly surrealistic quality, the doorbell interrupted proceedings, thank goodness. Answered the door. On the step was a figure leaning unsteadily on a stick, its head, arms and legs covered in bandages. A frail, quavery voice emerged from a crack in the bandages around the face.

'Please pray for me to be healed.'

I just don't believe Thynn sometimes. Told him to come in and stop being stupid. Incredible! Sat himself down in the sitting-room, bandages and all, and explained that he'd thought it would give my talks a 'bit of a boost' if he came along to the odd meeting in his 'cripple outfit' and got miraculously healed on the spot.

He said, 'It'd put God in a better light, wouldn't it?'

'But, Leonard,' I almost screamed, 'that would be telling lies, wouldn't it? We don't want people to believe in God because of a lie, do we?'

'Oh, don't we?' said Leonard, sounding genuinely surprised.

'You mean it's all right to tell the truth about everything?'

'Of course it is.'

'Everything?'

'Yes.'

'Oh, I see. Good! In that case I can tell everyone why I thought it was all right to tell lies. You see – well, you know the other night when Anne was away and we watched the late film at your house, Adrian?'

Glanced round nervously at the others and said warily, 'Ye-e-es.'

'Well, you know you and Gerald drank a whole bottle of wine each and I didn't have any because I can't?'

Glanced even more nervously at Anne. 'A bit of an exaggeration, I think, Leonard, don't you?'

Gerald said, 'Mmm, that is a bit of an exaggeration, Leonard. Dad had one and a half bottles – I only had about three glasses.'

'Oh, that's right, sorry, Gerald,' said Leonard, 'you were drinking out of a glass, I'd forgotten that. Adrian was lying on the sofa swigging straight out of the bottle – I mean bottles plural.'

Felt my face flaming. So much for wanting Thynn to tell the truth! How were my support group going to deal with this mental picture of the great evangelist sprawled across the living-room at midnight with a bottle of booze attached to his mouth like a baby's dummy?

'Just a minute, I don't understand,' said Anne, 'you can't possibly have drunk both bottles. There were only two to start with, and I remember seeing one left when I got the Hoover out the next afternoon.'

'Oh, I forgot that,' said Leonard, 'but I remember now. Adrian said he'd have to nip out quick in the morning and get another one to put in the cupboard so you wouldn't know.'

Mentally checked my life-insurance policies. Surely Thynn could see that not telling lies doesn't necessarily mean you have to tell the *whole truth*.

'Anyway, just before you finished the second bottle, you started talking about your meetings, and you got up and stood on the sofa with a Bible balanced on your head and said you were going to bring people to faith by hook or by crook. And when I asked you what that meant, you said it meant that it doesn't matter whether people are converted by bishops or con men. Then, just as you were going to say something else you fell off the sofa and rolled onto the floor and lay there singing "Roll me over, lay me down and do it again", and you said it was an old chorus about being slain in the Spirit. And that's why I thought it didn't matter if we told lies. Sorry.'

Felt strangely calm.

I said, 'Well, there we are then. It's nice to have this little group of people here to witness three significant endings – the end of my ministry, the end of my marriage and the end of Leonard Thynn's life when the rest of you have gone.' Shook my head in despair. 'I'm ever so sorry, everybody. Sorry, Anne. I can't tell you how embarrassed I am by all that stuff about the other night, especially going out and getting another bottle and all that. I really suggest the best thing is that you all go quietly home and we just forget about the whole thing. Sorry . . .'

'We can still have the food, though, can't we?' said Thynn sensitively.

Edwin cleared his throat and leaned forward, clasping his hands and resting his arms on his knees. He studied the floor as he began to speak.

'Now look, Adrian, the reason I chose the people who are here in this room to be the nucleus of your support group is that they are all people who love you. And we don't love you because you're perfect. You're not – any more than I am. We're fond of you because of lots of things, and despite a few other things. Do you understand that?' He looked up at me. I nodded, feeling a bit weepy. 'We don't want to support a writer or a speaker. We want to support *you*, the real you, not some shined up, falsely virtuous character who doesn't really exist. The things that happened the other night when Anne was away – well, let's just say I would have been embarrassed as well if they'd been described in front of other people, but, let's face it, every one of us here has almost certainly got some personal skeleton in the cupboard that we wouldn't be at all keen to put on public view. Something that God has forgiven but still makes us feel a bit guilty sometimes. Isn't that right, everybody?'

He looked enquiringly around at the other members of the group. Anne, Gerald and Leonard nodded agreement straightaway.

Richard looked terrified. Clutched his Bible to his chest with both arms like a comforter and said, 'Er, well, of course, Scripture does allow that a – a thorn in the flesh may be allowed by the Lord for purposes of growth in the area of humility, but er ...'

'It's all right, Richard,' said Edwin, smiling a little, 'you don't have to tell us what your particular thorn actually is. I'm just making the point that we've all got at least a thorn or two – *and* a load of marks from old thorns that God has got rid of, so none of us can afford to judge anyone else, can we?'

'Oh, no,' replied Richard, relieved to be back on safe ground, 'there is certainly no question of judgment of others. I – I would like to express my full support to Adrian in his ministry and I – I agree with all that Edwin er – all that Edwin has said about er ... it.'

I think Doreen might have liked to inform us that those who are in Christ are a new creation, and therefore without sin, but she contented herself with nodding in a slow, overtly compromising sort of way. 'We shall support Adrian as he seeks to do the Lord's work in every way possible,' she said.

Gerald whispered in my ear, 'I'm glad we're not going to compare thorns behind the bike-sheds.'

'The point is, Adrian,' continued Edwin, 'that as you get even more well known, I'm afraid most people will tend to lose sight of the real person behind the books and talks – they always do – and that's not going to be easy for you. That's what this group is for. We'll all still be dealing with the Adrian Plass that's frail and human and exactly the same as us – the person that we love. I think it's good that Leonard told us about what happened the

349

other night. It means we start clean – and, with a bit of luck, we'll stay clean.'

Doreen said, 'I am sure, Edwin, that when you speak of a "bit of luck", you are actually referring to the Grace of God?'

'Well, yes,' sighed Edwin, 'of course, Doreen, I meant that we shall stay clean by the Grace of God.'

'With a bit of luck,' added Gerald, making most of us laugh.

After that the meeting went well. We decided that the group would meet as and when needed, but at least once in every three months or so. Each session was to consist of a report from me on things that had already happened, including problems and difficulties that needed prayer and advice, followed by a look at my forthcoming diary and discussion about the future. We agreed that any of us could contribute any view we wanted as long as we were ready to discover that we were wrong.

Hmmm …

Finally, someone – a different person each time – would do a short Bible-study before we prayed together. Edwin said that he would 'enrich' the group by adding one or two other people as time went by, but refused to say who they might be. Didn't quite like to ask if Norma would be one of them. Not that she's – you know, special to me in any way …

Prayed for a while about a talk I'm doing in Derby on February sixteenth, and an outreach dinner on Saturday the nineteenth. Been trying to pretend to myself that the children's talk doesn't exist, but thought I'd better mention it. Hoped someone would have a word from God to say I shouldn't do it, but no one did. Think I'll cancel it anyway. I'll definitely call Vladimir tomorrow.

Had coffee and relaxed and chatted after that. One or two highlights. When Richard asked Anne to pass him the concordance, Thynn said, 'Oh, great, we're going to have a sing-song, are we?'

Incredibly, he wasn't joking.

When Anne explained what a concordance was, Leonard was absolutely scandalized. Said to Edwin, 'All those weeks you've stood up the front going from passage to passage to passage about the same thing, and I've always thought, "Blimey! I wish I knew my Bible well enough to do that." And all the time you were using a – a camcorder.'

'Concordance,' corrected Edwin, 'and you're dead right, Leonard, I cheat every time.'

A little embarrassing when Gerald took it upon himself to tell everyone that he thought I ought to be fully aware of the rules that govern something he calls the 'White Envelope Game'.

He said, 'I've seen Dad playing it ever so many times without realizing what it is, but I should think most Christian speakers play it at one time or another. What happens is this. The meeting finishes, and the bloke who's done the talk – let's call him Cedric the Speaker – knows that, at some point soon, one of the organizers is almost certain to approach him holding a white envelope with his name written on the front. And, of course, Cedric's very keen on this because the envelope has usually got some cash or a cheque in it. The trouble is – the first and strictest rule of the White Envelope Game is that the speaker isn't allowed to give any indication that he's even remotely interested in receiving such a thing, so he begins – '

Anne interrupted. 'If the time comes to leave and the envelope hasn't appeared yet, Cedric begins a sort of have-I-said-goodbye-to-everyone? dance, which consists of going around shaking hands in an impressively conscientious way, hoping that when he comes to the one who's got the cash, his or her memory will be jogged enough to get it out and part with it.'

Gerald looked admiringly at his mother. 'Good one, Mumsy! You're absolutely right. Anyway, sooner or later the person in question – let's call him George – approaches Cedric with the white envelope clutched in his hand, and it's at this point that the game begins in earnest.'

'Gerald,' I broke in, 'I'm quite sure that no one else wants to hear all this nonsense.'

Looked around seeking confirmation, but Edwin said, 'Oh, yes we do! Carry on, Gerald. As an occasional White Envelope distributor *and* collector myself, I find this all most interesting.'

'Right, well, having, as Mum said, hung around for ages to make sure he actually gets offered the White Envelope, Cedric now appears to be strangely incapable of perceiving the object when someone is virtually holding it under his nose. In fact, at this point Cedric will usually set off through the door, apparently leaving, but actually confident in the knowledge that he'll be stopped long before he gets outside.

'And, naturally, he is. Deeply impressed by the fact that Cedric the Speaker didn't miss even the humblest soul in his farewells, and that he's too ethereally absorbed to even *notice* money when it's offered to him, the holder of the White Envelope briskly pursues the saintly figure, stopping him in the porch and saying something along the following lines:

'"We thought – well, we just wanted to – you know – say thank you for – well, for coming and – well, we'd like you to accept this with our – you know ..."

'The time has now come for Cedric to role-play a subtle and quite endearing combination of confusion and puzzlement. He holds the envelope in his hand, peering curiously at it as though the concepts of "white" and "envelope" are completely new in his experience.

'"What on earth – ? What's this? Good heavens, I never expected ..."

'"Oh, it's just – just nothing," says George shyly, "really it's nothing – it's just nothing – just a little something to say – you know ..."

'A sudden revelation seems to hit Cedric like a thunderbolt. He's being given some money! Well, what a profound, totally unexpected, mind-numbing shock! He shakes his head with the wonder of it all.

'"You didn't have to give me this," he murmurs, nevertheless holding tightly on to the envelope as he speaks, "I certainly didn't do it for – well, for any sort of reward, except, of course, just knowing that the Lord is ..."

'"Oh, we know that!" replies George hurriedly, embarrassed that a spiritual giant of this magnitude should be burdened with something as vulgar as money, "but, for your ministry – well, just a small gift."

'Cedric quickly tucks the unopened envelope away in the inside pocket of his jacket as if its contents are of no interest to him whatsoever. It's quite possible, his manner suggests, that he will completely forget it's there and *never* bother to open it up to see what it contains. One more firm clasp of George's hand and a momentary engagement of his eyes in order to convey godly depth, prayerful good wishes, and warm gratitude, then outside and into the car for a dignified pulling away, a final wave and a sudden halt at a quiet spot three streets away to drag the White Envelope from the inside pocket and *rip it open* to find out how much he's got . . .'

Leonard said, 'Blimey! It's hard work being a speaker, innit? I don't think I could do all that.'

'Richard and I would be pleased to offer ministry to you, Adrian, if this pattern of deceit and wrong motivation is truly part of your experience,' offered Doreen.

Was about to reply but Edwin chuckled and said, 'Come on now, Doreen, that was a bit of a caricature that Gerald gave us, but I don't mind confessing that it wasn't so far from how I was a few years ago when the old shoe was pinching most of the time. You didn't want to look greedy, but you really hoped there'd be some cash involved because then you could do something unusual like – eat. Even now my motives are pretty mixed up. Always will be, I should think, but God knows about all that, because,' he finished simply, 'I tell him.'

Doreen cleared her throat slightly worriedly. 'Richard, have you er, encountered any of these er . . . feelings?'

Richard said, 'My own experience on those few occasions that I have performed a visiting speaker's role have differed from the hypothetical Cedric's in one particular way.'

Doreen looked relieved. 'And what is that difference?'

'Well,' replied Richard slowly, 'I never rip the envelope apart – I open it carefully so that I can save it and use it again . . .'

Tuesday 15 Feb

Everett Glander is like one of those splinters in the hand that you should have taken out when it first went in, but you didn't and now it's got so far under your skin that you can't shift it. Wish he'd either move to China or get converted and go to some church that isn't ours.

Hate me hating him . . .

Wednesday 16 Feb

Back at my hotel in Derby after speaking this evening. What a day!

I have had some extremely annoying conversations in my time, but this morning's encounter with a man who is paid regular money to supply the public with information about trains just about takes the biscuit. I realize that more and more people are being trained as counsellors, but if there aren't enough jobs to go round at the moment I really don't see why they should be inflicted on the general public.

Granted, it was me who made the mistake in the first place – I accept that. I forgot to set the alarm and ended up flinging myself down the road with a heavy case to the station. Flung myself on to the platform and found what I thought was the Derby train just about to go. Flung myself and case on, discovered instantly that it was the non-stop Flaxton train, flung myself off, remembered my case was still on, flung myself round intending to fling myself back on, and found that the train was moving out. Wanted to die. Worn out with flinging myself around. Knew I'd have to get the next train to Flaxton to get my case back, and then take a cross-country train to Derby. Just time if I was lucky with connections. Naïvely thought that I could find out about the next train to Flaxton from the travel centre. Arrived at the desk in a bit of a state, to find a young man with what I can only describe as a soppy grin on his face nodding at me like a toy dog in the back of a car. As far as I recall the dialogue went as follows.

ME: (WILDLY) Which train do I get to Flaxton?

MAN: (SLOWLY AND INSIGHTFULLY) Okay – which train do you want to get to Flaxton?

ME: (INCREDULOUS PAUSE) One that goes there, please. Soon! What are you talking about? Do you think I want a Flaxton train that *doesn't* go to Flaxton? Are you stupid or something?

MAN: (STILL NODDING AND SMILING) Thank you for sharing your anger with me.

ME: (COMPLETELY LOSING MY RAG AND HOPING HE DOESN'T READ CHRISTIAN BOOKS) I'll be sharing a left hook with you in a minute, if you –

MAN: (INTERRUPTING) Can I ask you something?

ME: (FAINTLY) *You* want to ask *me* something?

MAN: Do I remind you of your father?

ME: (APPROACHING HYSTERIA) No, you don't remind me of my father. My father was sane and helpful. Look! It's very simple really. I've left my case on the Flaxton train and I've got to get it back in time to get to Derby because I'm speaking there tonight. All right?

MAN: Okay, let's just unpack this.

ME: (ARRIVING AT HYSTERIA) I'd love to unpack it, you dozy pillock, but it's on its way to Flaxton!

MAN: (THERAPEUTICALLY APPRECIATIVE) Mmmm, oka-a-a-y! Humour's always good.

ME: (HAMMERING ON THE DESK WITH MY FISTS) Never mind humour! Never mind anything else! Just tell me which train I get to Flaxton. Tell me now!

MAN: May I tell you what I'm hearing you say?

ME: (A LOW GROWLING NOISE) Rrrrr . . .

MAN: What I feel I'm hearing you say – what I think I'm hearing the child in you say, friend, is that you don't want to go to Derby at all, and that's why you unconsciously made the

355

decision to leave your case on the Flaxton train. You actually never want to see that suitcase again. Am I resonating?

ME: (DEFEATED – HEAD DOWN ON THE COUNTER, MORE OR LESS SOBBING) Look, couldn't you please just tell me when the next train to Flaxton goes? That's all I want – I just want to go to Flaxton. Please lemme go to ...

MAN: (WITH WARM APPROVAL) All *ri-i-ight!* That's good, let it all out. Exteriorize the pain and we can deal with it together. (COMPASSIONATELY AND WITH IMMENSE SIGNIFICANCE) I guess that in a deeply real sense you've been wanting that case to become Flaxton's problem for a very, very long time. Am I right? (PAUSE – SUDDENLY EFFICIENT) Okay, well, I suggest you come back in a week's time, and in the meantime I'd like you to do some work on how you think you'd relate to Derby if it was a girl you were taking to the pictures. Who would pay? Would you sit in the back row? Might there be a subsequent pizza situation? That sort of thing. Now let me see ... (CONSULTS A DIARY) Yes, I can fit you in at eleven o'clock on Wednesday morning. And please – (PLAYFULLY) no spillage. Agreed?

ME: (HOMICIDALLY CALM) I really do suggest that, for your own sake, you should listen ever so carefully to what I am about to say. You are a person who is paid to provide information about trains to customers who need it. I, on the other hand, am a customer who needs a very small item of that information. If you do not provide a simple, factual answer to the next question that I ask, I promise you that I shall climb over to the side where you are, kneel on your chest, and make you eat the whole of the very substantial British Rail timetable that lies between us here on the counter. Now – when does the next train for Flaxton depart from this station?

PAUSE

MAN: Nine o'clock.

ME: Thank you for sharing that information with me.

Managed to get my case back and get to Derby all right in the end, but I was all hot and bothered by the time I got to the church where I was speaking. Stood out in the entrance porch for a little while signing books for people coming in.

Most embarrassing incident occurred.

A lady came up to me, held out one of my books, and said, 'Would you mind signing this for my friend, Eileen, only she's – well, she's inside.'

Pictured Eileen sitting in some lonely prison cell, and wrote in the book:

TO EILEEN
MAY YOU, BY SOME MIRACLE, BE FREE EVEN IN THAT PLACE.

Gave it back to the lady, who stared at what I'd written for a second, then said, 'No, no, I mean she's inside the church – she went in before me . . .'

Got her a new book and changed the message to BEST WISHES. Felt a real fool.

Good evening after that. People really seemed to eat up the idea that God loved them.

Later in the week, when I told Edwin the 'inside' story, he said that he knew the church in question, and thought I'd probably got it right the first time.

Tried to repent of my crossness with the British Rail man, but I didn't find it easy. I know Jesus never sinned, but I'm pretty sure that bloke would have stretched him close to breaking point.

Thursday 17 Feb

Couldn't stop thinking about this children's talk all the way back from Derby. Must phone Reverend Spool. All becoming a bit of a nightmare. Spoiling all my enjoyment of thinking about Australia. Too tired tonight – do it tomorrow . . .

Friday 18 Feb

Finally summoned up the courage to phone Vladimir Spool, but – PRAISE GOD! – he wasn't in.

Gerald, who was sitting by the fire with a book, looked up as I put the phone down and said, 'Is this vicar bloke really called Vladimir?'

'Yes.'

'Do you know if he was ever a smoker?'

Sensed that a very, very bad joke was imminent.

'No, why?'

'Because if he was, I bet I know what his congregation nick-named him.'

'And what might that have been?'

'Vlad the Inhaler.'

Saturday 19 Feb

Off to speak at an outreach dinner this evening with Thynn, who said he wanted to have a go at selling books for me, and Ger-ald, who, apart from anything else, likes free dinners.

Always feel a bit uneasy about these outreach affairs. When I think of all the planning and work and prayer culminating in me standing up for half an hour and saying silly things, I get quite panicky. Felt even more nervous this time, because the lady orga-nizing the dinner, somebody called Eve Worthington, had said on the phone that they were expecting the vast majority of the people who came to be non-Christians who had 'never been exposed to the raw Gospel' before. Not at all sure I was capable of produc-ing the 'raw Gospel' for them to be exposed to. As we drove up the motorway, Gerald said I shouldn't get too worried because, in his experience, anticipated 'vast majorities' of non-Christians almost always resolve themselves into rather small minorities when it comes to the crunch.

He was absolutely right.

When we got to the hotel where the dinner was happening I asked Eve Worthington, who turned out to be a jolly little round ball of a person, how many of the diners were Christians by her reckoning. Tried to sound as if I desperately hoped they would *all* be non-Christians so that I could expose them to the r. G. and convert every one.

She whispered confidentially in my ear, 'Well, it hasn't worked out quite as we'd hoped, I'm afraid.'

Thought – Yesss!

Said, 'Oh, I'm *very* disappointed to hear that. It'll be nearly all Christians, then, will it?'

'Actually, there's only one non-Christian here,' said Eve.

Deeply thrilled, but a little surprised. The gap between a 'vast majority' and 'one' seemed a bit dramatic, to say the least.

'His name's Brian,' whispered Eve, 'and he's a neighbour of ours. I asked him to come right in the middle of my husband George getting covered in oil and grease fixing his car when it wouldn't start one Saturday, so he couldn't really refuse, could he? He'd be so useful in the Kingdom – he's a bank manager.'

Obviously felt it unnecessary to decode this cryptic statement. Brought her mouth even closer to my ear, and hissed enthusiastically, 'He's very close, you know! We've sat you opposite him at dinner.' Drew her head back, smiling and nodding significantly at me. My heart sank. I always turn into a worm in the presence of bank managers, and I never know what to say to people I'm supposed to 'do my stuff' on. Really dreaded dinner.

Went to find the toilet before sitting down (at the dinner-table, I mean). Just stood by the wash basins talking to God. 'I feel useless,' I said. 'I feel nervous and stupid and ugly and faithless and I want to go home.'

'Hallelujah! Go forth in victory!' said a voice from one of the cubicles.

Nearly dropped dead on the spot.

There was a flushing noise and Gerald emerged, grinning. 'Not feeling too good, then, Dad?'

So relieved it was Gerald in the cubicle I didn't even get cross. I said, 'Gerald, I don't think I have ever looked forward to an event less. My faith is about the size of a pea.'

'That big, eh?'

'What?'

'Well, a pea's bigger than a mustard seed. Hey, Dad, you might even get to move that famous paper-clip at last.'

'Very funny.'

'Besides,' said Gerald, drying his hands at what he always insists on calling the Evangelist Machine ('hot air that takes a long time to produce a rather unsatisfactory result'), 'it can be quite dangerous to walk in victory – look what happened to Lord Nelson.' Patted my shoulder. 'Come on, Dad, you'll be all right.'

It's nice to have your grown-up son encouraging you, but what on earth has Lord Nelson got to do with anything?

Eve Worthington's belief that Brian the bank manager was 'close' didn't appear justified at all. Closer to getting up and walking out than becoming a Christian, if you'd asked me. He was a broad-shouldered man with grizzled grey hair and one of those lined, strong, capable faces that seem to be produced by years of dealing with people and situations on an official basis. Must have been near to retirement age.

When I sat down opposite him, he folded his arms and stared at me with one eyebrow raised, as if to say, 'Go on, then, convert me – if you dare!'

Shook hands and introduced myself nervously as the speaker. Managed to resist a strong temptation to tell him that my account was in perfect order at the moment, and that I would do my very best to ensure that it remained so in the future.

He said, 'So you're the chap who's going to bring us all to our knees, are you? Well, I wish you luck, because you're going to need it.'

He was so resonantly confident that, as the meal went on, my voice almost disappeared altogether, as it usually does when I feel overwhelmed. Not such a bad thing probably, because my bleating protests that I wasn't trying to convert anyone, and my pathetic attempts to engage him in conversation on the subject of banking, about which I know nothing whatsoever, were not worth hearing anyway. He seemed so sure and relaxed and self-contained in his brief answers to my questions, I couldn't imagine him identifying any area of his life that needed the sort of God who was misguided enough to allow himself to be publicly represented by a nerd like me.

(The Oxford English Dictionary, by the way, defines a 'nerd' as a feeble, foolish or uninteresting person, and that's *exactly* how I felt.)

By the time coffee had been served and someone had done an effusive introduction, I was experiencing the strange illusion, known to public speakers everywhere, that ice-cold hands belonging to people who didn't like me were gripping a selection of my internal organs as tightly as possible.

To make matters worse, Eve Worthington, bless her little Christian socks, had positioned herself in such a way that she was able to keep me and Brian the bank manager in view at the same time. She sent an excruciatingly unsubtle wink in my direction, whilst coyly miming her intention to pray throughout my talk by steepling her hands together for a moment in her lap. I resolved to avoid her eye at all costs until I'd finished.

Don't really know why I laid into the Church as heavily as I did when I spoke that evening. Maybe it was the only thing I could do with my confidence so low. It's always simpler to be negative than positive. You can get people laughing more easily when you look at what's wrong with the Church than when you talk about what's right with it.

Whatever the reason, I just know I went on and on about how Christians say silly things, and use silly voices, and sing silly songs, and have silly expectations, and do outreach in silly ways, and read silly books. In fact, on the basis of my talk, there was only one conclusion any outsider could have reached about the Church – it was silly.

One strange and embarrassing thing happened. About halfway through, when I was in full 'silly' flow, I had a sort of thought or feeling or understanding or – oh, I don't know how to describe it. I asked Anne what she thought it was afterwards and she said God was talking to me. I'm glad she said that, because that is what it felt like, but it seems so big-headed to say that God is *talking* to you. Anyway, just to be on the safe side I passed it on to all the people who were there.

I said, 'Look, I could be wrong, but I think God is saying to me that there are some people here tonight who need to forgive God.'

Panicked suddenly at what I could hear coming out of my own mouth. 'Of course,' I went on hastily, 'he can't actually do anything wrong to be forgiven for, but that's what's so difficult sometimes, isn't it? I mean – well, it's not very easy to have a real row with someone who never ever gets anything wrong, is it?' Suddenly seemed to know exactly what to say. 'I mean, there must be some of us who want to climb up onto God's lap like small children and bash at his chest with our little fists, and say, "I hate you! I hate you! I hate you! I asked you to help me and you *didn't* help me. You knew what I was feeling – you *knew* what needed to happen and you didn't do it. You say you love me, but you don't! If you did you would have done something, but you didn't! I hate you!"'

Suddenly spotted Gerald's face, his eyes wide with surprise at what I was saying. Remembered when he was just a little boy.

'When my son was very small,' I said, hoping Gerald wouldn't mind, 'he did exactly that once or twice. First, he'd be really angry, and then when he'd worn himself out with crossness, he'd cry, all curled up on my lap. Then, when he'd cried the last drop of energy away, he'd just fall asleep and I'd hold him for ages. And the important thing is – I think the important thing is that *he had to go through* all that fighting and fretting to get the nasty spiky feelings out of himself, and he did it all in the safest place he knew, which was in my arms.'

Gerald's not the sort of chap whose eyes mist over much, but when I glanced at him I'm pretty sure that's what they were doing.

I looked around at the other faces in the room. 'God doesn't mind you being angry with him,' I said.

What was I saying?

'He's used to taking the blame. In fact he'd rather you took it out on him than someone else.' Snatched a breath. 'We'll just spend about five minutes now – those who need to, that is – telling God about the resentment and anger they feel towards him. And anyone who doesn't need to do that can pray for the ones who do.'

Somewhat aghast at what I'd said, and five minutes lasts about three days when a hundred people are made to sit silently in the middle of what was supposed to be a talk. Kept wanting to cut the time down so that people wouldn't get bored or fall asleep or think I was being ridiculous. Five minutes was up at last, thank goodness. Got back into the silly flow, much to the relief of a little group of young teenagers who'd nearly died of containment during the 'Forgiving God' pause.

Could tell from the expression on Eve's face as I finished talking twenty minutes later, that, as far as she was concerned, I had quite definitely not delivered the evangelical goods. And when I risked a glance at Brian the banker, I could understand why she might feel like that. He looked *grim*. As I sat down to a mixture of applause, ranging from a polite patter to enthusiastic hooting from the teenagers, he leaned across the table towards me. Steeled myself to hearing that my overdraft facility was cancelled for all eternity.

He laid a hand on my arm and said, 'Let me help you sell your books.'

I gulped and said, 'All right – thank you.'

Walked over to the book table with him to find Thynn waiting for customers. Introduced Leonard to Brian the bank manager.

'Right, Leonard, my friend,' said Brian, still quite grimly, 'we're going to sell all these books now, and I'm going to need your help. You pass them to me as fast as I flog them, okay?'

Thynn nodded blankly, and said, 'We're going to sell them *all*?'

'No reason why not. Here we go!' Suddenly produced a huge voice that filled the room. 'Excuse me! Everybody look this way, please!'

Never seen anything like it in my life. Brian took a pile of books in his hand and literally sold them by the sheer force of his personality. Every time someone raised a hand to indicate that they wanted a book he flung it across the room to them like a frisbee, shouting, 'Pay at the table! Come on – who's next? Speaker's books! Buy one before they all run out! Thank you, madam – thank you, sir!'

People rather enjoyed it once they got the hang of it. And my self-appointed salesman was right. Every single book we'd

brought got sold. Wonderful! Thynn was in his element, handing books over to Brian as fast as he needed them, while Gerald took money and gave change, and I signed copies for anyone who asked me to. Ended up with the table a sea of notes and coins. There's something very satisfying about lots of money. Maybe there shouldn't be, but there is.

Afterwards, Brian sat at one of the tables with me, sipping at a glass of wine and staring into the distance for a few moments before saying anything. When he did look me straight in the eyes all I could feel was profound fear about what he'd say when he learned that I'd forgotten to fill my cheque stubs in properly, and wouldn't be able to accurately state the balance of my account.

'Wondering why I helped you sell your books, are you?'

'Er ... well, yes, I suppose so – very grateful, of course ...'

Brian gazed into the distance again. 'When I was a young man of twenty-one, I was quite into religion – well, Christianity, not just religion. Had been for a good few years. Involved a lot at school and college and so forth. And then, one summer when I was home from college, my kid sister, Millie, who was about ten years younger than me . . .'

The strong face crumpled a little.

'Millie was suddenly taken ill at about tea-time on a Wednesday – and I really mean suddenly. One minute she was right as rain, the next she'd collapsed and been whisked off to the local hospital in an ambulance with some – I dunno – some throat thing. They had to do one of those operations, a tracheotomy it's called, isn't it, actually *in* the ambulance on the way to hospital, although I didn't know that was going on at the time, of course. I just knew she was really bad. I'd heard these awful gasping noises she made as she was carried out to the ambulance, and I was left alone in the house. My mother had followed on in a neighbour's car to be there when the ambulance arrived.'

The resonant voice rumbled with emotion.

'I adored that little sister of mine. Full of life and sunshine, she was. A real innocent – can't have had more than about ten minutes of unhappiness in the whole of her life. Millie. My little sister. I wanted her to live so much. Went upstairs to her bedroom and knelt down among all her silly girly things – things she squeaked and laughed over with her friends, things that meant a lot to her, and I asked God – really *asked* him – to make her better and bring her home again. I wept. Could have sworn he heard me. And I couldn't see how he could refuse anyone who was raging with feeling like I was. I got up in the end, quite calm, and went downstairs to make a cup of tea. I knew it would be all right, you see. God was going to answer my prayer. Then – I'll never forget it, because the kettle began whistling at the precise moment the phone rang. An unforgettable combination. It was my mother on the phone to say that Millie had only lasted ten minutes after she reached the hospital. She must have died more or less the same time that I got up from saying my prayer – my useless prayer. Never did have that particular cup of tea.'

He took another sip of wine.

'After that I wanted nothing to do with God – if he existed. I'd asked him – begged him to save Millie, but he didn't. Why not? No one offered me any answers that sounded halfway reasonable, and I didn't particularly want to hear them anyway. I hated God, and I've gone on hating him ever since in a quiet sort of way.

'Tonight, when you started reading your stuff and going on about all the things that are up the creek with corporate Christianity, it – well, for a start it took me by surprise. I thought you were going to go through all the treacly gentle Jesus stuff, and I'd already decided treacle was just what I didn't want for my fourth course tonight. Your stuff seemed to – how can I describe something that doesn't make more than a ha'p'orth of sense? It seemed to open this narrow little back door that I might even want to squeeze through some time. And then, when you did that bit about forgiving God – look, I've got to ask you this – do you always do that bit? I mean, is it part of the act?'

Shook my head. 'Never done it before. It just – happened. Bit embarrassing actually.'

Brian the bank manager leaned forward and placed his hand on my arm, just as he had done before. 'Don't be embarrassed,' he said very quietly. 'You see – I went home this evening. Suddenly remembered where I live. Stomped in, tried to get cross, wept a bit, and tonight – tonight I'm going to sleep better than I've slept for a very long time.'

Told Gerald and Thynn all about Brian on the way home. Gerald just nodded slowly, stared out of the window and said nothing.

Thynn said, 'Maybe there's a God after all . . .'

Sunday 20 Feb

Thought about Glander in church today when Edwin was talking about loving your enemies. How can you love someone when you actually want to smash their teeth in? Prayed for him because Jesus said we should.

I said, 'Father, I hate Everett Glander, I really do. I wish he'd stop existing so that I could feel better about myself. You said

366

we've got to pray for our enemies, so I'm going to grit my teeth and do it now. Whatever I think of Everett, will you meet him somehow and give him all he needs, and if you've got any spare miracles hanging about, how about finding a way for me to stop hating him? Forgive me for being useless. Amen.'

Monday 21 Feb

Met Anne, Gerald and Thynn in town late afternoon to get some of those passport-size photographs taken for our big trip. Hate having my photo taken at the best of times, let alone in those little booths where you don't get time to comb your hair before the machine blinds you four times whether you've screwed the stupid stool to the right height yet or not, then delivers a strip of pictures showing an alien life-form dressed in your clothes.

We stood in a little bunch waiting nervously for our photographs to come down the slot at the side. Gerald was nearest when they finally appeared – after about a week. He was most annoying. Refused to let us even look at them until we were sitting round a table in the Army and Navy restaurant with tea and doughnuts in front of us. Then he said we had to finish our doughnuts before handling the pictures because they'd get all sticky. He may be grown-up, but he can be just as infuriating now as he ever was. Finally he cleared a space and laid the four strips out in a row.

Anne said, 'Oh, dear.'

Gerald said, 'Well, all I can say is that I'd certainly think twice or even three times before letting this little lot into my country if I was given the choice. Look at the state of us! Mr and Mrs Psychopath and their son Gerald Psychopath, accompanied by The Creature from the Black Lagoon.'

Gerald was absolutely right. In his strip, Leonard looked like one of those people in American police dramas who laugh maniacally as they're being released on a technicality, and are followed by Clint Eastwood and shot when they strike again in dark alleys, Anne's pictures reminded me of the Cabbage Patch dolls that were all the rage a few years ago (didn't actually tell her that), Gerald looked like James Dean trying to show emotion whilst under very heavy sedation, and mine bore a dismally striking resemblance to a very sad character called Alfred E. Neuman, who used to appear on the back cover of *Mad* magazine.

Thynn had to go right over the top, as usual, of course. Said my pictures reminded him of the faces of unidentified corpses that have been in the water for a very long time, the ones you sometimes see in touched up photographs in the papers. Charming!

Anne said it didn't really matter because they were only for official documents.

Gerald said, 'I suppose you're right, Mum. But we have to face the fact that if we arrive during daylight hours some immigration official may get very suspicious indeed when he discovers we're not travelling by coffin.'

Changed the subject. Wish I hadn't, because I ended up feeling extremely irritated. Very good example of how my family set out to deliberately annoy me sometimes.

I said, 'Anne, you know I was saying that Percy's roof badly needs repairing?'

(Percy Brain, our ex-actor neighbour is getting very frail now and can hardly walk, let alone climb ladders.)

'Oh, yes,' said Anne.

'Well, this morning, while you were out, I was in our garage looking for one of my tools that seems to have simply ceased to exist – *Gerald* – and I came across those slates left over from when we did our roof, so I thought I'd get the ladder out and put them up.'

'Oh, good, Percy'll be so pleased. He hates the idea of things falling apart around him. So you got it done, did you?'

Shook my head. 'Well, not properly. When I got up there the roof was in a much worse state than I'd realized when I looked at it from the ground. I used what I'd got, but the whole thing needs replacing if you ask me. Wasn't worth bothering really. I only had enough slates to patch one or two holes.'

Anne nodded sympathetically.

Thynn looked dumb.

Gerald said, 'A futile gesture in fact.'

Now, why, I have asked myself all day since that moment, did Anne and Leonard, and Gerald himself, fall about laughing at that comment? Why? Are all three of them mad? I asked them to tell me what was so funny but they downright refused. Said if I thought about it I'd see what had made them laugh. Well, I've thought – and I can't!

A FUTILE GESTURE IN FACT

There it is – this great joke of theirs. They keep saying it and then sniggering. Why, when it's not funny? I tried to mend Percy's roof with my bits of slate, and Gerald said it was a futile gesture.

WHY IS THAT FUNNY?

If one of them doesn't tell me soon I shall tie up all my special belongings in a little spotted handkerchief on the end of a pole and leave home – I shall really.

Tuesday 22 Feb

Funny how worrying things line up like horses in a race, isn't it? The leader, and odds-on favourite in the Adrian Plass Handicap is Vlad's Children's Talk, closely followed by Everett Glander's Existence, with What's Funny About A Futile Gesture coming up on the rails, and the outsider, Gerald's Future, biding its time at the back in fourth place.

Wednesday 23 Feb

My support group here tonight to pray about the weekend, when Anne, Gerald, Leonard and I are going to Scotland to do two meetings.

Support group has grown a bit since our first meeting. Tonight there was Edwin Burlesford, Stephanie Widgeon, a thin middle-aged lady with bright, blank eyes who moved to the area a few months ago, Leonard Thynn, Gloria Marsh, Richard and Doreen Cook and, of course, Anne and Gerald.

Looked round at them all as they sat in our sitting-room. They're a good crowd, but very sort of – real. Couldn't help wishing I was surrounded by mature, wise-faced, spiritual giants radiating quiet but powerful blessing in my direction as I bravely prepared to pour myself out for others. I'm sure Billy Graham doesn't have anyone in his group remotely like Leonard Thynn who, tonight, was wearing a pair of those trick spectacles with the eyeballs that fall out on a spring when you lean forward. Why? I mean – why?

Thynn really annoys me sometimes. Tonight, as part of my 'Reporting Back' I started to tell everyone about a conversation I had in Derby with a lady who came up to speak to me after the meeting. Rather looking forward to talking about this particular encounter because it was a bit like something out of one of those testimony books. Was planning to tell the story in a way that would show how wonderful I'd been, then finish by making it clear that it was God who'd done the work really. That way, you get to boast and be humble at the same time. Thynn ruined it.

Really tried to build up the tension. I said, 'The poor woman was in tears before I spoke to her, but when she'd finished listening to what I had to say, she quite suddenly lit up, and – '

'Smoker, was she?'

Short pause while everyone turned to Thynn.

I said, 'Pardon, Leonard?'

He looked puzzled and said, 'Sorry, only you said she suddenly lit up, so I assumed she must've been a smoker. What? *What?*'

Gerald enjoyed this enormously, of course. Story ruined.

As we came up to prayer time I confessed that I was feeling quite nervous about these two meetings up north, and asked the group to specially pray that I would hear the Lord's voice clearly in my preparation. Stephanie Widgeon, whom I've never spoken to very much, and who was here for the first time tonight, leaned towards me nodding and smiling significantly, and said, 'Adrian, has it ever occurred to you that the Church is not just a building made of bricks and mortar?'

I said, 'Yes, it has. Why?'

'I think it's the people, don't you?'

'Yes.'

Waited for a punch-line, but there wasn't one. Stephanie sat back in her chair, shaking her head in wonder, and biting her bottom lip as if to contain the ecstasy she'd experienced in passing on this shattering revelation. She obviously felt some great spiritual moment had occurred. Perhaps it had. Everyone else looked rather blank. Odd . . .

Prayer time disrupted at first by the arrival of Norma Twill, who'd come round to leave something for Anne. She put her head round the door just after everyone had lowered their eyes. Wouldn't have mattered at all except that stupid Thynn, who was sitting facing the door, raised his head just as she walked in, and she screamed loudly on seeing his eyeballs apparently hanging out of their sockets.

Why . . . ?

Was going to go out and comfort poor Norma, but Anne caught hold of the elastic waistband at the back of my Y-fronts under my tee-shirt and catapulted me back into my seat.

Quite a good time of prayer once we got settled again. Lovely to feel all these people caring about what happens to me. Prayed about Scotland, of course, and a meeting on March fourth that Richard has promised to drive me to. Asked if anyone had anything from the Lord about the children's talk, but no one had this time either.

Prayer time slightly spoiled by a rather disturbing prayer from Doreen Cook towards the end. I don't know what's the matter with her at the moment.

She said, 'Lord, we just want to ask that when Adrian – frail, weak, inadequate, incompetent and totally lacking in strength and talent as the world judges such things – stands up before those rows and rows of intimidating, judgmental, critical faces, his stomach turning to water, feeling that his trembling legs will never support him for long enough to deliver his unworthy message – that when he stands up there, Lord, he'll forget the ever-present possibility that his listeners will heckle, throw fruit, shout derisively and eventually jeer him off the stage and possibly pursue him with a view to committing physical violence on his person. Let him feel encouraged, Lord, by the knowledge that even though he may experience the lurching nausea of fear, the misery of abject humiliation and the searing pain of a steel toe-cap in the side of his head, it matters not as long as one person has found some small encouragement from his words. Yea, though he be systematically battered to death with half-bricks and lengths of lead piping, let him rejoice and be glad! Amen.'

Gerald murmured in my ear, 'Bet you can't wait for the weekend, Dad.'

Suddenly realized from the concentrated, straining expression on Richard Cook's face that he was either trying to control indigestion or about to have a 'picture'. Gerald said afterwards that he would have preferred the indigestion.

'God has given me a picture,' said Richard, in the peculiar, declamatory voice he adopts on such occasions. 'I see, as it were, a great multitude of folks of all ages on a hill, and behold they are singing and full of great joy concerning one who has brought them much refreshment ...'

'It's either Graham Kendrick leading a Make Way march or a Coca-Cola advert,' whispered Gerald.

'And behold I see the one who has brought this joy, and his name – his name is – Gordon Stillsby.'

Short puzzled pause.

'Gordon Stillsby?' echoed Gloria Marsh at last, looking up in surprise. 'Who's Gordon Stillsby? I thought you were going to say his name was Adrian Plass. I don't know anyone called Gordon Stillsby. There's no one called Gordon Stillsby at church, is there Edwin? Gordon Stillsby ...'

Prayer time degenerated after that into a discussion about who the mysterious Gordon Stillsby might be. Richard claimed he'd never heard of the name until it was vouchsafed to him just now, and Doreen wondered if Gordon Stillsby might be my spiritual name (whatever that might mean), and that perhaps I ought to call myself Gordon Stillsby when I was ministering publicly. Anne reduced to near hysterics by this, and we all ended up laughing, thank goodness. Edwin suggested gently that Richard might have got a bit carried away, and Richard agreed that it could be possible because Satan does seek to deceive even the elect. I hoped that would be that, and it was, except that Gerald annoyingly insisted on calling me Gordon for the rest of the evening.

Wish I could find a way to avoid blushing at the worst possible times. Very embarrassing moment as everyone was leaving. Gloria Marsh, who is, I suppose, from a purely objective point of view, attractively constructed, has never been anything but a sister in the Lord to me, despite silly comments and pointed remarks from Gerald and Anne respectively in the past. She was the last to leave and stood *very* close to me in the doorway. After saying goodbye, she added, 'I wanted to say, Adrian, that if you ever needed me to do a spot of warming up one evening, I'd be more than happy to share from the front.'

Felt my face turning bright purple and let out a ridiculous little bleating laugh. Why couldn't I have just said, 'Thank you very much, I'll certainly bear that in mind'? Anne and Gerald both saw my face burning. Very aware of them staring at my back as I closed the door behind Gloria. Anne didn't say anything afterwards. Just raised one eyebrow in a perhaps-it's-about-time-we-thought-about-having-single-beds sort of way.

After Anne had gone to bed, Gerald said, 'I've been thinking, Gordon.'

I said, '*Don't* call me Gordon – what about?'

'Well, you know Let God Spring into Royal Acts of Harvest Growth?'

'The Christian festival, yes.'

'And you know Gloria?'

'Ye-e-es.'

'Well, if Gloria ever – you know – shared from the front at Let God Spring into Royal Acts of Harvest Growth . . .'

Sighed heavily. 'Do get on with it, Gerald.'

'Well, I know where she'd have to do it.'

'And where might that be?'

'The Big Top.'

I said, 'Gerald, that joke is shallow, sexist and completely unfunny.'

He said, 'Sorry, Gordon.'

Thursday 24 Feb

Out for a drink with Gerald early evening to give Anne a chance to finish off the packing for Scotland. After getting our second pints, I spoke to him as casually as I could.

'So, how do you see the future?'

'How do I see the future?'

'Yes.'

'You really want to know how I see the future?'

'Yes.'

'All right, well, I suppose I see the future as a really very extensive period of time, beginning on the front edge of the present, and not a very great distance from the past. I guess there's a good case for assuming that each moment of the future, will, in its turn, become the present, and that those moments of present will, in *their* turn, eventually combine to constitute the past. So, how do *you* see the future?'

Realized I was wasting my time.

Gerald's Future has worked its way into third place, and the odds become shorter with every passing day.

Friday 25 Feb

Writing this in the car on the way to Scotland.

Away very early this morning with Anne, Gerald and Thynn. Love these early starts. Planning to stay somewhere tonight and do the last bit to our hotel near Edinburgh tomorrow. Gerald, who wasn't aware of this very simple, sensible plan, laughed and said that, as long as he drove and I didn't we'd easily reach our destination tonight.

Bit annoyed really. Asked him what was wrong with my driving.

He said, 'Well, not a lot, if you leave aside little things like your tendency to change down a gear when you come to bends on the motorway.'

Absolute rubbish! I am not a slow driver. I have just said to him that if he gets us to our hotel by six o'clock I will do ten press-ups and sing 'Three Blind Mice' in the hotel foyer immediately we arrive.

Totally confident that six o'clock is an impossible target.

6:15 p.m.

I am inexpressibly relieved that we are only staying in this hotel for one night. I shall not emerge from my room again until we leave.

Saturday 26 Feb

Really good meeting tonight. People came into the hall smiling, and went on smiling and laughing right the way through. Unfortunately a lot of them also laughed through all the moving bits. Still, never mind, I'm used to that, and it all made for a very warm time.

Had to rescue a customer from Thynn afterwards. Leonard was helping to sell copies of my books, and had just been approached by an elderly person as I arrived at the back of the hall.

'Are any of Adrian's books suitable,' the doddery white-haired man was asking, 'for a middle-aged nurse living in Hong Kong, who used to be a keen Christian and is just getting interested again, was divorced a year ago, is a passionate basketball fan and has an irrational but deep-rooted fear of pre-war Bakelite products?'

Stupid Thynn simply collected together my three books, held them out and said, 'Yes, Adrian wrote all these three specially with people like that in mind. That'll be fourteen pounds and ninety-seven pence, please.'

Rescued the man from Thynn's outrageous sales techniques.

Pre-war Bakelite products?

Stayed in a boarding house where the staff do not regard me as a very sad person indeed.

Sunday 27 Feb

Day off after going to the local church this morning.

Wonderful time exploring and relaxing. Staying tonight and tomorrow in a holiday cottage high up on a hill, kindly lent to us (the cottage, not the hill) by a local church member. Beautiful situation.

We're all sleeping in a row in a sort of dormitory bedroom reached by climbing an outside stairway made of wood. Should be a very comfortable place to spend the night, except that if you want to use the toilet you have to unbolt the bedroom door, go down the outside steps, unlock the front door of the cottage, use the toilet, lock the front door behind you again, climb the stairway, go back into the bedroom and bolt the door behind you. Gerald suggested just now that we use a bucket that's obviously been put up here for the purpose, but – well, it's one of those echoing, metal buckets and I just – couldn't. Made sure I went to the toilet before going to bed.

Too tired to write any more tonight.

Monday 28 Feb

11:45 p.m.
Back in the cottage at last after the final event of our little tour. Can hardly write about the events of last night without all the feelings of panic and fear coming back.

Should have been a good, peaceful night up here in our dormitory.

Dropped off quite quickly after writing my diary, but was awakened in the early hours by a voice in the distance calling, 'Help! Help! Help me!'

Said a quick prayer asking for God's protection and leaned over to the next bed to wake Anne up. Found she wasn't there! Suddenly realized it must be Anne calling for help. Threw my dressing gown on and headed for the door at top speed. Wish I'd known what had happened to Anne before going through that door.

Later, Anne told me that she'd woken up at about two in the morning and decided to go down the steps and into the house to use the toilet, but she forgot to turn on the outside light before leaving the bedroom. Setting off down the wooden stairway in the dark, she also forgot that the steps turned to the left halfway down, and walked straight over the edge, falling about six feet onto the stony ground below.

I forgot to turn the outside light on too. Only difference between Anne's experience and mine was that I *sprinted* down the steps forgetting that they turned to the left. Didn't just fall. I took off, a bit like a ski-jumper. Landed some way beyond Anne, who must have been deeply alarmed when a shadowy, Eddie Edwards-like figure launched itself into space above her head.

Ended up both crawling around in the dark moaning and groaning with pain. Learned later that Gerald and Thynn heard our wretched cries coming from what sounded like a long way away and thought there might be an axe-murderer or something on the loose – so they locked the door! Didn't bother to check our beds first. Cheers!

Found our way into the house eventually and gave each other first aid. Dozed for the rest of the night.

Had to go up on stage for my meeting tonight covered in plasters, bruises and bandages to talk about my victorious walk with

Christ. Noticed that people found the account of how I got my injuries much funnier than anything else I said. Rather annoyed at first, but realized, talking to people afterwards, that telling stories against yourself has a rather charming, self-effacing effect. Anne's right – I'll keep it in.

Caught up by a letter marked URGENT from Stephanie Widgeon today. In it she said that it had been revealed to her that the Church was actually the people and not the building, and she thought I ought to know immediately. Funny, I thought she said that in the support meeting. Odd . . .

Home tomorrow!

Tuesday 1 March

Why is the world of long-distance road travelling so obsessed with breakfasts? In one of the places we stopped at on the way home they did the 'All Day Fill-em-up Farmhouse' breakfast, the 'American Big-boy Texas Tummy Tempter' breakfast, the 'Super Gi-normous Three-meals-in-one' breakfast, the 'Bigger Than Any Breakfast You Ever Saw In Your Life Belly Buster' breakfast, and the 'Pile On A Platter For A Peckish Pachyderm' breakfast.

Asked for a small piece of dry toast and a weak tea.

The waitress, who can't have been much more than twelve and a half, said dispassionately, 'You mean, you want one of our "Sunshine Raft On The Old Mississippi" breakfasts.'

'I don't care what you call it,' I replied, 'as long as I'm not paying for the name.'

Arrived home late tonight. All a bit ratty. Not surprising after getting hardly any sleep the night before last. Axe-murderer on the loose! I ask you . . .

Still, generally, the trip went well. Thynn nearly drove us mad inventing bad Scottish jokes all the way down. Told him that if he carries on doing it now that we're back I shall donate his body to medical research before he dies. Some horrible examples:

Q. What does a Scottish owl do?
A. Hoots mon.

Q. What does a Scottish boxer call the fighters he trains with?
A. Sporran partners.

Q. What do you call a cockney who's looking down a rabbit hole?
A. Edinburgh.

Q. What's the difference between a kitchen appliance used for rapidly stirring a combination of foods, and a bottle of Scotch whisky?
A. One's a Food Mixer, and the other's a Mood Fixer.

Men have been killed for less.

Wednesday 2 March

Sle-e-e-e-e-e-e-e-e-e-e-e-e-e-e-e-e-e-e-e-e-e-e-e-e-e-e-e-p.

Thursday 3 March

Quite a lot of people send us their family newsletters, and some of them are fine, but when they're like the one that arrived this morning I feel really intimidated. Showed it to Gerald, who made being-sick noises when he'd finished it.

Dearest _____ (Please fill in own name),

It hardly seems possible that a whole year has passed since our last newsletter went out. What a lot has happened since then! Each of us has seen change, beginning with the youngest.

Naomi (age 5)

Little Naomi has become more spiritually alive than ever during the last twelve months. All four of us have the stigmata now. She is also very bright, but Rebecca and I are anxious that she should not be pushed too far, too quickly, where school work is concerned. She must certainly finish her reception year before taking maths 'A' level, and there is absolutely no question of her undertaking piano recitals in Europe until she has passed her seventh birthday.

Naomi continues to work hard at building up the Christian Union that she started at her junior school last term, and is very encouraged by a recent experience of personally leading her orthodox Jewish headmaster and several other members of staff (including the caretaker and three dinner-ladies) to Christ.

Naomi's after-school activities include a chess class on Monday (she earns her own pocket money by teaching that), applied thermonuclear dynamics on Tuesday, netball training with other members of the County team on Thursdays, and a soup-run into the East End every Friday evening. Typically, Naomi taught herself judo and karate to black-belt standard from textbooks before embarking on this potentially dangerous occupation.

Naomi is easily the most popular girl in her class, and was voted Miss Young and Humble at church this year, although she refused to accept the trophy saying that she was an unworthy winner. This act of pure unselfishness resulted in her being nominated for the award of Most Humble Church Member of All, an award which she subsequently won and decided to accept, feeling that it would have been uncharitable, churlish, and subtly vain to refuse.

Please pray with Rebecca and I that Naomi will learn how to put herself first from time to time. Failure to do this is her major fault.

Joshua (age 16)

Joshua has gained fifteen A grade GCSEs and nine spiritual gifts this year, including Sociology and Prophecy (the one to be most earnestly sought after, according to the apostle Paul – prophecy, that is, not sociology). Over the next two years he hopes to take the Word of the Lord to Communist China, and twelve 'A' levels.

Joshua spent his summer holiday converting Guatemala with a group of pals, constructing a life-size working model of Apollo 3 out of drinking straws, and practising the five Cantonese dialects in which he is now practically fluent.

It is not all plain sailing with Joshua, however. A typically wayward and rebellious sixteen-year-old, he has several times sneaked off to his room to do a couple of hours extra academic study when he knows he should be concentrating on tightening up his dressage skills in the back paddock ready for the Olympics, and on more than one occasion he has actually disappeared from the house altogether, only to be discovered guiltily shopping for the elderly lady who lives two doors away from us, or sitting and reading to her for long periods after cooking and serving her evening meal. When Rebecca and I gently pointed out that we can't always do exactly what we want, Joshua asked our forgiveness and repointed the brickwork of every house in the street as an act of repentance. Rebecca and I feel sure he'll come through in the end.

Both Oxford and Cambridge Universities have applied to have Joshua join them in two years' time, and he will probably fly up (as soon as his pilot's licence comes through) to look over both establishments before making a decision. Please pray for Joshua's feelings of inadequacy as he prepares to deal with fellow-students and their inevitable dependency on him during this next sixth-form phase of his life.

Rebecca

Rebecca continues to enjoy producing home-made jam, bread, cakes, wine, preserves, crocheted bedspreads, small animal models made out of baked dough, dried flower decorations, knitted baby-clothes, banners and kneeling mats for our local church, and meals for the housebound.

She has completed her first novel this year, held a successful one-woman oil-painting exhibition, been awarded a third Open University degree, and continues to single-handedly look after our twelve-acre ornamental garden, when her duties as mother, wife, amateur apiarist, semi-professional photographer, local magistrate, prison visitor, hospital volunteer, leading light in the amateur dramatic association, treasurer of the ladies tennis club, district council member and world chairperson of Women Against Poverty allow.

Rebecca is currently looking for some new challenge to occupy the spare time that she, in common with many non-working mothers, finds hanging so heavily on her hands. Next year, in addition to her present activities, she plans to become a special policewoman, stand as a prospective parliamentary candidate, complete a solo sailing trip around the world, and find a method of bottling gooseberries that doesn't lose all the flavour.

Please pray that Rebecca will develop a stronger sense of self-worth in the company of other women.

Simon

Simon has spent much of this year seeking the Lord's will for his life, and longing to serve in some more specific way. There has, however, been little space for this prayer to be answered as Simon's time has been filled with distractions throughout the twelve months, not least of which was the leading of twenty-five convoys of thirty lorries each to mid-European countries in need of aid. This took up most of the summer.

It did seem possible that the autumn would be free for Simon to concentrate on seeking guidance, but flying back from what had been an amazingly successful business trip in Hong Kong, his plane crashed into the Pacific Ocean and Simon, who was the sole survivor, swam ashore to an island inhabited by primitive natives who had never heard the Gospel before. In the two months that Simon was stranded on the island he managed to learn the native tongue, devise a written version of the language, and translate a large part of the New Testament (memorized) into a form that the islanders could understand. The entire population of the island became Christians as a result, and many of them set out in canoes to take the good news to thousands of other primitive peoples living on islands in that part of the Pacific.

Simon was eventually rescued by a passing ship which was named *The Dirty Digger* when it landed at the island, but had been rechristened *Redeemed* by the time it arrived at Portsmouth. Simon arrived home in the new year, frustrated by these delays, but as determined as ever to see if the Lord had some task that might be specially his.

In February he went into retreat in a monastery in Wales, and was just beginning to feel that he was getting somewhere, when, one night, the building caught fire, and Simon rescued twenty-two monks whose vows of silence had prevented them from calling for help.

Simon stayed in Wales with the monks for several weeks after the fire, helping to rebuild the monastery and telling the brothers about the new life of the Spirit that was promised to all Christians. All twenty-two made fresh commitments as a result, and the Prior pledged that he would spread the good news throughout the world-wide order of which they were part.

Simon therefore returned without the leading he had sought, and is hoping that next year might be the time when the Lord sees fit to give him a substantial task.

Pray that Simon will find the strength to ignore distractions from the evil one when they appear, and run for the finishing line in a more decisive and intelligent way.

That's all now from this very ordinary Christian family. See you next year!

Yours,

Simon, Rebecca, Joshua and Naomi.

P.S. We usually add a little bit at the bottom in Biro to make it more personal, but our time is the Lord's, not ours – if you see what we mean.

I think a firing squad would be the answer ...

Friday 4 March

Odd day today. Started badly and ended well.

The bad start was when, feeling a bit intimidated by the heroic exploits of Simon, Joshua, Rebecca and Naomi, I woke up determined to put into practice something I read in a magazine article last night about 'Praise Offered As Sacrifice'. The writer of the article said that we should be especially willing to give praise and worship to God at times when we don't feel like doing it. If we made this sacrifice, the article explained, God would reward us by turning our act of will into a veritable hymn of spontaneous joy that would bless us and all those around us.

Started as soon as I woke, feeling, as usual, like a dead slug, by saying 'Praise the Lord!' four or five times as I lay staring at the ceiling. Felt a bit strange and I sounded a bit croaky, but the article did say that one had to persist until one came through into the place of transfiguration. Occurred to me that if I got through a lot of praise very quickly the speed of 'coming through' might be concertinaed, as it were.

Said, 'Praise the Lord! Hallelujah! Amen!' very rapidly and repeatedly as I got out of bed and put my dressing gown on. Caught a glimpse of Anne's face peering over the bedclothes as I went out of the room. Her eyes were wild and staring. Continued praising by an act of the will all the way along the landing and into the bathroom. Carried on all through my shower and while I was in the lavatory. Flagging a bit by the time I made the return trip along the landing, but still managed to emit the odd 'Praise the Lord'.

No sign at breakfast that my act of will had been transformed into a hymn of joy that would bless me and all those around me. On the contrary – those around me (Anne and Gerald) looked more morose and unhappy and unblessed than usual.

Asked what was wrong.

Anne rubbed her eyes and said wearily, 'Adrian, I don't know what hare-brained scheme you're pursuing at the moment, and, to be honest, I don't really care. What I do care about is the way it affects me. I want to make it very clear that I don't appreciate being woken – early – out of what *was* a beautiful sleep by a religious maniac who is incapable of keeping his wretched outpourings to himself.'

'Wretched outpourings? I can't believe you're calling – '

'It really does puzzle me that, after all these years, and knowing what you know about the sheer – the sheer *sanity* of God, that you go on being sucked in by these half-baked twits who can't relax until they've got other people behaving in the same bizarre fashion as themselves.'

'I'll have you know,' I said with dignity, 'that this particular "half-baked twit" as you so uncharitably call him, has one of the most respected ministries in this country. More than twenty fellowships come under his umbrella.'

Anne said, 'Well, I hope the weather keeps fine for them.'

'That's not funny,' I said.

'Yes, it is!' cackled Gerald.

Really made me cross. 'And what about you, Gerald – have you got something serious to say about this morning? Or are you just going to make a joke of it as usual?'

Gerald shrugged. 'Well, I didn't have to suffer the awful awakening that Mum did, but I heard just about everything else after that. It was pretty awful, Dad. It sounded as though a Pentecostal convention was being held in our bathroom with a fringe praise-meeting going on in the loo. Then I heard you still muttering stuff along the landing on your way back to your room. It *was* a bit wearing.'

'I see. A bit wearing. And presumably you would agree with your mother's restrained description of my sacrifice of praise as the "wretched outpourings of a religious maniac", would you?'

'Oh, no,' said Gerald, 'I don't think I'd describe it like that. No – when I was listening to you in the bathroom and the toilet this morning it reminded me of something else, but I couldn't quite put my finger on what it was.' He paused and thought for a moment. 'Ah, yes, that's it! I know what it was. I think I'd describe it as a sort of – spiritual flatulence. Morning was breaking.'

Too angry to speak. Went up and shut myself in my study until they'd both gone out. Hoped that as the day went by they'd start to feel guilty and ashamed about the way they'd spoken to me. I planned to be hurt and not easily consoled, but eventually forgive them.

Had to leave for my evening speaking engagement before Anne and Gerald came home. Richard Cook had offered to drive me in our car so that I'd be fresh for the meeting when I got there. Set off about half past four.

Sometimes wish Richard's sense of humour was just a little more highly developed. We turned into a nearby garage to get some petrol, and just as we were approaching the pumps, Richard said, 'Is the petrol cap on your side?'

I said, 'Well, it's always been very supportive.'

He said, 'No, I mean – which side of the car is the petrol cap?'

Richard dropped me off at Wopsley Community Fellowship Church at about six-thirty before driving away to visit an aunt who lived locally.

First time I'd ever been to this church. Felt a bit lonely and isolated, especially after what had happened with Anne and Gerald in the morning. Had a bad attack of the 'What-on-earth-is-a-person-like-me-doing-here?' jitters. What would these trusting people say if they knew that their guest speaker was still in the middle of a giant sulk with his wife and son? Wished Anne and Gerald were there so that we could all say sorry and hug each other and make everything all right.

Talk went all right, I suppose, then afterwards coffee and cakes were served so that people could 'chat' while they circulated. Must say it was a very warm, friendly, relaxed atmosphere. Looked around the church for the first time (I never notice anything until after I've spoken) and saw that it was very plain except for a large, highly complex but very crudely carved wooden cross on the wall above the shallow stage at the front. Commented on it to an elderly lady carrying a tray of coffee around.

She said cheerfully, 'Ah, yes, that's our cross. We don't like that at all.'

She moved on with her tray before I could ask her what she meant.

Pointed out the cross a little later to a youngish man who was busy stacking chairs to make room for people to 'circulate'.

I said, 'That's a fine cross you have up there.'

He stopped for a moment, wiped his forehead and looked quite surprised. 'Do you really like it? We think it's hideous. Just the place for it, though, up in front there, don't you think?'

'Yes, but why – '

He'd gone.

Finally nobbled Daniel Bisset, the elder-in-charge, a large, happy man, who seemed to be everybody's friend, and asked him about the cross.

'Ah, yes!' Daniel nodded and beamed. 'We're very proud of that ugly old cross, we really are. You see, we always said we'd never have such things here. Had a special meeting, we did, eleven or twelve years ago when we got started, and the whole caboodle of us agreed that we didn't want any such stuff cluttering up the place. That's why it's so good to see it up there now – makes it even more important, if you see what I mean.'

I said, 'No, I'm sorry, I don't see what you mean at all. Everyone I talk to about that cross tells me how much you don't want it here, and in the same breath they tell me how proud you all are of it. I don't understand at all.'

Daniel guffawed loudly. 'See what you mean, see what you mean – okay, I'll tell you what happened. It's all about this old chap called Eric Carter – lived on his own up in one of those slummy cottages that used to be where the back of Sainsbury's is now. Eric was in his – ooh, his mid-seventies when I first met him, couldn't see too well and he was a real old pagan, according to his own estimate. We met him when some of the harvest stuff got taken round his house one Monday after the service, and whoever it was went round left a list of things going on at the church. Well, Eric was a wary old devil, and a bit crabby at first, but he was lonely, so he did turn up at one of our social evenings that we do, and he seemed to have a good time. After that – I dunno, one thing led to another – I saw him round at his home quite a bit as well as him coming to the odd service, and the long and the short of it is that, in the end, he became a Christian. Knelt down like a baby one evening up there at the front and said he wanted to give his life to Jesus.'

'And the cross?'

'One day, when I was round visiting him, Eric suddenly says, "Would it be all right if I said a word or two at the front next Sunday, and can someone pick me up and bring me down?" Well, I was a bit surprised at this because Eric always prided himself on making his own way down to the church whenever he came, but there was no way he was going to tell me what he was on about, so I just agreed to do what he'd asked and that was that.

'The next Sunday, Eric arrives at the church – can't remember who picked him up – and he actually walked into the building pushing the wheelbarrow that we keep in the shed round the back. And lying across the top of this wheelbarrow, not in it because it was too big, was this mystery object wrapped up in sacks and whatnot. Well, you can imagine, by the time Eric got up to do his turn everyone was agog. What *was* he going to say, and what was that *thing* in the wheelbarrow standing next to him? And then old Eric started to say his piece ...'

Daniel paused for a moment, his eyes bright with the memory.

'Eric talked about how lonely he'd been before he started coming down to church do's, as he called them, and how surprised he'd been at the friendliness, not just towards him, but among the rest of us. He said how he'd been taught as a kid that you keep yourself to yourself in church so as not to interfere with anyone else, and he'd been afraid it was going to be like that. I can still remember what he said.

'"You all seemed to be lookin' after each other," those were his words, "an' makin' sure each other was 'appy. It made me want to be in it. An' now I am. I didn't know it was Jesus doin' it, but I do now."

'And then he got a bit pink and said he'd made something for the church to thank us for being nice to each other and to him, so that he ended up meeting Jesus. He got one of the lads to come and help him unwrap the thing on the wheelbarrow and hold it up, and, of course, it was that cross that's up the front there now. It would be a sort of sign, he said, of how friendly Jesus wants us to be. Turned out he'd worked on it for weeks in the little shed at the back of his cottage, but, what with poor lighting and him having not very good eyesight anyway, the thing was all over the place, and some of it a very strange shape, as you can see.'

'But you put it up.'

'Course we did! That cross comes down over my dead body. It tells us and anyone else who bothers to find out that a man came to Jesus because we were nice to each other. We don't like crosses, but we like *that* cross.'

I glanced around. 'Is Eric here tonight?'

'Probably,' said Daniel with sudden gentleness, 'but you won't see him if he is. He died about four years ago – gone to put in a good word for us I hope.'

Richard arrived soon after that to take me home. Said he'd had a time of splitting and stacking at his aunt's house. Thought he was talking about some obscure area of dialectical religious philosophy until he explained that he'd been chopping firewood for her.

Both sat in silence for some time on the way back. Then Richard suddenly said, 'Ha! Always been very supportive – ha!'

Better late than never, I suppose.

Looking forward all the way home to telling Anne about my conversation with Daniel Bisset. Remembered, just as I walked into the kitchen where Anne and Gerald were sitting over coffee, that I was still in the middle of sulking and being deeply hurt about the reaction to my sacrifice of praise. Had about two seconds to decide whether to be nice or not . . .

I wonder if Eric Carter knows that his ugly old cross was still doing its work in our kitchen four years after he'd gone?

Anne and I away until Sunday night for a supposed-to-be-romantic-but-usually-begins-with-a-big-row-and-then-gets-a-lot-better-after-that-if-not-actually-romantic weekend. Anne says if I record a single word of it in here she's going to write a book about what happened on our wedding night.

Monday 7 March

Wonderful weekend. (I'm allowed to say that.)

I am absolutely determined to take this children's talk thing by the scruff of the neck and deal with it! I have been so *weak*. Every time I decide to do something about it I chicken out. Not this time! I'm going to phone Reverend Spool tonight when I get back from work and tell him I'm not doing it. What a relief!

11:00 p.m.

Chickened out. Do it tomorrow.

Tuesday 8 March

Chickened out.

Wednesday 9 March

Cluck, cluck!

Thursday 10 March

Laid egg.

Friday 11 March

Couldn't help moaning and groaning about the blasted children's talk while we were all watching television in the living-room tonight. Anne got really cross. Told me to either do something or shut up about it for ever.

Went through to the kitchen and, after a few minutes, found the courage to ring Reverend Spool. As soon as he heard who it was he said, 'Ah, Adrian, I cannot express to you in words the pleasurable anticipation that all of us are feeling about your visit to our church on Sunday. Quite a number of folk who are not regular attenders are making a special trip from a very great distance to be here for the occasion. I am quite sure that I would not be misrepresenting the general excitement if I were to say that, for many, it will be a high spot – if not *the* high spot – of our year here at St Dermot's. We are so *very* grateful to you for sparing us the time from your busy schedule!'

Couldn't very well say, 'Well, tough cheese, Vladimir, because I'm not coming', could I?

Told him I'd just rung to say how much I was looking forward to it, and how terrific it was of him to ask me. Felt like someone on Death Row having a good old chinwag with the electrician.

Went back into the living-room.

Gerald took one look at my face, and said, 'Get the Paxo out, Mum.'

Saturday 12 March

Really tried hard to feel ill this morning. Lay in bed for a long time straining to detect a problem in some part of my body. Nothing beyond a slight twinge in the left elbow. Went into the bathroom and made vague retching noises, hoping that Anne would hear and suggest I went back to bed.

Oh, the sweet, sweet fantasy of hearing her voice speaking to the vicar on the phone and apologizing on my behalf because I'm too sick to do the children's talk.

Staggered downstairs, leaning on walls and doorposts as I went, trying to look white and drawn. Almost believed in my sickness myself by now. Arrived in the kitchen at last, finishing with what I thought was a rather stylish little lurch from the doorway to a chair at the table where Anne and Gerald were eating breakfast.

Said in a hollow, sickening-for-something voice, 'Anne, I really don't feel all that good.'

Didn't even look up. She said, 'Well, stay in and keep warm, then, because you've got that children's talk tomorrow.'

How could she be so heartless?

'Anne,' I said, 'you don't seem to understand. I thought I was going to be sick upstairs just now.'

Gerald turned the page of his newspaper and said, 'Changed your mind, did you?'

I said, 'Are you suggesting that I was putting it on?'

'I don't know, but you certainly weren't throwing it up. Face it, Dad, thespian flu isn't going to get you anywhere. To get any sympathy from us you'll have to be actually in the process of being torn to pieces by wild dogs and on the absolute point of death. And even then one of us will ask the dogs to stop for a moment while we pass you the phone so that with your last breath you can tell the vicar you're not coming.'

Went and played a round of golf. No danger of compassion fatigue in my family.

Sunday 13 March

Woke at six-thirty with the thought of this blasted children's talk dragging my spirits down like a great lead weight. How could I have been so *incredibly* stupid? Made one last frantic effort to get Anne to phone them and say I was sick and she'd come and do it instead, but she got all hung up on trivial issues like 'truth' and 'keeping your promises' and 'learning through your own mistakes'.

Gerald said he'd come along to offer moral support. Accepted his offer just for the company. Slightly disturbed, however, when, just as we were about to leave, he shouted, 'Joyce Grenfell and I are off now, Mum.' Realized I was about to provide enough ammunition to last him a very long time.

As we walked through the door of St Dermot's at nine-fifteen, Gerald said, 'Bet you a bottle of claret you tell at least three lies in the next five minutes, Dad.'

I said, 'Don't be absurd, Gerald.'

The Reverend Spool, who, Gerald reckons, is the most vicarish vicar who ever vicared, hurried over when he saw us come in, clasped my hand earnestly in both of his, and said, 'I cannot tell you how grateful we all are to you for agreeing to come, Adrian. I expect the last thing you want is yet another speaking engagement on top of all the others.'

I replied, 'No, no, it's a pleasure to be here, it really is.'

Just behind my left ear Gerald whispered, 'One.'

'But, of course,' went on Spool, 'this is slightly different, is it not? Today you will be addressing our little ones.' He twinkled away appropriately. 'Something of a novelty for you, I dare say.'

'Yes,' I said, 'but I've been looking forward to it enormously, I really have.'

'Two and a half,' murmured Gerald from behind my right ear.

'By the way, you will let us know your normal fee for such a talk, won't you?' Spool was still unwinding. 'We shall need to alert Mr Frobisher, our treasurer. We naturally insist on paying whatever sum you usually charge.'

He really meant it. Suddenly wanted to appear as generous as he was.

'I don't think we'll bother about that on this occasion,' I said, hoping he'd sense how great a sacrifice I was making. 'To be honest, money has never been very near the top of my list of priorities.'

'Sixteen and three quarters,' hissed Gerald's scandalized voice in stereo from directly behind the back of my head.

Reverend Spool beamed in appreciation of my magnificent gesture, and said roguishly and somewhat confusingly, 'Yes, yes, no, no, well, well, we shall see. By the way, we are planning to tape-record the service as usual for the homebound. I trust you have no objection to that?' (vaguely) 'No problems with er . . . copyright?'

Said, 'No, of course not.'

Thought, Oh, thank *you*, God! They're going to carefully preserve my humiliation and pass it round the universe.

Nearly died of nerves as I sat on one of the front pews next to Gerald waiting for the service to start. All the small children had been shepherded into the front five or six rows on the other side by lady helpers, and already one or two of them were pointing me, a stranger, out to each other, and producing giggling mini-explosions as though there was something excruciatingly funny about the way I looked. Those little monsters were never going to listen attentively to anything I said to them, for heaven's sake!

Wondered again – how *could* I have been so stupid?

A little distracted, thank goodness, after things got started, by Reverend Spool's notices.

Later, Gerald said that they were even more vicarishly vicarish than the vicarishness he had witnessed from any number of very vicarish vicars in the past. He clearly thought this comment of *his* extremely funny, but when I riposted with an observation that he must be very fond of Vicarish Allsorts, he looked at me in a very puzzled way, as if I'd said something completely meaningless.

Spool's staggeringly convoluted notices, transcribed this afternoon by Gerald from the tape of the service, were as follows:

'Good morning. A few brief notices before our service commences.

'In the forthcoming week Tuesday will be the fourth Tuesday in a month that has five Tuesdays, so, as is our normal practice, we shall be bringing the Wednesday meeting back to Monday, and holding the Tuesday meeting on Friday. Please study these details carefully, as we wish to avoid the most unsatisfactory situation that occurred on the last occasion that Tuesday was the fourth Tuesday in a month of five Tuesdays, when a number of folk attended all four meetings in the hope that they might hit upon the right one by chance.

'I have been asked to remind everybody that the key to the side-chapel is on a hook in the junction box just outside the vestry door. The key to the junction box is kept in the tall cupboard at the back of the church, and the key to the tall cupboard can be found in the robing chest which is situated just outside the vestry door immediately beneath the junction box. The key to the robing chest is held by Mr Frobisher, who has kindly agreed to make it available for collection on the first and third Mondays and the second and fourth Tuesdays of each month. On those months which actually commence on a Monday the key will be available on the first Wednesday, the second Friday, the third Thursday and the fourth Wednesday of that month.

'The side-chapel has been rather underused of late, and we hope that more folk will take advantage of this facility.

'May I ask that, when the time comes for communion, those occupying the left-hand side of the rearmost block of pews should make their way up the north aisle, through the door into the passage between the church and the hall, turn right just past the disabled toilet, proceed round behind the altar and approach the rail through the north door of the Lady Chapel.

'It really is impossible, incidentally, to emphasize too strongly the need to remember that right turn immediately after passing the disabled toilet. The week before last Mr Tooley, whose sight is poor, failed to turn to the right, spent a lengthy and distressing time in the church boiler-room, and finally arrived at the altar rail just after the commencement of the opening hymn in the following service.

'Similarly, last week, Mrs Cardew-Fitt, who is really quite frail and elderly, and just a little confused, walked straight on out of the east door, and along the High Street, eventually lining up for communion in the public bar of the Blue Cockatoo. Both incidents very upsetting for all concerned, and quite unnecessary if the two people involved had borne these very clear instructions in mind.

'Procedure for those in the right-hand side of that rearmost block of pews is, if anything, even simpler. They should go out of the west door, circle around the building in an anti-clockwise direction, re-enter through the south door of the Lady Chapel, and, with due sensitivity to those of the left-hand side of the rearmost block of pews who might be passing through at that moment, approach via the north door of the chapel, bearing in mind as they do so, that folk from the main body of the church will be approaching and departing at the same time.

'It is, may I say, a matter for sad regret that some flippant person has seen fit to scrawl the words "COMMUNION CONGA – THIS WAY" on the passage wall. Communion is a solemn matter, and these measures are designed to ease the involvement of all in that solemnity.

'I am happy to announce that the new arrangements for after-church coffee are working extremely well. Each Sunday we are adding to the number of folk who want coffee and actually manage to get some.

'Finally, I am told that some people have expressed concern regarding the complicated nature of our arrangements here at St Dermot's. Well, you know, friends, if you don't come and tell me, your vicar, the things that are troubling you, how on earth am I ever going to find out? Eh? Come and talk it over. I am, as always, regularly available on the fifth, seventh and twelfth odd-numbered days in each month, other than those which fall on a weekend, except where that weekend is the penultimate weekend in the month, when such exceptions do not apply. Whatever the problem, I'm sure we can work it out – in time.

'Good – and now may I say, on behalf of all of us, and especially the little ones, how pleased we are to welcome Mr Adrian Plass, who will be doing our children's talk this morning. Mr Plass has written some gloriously funny books and is well known as a very fine speaker, so we all look forward with immense pleasure to hearing what he has to say to us.

Thank you.'

Nearly paralysed with nerves by the time I stood up to talk to the children. Felt as if I was trying to swallow a large apple whole, smile and speak simultaneously. Decided the only hope of keeping their attention was to make an impact right at the beginning.

I said, 'Right, who'd like to hear a *really* scary story?'

So far, so good. All the children and a selection of indulgently smiling, roguishly uninhibited, crinkly-eyed adults put their hands up.

'The only thing is – I'm not sure if I ought to tell you this story, because it's very, very, *very* frightening. In fact it's *so* frightening that I might make myself scream with fear just by telling it to you. In fact, it's probably the most terrifying story *anyone, anywhere* has *ever* heard in the whole history of telling stories.'

Certainly seemed to have succeeded in making an impact on everybody. Noticed that the indulgent smiles on the faces of most of the crinkly-eyed adults had faded. A small, round-faced, rosy-cheeked, pigtailed girl of about three glanced worriedly over her shoulder to check Mummy and Daddy were still in the church.

I said, in low, menacing tones, 'Ready to be sick with fear, then?'

Might have overdone it a bit. The children were a solid block of tension and dread, holding on to each other for safety and staring at me, wide-eyed with apprehension. Certainly paying attention.

Ruined the whole effect right at the beginning with a stupid, unintentional spoonerism.

I said, 'Once upon a time, there was a crappy little gab called Hordon . . .'

Short, shocked, uncomprehending silence. An elderly lady at the back of the church cupped her hand behind her ear and said, 'Once upon a time there was a *what*, did he say . . . ?'

The small pigtailed girl turned round and said in a loud, clear voice, 'He said there was a crappy little gab called Hordon, but I don't know what crappy means, and I don't know what a gab is, and I've never heard of anyone called "Hordon". What is a crappy little gab called Hordon? What does *crappy* mean? Is it –'

Panicked and interrupted hurriedly. 'I didn't say the story was about a crappy little gab called Hordon.' Expressions of outraged disbelief appeared on the faces of the children. 'Or rather – sorry, sorry – I did say that, but it was a mistake. What I meant to say was that once upon a time there was a happy little crab called Gordon. And one day Gordon's big brothers and sisters forgot what their mummy and daddy had told them about looking after Gordon, and while they were doing something else he wandered off into a different rockpool and was very frightened because a seagull nearly ate him up and his mummy rescued him just in time.'

Short silence.

The little girl said, 'What happened next?'

'Er, well, that's it – that's the end.'

Filled with despair as I realized that I'd left out all the funny crab voices and the conversation between the brothers and sisters and the frightening bit leading up to Gordon's mummy finding him. I'd managed to finish the story in thirty seconds flat.

'That's not what I'd call a very, very *scary* story,' said the pig-tailed girl. 'That's what I'd call a very, very *short* story.'

Tried to carry brightly on.

'Right, now who'd like to suggest what the story teaches us?'

Lots of arms went up. Pointed at a thin little girl with huge glasses.

She said, 'The seaside is a very bad, nasty, dangerous place for small children?'

Two toddlers opened their eyes very wide at this suggestion and, to my horror, seemed to be on the verge of tears.

'No,' I said hurriedly, 'of course it doesn't mean that. The seaside is a *lovely* place for children. Of course it is.'

The two toddlers cheered up immediately. The thin little girl's face crumpled.

'But er ... it was a very good suggestion – very good indeed. Well done!' Could hear my own voice rising to a hysterical pitch. 'Come on, somebody else – what does the story show us?'

A little lad with wide staring eyes and hair standing up on end, who looked as if a powerful electric current was being passed through his body, called out, 'Does it show that we must never trust our brothers and sisters, because they just don't care when we get eaten at the seaside?'

Felt as if I was going mad. I know I'd started it, but the whole thing was turning into something out of Edgar Allan Poe. Children's talks aren't supposed to leave the congregation emotionally scarred for life.

'Of course our brothers and sisters care when we get eaten at the seaside. I mean' – hastily – 'we're not going to be eaten at the seaside – or anywhere else for that matter, but if we were – *if* we were, then our brothers and sisters would certainly care, of *course* they would. Look, doesn't anyone think,' I pleaded desperately, 'that the story might show how important it is for us to look after each other? Do you think that's what it shows?'

At this, a pretty little dark-haired thing pushed her hand into the air as far as it would go, waving wildly, rocking her whole body and clenching her teeth with the sheer eagerness of her desire to reply. I nodded encouragingly.

'Do you think that's what it shows?'

She said, 'No.'

Could feel my whole being moving rapidly into Basil Fawlty mode.

'All right – all right! Everybody put their hands down and I'll go over it again, okay? No, I said put your hands *down*, didn't I? You all had your chance to say what the story meant just now, and no one's got it right. Now it's my turn, unless of course someone wants to object.'

Glared challengingly at the children. They huddled fearfully together for mutual protection and said nothing.

'Now! There's a crab called Gordon. Right?'

Anxious nods.

'He's happy. *Right?*'

More nods.

'His brothers and sisters are supposed to be looking after him. Right? Anybody find that difficult to understand?'

Solemn head shakes.

'But they forget to look after him and he nearly gets eaten by a seagull. *Right?*'

Slightly more confident nods.

'But Gordon's mother rescues him. *Right?*'

Smiles and nods.

'Good! Excellent! So – what does the story teach us?'

Uneasy pause. Children all looked at each other. At last, a slightly odd, serious-looking, short-haired boy of about ten, dressed in a dark suit and tie, raised his hand.

'Yes?'

'It shows that Satan will sometimes appear to us as a seagull.'

Depressed silence.

Gave up, and said, 'Amen.'

Afterwards, Reverend Spool reacted as if I'd converted the whole of Great Britain.

'*Wonderful!*' he enthused, clasping my hand again, 'I'm sure our children were greatly challenged by your message. So much more likely that a lesson will lodge in tiny minds when it comes wrapped up in a well-told story.'

Frowns of annoyance directed at me from some of the parents who were trying to soothe their disturbed small children suggested that, given half a chance, they'd like to have lodged something in my tiny mind – a hatchet, for instance. Detached myself as soon as possible from the vicar, who said, just as we were going through the door, 'By the way, I have instructed Mr Frobisher that he is to ambush you – yes, positively to *ambush* you – before you leave the church premises. He will be thrilled to defray your expenses. Thank you so much for inspiring us. You must come and speak to the kiddies again soon ...'

Asked Gerald what he'd thought of my talk as we passed through the church porch.

He said, 'May I phrase my answer in the form of a cryptic crossword clue?'

Sighed. 'If you must.'

'Well, I think it would be something like this.'

Handed me another of his infernal backs-of-envelope-jottings. I read it. It said:

RUBBISH FROM CANADA AND FAST MOVING RHYTHMIC VERSE PERFORMED TO MUSICAL BACKING (4 LETTERS)

Gerald said, 'And the solution is – '

I said, 'I've solved it, thank you very much, and I agree.'

In the churchyard we were accosted by Mr Frobisher. He turned out to be an immensely fat young man with a very small purse, a common phenomenon among treasurers, perhaps, Gerald surmised rather obscurely later. Reverend Spool's assurance that Mr Frobisher would be thrilled to defray our expenses erred on the side of optimism. On the contrary, Mr Frobisher seemed to regard us with deep suspicion, and, judging from his general manner, was actually very reluctant indeed to defray our expenses.

Having taken out a small notebook and pencil as well as the small purse, he said in a high-pitched, officious voice, 'May I enquire as to the fee?'

I went through my modest, head-shaking, no-need-to-bother routine, but he didn't even try to argue. He just moved on to the next question.

'May I enquire as to the means of transport?'

Gerald twisted his head round until he was looking at the page on which Mr Frobisher was about to write, and said in friendly, helpful, I'll-say-it-and-you-write-it-down tones, 'Er, we came by helicopter. That's h, e, l, i – '

'We came by car!' I interrupted hurriedly, as Mr Frobisher started to inflate to an even greater size. 'And there's no need to pay us anything for that. The trip is no more than seven-eighths of a mile – it's not worth bothering with, really it's not.'

'The Reverend has instructed me that I am to defray your travelling expenses,' squeaked Mr Frobisher, 'and we pay thirty pence for every mile travelled. In this case the total mileage comes to twice seven-eighths of a mile which is fourteen-eighths of a mile which is one mile plus six-eighths of a mile which is –'

Forced to stop because he couldn't work out the sum in his head, Mr Frobisher produced from his pocket a calculator as minuscule as the rest of his equipment, stuck his tongue out of the side of his mouth and prodded buttons for a moment.

'That comes,' he said at last, 'to fifty-two and a half pence. I feel sure Reverend Spool would wish me to round that up to fifty-three pence.'

Solemnly, he counted the coins into my hand before producing a Lilliputian receipt book, which I duly and solemnly signed.

'Well,' said Gerald, as we climbed into the car, 'that was a nice little earner, wasn't it? Fifty-three pence! Wow!'

'There's one consolation,' I replied.

'Which is?'

'That's just a little more than my talk was actually worth ...'

Monday 14 March

Felt embarrassed this morning just thinking about yesterday's fiasco. Not helped by Gerald pointing out that, as I owe him a bottle of claret, I'm actually about four pounds out of pocket. All

I could see in the bathroom mirror was a crappy little gab called Adrian. At breakfast Anne was quite sympathetic (now that I've done it!), but she said it's all part of learning what my limitations are, and then saying 'No' to things that I've got no talent for.

I said, 'But we're not supposed to limit God, are we?'

Gerald chipped in and said, 'No, but if Moses had decided to bake a chocolate cake gigantic enough to feed several hundred thousand Israelites just at the point when he was supposed to be getting on with parting the Red Sea, I don't think there would have been any culinary miracles available, do you? God would have got cross and made it sink in the middle.'

He paused, then said reflectively, 'I feel really sorry for old Moses, you know. Fancy going all that way and then not being allowed to enter the Promised Land. Can't you just picture him standing up on Mount Nebo, a hundred and twenty years old, eyesight as good as ever, gazing out at Naphtali, and Manasseh, and Judah stretching all the way to the Mediterranean, and the Negeb and the Jordan Valley and Jericho and Zoar, and realizing he'd never get there? And then, like a sort of Old Testament Frank Sinatra, knowing it was his last appearance, he'd have turned to the hordes of Israelites down on the plain and sung the old song just one more time.'

'Old song? What old song?'

'I did it Ya-a-a-hweh!' warbled Gerald.

Tuesday 15 March

Happened to mention to Gerald this morning that an awful lot of the Christians I meet don't seem to feel they've ever really met God and been properly forgiven by him. You'd think, I said, that Jesus had never told the story of the Prodigal Son. When I got back tonight from a Glander-filled day, he showed me another of these Scripture rewrites of his. Said our chat in the morning had inspired him. Felt quite flattered really.

Oddest feeling is creeping up on me that Gerald is the adult around here, and I'm a sort of earnest adolescent. Quite nice in a way – I think.

At last he cometh to his senses and saith, 'All my father's hired workers have more than they can eat, and here am I about to starve! I will arise and go to my father and say, "Father, I have sinned against heaven and before thee. I am no longer worthy to be called thy son; make me as one of thy hired servants."'

So he arose and came to his father.

But when he was still a long way off his father seeth him and runneth to him and falleth on his neck and pulleth his hair and smacketh his backside and clumpeth him on the ear and saith, 'Where the devil do you think you've been, Scumbag?'

And the prodigal replieth, 'Father, I have sinned against heaven and before thee. I am no longer worthy to be called thy son; make me as one of thine hired servants.'

The father saith, 'Too right I'll make thee as one of my hired servants, Master Dirty-stop-out-inheritance-spending-stinker-pinker-prodigal! I suppose thou believest that thou canst waltz back in here without so much as an by thine leave, and conneth me with thine dramatic little speech? Thinkest thou that this is "Little House on the Prairie"? Or mayhap thou reckoneth that I was born yestere'en? Oh, no. Third assistant bog-cleaner, unpaid, for thee, mine odorous ex-relative.'

Then the prodigal saith dismally unto him, 'Oh, right, right – fair enough. So, er, just to get it straight, there existeth no question of lots of nice presents and instant forgiveness and an large celebratory meal involving the fatted calf, or anything of that nature?'

'In thy dreams, son!' replieth the father. 'The only gift thou art likely to see is the personalized lavatory-brush with which thou shalt shortly be presented.'

And the father taketh the prodigal by that ear which previously he clumpeth, and hauleth him back to the farm.

And lo, the fatted calf beholdeth them approach from an long way off, and, summing up the situation perfectly, throweth an big party. And the fatted calf's family and guests rejoiceth and doeth an bit of discow-dancing, and mooeth sarcastically over the fence at the prodigal as he passeth by in his tribulation.

And behold, as nightfall approacheth, the prodigal's elder brother heareth distant sounds as of an bog-brush being applied, and strolleth out to the edge of the cess-pit after supper holding an large brandy, and he stretcheth luxuriously and picketh his teeth and lighteth an enormous cigar and looketh down and saith, 'Evenin', Rambo. I see thou hast returned, then? Likest thou thine rapid progress from affluent to effluent?'

And the prodigal looketh up and saith, 'Verily, thou rebukest me justly with thine clever barb. When I had great wealth I shared it not with thee, but now I freely offer thee an good share of what is mine.'

And he flicketh at the elder brother with his brush, so that an weighty portion of something exceeding unpleasant ploppeth into his brother's brandy glass, and his brother retireth, threatening to tell on him.

And the prodigal findeth his father and saith unto him, 'Behold, all these years during which I was in an far country, mine smug, pie-faced, hypocritical, dipstick of an brother must have caused thee to gnash thine teeth on an daily basis, so how come he getteth all the perks like brandy, cigars and suchlike, while I remaineth up to mine elbows in other people's poo?'

But his father replieth, 'Thine brother is boring but biddable. Get on with thine work, thou less than Baldrick, and think thyself lucky.'

The father departeth and the prodigal saith to himself, 'Blow this for an game of centurions. I wisheth I hadn't come home now. Behold I am just as hungry, twice as guilty and four times as smelly. Verily, if, by an miracle, any time off ever presenteth itself, there existeth in my mind no doubt about how I shall seek to occupieth it. Definitely – it's an day-trip to the pigs for me . . .'

Wednesday 16 March

Spent quite a long time today trying to work out whether the sort of thing Gerald wrote yesterday means that he's getting closer to God or further away. At teatime, when he wasn't around, I said to Anne, 'I think Peter O'Sullevan's going to get his knickers in a real twist over Gerald's Future.'

She said, 'Past experience tells me, darling, that what you've just said almost certainly means something to you, even though it appears to be complete nonsense to me. Unravel your thought processes gently and I might even end up agreeing with you.'

She did.

Thursday 17 March

Thynn round today. Cornered him in the sitting-room.

I said casually, 'Oh, by the way, Leonard, I've worked out why the thing about Percy Brain's roof made you all laugh so much.'

'Oh, you have, have you?' said Leonard. 'Well, what was it, then?'

Said I'd hit him if he didn't tell me, but Anne and Gerald burst in and rescued him. The three of them put me under the cushions on the settee, then sat on me and said my attempt to trick the information out of Thynn was a futile gesture. Not something St Paul ever had to put up with. He never denied his faith when he was being shipwrecked, beaten, starved or imprisoned, but if he'd had to endure being put under sofa cushions and sat on by his immediate family and friends who wouldn't tell him what their stupid joke meant, it might have been a different story.

He and I could swop a few yarns . . .

Friday 18 March

Going out for an Indian meal later this evening with Anne, Leonard, Gerald, Edwin and Richard (Doreen wouldn't come, but I don't know why) as a sort of get-together before our big trip to Australia next week.

I enjoy Indian food very much – I mean *very* much, but the business of ordering it drives me completely mad. I start getting tense long before we leave home. Can't bear the prospect of everyone fussing and faffing around with the menus, choosing something at last, then changing their minds, then changing their minds back again, then forgetting what they've decided as soon as the waiter comes. And as for the business of paying – oh, the whole thing really does drive me round the bend.

Decided to prevent all the hassle this time.

Waited until about five o'clock when Anne and Gerald went off to the supermarket, then rang Edwin, and asked him to choose within the next half hour what he was going to have and tell me what he'd decided when I rang him back. Sounded a little surprised but said he'd do his best.

Then I rang Leonard. Speaking to Thynn by phone is like using a megaphone to communicate with another planet – a complete waste of time. The conversation went as follows:

ME: Hello, Leonard, is that you?

THYNN: Yes, it's me.

ME: I want to talk about tonight.

THYNN: All right, then.

ME: You haven't forgotten, have you?

THYNN: Oh, good.

ME: Well, it's not good if you have forgotten – so have you?

THYNN: I don't know.

ME: You don't know what?

THYNN: I don't know if I've forgotten, because I can't remember what it is I'm supposed to have not forgotten.

ME: You haven't forgotten what's happening tonight.

THYNN: What is happening tonight?

ME: Leonard, you *know* what's happening tonight.

THYNN: I don't know what's happening. I've forgotten.

ME: We're going out for an Indian.

THYNN: I'm sorry, George, I can't – I'm already going out for an Indian with Adrian and Anne and the others.

407

ME: This is Adrian speaking, you blithering idiot!

THYNN: Oh, sorry, I thought you were George, but – hold on a minute – if you're Adrian, you *know* what we're doing tonight.

ME: Well, of course I know that I know, don't I! I was just checking that – oh, never mind. Listen, Leonard, I want you to tell me what you'd like to eat tonight.

THYNN: Well, personally, I'd be quite happy with an Indian meal.

ME: (PAUSING TO GRIND THE TIP OF A PENCIL INTO THE BRICK-WORK UNDER THE WINDOW-SILL) Leonard, tell me which main dish you would like to eat at the Indian restaurant tonight or I shall come round there and puree you in your own blender.

THYNN: (PANICKING A LITTLE) Sweet and sour pork would be fine.

ME: That's Chinese.

THYNN: No it's not, it's English. I said –

ME: Sweet and sour pork is a Chinese dish. Which Indian dish would you like?

THYNN: (A WILD GUESS) Tandoori, then?

ME: Tandoori is a generic term.

THYNN: That's fine – I like it generic. Can I have pilau rice with it, and lots of poppadoms to start?

ME: (CURIOUSLY NUMBED) Tandoori is a style of cooking. I'll put you down for a chicken tikka, shall I, Leonard?

THYNN: Oh, yes, fine, if you think I'd like that better than a – a geriatric tern, was it? I don't think I fancy that much anyway, now I think about it. Sounds vile, but I suppose if you're very poor in India and you live by the sea, you have to –

ME: (WEAKLY INTERRUPTING) I'll see you at eight o'clock tonight at the restaurant, Leonard. You know which one we're going to, don't you?

THYNN: Yes, the one next to the cinema.

ME: That's right, it's called All the Raj. See you later.

THYNN: See you later.

After recovering from my dialogue with Thynn I rang Richard at work and asked him what he fancied. After a brief but utterly ludicrous discussion on the dangers of accidentally ingesting occult spices, he settled on a prawn biryani with a stuffed paratha. Wrote it down carefully.

Rang Edwin back and asked if he'd chosen his food. Hallelujah! He had. He went for a tandoori mixed grill with a main-course vegetable curry and nan bread.

Began to feel quite optimistic about the coming evening, although I knew I still had the toughest nuts to crack. Somehow I had to find out what Anne and Gerald were likely to order without them realizing what I was doing. Devised a cunning plan.

When they came back with the shopping and I was helping to carry the bags through to the kitchen, I said casually, 'I suppose you two wouldn't rather give the Indian a miss this evening? We could go to a pub or something instead.'

Went on stowing stuff away in the larder and fridge, conscious that Gerald and Anne were standing in flabbergasted silence behind me. Turned round and noticed them.

'What?'

'Dad,' said Gerald at last, 'I can't believe you're saying this. You salivate like a starving mongrel at the very mention of Indian food.'

'Thank you for that delicate observation, Gerald,' I replied, 'and you're quite right usually, of course. It's just that – well, I've tried most things on the menu and I'm getting a bit bored. Time for a change, perhaps.'

Anne shook her head disbelievingly and said, 'Darling, you have *not* tried most things on the menu. On the contrary, you choose precisely the same things every single time we go.'

'Mum's right, Dad,' contributed Gerald, 'you're more regular than a Prussian on a diet of prunes.'

'Well, what do you suggest I have then? What are you both going to eat?'

'I know what I'm going to have,' said Anne. 'I don't want any old pub dinner. I want chicken korma and that lovely lentil dish and lots of special rice, and I'm going to have it, so there!'

'Come on, Dad,' coaxed Gerald, 'you know you want to go really. Have the same as me. I'm going for lamb curry and those onion things that look like balls of shoelaces tied together, and about a million poppadoms with that heavenly mango chutney.'

Tried not to let them see my mouth watering.

'Oh, all right,' I conceded, 'we'll go to the Indian. After all, Edwin and Richard and Leonard are probably looking forward to it. Can't let them down.'

Hurried upstairs to jot down Anne and Gerald's choices. Felt quietly triumphant. Nice to leave my wife and son feeling a trifle bewildered for a change. I'll write about the meal when I get back.

11:30 p.m.

Some are born ignominious, some achieve ignominy, some have ignominy thrust upon them. I must be one of the very few people in the history of the world who qualify on all three counts.

If only I'd bothered to check that the sheet of paper I picked up before we left for the restaurant was the one with the list of Indian dishes on it. The one I actually grabbed came from the same jotting pad, the one beside our bed, and was also a list, written with the same pen. Because, as usual, we were in a tearing hurry, I snatched it up quickly and just assumed I'd got the right one. Even then it might not have been so bad if I'd taken the trouble to glance at the stupid thing in All the Raj before handing it to the waiter with – well, I suppose it might have appeared a rather lordly air. I'd so enjoyed producing it with a flourish and announcing that menus would not be necessary because I had a complete list of everyone's requirements. I wasn't even too put out by Anne's glare of disapproval. I felt good, a bit like Hercule Poirot at the end of a book, blinding the assembled company with his brilliance.

The difference between the great detective and me being, of course, that he was a private dick, whereas I was about to perform in public.

The smartly dressed waiter took my sheet of paper and studied it attentively for a moment or two. A puzzled expression appeared on his polite features.

He said, 'Please excuse me, sir, but this food order begins itself with "Widgeon's bottom", and finishes itself with "Moving parts in oil". Neither of these are common Indian dishes.'

I snatched the piece of paper from his hand.

Anne said, 'You've brought your list of weekend-jobs-to-avoid-at-all-costs by mistake, haven't you? Serves you right!'

Everyone in stitches. Gerald loved it, of course. Wanted to know what 'Widgeon's bottom' could possibly mean. Explained with what rags of dignity remained to me, that Stephanie Widgeon had asked me if I would clear the end of her garden so that she could grow vegetables. Declined to explain 'Moving parts in oil' on the grounds that there had already been enough hilarity at my expense.

Thynn nearly got us thrown out at this point. He said that it didn't matter me bringing the wrong list because we could probably all remember what we'd ordered.

'Take me, for instance,' he said, turning to speak to the waiter. 'I'm pretty sure I can remember what I was having.'

The patient waiter poised his pen above his order pad respectfully.

'Yes,' said Thynn, assuming a ridiculously unconvincing man of the world air. 'Adrian tells me that one of your specialities is elderly seagull cooked in the tandoori style.'

A sort of microcosmic Indian Mutiny was only avoided by giving the impression to the deeply affronted waiter and two of his colleagues who were summoned to witness this vile slander against the establishment, that Leonard was a sadly deranged but harmless person who was in the habit of making wild, meaningless statements (more or less true, come to think of it) and that we were present in the role of keepers or minders.

Felt a bit guilty about this. Tried to explain to Leonard, but he was so inextricably confused that I had to abandon the attempt to take him on a mental journey from 'generic term' to 'elderly seagull', and simply said it had all been my fault, which, of course, as Anne unhesitatingly pointed out, it had.

Felt a bit depressed after that, not least because we still had to go through the whole nerve-jangling business of ordering, but I didn't dare utter a word of complaint.

Edwin must have realized that I was feeling a bit low. Once we had our food in front of us, he took a postcard from his inside pocket and held it up. On one side there was a picture of semi-naked African dancers.

'Look at this,' said Edwin, 'it arrived from Victoria Flushpool in Africa this morning. I'll read you what she says:

> 'Dear Edwin and all at church,
> Work going very well here.
> Great blessings. Impertinent
> mosquitoes. Watched this tribal
> dancing on Tuesday. Enthusiasm
> and modesty disproportionately
> related. Stenneth studying
> Titus as before. Africa needs
> a good clean. Have begun.
>   Love, Victoria.'

Anne, Leonard and I burst into laughter on hearing the contents of the postcard. Even Richard emitted a restrained, hissing little chuckle. Gerald looked blank.

He said, 'What are you all laughing at? I mean – it's quite funny, but nothing to get hysterical about – is it?'

Edwin said, 'Oh, it's just the bit about Stenneth and Titus. If you ever wanted cast-iron evidence that Victoria has genuinely changed for the better, it's the fact that she can mention something like that in a postcard for the whole church to see. Wonderful, really.'

Gerald still looked blank. 'I don't know what you're talking about, Edwin. What about Stenneth and Titus?'

Suddenly realized that Gerald had not been at church on the memorable occasion to which Edwin was referring. In fact, he had been away from home altogether on some kind of hiking holiday with William Farmer. Wondered why I'd never told him, but I knew the answer even as I asked myself the question. He would have made *such* a meal of it.

I said, 'Gerald never heard what happened that day, Edwin. You tell him.'

'All right,' agreed Edwin, 'as long as Anne doesn't mind. It's a bit er . . .'

Anne laughed and said, 'Edwin, the expression on Victoria's face that morning is one of the memories I use to cheer myself up with when life is at its darkest. I'm glad we didn't tell you about it at the time, though, Gerald.'

'All right, then,' said Edwin, 'I'm sure Victoria wouldn't object to me talking about it now. I'll tell you what happened, but don't blame me if I collapse before I get to the end.'

Before starting he gazed into the distance for a moment with an almost beatific smile on his face.

'It was several years ago on a Sunday towards the end of August, and a lot of folk were still away on their holidays, so there weren't all that many people there. Stenneth was supposed to be doing a sort of little Bible-study during the service, not the actual message, because – well, frankly, at that time I wasn't very keen on the idea of exposing the church to what you might call the Flush-pool way of thinking. But Victoria had been going on and on at me all year about letting Stenneth get involved in "the ministry of the word". Not, she insisted, that the impetus came from her, because that would not have been Scriptural. No, Stenneth was the head of the woman, and woe betide him if he dared to argue the point. So, in the end, I gave in, and offered Stenneth this particular Sunday just because I knew it wouldn't be all that well attended. To be quite honest, poor old Stenneth didn't want to do it anyway, but he was a man under orders, and, as he put it, rather dolefully, "Most of the choices I'm allowed to make in life are between one thing that I don't want, and another thing that I want even less."

413

'Now, the other thing you need to know, Gerald, is that the Flushpools themselves had come back from holiday on the Friday just gone, and –'

'They didn't used to call them holidays, though, did they?' interrupted Gerald. 'Didn't they call them "periods of recreational outreach"?'

'That's right,' agreed Edwin, chuckling, 'recreational outreach, that was it. Well, this particular period of recreational outreach was a prize that Victoria and Stenneth had won in some kind of competition – can't have been a raffle, because raffles were about on a par with mass murder on the sin scale – anyway, they won it, and, after a lot of iffing and butting and persuading on my part, they decided to go. It was a week at one of those sunny Mediterranean resorts, and it was only after they'd gone that I suddenly realized the beaches near their hotel were pretty well bound to be full of topless bathers. I had this picture in my mind of Stenneth, still formally dressed in suit and tie, sitting on a deckchair with his gaze rigidly fixed on the far horizon, with Victoria in very close attendance, grimly policing the movement of his eyeballs.'

We all sat in fascinated silence for a moment, picturing the scene as Edwin had described it.

'Well,' continued Edwin, 'somehow, not via me, I can assure you, word got around that the Flushpools had gone off to a nudey-beach in the South of France, and by the time they came back there were a number of jokes on the subject in currency, and I had to actually ask some people to cool it a bit, because I didn't want Victoria and Stenneth to get upset.

'So, Sunday morning comes along, and old Stenneth had decided he was going to say a bit about the New Testament book that he'd been reading and thinking about in his devotional time during the holiday. Give him due credit – on the Saturday he'd contacted five small children of parents who'd definitely be there that weekend – it was Family Service, you understand – and asked them to help him introduce his subject. Then, on the Sunday morning, just before the service began, he gave each child a large

414

square made of card with a letter on it to hold up when he began his talk . . .'

A sudden convulsion of laughter choked Edwin for a moment. He pulled himself together and continued.

'Sorry about that. The first bit of the service went all right, and then it was time for Stenneth to do his stuff. Victoria was sitting right up on the front row, ready to fuel her husband with the power of visible expectation, as it were, and Stenneth was shuffling pieces of paper nervously, trying to find the courage to actually open his mouth and say something. Then he got going at last.

'He said, "May I ask the children at the back to join me up here, so that everyone can see what we shall be talking about."

'So this little troop of children marched solemnly up to the front and positioned themselves in a neat line to the side of and just behind Stenneth, holding their cards down ready for when they were told to lift them up.

'"Right, children," said Stenneth brightly, ignoring the fact that the children were looking mildly perturbed about something, "show everybody what I've been studying all this last week on holiday."

'When the children lifted their cards they should, of course, have spelled out the word "TITUS". They didn't. Unfortunately for Stenneth, "U" had nipped into the lavatory just before being called up, and the ensuing gap was –' he nearly choked again ' – a rather significant one.'

I have never seen Gerald laugh as much as he did when Edwin came to this point in his story. He ended up quite red in the face, and had to be patted on the back and told to sip water. When he'd recovered, he asked Edwin how the rest of the congregation had reacted.

'Well, all I can say is that human beings are capable of quite incredible restraint on certain occasions. I don't think anyone actually laughed out loud at that point, but when "U" suddenly came rushing from the toilet to take up his position between "T" and "S" one of the teenagers at the back just seemed to burst. She put her head down in her lap, and started to literally sob with laughter. Stenneth, who still had no idea what was going on, asked for someone to take her off into another room for ministry. How the rest of us kept straight faces I shall never know. There was a tremendous feeling of togetherness in church that day – the fellowship of suffering and all that, I suppose. But, oh, my, what a moment!' He held up the postcard again. 'And that's why this means so much.'

'Goodness, yes,' said Anne, 'at the time Victoria was in a state of utter dumbfoundedness. She looked like someone who wants to blame the council for a mountain falling on her head but knows in her heart that it was an act of God.'

'Perhaps it was,' smiled Edwin.

When we got home tonight Gerald said to me, 'There's one other question that I'd have asked about the Titus episode.'

'Yes,' I said, 'what's that?'

'Which inspired member of the congregation bribed "U" to disappear with such perfect timing?'

Saturday 19 March

Frantic preparation for Australia. We're allowed one large suitcase and one small bag each. I hate packing. It's like a grenade going off in a jumble sale. Left it to Anne.

Thynn, very proud of himself, brought his case round this evening and asked Anne to check it. She found it was full of thick pullovers and scarves and fishermen's socks and a very large overcoat. Anne gently pointed out that Australians would be in the middle of their summer, so we'd be wearing shorts and tee-shirts most of the time. Thynn laughed as though she'd made a really funny joke. Spent the next half hour helping Leonard to catch up with Galileo. Only about four hundred years late.

Anne went home with Leonard to sort him out, then brought him back to stay tonight and tomorrow night.

We really are going!

How come the only person in Great Britain who still qualifies for the Flat Earth Society understands a joke about futile gestures, and I don't?

Sunday 20 March

Edwin called Anne and me and Gerald and Leonard up to the front in church this morning and said a blessing over us. Felt very weepy and uncertain suddenly. Suppose Britain sinks while we're away?

Went for a walk after lunch. Wonder why I've never noticed how attractive our home town is before? All those nice, safe, familiar buildings and trees and streets and people. Wish something would happen to stop us going.

The night's come now. Help me, Jesus, I'm frightened.

Monday 21 March

Mornings are magic. Yesterday's fears all disappeared with the night.

Good luck card from Stephanie Widgeon through the door just before we left. Little note on the bottom urging us to bear in mind that the church is not the building but the people. Beginning to annoy me a bit now.

Drove to Heathrow in the afternoon feeling very excited. Plane took off at about ten-thirty in the evening.

We've been on this plane now for about six weeks. During the early part of the trip I walked up the gangway to the toilet three times, but couldn't work out how to get in. Did a lot of stretching and deep breathing outside the door each time to convince people that I'd just come for a little exercise. Finally managed to open one, then couldn't for the life of me discover how to get out. Spent half an hour in there (missed four meals) before Anne sent a stewardess to see if I was all right. Very embarrassing. Guided me carefully back to my seat from behind as if I were suffering from some severe mental deficiency.

Got back to find Leonard, still coiled and folded into his sardine-class seat-space, muttering to himself with his eyes closed. Tapped him on the shoulder and asked what he was doing.

He said, 'I'm doing what Jesus said we must do.'

'Which is?'

'Praying for the people I hate.'

I said, 'And who are they?'

'First-class passengers.'

Think I've mastered the toilets now.

Anne and Gerald have been asleep for three or four hours. Very tempted to wake them and tell them that I haven't. All there has ever been or ever will be is this plane droning dozily on through the night, pretending to be on its way to Australia.

Tuesday 22 March

Can't work out whether Tuesday is now Monday, Wednesday or still Tuesday, but a different bit of Tuesday than it would have been if we were still in England. All I want in the world is a space big enough to be horizontal in.

Wednesday 23 March

Landed at last. Everything in me said it was time to go to bed, but everything around me said it was time to get up. Came out of the airport terminal at Perth into heat that hit me on the head like a hammer. Met by our hosts who were kindness itself. Took us to their big shady house with a swimming pool and sunbeds and lots of cold drinks and cicadas chirruping, and were told to relax and take it easy for the rest of the day.

Jet lag is a very strange sensation. Your will takes a step forward, or reaches out for a drink, but then you have to wait a second or two for it to actually happen. Like being in a dream.

Thynn rather disconcerted to find that our hosts' two children, little girls of about five and six, came running out to the back when they came home from school, and stood staring at him in awe.

They said, 'Are you really Leonard Thynn?'

Leonard said, 'Well, yes, I am.'

They said, 'Do you want to borrow our cat?' then burst into giggles and ran back inside.

Naturally I didn't mind the fact that they didn't come and gaze at *me* in awe – much. I mean, why should they? After all, I only wrote the books, didn't I?

Should get a really good sleep tonight – looking forward to the play tomorrow. Hopefully, my shy yes-it's-me-but-I'm-no-different-from-anyone-else-look will be a bit more effective there than it was at the Reginald and Eileen Afternoon Tea Club.

Thursday 24 March

Off to Bongalinga Creek this afternoon. Had to leave fairly early. Apparently, when Australians say somewhere is 'just down the road' they could mean anything from fifty to five hundred miles.

What a welcome we got at the theatre! Had a huge seafood meal with the whole cast and technical crew before the performance. These Ozzies really know how to look after you. Thought personally that Thynn was a bit flamboyant. He'd bought a big bush hat complete with corks and insisted on wearing it to the theatre. They seemed to think he was wonderful, though. Hung on his every word. Very nice to the rest of us, but there was no doubt about who the star was. They laughed at everything he said as though it was a marvellous witticism, including his request for exact directions to Ramsey Street, which was just as well, because he was dead serious.

Play went ever so well, and the audience gave us a round of applause at the end, as well as giving a standing ovation to the cast.

Compared notes afterwards when we got back to the house where we were staying.

I said, 'The person who played you was really good, Leonard. It's amazing that he'd never met you before – it was so like you.'

'I don't think so,' said Leonard rather indignantly, 'the Leonard Thynn in the play was a strange, loony sort of person who kept getting in everyone's way and didn't know what he was talking about half the time.'

I laughed and said that proved my point. Leonard got quite annoyed. Said that the person who played me in the play was even more like me than the person who'd played him was like him.

What nonsense!

'The character who had the same name as me,' I said, 'was a pedantic, stolid, po-faced, self-deluded type of individual who was incapable of seeing things happening right in front of his face. Amiable in a bovine sort of way, but basically thick. Now you're not seriously trying to tell me that I'm like that, are you?'

There was a short silence, then Anne said, 'Let's talk about something else, shall we?'

So like Anne to rescue Leonard from getting too embarrassed.

Friday 25 March

Free time today. Seem to have woken up properly now. Did a little tour of the city – so beautiful. Thynn on and on about the heat. Had a point, though. Couldn't spend long in direct sunshine. Temperature was up near the thirty degree mark during most of the day, and beyond for some of the time.

Decided to visit one of Perth's fine art galleries this afternoon. Not at all Thynn's cup of tea, really, so I was amazed and rather pleased to spot him in the distance standing, quite motionless, in front of one of the exhibits, staring straight at it with an expression of ecstatic rapture on his face. Moved a little closer to find out which particular work of art was so enthralling him. Appeared from a distance to be some sort of abstract, a rectangular, box-like shape filled with rows of little square apertures. Didn't want to get too close in case I broke the spell for him.

Whispered to Gerald, 'Look at that! Leonard's really taken with that modern piece. What is it about that particular exhibit that happens to speak just to him? I wonder what it's called?'

Gerald peered at Leonard's abstract and said dryly, 'I don't think that particular piece has a name, but if it did I think it would be simply entitled "Air-conditioning".'

Saturday 26 March

11:30 p.m.

Really good meeting tonight at a little town just outside Perth. Felt quite proud of my little team, who sold books and showed people to seats and generally helped out.

Had to reject one of Thynn's loony schemes before we got going. Keeps coming up with 'tricks' at the moment to help with the speaking. Wish he wouldn't.

I was on my own in the little room at the back just before we were due to start, when he came rushing in clutching a book in one hand and half a large onion in the other.

Held the onion in front of my face and said, 'Use this!'

Looked at him blankly. Can't help feeling sometimes that, on some far distant planet, way out in space, an alien being is wondering why Leonard has been away from home for so long.

'Use what?' I said.

'This onion!' he said with wild enthusiasm. 'I bought it today. Use it just before the bit where you always make your voice break.'

'I do not *make* my voice break, Leonard,' I said with dignity. 'If and when my voice breaks, it is with genuine emotion.'

'Well, use it just before the bit where you always make your voice break with genuine emotion,' he persisted.

Hate it when Thynn says things like that. So diminishing. Very tempted to insert the half onion into him. Resisted the temptation. You're supposed to pray and meditate before talking about God, not insert vegetables into people. Decided to explore the fog of his mind.

I said, 'Leonard, please tell me as quietly and clearly as you can how I could possibly think half an onion essential to the success of my talk this evening.'

'You rub it on your hymnbook before you go on,' he said, in the tone of voice you use when someone is being wilfully dense.

'Rub it on my hymnbook?'

'Rub it on your hymnbook, yes, and then, when you come to the bit where you always – where you always *genuinely* make your voice break, put the open book over your face as if you're really upset and sniff the page you rubbed the onion on. People like tears, don't they? They'll think you really mean what you say. Good for business.'

'Good for business?' Shook my head in disbelief. Couldn't think of anything else to say.

'I read about it in this book I brought with me from England,' continued Thynn. 'There are lots of good tips in here.'

Took the book from his hand. It was a faded paperback printed in the fifties entitled 'HOW TO BE A SUCCESSFUL EVANGE-LIST' by someone called Conroy Orville Nathanburger the Third. Opened it at random and read the following passage aloud:

' . . . as the close of the meeting approaches, close your eyes tightly to indicate that you are concentrating on the instructions of a mystical inner voice. In suitably hushed and solemn tones, request all present to bow their heads and close their eyes while God ministers to his people. After a short but – hopefully – significant pause, invite those who feel that God has touched them to raise a hand in grateful acknowledgement, whilst insisting quite sternly that all eyes should remain shut. It may be necessary at this point to, as it were, "massage" the response of your congregation. I myself find it most helpful, if no hands at all are raised, to murmur humbly, warmly and appreciatively, such phrases as, "Thank you, Sir. Thank you, Madam. Thank you, young person – your obedience will bring you great blessing." This mild and harmless deception is guaranteed to have an almost magically stimulating effect on reluctant congregations . . .'

Leonard said, 'Good stuff, eh?'

'No, Leonard,' I replied, 'it is not "good stuff". It is appalling, dreadful stuff. I don't want to deceive people – I want to tell them the truth.'

Anne and Gerald came in at that moment to say it was time for the meeting to start. Anne asked what we were doing.

I said, 'I'm just explaining to Leonard that anyone the Lord's calling to salvation will come to faith whether or not I deceive them with an onion.'

Gerald and Anne studied me for a moment before exchanging the kind of pitying, concerned look that has been part of my life since Gerald was about six. Occurred to me that I might not have communicated with total clarity. Was going to explain, but Gerald didn't give me a chance.

'You know, Dad, you're a sort of theological Captain Kirk, aren't you? Boldly going where no man has gone before. I don't suppose anyone else has yet had the courage or the – the originality, to seriously tackle the shamefully unacknowledged problem of onion deception in the modern church. How will you go about it? I suppose the evil will have to be exposed layer by layer.'

Was about to thank Gerald for his rather heavy-handed satire, and point out that there was a perfectly reasonable explanation for what I'd said, when I suddenly heard myself being introduced and had to go.

Explained to Anne later.

Really excellent evening after Thynn's nonsense. Lots of laughter and a few tears – even without the onion. Australian people don't seem to mind you taking the mickey out of them as long as you begin by taking the mickey out of yourself. Things seem pretty good now as I lie in bed next to Anne writing this. And we've got seven days off with a borrowed, air-conditioned car to have a holiday. Thank you, God!

Won't bother with any more diary entries until next Friday, which is the day before my next meeting (a big one, apparently) is scheduled.

Friday 1 April

Wonderful holiday travelling from motel to motel, falling into the pool at each one as soon as we arrived. Eating out at the excellent Sizzlers restaurants that serve steak and pasta and as much ice cream as you can eat. Walking through warm sea water on the edge of the ocean in the late evening. Cuddling koalas in sanctuaries. Trying to entice possums down from the roof with apple cores at night. Wrestling with the mosquitoes that love to eat pink, ripe poms. Even the 'mozzies' didn't put us off. We love Australia.

Rather surprised halfway through the week, when Gerald, who'd been scribbling on a piece of paper for the last five minutes or so, suddenly said, 'I think it ought to be a tour of New Zealand next year, Dad.'

Asked him why.

He said, 'Well, I've been reading about a place in New Zealand called Rotarua, a big tourist draw, apparently.'

'And you'd like to go there?'

'Only if I can go with a girl called Rhoda, or meet someone called Rhoda when I get there.'

'What – *any* girl called Rhoda?'

'Well, just three qualifications. She has to be more impolite and more likely to blush than another girl called Rhoda, she has to be willing to join us in a largish rowing boat some distance from Rotarua, and she has to be responsible for drawing up a list of pairs for rowing duty so that we can get there by sea.'

Stared at him for a moment. I said, 'You want me to ask you why, don't you?'

'Well, I've wasted a good ten minutes working this out if you don't.'

Sighed. 'All right, then, go on – why?'

'Because afterwards I want to be able to say – "The redder ruder Rhoda wrote a rota to row to Rotarua."'

You have to understand that it had been *very* hot …

Saturday 2 April

Rather taken aback by the size of the meeting tonight. Must have been about a thousand people there. Felt quite nervous looking out at such a vast sea of faces while the worship session was going on. Shut my eyes and tried to concentrate on God, but got distracted by the thought of how much money I'd have made if each person had paid three pounds to come in and I'd been due to get sixty per cent of the profits after all expenses on both sides had been taken out. Something like three thousand pounds minus, say, three hundred for their expenses and a couple of hundred for mine would have left something in the region of –

'Excuse me, brother, I know how important and precious time with the Lord is when you're about to speak, but I just wanted to make a quick point if you don't mind.'

It was the organizer of the meeting, Gary Turnbull, who was sitting next to me. Felt rather ashamed. Tried to look like someone who's been dragged back from the seventh heaven, but is willing to sacrifice further spiritual ecstasy for the sake of another's earthly needs. Crinkled my eyes and whispered, 'It's okay, carry on.'

He said, 'Just to let you know that we've allowed half an hour at the end for your ministry.'

Stared blankly at him.

I said, 'Oh, have you? Er ... what is that, then? When you say my ministry, you mean er ... ?'

'Well, you know, commitment to Christ, recommitment to Christ, healing of the body – all that sort of thing.'

Suddenly felt terrified. Said in a feeble voice, 'I don't really do – ministry.'

Looked at me for a moment then said, 'No problem, I'll do it for you.'

Felt even more nervous after that. Not at all helped by the introduction Gary gave me when the worship had finished.

He said in a deep and thrilling voice, 'Friends, through the words of the man who's about to come to this microphone now, the Lord is going to change your lives, I can promise you that. Friends, he'll make you laugh. He'll make you cry. He'll bring the power and the light of God winging into the very centre of your hearts. Friends, as you leave this place tonight you will indeed know that you have been in the presence of the Most High. The justice of God and the love of God will be revealed to you in a wonderful way as this brother witnesses to the mighty twofold dispensation.'

Mentally abandoned my opening story about a vicar, a balloon and a mutant pineapple.

'Open your hearts, friends,' went on Gary, 'to receive the blessing you've craved for years. Please greet the messenger of God who stands before you now with sanctified lips and an anointed tongue.'

So nervous by now that when I *was* finally allowed to actually come to the microphone and I tried to speak, my sanctified lips and anointed tongue were too dry to produce anything but unintelligible sounds for a few seconds. Tempted to stop and wait in stern silence for an interpretation, but decided God wouldn't be very pleased.

Afraid my talk failed signally to live up to Gary's advance publicity. Mainly because I tried to make it do just that. There's something about people saying I'm going to witness to the mighty twofold dispensation that really glues up my delivery.

Finished my address hoping the gloomy silence was evidence of people being deeply moved. Don't think it was. More likely to have been evidence that I should have told the story about the vicar, the balloon and the mutant pineapple. Suddenly realized how stupid it was to be so affected by someone else's expectations. Sank miserably back in my seat and got on with dying quietly.

Gary wasn't put off in the slightest. Garys never are. Uncoiled himself in slow motion from his chair in that hushed, carefully-not-destroying-the-atmosphere sort of way, exuding significance from every pore, and spoke through the microphone in an even deeper and yet more thrilling voice than before.

'I'm sure you were as moved and challenged by that inspired word as I was, friends' – I'm quite sure they were – 'and I want to give you a chance now to respond to the touch of God on your heart. Don't leave here tonight, brothers and sisters, without doing business with the living God, I beg you.'

Suddenly became businesslike.

'Right! Our counsellors are ready. All those who want to make a first-time commitment to Christ, perhaps you could line up down here at the left-hand side of the stage. All those who want to make a recommitment to Christ, could I ask you to form a line down on my right-hand side? Those requiring healing of the body just queue down the middle between those two lines, and anyone who doesn't fit into any of those categories, perhaps you could form up by the steps over on my *far* right-hand side and beside the swing-doors on my *far* left-hand side if the numbers involved demand a second line.'

All very straightforward in theory, but it actually ended up with hundreds of people milling blankly around saying things like, 'Thing is – I want to make a recommitment, but I need healing of the body as well, so should I go in this line or that line, or the one over there?'

Whole thing began to feel like some badly organized divine car-boot sale, with people wandering from line to line seeing what was on offer. Glad to get back to the hotel tonight. Told Anne all about the evening and asked why she thought I was feeling so guilty and unhappy.

She said without even pausing for thought, 'You're feeling guilty because you tried to do a Gary instead of an Adrian, and you're unhappy because you probably bored the socks off them in the process.'

I said, 'No, don't hold back, Anne, say exactly what you think.'

She said, 'I did.'

Perhaps I'll save the satire for my next book . . .

Sunday 3 April

Spoke at an Anglican church this morning. Left Gerald and Thynn in their beds this time, and went with Anne. Funny how the events you dismiss as being trivial turn out to be the really meaningful ones. God seemed to be absolutely in charge of what I was saying for the half hour I was preaching.

Back to the vicarage afterwards for Sunday lunch. As we went in through the door, the vicar, whose name is Col Bevin, said very graciously, 'I believe you're bringing something very fragrant into our house today.'

He was right about me bringing something into the house, but I'm afraid it wasn't very fragrant. I brought it in on the sole of my shoe. We'd flopped gratefully into the soft, comfortable sitting-room chairs, and sherries were being poured, when Col's son, Jimmy, who's about fourteen, suddenly screwed up his nose and said, 'Blimey, Dad, someone's trod in something!'

Don't know why I assumed it couldn't be me. Something incongruous about delivering the word of God one moment and distributing dog poo over somebody's carpet the next, I suppose. You really would think that an interventionist God worth his salt might have done something about that, wouldn't you? An angel with a pooper-scooper or something?

Everyone except me was studying the soles of their shoes and sniffing round the room when Col's wife Noelene screamed and pointed to the piece of pale lilac carpet under and around my feet. It was covered in the stuff. That scream said 'NEW CARPET!' as clearly as if she'd used the words themselves. Anne was furious. Dragged my shoes bodily off my feet, hissing imprecations as she did so, and hurried out into the garden to clean them up. I jumped up and started hopping around making clicking noises with my tongue, hoping to express remorse through activity, pointless though the activity actually was. Col was determined not to make a big deal of it.

He said, 'No worries, Adrian, please don't distress yourself. Anyone could have done the same. A carpet is just a thing, and things can be replaced. We'd rather have your words this morning than a perfectly clean carpet, wouldn't we, Noelene?'

Noelene, who was already frantically at work on the carpet with a cloth and some kind of spray, forced a twisted smile onto her face, but I knew the real answer to her husband's question was:

'No, frankly, I would swop a carpet with no dog poo on it for the words he spoke this morning any day if such an exchange was an option, which it isn't. Furthermore, as you well know, this brand new *thing* has replaced the threadbare old *thing,* which I put up with for years and years and years. I would like him to feel free to distress himself as much as possible, thank you very much.'

Worked as hard as I could to redeem myself after that, talking to Jimmy about cricket, complimenting Col on the atmosphere in his church, and being utterly overwhelmed by the quality of the lunch, but it was no good. Poor Noelene was unable to prevent her eyes from continually drifting down towards my now poo-less shoes. I had sullied her pride and joy, and she just didn't trust me any more.

Said to Anne on the way home, 'Why is it that preaching and poo always seem to go together in my life?'

She replied rather coldly, 'Because you don't always look where you're walking.'

Hmmm ...

Monday 4 April

Explosion in jumble sale repeated. Sad to be thinking of leaving, but excited to be going home.

Tuesday 5 April

Anne, Gerald, Leonard and I entertained before leaving for the airport by *the* perfect Christian family.

Father warm and loving yet balanced and strong, mother clearly a perfect manager, yet flexible and fully involved with her children's lives, two beautiful teenage daughters alive and vibrant, yet sensible and self-disciplined, small boy endearingly mischievous, yet obviously good-hearted. *All* the children were polite but entirely natural, and all talked about deep experiences they'd had with God over the last few months. Everyone helped quite spontaneously with anything that had to be done, and there was not a single hissed threat, warning, bribe or entreaty from parents to offspring. To top all this, when we'd finished our snacks and drinks (prepared willingly by one daughter, served with humble elegance by the other, and passed assiduously by the little brother) the whole family *sang Christian choruses in harmony* to us!

A disgusting display altogether, in fact. We all felt obliged to role-play bubbling joy to match theirs. Very wearying. Tempted to pinch the small boy hard to make him swear or something. He'd probably have forgiven me, though ...

To make matters even worse they all insisted on treating me as if I was some kind of spiritual expert or guru. When the singing had finished the perfect father turned to me and said, 'My wife and I wondered if you would mind very much giving us the benefit of your wisdom and experience in a certain matter.'

Tried to ignore Gerald's sardonic eye and Thynn's look of blank puzzlement.

'Er, yes, of course, if there's anything I can help you with – of course.'

'Well, we know that your son –' he smiled in Gerald's direction, 'is grown up now, and often there will just be the two of you at home, but we were hoping that you could tell us which model of family worship you have used over the years.'

I said, 'Ah!', as if this were the very question I'd been longing for them to ask.

Anne and Gerald and I looked at each other. I asked a silent question. They answered in the affirmative without nodding or speaking. Sometimes loyalty embodies a greater truth than the truth itself.

I said, 'Ah, yes, family worship, yes. Which model ... yes. Well, er ... yes. Actually, we've always tried to be as flexible as possible with family worship –'

The perfect parents leaned forward, frowning and nodding interestedly, anxious to benefit from my great wisdom as much as possible while they had the chance. Any minute now they'd start taking notes.

'How exactly do you mean?' asked the perfect mother.

'Well, flexible in the sense that if anyone didn't want to come they didn't have to be there. And that er ... that always worked out very well, because, generally speaking, none of us wanted to come so, er ... we didn't.'

The whole perfect family fell about laughing at this point, clearly believing this unplanned moment of honesty to be a deliberate and hilarious joke on my part. No family worship time? What a rib-tickler! The perfect father patted me on the back while he chortled, as if I really was his sort of Christian-fun-chap. Taking the line of least resistance, Anne, Gerald and I laughed heartily with them (Thynn overdid it, of course, ending up rolling around on the floor), and then, thank goodness, it was time to go to the airport in their enormous, clean, perfect, rubbish-free Christian vehicle.

Whispered to Anne in the back of the car, 'Can't wait to be on our own so that we can be unholy in comfort.'

Called a final farewell some time later as we passed through the departure gate. The perfect family stood in a little shining group, still exuding love, joy, peace and harmless high spirits in every direction as they waved a vigorous goodbye to the departing spiritual guru and his lucky family and friend.

As soon as they were out of sight we all relaxed like four human balloons deflating.

Gerald said, 'Blimey! I've never been so relieved to get back into morose mode. The muscles in my face were beginning to ache with all that victorious smiling.'

Anne suddenly said, 'Look out! Bubbly smiles on! There they are again.'

Sure enough our erstwhile hosts had found their way round to a place from which they could see into the glass-walled walkway that led to the boarding gates. There they stood, smiling and waving as before. Instant resurrection in the Plass family. Thynn grinned like a maniac. We all waved back with guru-and-his-family-type smiles on our faces, then collapsed again with exhaustion as we passed on out of their sight.

Could feel my face crumpling into a visible groan. 'Oh, dear! I honestly don't think I could manage to get myself -'

'They're there again!' screamed Gerald, as we rounded the corner. 'I don't believe it! Look! They're there *again!* Smile to attention, everybody!'

With the mental ingenuity we should have expected from them, the perfect family had indeed found, and rushed to occupy, yet another point from which to salute us as we headed for the safety of our plane. You could tell they were *immensely* excited and happy about being able to give us such a wonderful and unexpected surprise. We produced another frenetic burst of robotic joy before continuing on our way. But we were broken people now. Our false smiles stayed glued to our faces as we stumbled defeatedly along. Who could tell when they might be needed? We were ready to believe that our persecutors were capable of appearing at any time and in any place.

Even after the plane had taken off and we were thousands of

feet in the air, I hardly dared look through the window beside me, in case, by some impossible but perfect means, the Australian Von Trapp family turned out to be standing happily on the wing, smiling and waving and singing choruses in harmony and reminding us that we were not a perfect family, all the way back to Heathrow airport.

If only they hadn't been so *nice* as well as everything else ...

Wednesday 6 April

All there ever has been or ever will be is this plane ...

Thursday 7 April

3 p.m.

Only an hour to Heathrow now.

Very relieved to have my diary to write just at this moment. Struck up a conversation a while ago with the very smart American lady sitting on my left. All right at first, but took a rather unfortunate turn after a while. Discovered as we talked that she's married to a very well known Christian speaker who I met for about three seconds at Let God Spring into Royal Acts of Harvest Growth a few years ago.

I said, 'Ah, yes, I know your husband well, he's a terrible man!'

She gave me a very straight look and said, 'He's not a terrible man – he's a very *good* man.'

Occurred to me that English irony might not be completely understood in the New World.

'I know,' I said, simpering and wriggling with embarrassment, 'that's what I meant. I was er ... joking.'

She said slowly, and without even the ghost of a smile, 'I see – so when you said he was a terrible man, what you actually meant was that he's a good man?'

Cackled foolishly and said, 'Yes.'

Where is death when you really want it?

Now I know why nobody buys my books in America. I shall tell everyone the problem is that Americans just don't understand irony. That sounds much better than saying they don't find them funny.

Friday 8 April

Forgotten how green England is. Can hardly write this, I'm so tired. Still, we did it, didn't we? Not sure who, what, when, where, how or why, but we did do it ...

Saturday 9 April

Australia's just a dream. We never really went. Took our films in to the chemist so that we can prove we went. Should be ready on Monday.

Richard phoned, sounding very strained, to ask if his son Charles, who's visiting at the moment, could come to lunch or something next week. Anne's always got on well with Charles, so I expect Richard's hoping she'll talk to him about – what?

Anne said she'd ring Charles and ask him to eat with us on Monday evening.

Sunday 10 April

Really good to be home.

Actually managed to get to church this morning. Walked in trying to look like someone who is hardly aware that others regard him with a certain awe because of his position as an international Christian speaker. When am I going to learn? Whole church distracted by talk of a new movement of the Spirit that apparently started in the Far East and is known as the Taiwanese Tickle. Whole thing appears to centre on fish! I gather Doreen Cook went off to some other church somewhere and – well, caught it, and brought it back.

Never seen anything like it. In the course of the service Richard Cook undulated around the hall like a very solemn eel taking bad news to someone, Elsie Burlesford – or Elsie Farmer, as I shall have to get used to calling her – flapped her arms like fins and made 'BOB' noises, and George Farmer leapt around energetically being a salmon travelling upstream. Lots of people fell on the floor, wriggling like happy sardines in a net and laughing out loud (presumably not at George Farmer). Young William Farmer conducted a time of healing at one stage. Lots of noise, but nobody seemed to actually be healed, as far as I could see. Didn't seem to bother William much. Presumably he got used to producing an opposite effect to the one intended when he was singing with Bad News for the Devil all those years ago. He certainly went happily back to doing lobster impressions after the prayer time. Hard to know what to make of it all.

At coffee time Gerald and Anne and I sat with Richard and Edwin. Richard asked us what we thought of the 'new wave'.

Gerald said, 'Richard, one very serious thought has occurred to me.'

Richard leaned forward and nodded encouragingly. 'Yes?'

'Well, it's going to be very tough on evangelists from Taiwan coming into this country, isn't it?'

'In what way?'

'Well, six months in an aquarium in quarantine is no joke if you're being a herring for the Lord, is it? I'd be gutted.'

Edwin chuckled, but Richard, unbelievably, said, 'You don't seriously think that will be a problem, do you?'

Anne told Gerald to stop being annoying and get some coffee for us all. Richard went to help with the carrying.

Anne said, 'Seriously, Edwin, what is it all about? It does look a bit odd when you walk into the middle of it like we did this morning.'

Edwin shrugged and smiled a little wearily. 'I'm glad you asked that, Anne. You know how it is. God starts something off and it's really good, then it gets – well, I suppose the word is hijacked, by some of us people in the churches, and we try to give it a shape and a name that it never really had, and then other people think we're the experts and copy our mistakes in a slightly different way, and more folk follow their lead until it's difficult to know if the thing you've ended up with is the same as the thing that God started in the first place. It's a bit like Chinese whispers. I mean – everything that's genuine in this "tickle" thing is originally from God, not from Taiwan, for goodness' sake.'

Wish I was like Edwin. Whenever he says anything vaguely critical he always talks about 'us' and never 'them'.

I said, 'You think it's from God – all the fish stuff?'

Edwin shrugged. 'Well, I do think God is anxious to bring a bit of lightness and relaxation into the business of being a Christian, and some people I know have had really wonderful experiences. I also think ...' Shifted his position and thought for a moment before going on – I love it when Edwin has things to say about things. 'I think a lot of Christians have got very disappointed over the last few years. So many promises in such fine, combative language about mighty works of revival and healing and goodness knows what other victorious events that are going to happen at any moment, and an awful lot of those promises don't seem to have been ful-filled – at least, not in the ways that people expected. There's a sort of weariness around, and I think maybe God, who is after all –'

'Very nice.'

'Yes,' smiled Edwin, 'fancy you guessing I was going to say that – God, who is definitely very nice, is probably offering us a kind of pick-me-up, which is great. And we should be able to han-dle some of the more er ... vivid manifestations without too much trouble. I think Elsie will –' He stopped and looked guardedly around the room. 'Where is she? Oh, good, she's right over there. I think Elsie will be starting on a diet of ants' eggs any day now. No, seriously, I welcome it and I'm wary of it, and I hope it helps people to see and accept that the real victories are a bit more costly and more local and more boring and more Jesus-like than a lot of these grand-sounding things that never quite happen. The hardest thing, Anne, when you're a twit like me, and you're sup-posed to be running a church, is working out how you get people to actually *do* things. They all want to laugh and cry and even be deeply moved as they watch the play, but not many want to be in it. I know I'm a bit old-fashioned, but I do prefer James' defini-tion of true religion to most other people's.' Suddenly clapped his hand to his head. 'Oh, dear – forgive me for rambling on like this. I've thought a lot about all this lately, and there aren't many people I can open up to.'

Pretty sure he was talking about Anne. She always makes people feel safe.

Richard and Gerald came back with the coffee. Gerald said, 'I was just asking Richard if he feels there can be salvation without salmon-leaping, but I've just remembered what Paul said on the subject.'

Edwin said, 'This should be interesting, to say the least.'

'There were three things,' said Gerald solemnly. 'First, the apostle enquires rhetorically, 'Do all leap like salmon?', and then, a little later in the same book, "I thank God that I leap like a salmon more than any of you", and again, 'The spirits of salmon-leapers are subject to the control of salmon-leapers".'

Short pause while Richard's brain double-declutched.

He said, 'I always thought those passages were about tongues.'

Monday 11 April

Anne collected our films from the chemist today, and Leonard came round for lunch so that we could all look at them. Like peering through little bright windows at a different part of our lives. Hope we go back one day.

Charles Cook to dinner today.

Easy to see why Richard and (presumably) Doreen are so worried about him. Years ago, when he was studying at Deep Joy Bible College, Charles made Billy Graham look like a backslider. He wrote long, passionate, epistolary letters full of religious language, dire warnings and exhortations couched in vaguely prophetic tones to various members of the church. He wasn't just on fire for God – he was a human torch. In those days it was Gerald who took the mickey out of Charles (fortunately, Anne reckoned) and Charles who remained earnest and unremittingly spiritual regardless of what was being said or done around him at the time. Hardly seemed possible that the silly but rather engaging young man we'd once known could have altered quite so much. So floppy and cynical. Didn't seem capable of being anything but morose or sarcastic today. Even Anne, who used to get on really well with Charles, was obviously puzzled about the change that had come over him.

Compared notes afterwards and found that both of us were dying to ask what had happened to alter him so much, but didn't like to at first.

Not a little interested to find out how Gerald would react to someone who was in a much more sceptical state of mind than he had ever been. Quite pleased when he made a real effort to get Charles talking about a big Christian festival that Gerald loves and tries to get to every year. Charles has never been.

Gerald said, 'You'd love the huge open-air service at the end. It's completely non-denominational and unbiased. Ever so moving.'

Charles frowned. 'Oh, yes,' he said, 'I've heard about that service. You're right. It's completely undenominational and unbiased and free, except that – correct me if I'm wrong – it *has* to include somebody Scottish and impressively uncompromising teaching tunes and telling people off, and it's compulsory that there's a long, incomprehensible song written by a black, female, African, bi-sexual, disabled terrorist, and it's essential that there's a ten-minute section in which someone, preferably from the Middle East, shouts out great truths in a bellowing monotone. That's about it, isn't it? Oh, no, sorry, I missed out the fact that the liturgy has to be flexible enough to avoid excluding our brothers in the Tractor Worshipping Assembly of Northwestern Latvia, and particularly those members of that assembly (every single one of them, that is) who have never and will never, hear of, or have any connection with, the festival that strains so hard to accommodate their proclivities – very important point, that.'

Gerald completely nonplussed by all this. Later, Anne said that, over the years, Gerald has got into the habit of using Charles as a sort of symbol of silly Christianity, so it was no surprise that he couldn't handle the transformation that seems to have happened. Sounds a bit complicated to me, but Anne's probably right – she usually is.

Anne said, 'Now come on, Charles. You've never been. Honestly! How can you be so critical when you haven't got the first idea what you're talking about?'

'You ought to come one year, Mum,' said Gerald, grateful for the support, 'they had a whole series of banner-making seminars this year. Not quite my sort of thing, but you would've really enjoyed going to those.'

Anne and her friend Liz have made several beautiful banners for our church. Lots of people have said how much they add to the feel of the place. I never quite know what to think about them, but Charles seemed to have no doubt about his opinion.

'I've always thought,' he said, 'that – '

'You mean you've only just thought,' interrupted Gerald dryly.

'I've always thought that I'd like to lead a banner *ripping* seminar at a festival like the one you're talking about, Gerald. I'm sure an awful lot of people would turn up, don't you agree? I can just imagine it . . .'

Charles stood up, clapped his hands, and addressed us from the end of the table in those jolly, let's-have-a-good-time tones that one somehow associates with Christian workshops.

'Right, everybody, one or two still coming in, but I think we'll make a start. Can I ask everyone to just move into small groups of four or five, and what I want you to do is just share with each other as openly as you can – no pressure – the different reasons why you hate all these blinking silly banners that infest our churches, okay? And perhaps one person in each group wouldn't mind acting as a scribe – ha, ha! – so that you can write down what everybody says, and then, in about – ooh – five minutes, we'll have a time of reporting back and brainstorming and I'll just write it all up in black marker-pen on this big sheet of paper. Okay? Off you go into your small groups, and let's have you mixing with folks you don't know, so that you'll feel more uncomfortable, eh?'

Anne opened her mouth to say something, but Charles was in full, unstoppable, pseudo-jolly flow by now.

'Right, well, we've had our feedback session, and it's amazing, isn't it, folks, how we come to a session like this thinking that we're the only people in the world who hold the views that we do, only to discover that we all loathe banners for exactly the same reasons?

'Good! Now we come to the practical bit, and, look, please don't worry if you don't get the hang of it straight away. Just watch what someone else is doing and copy them and you'll be fine. After all, that's the way the church has worked for years, isn't it? Okay, well, if you look around you'll see that we've got scissors, we've got knives, we've got matches – do please use the sand-bins provided – and we've got a couple of little vats of acid for those who are into that, and, listen folks, there's absolutely nothing wrong with tearing the things to bits with your teeth and bare hands if that's the way you feel you're being led. Okay? So, I want a group of fifteen or so over here with the scissors – thank you. And let's have four or five on the knife table – good. A couple of volunteers for the acid? Great! And I'll lead a bigger group over on this side for the teeth and hand-tearing activity. And every time you hear this, folks,' Charles clapped his hands playfully, 'it's all-change time, okay? Ha, ha!

'Kids, no need for you to feel left out. As we destroy each banner we'll pass on the fragments to you, and Uncle Stan, who's over in the corner there wearing the Thompson's gazelle costume – cheer up, Uncle Stan? Isn't he great! – Uncle Stan will lead you in a time of jumping up and down on the remains.'

Raised his voice as if speaking over a busy hubbub of activity.

'Plenty of banners around, everybody – all absolutely sick-making. Some specially chosen because they were made in prophetic banner-making sessions – have a really good time with those. And, a final word, if you run out of puff – ha, ha! – or motivation, have a butchers at the list we've made, all the reasons why we loathe and despise the ghastly, flappy, banal objects, and I'm sure you'll feel a new surge of energy and commitment! Go for it, folks!'

Gerald smiled dutifully, but I could tell he didn't really find it funny. Well, it wasn't. It was full of anger and bitterness.

Somehow knew Anne wasn't going to let Charles go without making sure he knew how she felt. I was right.

Anne said, 'Charles, dear, what's happened to you?'

Isn't it funny when a person who's not being themselves knows exactly what another person's meant, but they have to pretend they don't understand the other person because they're so busy being this other kind of person who would never be able to understand what the other person meant.

(Read that last bit to Anne, and she said she knew what I meant, but didn't think anyone else would. Still, I'll leave it in.)

Charles said morosely, 'Nothing much. I get up, eat, go to work, come home, eat, watch telly, go to bed, sleep – then it starts all over again. I don't know what you mean by "happened". Nothing's happened to me.'

Anne said very gently, 'We've all known you ever since you were a little boy, Charles, and for most of that time your belief in God was the most important thing in your life. You talked about it all the time, you went away to college to study the Bible so that you could pass on your faith to other people more effectively, you wrote us long letters telling us what God was doing in your life down at Deep Joy College, or whatever it was called – I've still got those letters upstairs – and you actually went on to be assistant pastor at a church up near Gillingham, didn't you?'

Charles nodded, but just stared into his coffee cup without saying anything.

'And then,' went on Anne, 'after quite a short time, didn't you leave that job and get another one in a shop in the same town –'

'A newsagent's, wasn't it?' said Gerald.

'A newsagent's, that's right, and neither your Mum nor your Dad, nor us – although it's nothing to do with us really – nobody knows quite what went wrong.'

Anne waited for a moment, but Charles still said nothing. He seemed to be carrying out some very delicate surgical work with a spoon on the bottom of his cup. Decided it was about time I said something. Just a bit nervous because Anne always seems to have a sort of script ready written for her at times like this, and I don't. Didn't want to say the wrong thing.

'And then, Charles,' I said, 'today – you seem to want to make fun of everything anyone says about the Church, and there's something not quite right about – '

'Gerald always did,' mumbled Charles, looking up briefly from the operation he had been performing with such concentration. 'Edwin always laughed when Gerald said things. He said things about me and Dad sometimes.'

Anne and Gerald and I looked at each other helplessly. I opened my mouth and shifted around in my chair as if I had something useful to say but wasn't quite sure how to put it, hoping that Anne would get in before me with something that *was* useful. She did.

'Charles,' she said in a firm voice, 'there were times in the past when I could have cheerfully murdered Gerald.'

'Thanks, Mumsy,' murmured Gerald.

'Well, it's true! In your endless quest to be funny and clever you quite often went right over the top when you and Charles were younger. I suppose you don't remember referring to Charles' college as "the old Muppet factory", do you? And what about that New Year's church party when Charles' Dad asked you if you had assurance? Come on – what did you say to him?'

'Forgotten,' lied Gerald.

'You said, "Yes, I'm with the Woolwich", didn't you?'

'Well, yes, but – '

'And have you also forgotten your contribution to that meeting we had once to discuss what form the Easter service should take? You suggested, if I remember rightly, that a huge artificial chicken should be slid along a wire over the heads of the congregation, and when it reached the middle it would "lay" a large egg onto the centre aisle.'

'That's right,' I said, remembering, 'and the egg would burst open and Charles' Dad would step out dressed as a baby chicken and shout, "New Life!". Was that right?'

'You've left out the bit about releasing live chickens into the congregation,' said Gerald.

Charles said without smiling, 'And you've left out the bit about Dad asking where you'd get the chicken from.'

'The point I'm making,' said Anne, still sounding quite firm, 'is that you're right. Gerald has done a lot of mickey-taking when it comes to the Church, and sometimes he's done it thoughtlessly, and perhaps even ended up hurting folk from time to time. I don't defend that. But the things you've said today . . .' Anne's voice softened as she went on. 'They're not the same, Charles. And I think the difference is – I think it's that Gerald always said what he said from *inside,* if you know what I mean. The things you're saying and the way you're saying them – well, they sound as if they're coming from someone who's right outside the Church – the *real* Church, as our friend Stephanie would hasten to remind us. So that's what my question meant, I suppose. What's happened to put you outside instead of inside? You're our friend, Charles, and we care about you –' Anne looked at Gerald and I '– don't we?'

We both nodded enthusiastically.

'I let go of the rope,' said Charles, in such a quiet voice that we had to strain to listen, 'and no one caught me.'

Somehow conquered the desire to say, 'What rope? Who didn't catch you?' There was quite a long silence, then Anne spoke.

'Charles, do you remember when you were in the middle of your college course and you decided to give it all up because the Lord was calling you to Israel?'

Gerald and I glanced at each other, exchanging an unspoken agreement that neither of us would laugh. On the occasion Anne was referring to, Charles had announced with great earnestness that every time he opened his Bible there seemed to be some reference to Israel, and that he felt this was a sign that he should abandon his course and head for the Middle East. Anne had seemed to know, as if by magic, that that wasn't really the problem at all, and everything seemed to get sorted out in the end.

Charles nodded sadly into his mug. 'Wish I had given it up then. Would've saved a lot of trouble.'

Anne said, 'But do you remember what it was that really helped on that particular evening? There was one of God's gifts that brought at least a glimmer of light into the darkness, wasn't there? Actually, it's something that always helped you from when you were a little boy.'

Charles looked up at Anne, curious despite himself. I was curious as well. What was she talking about? Prayer? Counselling? A particular verse from the Bible, perhaps?

'What was it, then?' asked Charles.

Anne opened the cupboard behind her and took out a large round tin. 'Cake,' she said, 'and especially chocolate cake.'

A little public smile trespassed on the surface of poor old Charles' private misery for just a moment. 'I do still like cake,' he said.

All munched for a while.

'You believe everything your Mum and Dad tell you when you're little, don't you?' said Charles a minute or so later. 'My Mum and Dad made me believe that you ought to feel excited and strong and hearing God all the time and – oh, I don't know – like them, I suppose. And for years and years I tried as hard as I could to at least look as if that was how I really was inside. I tried ever so *hard,* you know . . .'

A tear plopped into the coffee mug with a surprisingly loud sound. We ate cake and passed tissues and waited.

'I learned how to pray and sing choruses and quote bits from the Bible and do all the things that Christians are supposed to do, and, looking back, I can see that I was making a real idiot of myself. Because it was never really happening inside, you see. I didn't feel Jesus in me or any of that. I wasn't H-A-P-P-Y, or whatever it was we used to sing. I was P-A-N-I-C-K-Y. I wondered how long it would be before this God that Mum and Dad talked about all the time noticed what an effort I was making and showed himself to me in some way and *made* it all real. That's what I meant about the rope just now. It got more and more difficult to pretend. It was like dangling over some awful pit, hanging on to the end of a rope by one hand like grim death, terrified that, at any moment, I'd let go and fall. But a bit of me . . . A bit of me hoped that if – when – I did let go, God would sort of catch hold of me and take me somewhere safe. But he didn't. As soon as I started the job in Kent I knew it wasn't going to be any good. You can't go round door-to-door trying to sell something you haven't got, can you? I couldn't anyway.'

Gerald said, 'What's in this pit of yours, Charles – the one you've landed in?'

'My Dad's disappointed face mainly,' said Charles miserably. 'I know Dad's a bit of a twit sometimes.' (Gerald blushed faintly,

I'm pleased to say.) 'But he's always been – he's always cared a lot about what happens to me, and he was so excited when I went to college, and then when I got the job. I knew Mum and Dad would never really be able to understand what's happened to me because they're not made like that. Dad especially just *knows* everything about God is true and all right, and that's that. He really does – he's not kidding. The thing about Dad is that if he finds out he's wrong about something he'll change it, even if he's been going on and on about it in the wrong way for ages. He means it all, you see. So, even if I told him that all that trying had really been for him I don't think he'd have the faintest idea what I was talking about. And if he did understand he'd be so upset and guilty that I couldn't stand it. That's why I stayed up there and found a job after leaving college. I couldn't face seeing that puzzled, hurt, wanting-to-do-the-right-thing look on his face all the time.'

Anne said, 'So that's where all the anger's coming from, Charles – the feeling that God's let *you* down, and you've let your Dad down and everything's just ghastly?'

'More or less,' replied Charles, then, trustingly, like a small child, 'What shall I do, Anne?'

'There are two things I want to say to you, Charles,' said Anne. 'First, I think that all of us here in this room owe you an apology, don't we, Adrian?'

Rather taken by surprise.

'Er, yes, yes, certainly we owe you an – an apology, Charles, for – well, for er . . . obvious reasons.'

'You mean about the past, Mum?'

Anne smiled. 'Yes, Gerald, about the past. I don't know what's the matter with us Christians. We're so busy being civilized that we forget to be helpful, don't we?'

I nodded gravely, and said, 'True, true.' Hadn't got even the remotest idea what Anne was talking about.

'The thing is, I could have told you years ago that this was likely to happen one day, Charles, but I didn't, because it – well, it's pathetic I know, but it didn't seem to be any of my business. I could

444

see you desperately trying to be what your parents wanted you to be, and if I'd had a bit more courage, or whatever it needed, I'd have told you that's not the same as being a Christian, and maybe saved you at least a bit of all this pain. I'm really sorry. It seems to have always been a problem in our sort of church that as long as people are making the right kind of noises we just let them get on with it, even when we're quite sure there's a real vacuum underneath. Please forgive me – us – for letting you down like that.'

'Course I do, Anne,' said Charles. 'It wasn't your fault anyway. You've always been kind to me. What – what was the other thing you wanted to say?'

'Just that I think you're underestimating your father. Just at the moment I don't think it matters a jot what you believe or don't believe. You're far more worried about it than God is – if he exists, that is, of course. I think your Dad would handle actually knowing what's going on far better than he's coping with worrying and guessing. Why don't you just tell him? I think you'd be surprised.'

'Just tell him?'

'Mm.'

Charles always was like a little doggy with Anne. He got straight on to the phone and asked his Dad to come round to our house because he'd got something to say to him. Poor old Richard was knocking on the door within minutes, his face a mask of tension and worry when I let him in. We left the two of them alone in the kitchen and waited in the sitting-room for what seemed like hours. When father and son emerged at last – well, talk about two little rays of sunshine! Richard didn't know where to put himself, he was so pleased. He fiddled excitedly with the inevitable tie around his neck as he spoke.

'Charles has er, explained some of the er, problems that he has er, faced over the past few years, and I am so pleased that he has told me about – told me about – well, told me about them. I feared that he might simply be angry with me for being – for being – well, for being me, I suppose, but I'm quite sure now that we shall be able to . . .'

Richard scratched his head, clearly not quite able to express what it was that they would be able to do, but it didn't matter. I think we knew what they meant. They knew they loved each other and that wasn't a bad beginning.

Came across Gerald in the kitchen much later, laughing quietly to himself. Asked what he was finding so funny.

He said, 'Oh, I was just thinking about old Charles' banner ripping seminar. It may be a very negative concept, but, you know, I think he was probably right. An awful lot of people would turn up . . .'

Found myself thinking about the Cooks just before settling down for the night. Why did Charles hardly mention his mother? Why didn't she come round with Richard?

Tuesday 12 April

Can't bear the thought of going back to work next week. I know it's awful, but I feel as if Glander's a sort of blockage in my main pipe. Disgusting image, I know, but that's how it feels.

Wednesday 13 April

Prayed with Anne about Glander at lunchtime today. The whole thing's filling my mind in the most ridiculous way. Anne says we must trust God now that we've prayed, but my experience is that he hardly ever does exactly what I want in exactly the way that I want him to do it.

Thursday 14 April

11:00 a.m.

Tremendously excited and tremendously annoyed and all sorts of other things by a phone call from Everett Glander just now. The only time in my life I can remember God replying by first post.

Conversation began as follows:

'Adrian? Glander here – Everett Glander. How was Oz?'

'Oh, fine, thanks, Everett. Had a great time, yes. It really went well. How are you?'

'Well, have you got a minute? I know you international speakers are terribly busy.'

'Don't be silly – yes, of course, what can I do for you?'

Always get very tense when Glander phones. Find myself clenching my teeth and plucking nervously at the telephone wire. Why on earth would he be ringing from work on a Thursday morning? I wasn't supposed to be back, was I?

'Well, the thing is, old man – hold your hat – I think I've become one of them – or rather, one of you.'

'Become one of me? What do you mean?'

'I mean I've become one of your lot, old man. I've joined – taken the King's shilling. I am of the elect. You and I are little brother sunbeams.'

Pause while it sunk in.

'Is what you're trying to tell me that *you* have become a *Christian*, Everett?'

'Well, that's about the size of it, chief, and I must say I feel pretty damn good. Wish I'd taken the plunge years ago.'

Glander made it sound like joining a swimming club, but I suppose that's just his way. The thing that really bothered me was the conflict in my own reactions to this news. Part of me was very pleased – of course – but, despite my prayer of yesterday, another part of me was horrified. Everett has always managed to diminish me in my own eyes. Everything that I've thought worth anything seems to shrink and feel silly when I'm with him. What's it going to be like if he's in our church or even in our Bible-study group? What if – heaven preserve me! – what if Edwin decides that Glander is a candidate for my support group? The thought of him sitting there listening to intimate things about me and then making his caustic comments in front of everyone else just makes my blood run cold.

Tried to respond as enthusiastically as I could. Not easy.

'Well, that's terrific news, Everett! A real surprise.'

'You mean you're surprised that a black-hearted pagan like me has enough strength left in his sin-raddled body to drag himself up to the mercy seat, old man?'

'No, of course I didn't mean that. I just meant – I don't know what I meant,' I finished lamely. 'Anyway, tell me how it happened.'

'Well, I guess there must have been statues running blood and ladybirds coming to life in children's tee-shirts and signs in the sky and sundry other portents all over the place last Friday if one had but known where to look, because it all happened by chance, saving his presence, if you know what I mean.'

'What happened?'

'Went for a couple of jars at the King and Country as is my wont on a Friday night, and on the way back – you know that little old-fashioned chapel-type place set back between the Q8 garage and the Chinese takeaway?'

'Yes, but they're not really what I'd call – '

Suddenly stopped as I realized what I was saying. In the past, I'd tended to dismiss the church Everett was talking about as being dowdy and lifeless. Now I realized I didn't know anything about it at all.

'Not what you'd really call what, old man?'

'Oh, I just meant I've never actually been there, that was all.'

One of the things that's always frightened me about Glander is the way he seems to be able to see behind what I've said and then comment on it. That's what he did now.

'Well, that's a great relief, old chap. I thought for one dreadful moment you were going to say that they were some sort of spiritual lowlife down there. You weren't going to say that, were you?'

'Er, no, of course not.'

'Oh, good. Anyway – where was I? Oh, yes, on the way back from the hostelry I just happened to notice that there was some sort of knees-up going on in this little chapel place and I sort of drifted through the door and slotted in at the back while they were singing. Tried not to breathe on anyone – fruit of the hop must have wafted out on the wings of 'Shine Jesus Shine', I fear. And then this bloke did a talk. Didn't appear all that promising at first I have to say. In fact, you know they sometimes reproduce those little Edwardian books with pictures that told you what to wear and how to comb your hair and behave properly in company?'

'Yes, I – I think I know the sort of thing you mean.'

'Well, this character reminded me of the pictures they put in to show you how it *shouldn't* be done. Norman Wisdom without cap or jokes – that's about the nearest I can get to it.'

'But it was a good talk?'

It was the first silence since the beginning of the phone call, but I could almost hear Everett struggling to find a way of saying something without wrapping it up in flippancy like coloured cellophane.

'Not so much a good talk. Just that – it suddenly all made sense.'

'What made sense?'

Rather enjoyed pressing Glander to make him say something he really meant.

'You know, all the stuff about going home – all the old prodigal stuff. That's what this geezer was on about, going home and everything being good – being forgiven. All that. Collared the bloke afterwards and asked him to come back to the King and Country with me. Bit of a challenge, I suppose. Blow me down if he didn't do exactly that. Tell you what, old man, if you haven't sat in the public bar of a working men's pub, with darts and farts and filthy jokes flying all round your head, listening to a Norman Wisdom lookalike talking about religion, you just haven't lived.'

'What did this man say that you hadn't heard already, then?'

'What *didn't* he tell me that I'd never heard, you mean. All the meaty stuff about being a new man in Christ, for a start.'

'But I told you – '

'And then there was the link-up between the Old Testament and the New Testament. All those bullseye prophecies, old man. Amazing!'

'But I explained – '

'And just the fact that little old me, E. Glander himself, is a bit of a twinkle in the boss's eye. Never even guessed at it.'

'I can't remember how many times I tried to tell you – '

'Most important of all, though, old man, is that I can actually get it together, have what you'd call a real relationship with this Jesus of yours – mine – ours, I should say.'

'I can't *believe* you don't remember – '

'I must say, old man, I think you could've filled me in on a few of these bits of info before now.'

Felt ever so cross. All those years of listening to Glander's cynical comments and trying to tell him what my faith was all about, and in the end God sends Norman Wisdom along to tell him things he's already heard, and convert him in a pub.

'Went home after that,' continued Everett, 'and told the wife I wanted to sign up with "Big J", and she did a total dissolve on me. Cried all over the carpet, then said she'd been waiting for this to happen for years. She was way ahead of me.'

Felt very guilty suddenly. I suppose the Holy Spirit can do what he likes, when he likes. Well, I mean, of course he can. Tried to be more positive.

'Well, this is great news, Everett, it really is. I suppose you and Joyce will be going along to the chapel on Sunday, will you?'

Prayed silently that he would say yes.

'Good heavens, no, old man! We'll be coming to your place, of course. Wouldn't go anywhere else. That's the other reason I rang. Do you think Edwin, your elder fellow, would let Joyce and me do a little public announcement up front if I kept it shortish? Just to make it stick, as it were.'

Said I was sure Edwin would be pleased to let them do that, and promised to ring him myself and fix it up.

Everett said, 'Oh, one last thing – something else happened last night that I haven't told you or even Joyce about – '

'A spiritual experience, you mean?'

'Oh, yes, definitely one of those, old man, a real clincher, it was, but I think I'll keep it as a surprise for Sunday.'

Put the phone down with a rather heavy heart. Everett Glander is going to become a member of my church. Real life sticking its nose in again where it's not wanted.

later

Told Anne and Gerald what had happened at lunchtime. Gerald was too deeply buried in the paper to take much notice, but Anne received the news with genuine joy, as I thought she might.

She said, 'I'm so glad for Joyce, she's been so patient. I wouldn't have been able to stand the man all this time.'

'You don't mean he's even more annoying than me, do you?'

'No,' said Anne, who never indulges my fishing exploits, 'just annoying in a different and even less acceptable way.'

Explained to her how galling it was that Everett had heard all those things from Norman Wisdom about Christianity as if they were completely fresh, even though I'd been saying them to him on and off for years.

She said, 'I think you're underestimating the effect you've had on him over the years, darling. It's like the old Chinese water torture, isn't it? A little drop falling at regular intervals has an enormous impact over a long period, I'm quite sure. Why don't you suggest to Edwin that you interview Everett and Joyce in church on Sunday, seeing as you know him better than anyone else.'

Thought the use of the Chinese water torture as a metaphor for my Christian witness was a little ill-chosen, but I see what Anne means. And I really like the idea of me interviewing them. Can't help hoping that people will see Everett and Joyce as fruits of my long-term labours, as it were. Maybe Everett won't be such a pain now that he's a Christian – have to wait and see. I wonder what this 'something else that happened' was. Quite looking forward to Sunday now.

As I was leaving the table, Gerald suddenly looked up from his newspaper with a puzzled expression on his face and said, 'Dad?'

'Yes?' I said.

'Was I imagining it, or did I hear you say just now that Everett Glander has been converted by Norman Wisdom in a pub?'

'That's right,' I said casually, enjoying not explaining.

'Is that meant to be a joke?'

'A joke?' I said lightly. 'Everett Glander being converted by Norman Wisdom is no funnier than – let me see – well, no funnier than you saying my attempt to mend Percy's roof was a futile gesture. Or perhaps just about as funny as that.'

Very seldom I defeat my son.

He sighed and said, 'All right, Dad, you explain Everett Glander and Norman Wisdom in the pub, and I'll tell you why your futile gesture made everyone laugh.'

Agreed.

He told me.

Well, now I know! It really wasn't worth waiting for. Certainly not worth entering for a decent horse race . . .

Rang Edwin this evening to suggest the interview. He's known Everett on and off for a few years now, so he was really pleased to hear what had happened. Agreed enthusiastically with Anne's idea that I should ask Everett and Joyce a few questions – sort of draw them out, but thought I should phone them first to check that they were happy to do it that way. Phoned Everett straightaway and asked if he minded being interviewed.

He said, 'Joyce'll be a bit nervous, I should think, so go easy, old boy, won't you? But, yes, by all means do a Wogan on us – spot of kudos for you there, eh, old man?' How does he *always* know? 'Just so long as you don't forget to ask me about this other experience of mine, okay?'

Must jot a few questions down before the weekend. I really am quite intrigued by this 'other experience'. Roll on Sunday!

Friday 15 April

Photocopies of two magazine reviews of my last book arrived in the post this morning, sent by someone at the publishers. Decided to prove Anne and Gerald wrong about my so-called inability to accept criticism. I shall read the first one now, and then comment on it in my diary, being as objective and mature as possible in my response.

five minutes later

Well, I must say, this first piece is a fine, balanced piece of work. In style, structure and general presentation it can hardly be faulted. Here is a man or woman, one feels, with whom one would like to establish a warm personal friendship. Through the very words that are written the author seems to reach out to you, the reader, to say, 'You are safe with me – relax and trust me to lead you into paths of perception that will stimulate and enrich you.' Very impressed indeed. It is true that the specific comments contained in the review are almost all very pleasingly positive, but I honestly do believe that I would have arrived at the same conclusion if the general content had been negative.

Now I shall read the second review in exactly the same spirit of calm, unbiased objectivity.

ninety seconds later

I'm sorry, but what's the point of trying to be objective when you're presented with garbage like this? I mean, if they really do insist on having reviews in this sad little rag of theirs, they might at least make sure that the person doing the review (a) is a human being who knows what a sentence is, and (b) has actually read the book he's supposed to be reviewing. It makes me want to vomit, it really does! Jumped-up, arty-farty drip of a person, I have no doubt, who's never written a book in his life, being allowed to comment publicly on the product of somebody else's hard work. Miserable parasite should be shot! Love to do it myself. Sod!

Saturday 16 April

Meant to tear yesterday's entry out before Anne and Gerald got a chance to see it. Forgot! Rushed down this morning, but it was too late. Gerald's threatening to frame it and give a copy to all our friends as an Easter present.

Sunday 17 April

Woke up this morning with that funny feeling you have when you know something's going to happen but you can't quite remember what it is, and you know you're either looking forward to it very much or absolutely dreading it, but you're not sure which. Mind you, once I *had* remembered what it was I still wasn't sure.

Felt quite good by the time I got to church, though. Looking forward to modestly facilitating a public demonstration of what the Lord can do through his battle-worn servants. Just a little concerned that Glander might reveal one or two of the less admirable excesses of this particular battle-worn servant. Decided to make sure the questions avoided any chance of him commenting on me.

Everett and Joyce had been given seats on the front row by Edwin, and they were already there, Joyce looking glowingly happy but darting little nervous glances around her all the time, and Everett relaxedly leaning his elbows on the back of his chair, just as he's always done at work.

Got a bit impatient during the early part of the service. Someone got up to bring us one of those 'thoughts' that always make me want to beat up the thinker. Such a nuisance, because then you wish you hadn't reacted like that and you feel you ought to repent and – oh, it all gets so tedious. This time it was Sadie Wingford, who's soupily devout and dresses like Alice in Wonderland even though she's in her mid-twenties. She jumped out of her seat just as we were about to sing one of my favourite choruses (the one that goes to the tune of 'Danny Boy'), and daisy-chained her way up to Edwin at the front, who listened with his usual patience as she whispered something in his ear.

Edwin said, 'Sadie's asked if she can share a thought with us, everybody. It's all yours, Sadie – away you go.'

'Well,' said Sadie in her breathless voice – Gerald says it makes her sound like a cross between Snow White and Marilyn Monroe – 'I just had a sudden precious little thought last night, and – well, it just seemed too beautiful to be kept to myself, so I said to the Lord, "Pretty please, can I share it with all my brothers and sisters at church tomorrow morning?" and he said, "Oh, yes!!". Who wants to hear my special thought?'

She cocked her head on one side, swivelled her eyes skyward and opened her mouth to the size of a golf ball, like someone listening for an echo on a mountainside in one of those bad musicals. The congregation stirred uneasily and produced a sort of assenting mumble. Interpreting these wretchedly uncomfortable murmurings as an enthusiastically positive response to the prospect of hearing her special thought, Sadie continued.

'My little thought was this. Isn't the Good News of the Gospel just like jam?'

'Oh, God!' groaned Gerald irreverently beside me in a whisper, 'I don't think I can stand hearing why the Good News of the Gospel is just like jam. Have I got time to get to the lavatory?'

He hadn't.

'The Good News of the Gospel is just like jam because –' Sadie paused dramatically, 'it needs to be SPREAD!!!'

Gerald suggested grimly that Sadie Wingford was just like cod because she needed to be battered. He was only joking, but I know what he means. She's very annoying at times.

Much more enjoyed a thought that Edwin told us he'd had.

He said, 'I came across a Bible verse that might possibly be a great encouragement to those ladies in the congregation who are not yet married, but would like to be. It's the first verse of psalm fifty-six: "Be merciful to me, O God, for men hotly pursue me ..."'

Raised quite a laugh around the church, including a rather raucous guffaw from Everett Glander at the front. Leaned across and said to Anne, 'Hope to goodness he really is redeemed.'

At last the time came for me to interview Everett and Joyce. Edwin invited us all up to the front without saying what was going to happen then sat down on the front row to listen.

Suddenly felt really good. Told everybody how I'd worked with Everett for a good few years and always longed that he might one day become a Christian (didn't actually mention how extremely irksome I'd found him for most of that time, nor that I'd rather hoped he would die when he had a cold recently). Went on to say that Everett had phoned me the other day with some good news and that he and Joyce wanted to share it with the congregation today.

(Isn't it funny how you slip into role on these occasions without even thinking about it. Gerald told me this evening that I was displaying all the bobbing, hand-washing, bottom-lip-between-the-teeth-grinning mannerisms that I'd noticed in others when they're doing similar things. 'Ah, well,' I said to him, 'don't suppose it really matters.' He said, 'No, as long as you're insincere. That's what counts.' Perhaps I misheard him.)

Glander explained with surprising simplicity about events at the chapel and the pub afterwards, and then I asked Joyce to tell everyone what had happened when he came home. People really warmed to Joyce, who is a slight, neatly dressed lady with a quiet voice, as she talked about how drawn to Jesus she had been for a long time, but how she'd more or less kept it to herself because she knew that Everett would not only be unable to handle it, but would probably have been driven even farther away from believing if he'd known. She nearly cried, but not quite.

One tricky bit just after Joyce had finished, when Everett said that working with me all these years must have had something to do with what had happened, despite, as he put it, 'one or two things that I'd better not mention'. My heart was in my mouth for a moment, thinking he was going to describe the awful occasion when I drank more than was good for me at the office party and told Everett to 'stuff his beliefs' after he'd told me yet again that he didn't agree with mine.

But he didn't, and I was beginning to feel a very satisfactory, warm, proprietorial glow about the whole thing. This man who had been a colleague of mine for all those years was standing beside me in church confessing his faith in Jesus. What a privilege!

'Don't forget, old man,' whispered Everett, interrupting my bask, 'you were going to ask me about my experience last night.'

My big mistake at this point was, of course, in deliberately giving the impression that I knew what he was about to say. I'd just got a bit carried away with the old proprietorial bit, I suppose.

What I actually said was, 'Ah, right! Everett's got one other thing to say, everybody, and I can tell you that this is quite something. The Lord has really been working in his life. Tell people what happened, Everett,' and I smiled, as if recalling some earlier account of whatever the occurrence had been.

'Right,' said Everett, 'well, folks and folkesses, I guess this was the icing on the old cake, as it were, and I want to say a big public

thank you to – well, I suppose I shall have to call him God from now on, won't I? Not that I didn't call him God before, you understand – I just didn't er – thank him for anything.'

I have to admit that it was good to see Glander floundering for once. I rather enjoyed being kind.

I said, 'Okay, Everett, take your time, old chap. Just relax and tell everyone how the Lord spoke to you.'

'Well, to be honest, old man,' said Everett, 'it wasn't so much the Lord who actually spoke to me – more my dead grandmother.'

Totally paralysed for a moment. Dead grandmother? We didn't allow dead grandmothers in our fellowship – not ones that spoke to their live grandsons anyway. What did he think he was doing? Decided I'd have to stop him somehow. Glander's voice is a very difficult one to stop, though. I writhed inwardly with embarrassment as he went on.

'Fact of the matter is, I always had a bit of a thing about old Granny, who, interestingly, was very much into the old Jesus stuff herself. You see, not having anything approximating to what you might call parents around for most of my natural born, I sort of depended on old Granny. Used to troddle down to Newhaven most weekends to check out this or that. She'd say what she thought, then I'd say thank you very much but I think you're probably wrong, then she'd smile in a way she had, then I'd go off home and find she was absolutely right. So, when, after all these years of being pummelled at work by our resident poor man's Billy Graham here (prolonged laughter from congregation – thank you, Everett), this funny business at the chapel and down the old Kings happened, everything in me said, "Glander, before you finally pop the parcel in the post, as it were, get yourself down to Newhaven and check it out with Granny." Stupid thing for Everything In Me to say, of course, because poor old Granny popped her clogs half a decade ago. Still – '

There was a pause as Everett's glasses steamed up a little. Joyce moved closer and took his arm. Here was my opportunity to stop this before it went any further.

'Well, on behalf of everyone here, Everett, I'd really like to thank you and Joyce for being so – '

'Hold on, old man,' said Glander, 'I haven't had a chance to tell everyone what happened yet.'

I peered ostentatiously at my watch before clicking my tongue against my teeth and sighing, as though deeply disappointed.

'It really does seem as if time's beaten us,' I said desperately, 'and I'm sure Edwin would agree that it's very important to – to stick to the timing that people are expecting – wouldn't you, Edwin?'

Threw an intense look at Edwin on the front row, a look which was designed to communicate, in that split second, the following:

'Have you understood, as the elder of this church, that the lunatic standing next to me, this mega-annoying person who has made my life miserable at work for more years than I care to remember by pulling just this kind of stunt, is about to support his claim to conversion by describing some kind of conversation with an elderly person who's been dead since the mid-eighties?

Do you realize that one or two people here will almost certainly attempt to deliver him on the spot if he goes on much longer? Will you please, please agree with me that we haven't got time for any more?'

I am quite sure that Edwin interpreted my burning stare with total accuracy, but he wasn't having any of it.

'No, you're okay for a while, Adrian,' he called out casually. 'In any case, I'm quite sure lots of people will be more than happy for me to lop five minutes of dead wood off my talk so that we can have a bit more of Everett's green stuff. You just carry on, Everett – plenty of time.'

'Yes, carry on, Everett,' I echoed limply, adding under my breath, 'with your heresy.' There was nothing else I could do.

'Ta muchly,' said Everett, adding slightly tartly, 'be nice to just finish. So, anyway, last night, after Joyce had gone up the wooden hill and I'd finished locking the cat and feeding the front door, as I always say, I thought I'd just sit in the dark for a second or two in Granny's old basket-chair in the corner of the sitting-room, and have a little think about what she'd have said if she could have seen Joyce and me actually praying together earlier.' He shrugged. 'Couldn't really say if I actually dropped off or not. Might have done, but it doesn't matter a row of beans when you come right down to it. I just seemed to see old Gran's face right there in front of me, and the thing of it is – well, Gran was smiling and nodding like she used to, and she said "yes". And that seemed to put the cap on the whole thing. I say,' he suddenly said to me, sensing my reaction as usual, 'I'm not embarrassing you by going on about Granny, am I? You haven't got the Spanish Inquisition hiding inside the lectern ready to jump out and torture people who talk about their deceased grandparents, have you?'

I stood there speechless, my mouth opening and shutting like an insulted guppy. Edwin rescued me by getting up and coming to the front to take over. Standing between Everett and Joyce with his arms around their shoulders, he said, 'I'm sure we'd all want to thank both of you for being brave enough to stand up here this morning so that we could hear about Jesus calling you to follow him. We're so glad that you're part of us now. As for that wonderful experience of seeing your grandmother last night – well, God is very good and very wise. My guess, Everett, is that you probably did doze for a while in that chair, and that God let you see in a dream the sort of reaction you'd have got if there was still someone down in Newhaven for you to go and see. He knew you needed to see that. In fact, I'm sure that's exactly how she is reacting in the place where she is now. Let's welcome Everett and Joyce, everybody.'

As I joined in the applause, I thought, yet again, of the way in which Edwin's personal faith and set of beliefs have a sort of elastic quality. Sometimes he seems to let them stretch to accommodate a person, or something a person thinks or says, but they never go out of shape. They always come back to where they started in the end, and at least one good thing usually happens in the process. Wish I was like that. Perhaps I will be one day.

Couldn't help feeling a certain satisfaction at seeing Stephanie Widgeon bear hungrily down on Everett as the service ended, presumably to share for the first, and hopefully by no means the last time, her novel insight into the nature of the Church.

Said to Anne this evening, 'The thing that worries me a bit is that the Spanish Inquisition wasn't hiding inside the lectern – it was hiding inside me.'

Anne looked up from what she was doing and said, 'Why don't you concentrate on being forgiven, and let God concentrate on being perfect?'

Monday 18 April

Must remember to look up 'cleistogamic' in the dictionary.

Tuesday 19 April

Horrific scene with Doreen this evening.

First of all Richard phoned, almost incoherent, to say that Doreen was on her way to see Anne and me, and that she was, as he put it, in a 'strongly rebuking mood'. Fact is, she was just plain seething. Refused anything to drink and wouldn't sit down. I asked her why she was so angry.

She looked at Anne as she replied, 'My son came to you in need of Christian counsel and you – you supported him in his sin and in his backsliding.'

'Doreen,' said Anne gently, 'I honestly don't think – '

'Did you tell him – ' Doreen raised her arm and pointed at Anne like some Old Testament prophet declaring judgment on Israel, 'that what he believes or does not believe is of no consequence?'

Anne shook her head in frustration. 'Yes, but it was – '

'Did you encourage Charles to believe that the Lord is unconcerned with his sin of doubt, and did you –' Doreen's face was suffused with colour as her voice lifted almost to a shout, 'did you yourself cast doubt on the very existence of God? Did you lead him to believe that all his past experiences were meaningless because they really meant something else, something that *you* should never have allowed to happen? Did you do that?'

'Doreen, that's a distortion of what really happened. I wanted Charles to relax so that his feelings about his father could – '

'You wanted! You wanted! You wanted! Why is what you wanted important? Tell me why the things you say and think and – *want,* have always been so much more important to my son than what I want. Why? Tell me why that is! I rebuke you in the name of the Lord for the way in which you have seduced him in the direction of your own ungodly liberalism and half-hearted adherence to the things of the Spirit and the word of God!'

This, obviously, was the speech that Doreen had been rehearsing on the way over to our house, and I have to admit that it left me quite speechless. I had a vague notion that, as the head of the household, I ought really to do something, but I couldn't think what to say. I needn't have worried. Anne suddenly stopped looking distressed and directed a very steady gaze towards Doreen. She spoke with a calm assurance that I've rarely heard, and, as she went on speaking, her voice was like the sound of a bell.

'There is nothing liberal about coming down the road that another human being is travelling, to meet them and bring them to safety. If that is liberal, then God is a liberal. There is nothing liberal about helping people to smash the false gods and images of religion or worldliness that have let them down and given them nothing over the years. If doing that is liberal, then God is a liberal. There is nothing liberal about using divine gifts of creativity and flexibility and ingenuity to open doors of understanding and delight in those who desperately need to know that compassion and care really are waiting for them in the arms of the Father. If that is liberal then the God who created this world is a liberal. There is nothing liberal about treading the narrowest path imaginable yourself, but throwing your arms as wide as they'll go to greet and enfold as many others as possible. If that is liberal, then all the most godly men and women I've ever known are liberals. There is nothing liberal, Doreen, about staying at the back of the expedition to tie shoelaces, and to encourage the fat ones and the slow ones and the ones whose feet hurt, rather than pushing triumphantly to the front of the line so that you can be first to the ultimate destination. If doing that is liberal, then Jesus was the greatest liberal of them all.'

There was a pause, and when Anne spoke again her voice was much softer.

'Doreen, I know you're really hurting, and I know a lot of it's to do with feeling that Charles isn't turning to you when he's so needy. If I've ever, in any way, made that worse, then I apologize without reserve, but don't you think that if you just – if you were to just freely offer him your love and support without worrying too much about the Christian side of things, just for a while – don't you think it might make all the difference? We all love him, don't we? Please don't let's be enemies, Doreen. Won't you come and give me a hug?'

Anne extended her arms and took a step forward. For an instant Doreen's expression crumpled and softened, like a small child's when she is suddenly overwhelmed by her own feelings, and I thought she was going to respond, but the moment passed, and a second later she was gone, slamming the door behind her.

'I feel very sorry for that family,' said Anne sadly, as I gave her a hug instead. 'Finding a new way will be so difficult ...'

Wednesday 20 April

Anne came downstairs this evening holding a sheet of paper and a photograph.

'Look,' she said, 'here's an old letter of Andromeda's. I don't think we've looked at this for years. It was right at the back of the bottom drawer in our room, with the photograph she sent. So sweet! Have a look.'

We first knew Andromeda Veal, who happens to be Edwin's niece, when she was a little girl of about six. She came to stay with us for a while, and, influenced very heavily by her mother and her mother's friend Gwenda, she constantly criticized me and just about everyone else, for being anti-feminist and not sufficiently committed to the socialist cause. Her favourite phrase, I seem to remember, was 'I'm afraid I don't find that very funny.'

Later, Andromeda went into hospital with a broken femur, and was in traction for some time. We became quite good friends then through letters and visits, and Andromeda actually became a Christian round about that time. She adored Anne and was deeply in love with Gerald, who lent her his personal stereo for the duration of her hospital stay, although she invariably referred to it as his 'personal problem'.

Nowadays, Andromeda lives with her stormy but reunited parents in London. The letter Anne found must have been written not long after Andromeda came out of hospital. This is what she said, exactly as she spelt it:

Dear Anne and Geruld and nice fashist, *(That's me, by the way)*

As you awl knoe, my lemur is suffishently reecoverd and nittid togetha for me to stop being an attraction and go home with mother and Gwenda, who hav temper rarilee stoppt being green and common wimmen becos the docter says I need sum comeforlessons or sumthing, so I am back in my own room exept that Gwenda says in a I deal world nobody wood own ennything but evrybody in the werld wood own evrything. I ecspect shes right, but awl I knoe is

I cried a bit when I got back to my room that evrybody in the werld owns and Im glad the rest of the werld was out.

Mother and me bowth have secrits from Gwenda now Anne. My secrit is Lucky Lucy the dolly that you choze becos shes gott tuff nickers. You left her for me when I was asleep and horizontall. O Anne I do *luv* Lucky Lucy even if she is sosieties tool for reinforsing the subjektiv female roll. As you knoe the ownly uther dolly I ever had was a littel plastic man that Gwenda made me call Bigot and he becayme a victim of dumbestick vilence. I had to snuggle Lucky Lucy out of the hospitall and now she livs in a little cubbord in my room like Ann franc in Hampster damn. Daddy says Gwenda makes the gestarpo look like soshul werkers so I hope she dosnt find Lucky Lucy.

Mothers secret is that daddy came to the hospital and thay got awl luvvy duvvy and she keeps glarnsing at daddys foto on the side and hes cumming to see her soon and Mothers trying too summun up the curridge to tell Gwenda enuff is enuff. O Anne I so wont to hav my mummy and daddy togetha again.

Ennyway the reeson I rearly rote was to say that my cuzzin Merle is getting marrid soon and o Anne she wonts me to be a brydesdmade and where a pritty dress and awl that. Imma-gin working up the I'll behind the bryde Anne eh? Acey-pacey ecsiting! Gwenda poopood in the hole idear becos she said marrige is a mail device to enshore feemale submishon and Mother pritended to agree with her but O Anne she secritlee bort my dress and took a pickture of me atchewally in it and hear it is in this letta. Daddy says Mother is week but luvvlee.

Just supose it was me who cort the bucket when the bryde throse it Anne. That wood mean its me next! Geruld isnt marrid or ingaged or enny of that is he?

Logical bonds,
    Andromeda and Lucky Lucy.

P.S. Tell Geruld if hes feeling a bit lost withowt his persun-nel problem heel have to cum and get it.

Had a look at the photograph. It showed a radiant Andromeda in her bridesmaid's dress, with Mum peeping nervously out from behind her shoulder. That photo can't have been taken long before the infamous Gwenda moved out and hero daddy moved back in.

Must invite Andromeda down again some time, and see what sort of sixteen-year-old she's turned out to be.

Thursday 21 April

Anne phoned Doreen today and tried to talk to her, but all she got was icy politeness. Glad she tried, though.

Friday 22 April

Gerald very quiet at dinner tonight. As we finished eating, he leaned back in his chair and said, 'Any chance we could have a bit of a chat on Sunday evening?'

Anne and I froze, me with a piece of Cathedral Cheddar halfway to my mouth, she in the act of scraping scraps from one plate onto another. Knew we were both wondering the same thing – was Gerald intending to solve the mystery of his three months off work and the long walks and the occasional unexplained absences? Very slowly and casually brought my piece of cheese to its intended destination. Anne continued with her scraping, but went on absentmindedly moving her knife across the plate for a few seconds after there was nothing left to scrape. Both so anxious not to overreact that neither of us said anything at all.

Gerald said, 'Hello! Anyone out there? I know it wasn't the most dynamic of questions but I'd appreciate even the briefest of replies – if it's not too much trouble, that is.'

Anne and I immediately launched into high-pitched laughing, compensatory babbling mode. One of the things I really like about Anne is her vulnerability when it comes to anything important connected with Gerald. She's so wise and calm with everyone else, but with him it's different. I must tell her that sometime (perhaps).

Agreed to 'chat' on Sunday evening.

Saturday 23 April

Went for a long walk over the hills with Richard today. Poor old chap finds it very difficult to communicate easily when real feelings are involved. Told me that he and Charles are getting on very well, although Charles is still adamant that the whole Christian 'thing' is not for him. Felt like crying when Richard said that he'd privately repented before the Lord for piling religious expectations on his son instead of simply loving him.

Asked how Doreen was.

Richard said she's very angry and tight-lipped. Will hardly speak to Charles, and blames just about everything on Anne and one or two other people in the church. Says he doubts if she'll continue her involvement with my support group.

'I wish,' said Richard dolefully, 'that we were like you and Anne and Gerald. You must feel so glad that Gerald's settled in his faith and everything.'

Agreed automatically, then suddenly realized that for all I'm supposed to be so open about myself I very rarely share what's troubling me *now*. I suppose that's why so many Christian speakers only ever seem to have problems in the past. Told Richard about our forthcoming 'chat' with Gerald, and how nervous we both were. He was so pleased to have something to comfort *me* about. Prayed together on a wooden seat overlooking the valley, then strolled down to a little pub I know where they do the most *excellent* pint of bitter. I know heaven is different things for different people, but settling down into the corner of a pub with a pint and a friend takes some beating.

Can't get to sleep tonight. Find myself wondering, as I used to wonder in the past, whether I would ever have been able to offer Gerald as a sacrifice, like Abraham with Isaac. Funny to think about all those times in the past when I used to apologize to God for loving Gerald more than I loved Jesus. Couldn't and can't imagine choosing between them. I tell myself I don't have that problem now that I understand God a little bit better. Not quite sure though. Wonder if Gerald knows how much I love him. Don't suppose he does. Should say these things more perhaps.

Yes, and mmmmmmmmmmmmmmmmmmmmmmmmmm
mmmmmmmmmmmmmmmmmmmmmmmmmmmmmmmm
mmmmmmmmmmmmmmmmmmmmmmmmmmmmmmmm

Easter Sunday 24 April

Woke up at midnight last night to find that I'd stupidly nodded off with my finger on the 'm' button of my portable word processor. Did thirty-five pages of 'm' before waking up. Deleted them and went back to sleep. Thought I'd leave a few in just to keep the record accurate. Anne says that this decision is my final qualification for long-term institutional care.

Sometimes think my word processor despises me. It says scathing things like: DO YOU REALLY WANT TO SAVE THIS?

Easter Sunday is my favourite service, I think. Anything seems possible on Easter Sunday. Come to think of it – I suppose anything's possible *because* of Easter Sunday.

Didn't want the service to end today. Didn't want the evening to come.

Tea predictably a rather tense meal this evening. Anne ate hardly anything.

'Let's leave the washing-up,' Gerald suggested as we finished, looking at me because it was my turn. 'You and Mum go through to the sitting-room and I'll bring you a coffee.'

Went down the hall to the sitting-room with Anne, feeling, for some reason, as if we were joint job-applicants who had lied in pursuit of the post for which we were about to be interviewed. All sorts of nightmare scenarios flitted through my mind as we sat neatly together on the settee. Tried to blank them off. Felt a shiver go through me as I heard him coming along the hall. Everything could change in the next five minutes.

Looked at Anne. She blew out a breath she'd been holding in for some time and said, 'Well, then.'

'Yes,' I said, 'just what I was thinking.'

Gerald fussed around with our coffee for an unnecessarily long time before sitting down in the armchair facing us. Took a few sips from a glass of something that was definitely not coffee.

I said, in what was supposed to be a joky tone, but came out like something from the darkest bits of Macbeth, 'We're not going to need one of those, then, Gerald?'

'Well, I'm not sure,' said Gerald without smiling. 'You might, actually. Do you want me to get you one?'

'Please, Gerald,' Anne was looking rather white, 'please say what it is you have to say. I'm not very good at dentists' waiting rooms.'

'Nor am I,' I said, suddenly very much not wanting to hear what Gerald had to say. 'When I was at college a little group of us who all hated the dentist got together and pledged that whenever one of us had to go to have a tooth out, at least one of the others would go with him or her to make it a bit more bearable. As far as I can remember, we called ourselves the Action Faction for Distraction from Reaction to Extraction, and we met – '

'Adrian,' said Anne.

'Yes?'

'Please be quiet.'

'Sorry.'

'Right,' said Gerald, 'here we go then.' He looked at us for a moment. 'What I have to say to you may come as a bit of a surprise. To be honest, it surprised me when – well, when it happened. Let me tell you what it isn't, just to put your minds at rest. For instance, I'm not gay.'

Anne and I fell about laughing on the sofa. Gay indeed! As if we'd ever worried about such a thing! What a hoot! In any case we have a warmly compassionate view of such things, so we'd have handled it, wouldn't we?

Breathed an inward sigh of relief. Nightmare scenario number one out of the way, thank God.

'Nor am I pregnant,' said Gerald solemnly.

Well, this *was* turning out to be a jolly session! Not pregnant – ha, ha, ha!

'Nor have I impregnated anybody else.'

Phew! That was n.s. number two disposed of. Perhaps it wouldn't be anything very alarming after all. Perhaps it was just going to be –

'I'm going to be a male stripper,' said Gerald.

Sat and stared in utter amazement. Hurriedly scanned my list of nightmare scenarios. Not a male stripper in sight.

I said, 'Gerald, I'm absolutely – '

'Adrian,' interrupted Anne, 'I think that might have been a joke, don't you?'

'Sorry, Dad,' said Gerald penitently, 'finding it a bit tricky coming to the point.' He cleared his throat. 'It's about my faith, actually.'

Found myself harking back nostalgically to those dear distant days, a few seconds ago, when I'd thought my only son was planning to make a living as a male stripper. After all, what was so very wrong with taking your clothes off in public? Found myself pleading silently with God:

'Don't let it be that Gerald doesn't believe anything any more. All those nights when he was little – you must remember how I'd creep into his bedroom when he was asleep and talk to you about him – ask you, sometimes with tears in my eyes, to look after him and keep him close to you? That was a prayer, and you answer prayer, don't you? Don't you?'

'Do you remember, Dad,' said Gerald, 'that time when Father John came to speak at the church, and said heaven would have to involve some cricket just for you?'

'Mmm.' I nodded and smiled, remembering that particular service very well indeed. It had solved a long-standing problem for me.

'Well, at coffee time afterwards I was having a bit of a chat with him, and he said, right out of the blue, "Ever thought that you might end up in the Anglican ministry?" I didn't know what to say, so I suppose I was a bit flippant. I said that, firstly, I didn't really know what the Anglican Church was, secondly, I hadn't got anything to preach, and, thirdly, God was still a complete mystery to me. He laughed and said, "In that case you precisely fulfil the normal qualifications. In fact, I'm pretty sure that, if he was here now, the bishop would ordain you on the spot." I thought it was quite funny at the time, but I certainly didn't take it very seriously.

Over the years, though – it's funny really – I've heard Father John's voice asking me that question in my mind over and over again. It's been like a sort of pointless secret that's not worth sharing with anyone else, but, then, one Sunday about a year ago, I went to this Anglican church just up the road from where I was living. I'd been there a few times before, actually, but I don't really know why. It wasn't particularly lively, and the vicar looked kind of defeated. I knew he must be feeling threatened by his congregation the first time I went there – I mean, you're supposed to begin your sermon with "Dearly beloved", aren't you, not "Ladies and gentlemen of the jury"?'

I tittered dutifully, filled with relief that my son was neither gay nor pregnant nor about to become the unscheduled male stripper. Anne didn't laugh. She clicked her tongue impatiently.

'Sorry, Mumsy,' said Gerald, 'silly joke – bit embarrassed. I was sitting in the evening service on this particular Sunday, my presence probably having lowered the average age of the congregation to about eighty-three, and I'd just been asking myself what on earth I thought I was doing there, when a sort of feeling went through me. That's the only way I can describe it – like a beam of light filling me up and passing on, but – but leaving behind a quiet sort of sureness that I was going to end up . . .'

Gerald didn't seem to be quite able to finally say the words.

'Say it, Gerald,' said Anne.

'I heard that same question again, even clearer than before – just the same words, except that this time it wasn't Father John asking, and this time I said 'Yes'. I think God was asking me to become a priest in the Anglican Church. I know one or two people would attack me with several specially sharpened chunks of Scripture for saying that, but that's their problem, I'm afraid. I don't mean that nastily, but I sure as eggs do mean it.'

Anne said, 'Of course.'

'So, over the last few months,' continued Gerald, 'I've been walking and thinking and praying and doing bits of writing for you, Dad, and just checking that I've not got carried away by my own imagination. I was sure before, but I'm even surer now. That's what I'm going to do, and I've been to see the director of thingummybobs and set the whole thing in motion.' He smiled at us as he's been smiling at us for twenty-four years. 'What do you think?'

Finished the bottle of not-coffee between us.

Anne and Gerald have gone to bed now. Anne seems very peaceful about Gerald's news, and I think I am, but there are one or two little worries. What will Edwin think about him going off into one of what some people describe as the 'dead limbs' of the body? What do I think? What does God think? Well, I suppose, as he's the one who suggested it, he must think it's quite a good idea. Can't imagine Gerald in a backwards collar, like my friend Vladimir. I know it's late, but I think I'll give Edwin a ring and see what he says.

five minutes later

Edwin already knew. Says it was him who advised Gerald to go for it. Asked him if he agreed with the people who say that traditional denominations are dead limbs.

He said, 'People who mend shoes. Good night.'

Monday 25 April

Just occurred to me that all my worry horses fell before the final fence – thank goodness. Trouble is (in my life anyway) there always seems to be another race with plenty of runners, all ready to begin, just around the corner.

Tuesday 26 April

Very odd being at work with Glander now that he's a Christian. We're a bit uneasy with each other at the moment, trying to work out what's going to take the place of my defensive bleating and his sarcastic retorts. He's putting up with a lot of stick from some of the other blokes at work who used to enjoy hearing him put me and my faith down. Have to admit feeling a fair bit of admiration for the way he's sticking to his guns. But I still don't like him.

Anne says we should ask him to come and eat with us soon, so that we can start to make real friends.

Oh, Lord, couldn't I do something more pleasant, like turning frogs inside out and eating the squidgy bits?

Sorry – I will try.

Wednesday 27 April

Amazing evening at our house. Started quite normally with the support group coming round for one of our usual meetings. Surprised to see that Doreen turned up after all. Didn't look very happy, and didn't say much, but she was there.

All seemed to be going well except that I was a bit worried about Leonard. Didn't say or do *anything* silly or loony during the main, business bit of the evening when we were giving some feedback on the Australian trip, and he looked very low. When coffee time came, and everyone had stopped talking for a minute, I said, 'Leonard, is there something wrong that we could help you with? You don't look very happy at all.'

Leonard usually loves being the centre of attention – that's why I waited till everyone was listening. Didn't perk up at all now, though. He said, 'Sorry I've been miserable, everybody. With giving up the booze and then Mother dying and' – glancing at Edwin – 'that not being a good enough excuse to start drinking again, I think I'm going through – ' pause, as he screwed his eyes up as if trying to remember something. Suddenly raised an index finger. 'That's it – I think I'm going through the long dark night of the haddock.'

Rather tense silence punctuated by suppressed choking sounds from one part of the room.

Edwin didn't even smile. He said seriously, 'Leonard, I think you mean "soul", don't you?'

'Oh, yes, that's right,' said Leonard mournfully. 'Well, I knew it was a fish. Anyway, that's what I'm going through. I keep crying on my own at home.'

Murmurs of concern from everyone at this plaintive confession.

'Oh, Lenny-baby, come to Glor-bags!' Gloria Marsh, who is very kind as well as being – the other things she is, was sitting beside Thynn on the sofa. Bottom lip thrust out in sympathy, she was almost crying herself. Flung her arms round him and cuddled him so closely into her chest that his head completely disappeared. Slightly distracted by this for a fleeting moment, but I really was worried about Leonard.

Richard said, with real concern in his voice, 'Leonard, have you asked the Lord to uphold you in this time of trial?'

Strange, muffled sounds floating up from the area of Gloria's bosom suggested that Leonard was doing his best to reply. When she released him he came up crimson-faced and breathless. Later, Gerald said he'd had the air of a half-drowned man anxious to be given artificial respiration so that he can get back in the water as soon as possible.

'I'm sorry,' he said, after getting his breath, 'I didn't quite catch the question. My ears were – were covered.'

'I was enquiring,' repeated Richard, 'as to whether or not you have asked the Lord to uphold you in this time of trial.'

'Yes,' said Leonard simply. 'It didn't work.'

Richard nodded, but a strangely determined expression appeared on Doreen's face. 'Leonard, the Lord always upholds his people in their time of need. Would you like me to lay hands on you and pray his blessing down upon you, as I have done in the past?'

'No, thank you, Doreen,' replied Leonard, his voice flatter and wearier than I've ever heard it before. 'It's quite hard work pretending to feel better – don't think I can manage it today. Sorry.'

Leonard wasn't being nasty. He was just too depressed to come out with anything but the truth.

Doreen went white, stood up and said to Edwin, 'This is a mockery of the Lord's work. I refuse to involve myself any further. I shall now leave.'

As Anne said later, Doreen had clearly come in order to go, as it were, and this was the trigger she had been waiting for. Edwin didn't try to stop her. He just nodded gently.

As she reached the door, Doreen stopped, and in a voice so brittle that it almost broke, she said, 'Richard, are you coming?'

We all wanted to be somewhere else at that moment. Richard, who was sitting with his face in his hands, didn't move. He replied, with a pathetic attempt to keep his voice normal, 'Er, no, you go ahead, dear, I'll follow on a little later.'

She looked at him for just a moment, and then went. Something important had happened.

Nobody spoke for a while, then Edwin said, as if to himself, 'As Father John used to tell us, there's never anything but trouble when you allow vulgar truth to creep into the Church. Let's get back to business.'

He turned to Leonard.

'Look, Leonard, forget for the moment what anyone else says. If you want to, and *only* if you want to, just tell us exactly how you feel. Never mind what you're *supposed* to think or feel – that's not important. And we'll just listen, okay? Or if you prefer, we won't say another word about it now – we'll talk about something else, and you and I can have a chat later. It's up to you.'

Gloria held Leonard's left hand tightly in both of hers and smiled encouragingly at him.

'Well,' said Leonard, 'it's just that – ' He looked round at us all and sighed dismally. 'I don't think I've ever really believed any of it – all the God things, I mean. Not like the rest of you, anyway. Adrian gets all excited about it when he's talking to lots of people, even if he is different in real life.' Tried to avoid blushing by an act of the will. 'But I don't. And I haven't heard God speak to me like he speaks to Richard and – and Doreen all the time. Why does he always say lots of things to them and never anything to me?'

Not a complaint, just a question.

(Couldn't help remembering the conversation Anne and Gerald and I had with Charles in our kitchen. How many others are there, for goodness sake?)

Edwin shook his head slowly. 'Well, I'd have to line up with you on that one, Leonard,' he said quietly, 'I'm afraid God doesn't have an awful lot of specific things to say to me either. Mind you, I'm probably not very good at listening ...'

'But you do believe in him, don't you?' said Leonard, a trace of alarm sounding in his voice. Some walls, after all, are supporting ones.

'Oh, yes,' answered Edwin, his voice barely a whisper, but filled, as Anne put it so well afterwards, with the warmth and passion of a man who is deeply in love. 'I do believe in him – I always have done. I belong to him.'

'I don't think I belong to anything, really,' said Leonard dolefully. 'I'm not very good at the things you all are.' There was a short silence, then he frowned suddenly, and the very essence of his deepest trouble was etched into the lines of that dark expression. 'I think he doesn't want me because I'm silly.'

Leonard's eyes filled with tears and so did most of ours.

At this moment, Stephanie Widgeon, who had contributed virtually nothing to the conversation all evening, leaned towards the sofa and said, 'Leonard, dear, I know that we have been friends for only a very short time, but I would like to pass on to you something that has been a great comfort to me.'

'Oh, no,' I muttered under my breath, 'please don't say we're getting the bloody Church-is-not-the-building bit now – *surely* not now! Stop her, Edwin!'

But he didn't – this man who never hears from God didn't stop her.

'You see,' went on Stephanie, her eyes sparkling, 'the Church is not just a building – it's actually the people inside who are the Church. Have you ever heard that idea before, Leonard?'

'Yes,' said Leonard, his truth-telling mechanism still very much in operation, 'from you – every time I see you. And I never have understood what you mean. The Church is a building, usually a big grey one made of stone, and the people who go to it aren't churches, they're people.'

'Ah, yes,' trilled Stephanie, undaunted, 'but that is in a material sense. I am speaking spiritually.'

She sat back and beamed at us all, clearly convinced once again that she had introduced the group to an entirely novel concept. I decided we'd had enough of this.

I said, 'Edwin, don't you think this is the wrong time for this sort of – '

He put up a hand to stop me (very unusual for Edwin to stop

anyone in mid-sentence). 'No, Adrian, I think that what Stephanie has said is the most important thing of all for Leonard to hear.'

Stephanie's beam became a positive beacon.

'You see, Leonard,' continued Edwin gently, 'Stephanie is absolutely right when she says that the *real* Church – not the building, but the people who have to be Jesus in the world until he comes back – is, well, it's just us. If there was *only* you and I left, then we would be the Church – us two, Edwin Burlesford and Leonard Thynn, the body of Jesus on earth. And neither of us would be more important than the other because the Bible says that all the parts are equal and that we belong to each other. Do you understand that?'

Leonard nodded his head vigorously and said, 'No, not really.'

Edwin said, 'Anne, do you have a candle we could use, please?'

A couple of minutes later our only light source was the flickering flame of a white, household candle, balanced in a saucer on the coffee table in the middle of the room. Edwin asked us to all hold hands and sit in silence for a moment. When he spoke his voice was very clear and deliberate.

'Leonard, I am an alcoholic, managing by the skin of my teeth to avoid having a drink each day. In the past I have been arrested on the street, and sometimes ridiculed by people who hear me claim to be a Christian when they know me only as a drunk. Nobody really knows how hard I have to fight to live without alcohol.'

Even in the dim light thrown by the candle it was easy to make out the expression of astonishment on Leonard's face. 'But, that's exactly what I – you never told me that you were a . . .' Realization dawned. 'You mean that you . . .'

'I am very proud,' said Edwin softly, 'to own and share the good and the bad, the sense and the silliness in you, Leonard, my dear brother. I want you to know that your fights and victories are my fights and victories. Your failures are my failures. I hope that you can share the good and the bad in me as well – much more bad than you think, I'm afraid. But I do believe in God – this week anyway – so, I tell you what, since we are brothers, and parts of the same body, I'll hold your unbelief and you can hold my faith.' He smiled. 'That'll confuse God so much that he'll put up with both of us. I think that's the kind of confusion he likes. Jesus so wanted us to love each other. Tell me, Leonard, do you believe in the hands that are touching yours at this moment?'

'Yes,' said Leonard, 'they're real people.'

'That's right, and these real people are parts of Jesus, so when you hold their hands you are actually holding hands with God. Whatever one of us lacks, all of us lack. Whatever one of us owns, all of us share.'

Leonard looked slowly from Gloria on his left to Anne on his right and smiled his first watery little smile of the evening.

Edwin glanced around the group. 'You know, I feel more lucky than I can say to be serving as an elder. When I look at just this little group here I realize how rich I am. Stephanie has shared that little piece of truth with us – more than once, it's true, but what a great truth, and so right for what's happening here tonight; Leonard, lovable and quite unique; dear Anne, so warm and wise; Gloria, full of compassion and need; Gerald, who has brightened my day on many, many occasions, and is now being called by God to a very specific task; Richard and Doreen, troubled at present, but loyal friends in the past, anxious to serve God – too anxious sometimes, perhaps, and Adrian, who undervalues all his strengths and has made the world a gift of his weaknesses. I don't want to sound too soppy, but it's such a pleasure to know that all those qualities are mine as well as yours. As for the more negative things – well, we share all those as well, and because of that we do need to take turns being Jesus for each other, don't you think? I certainly need all of you to do that for me.'

We sat quietly looking at the flame for quite a long time after that.

I don't think I shall go on writing a diary after this, but there's one last thing I want to put down. It's what I tried to say to Anne just now before she went to sleep.

I tried to say that there are days when I feel very worried and confused about the Church – a little frightened even at times. But, as we sat in the darkness of our sitting-room this evening, with that tiny light shining in the middle of our group, I knew in the very heart of my heart that the Church – Stephanie's real Church – will be all right in the end. And it will be all right because there will always be just a few people like Edwin around in every generation – people who, when the tongues have stopped, and the prophecies have ended, and the kangaroo-hopping has come to a standstill, and the religious posing and posturing fools nobody any more, will still be ready and willing to genuinely share the burdens of the little people who are close to them, committed to the staggering eternal truth that we are one body because we all partake of the one bread.

And I guess they'll be like that because they want, if only in some small way, to be like their master and friend, who long ago hung on a cross, not ashamed at all to be as broken and as silly as Leonard Thynn, and Adrian Plass, and Everett Glander and the others in my church, and the whole of the rest of the world, because he loved us.

Thursday 28 April

One last thing.

Said to Gerald today, 'It's just occurred to me that you used to produce a constant stream of anagrams. What happened to all that misdirected creative energy?'

He smiled as he went out of the room and said, 'Oh, I just grew out of it, I suppose.'

Five minutes later he reappeared with a very serious expression on his face, and a piece of paper in his hand, and said, 'Dad, something quite important's come up.'

'Yes,' I said, 'what?'

'Did you know,' replied Gerald, 'that TORONTO BLESSING is an anagram of something an obedient angel probably said to his squadron leader immediately after launching the new wave?'

'No, I didn't know that. What did he say?'

'He said, "LO, GRIN BOOST SENT!"'

478

Friday 29 April

One absolutely, definitely last thing.

Today I finally solved a problem that's troubled me for years. I have never received anything like a satisfactory answer to the following question:

WHY DID LEONARD THYNN BORROW OUR CAT?

Everywhere I go, people who've read my first book want to know why Leonard came round one day to ask us to loan him the cat. Today I decided to finally get the truth out of him. Sat him down at the kitchen table and put it to him straight.

'Leonard, do you remember when you borrowed our cat?'

Troubled look. 'Yes.'

'Why did you?'

'The truth?'

'Yes, the truth.'

'Well, I'd never had an animal, and – '

'The truth, Leonard!'

'The truth?'

'The truth.'

'I had this tape recorder and – '

'Leonard!'

Pause – very small voice, 'Ran out of excuses for coming round, Adrian . . .'

Must look up 'cleistogamic' in the dictionary.